To Dorothy

CONTENTS

ABOUT THE CONTRIBUTORS

CHARLES ATKIN is Assistant Professor in the Department of Communication at Michigan State University. He obtained his Ph.D. in Mass Communications at the University of Wisconsin. His published research involves mass media and political behavior, television effects on children, and determinants of media exposure patterns.

RICHARD F. CARTER, currently a professor in the School of Communications, University of Washington, received a Ph.D. in Mass Communications Research from the University of Wisconsin. He has taught at Stanford University and the University of Wisconsin. His current research interests derive from consequences of discontinuity theory—including stopping behavior, picturing behavior, and control capabilities.

PETER CLARKE is Professor and Chairman of Journalism, University of Michigan. He received his Ph.D. in Mass Communication from the University of Minnesota and has taught there and at the University of Wisconsin and the University of Washington. His research interests include communication and political behavior, as well as use of mass media by the young.

LEWIS DONOHEW is Professor and Acting Director, School of Communications, University of Kentucky. He received his doctorate from the University of Iowa. His research interests are in information seeking and in communication and development.

GEORGE A. DONOHUE is Professor of Sociology at the University of Minnesota. His areas of specialization include social theory, socioeconomic development, and community organization.

ALEX S. EDELSTEIN is Professor and Director of the School of Communications at the University of Washington. He is the author of *Perspectives in Mass Communication* and the forthcoming *Uses of Communication in Decision-Making*. His most recent studies have been in cross-cultural mass media research and in methodological innovations in data gathering for media and opinion research.

M. BETH HEFFNER is currently working for the Du Pont Company in Wilmington, Delaware. She received a Ph.D. in Communication Theory and Methodology from the University of Washington. Her research interests include communicative accuracy and understanding via communication.

KENNETH M. JACKSON, Associate Professor in the Department of Journalism and Mass Communications Program at Indiana University, received his doctorate in Communication Theory and Methodology from the University of Washington. His research interests include journalistic practices—in particular the impact and implications of technological development, the reporting of science and other specialized topics, and the relationships between media and society.

NATHAN MACCOBY is Professor of Communication and Director of the Institute for Communication Research at Stanford University. He received his Ph.D. in Psychology from the University of Michigan and has served as Chairman of the Department of Psychology and the Division of Research, School of Communications, at Boston University. His primary research interest lies in the area of persuasion and learning, particularly as they relate to the mass media.

CLARICE N. OLIEN is Associate Professor of Sociology at the University of Minnesota. Her research specialties include community organization, youth development, and mass communication.

W. BARNETT PEARCE is Associate Professor of Speech in the School of Communication at the University of Kentucky. He received his doctorate in International Communication from Ohio University. Before moving to Kentucky he was Assistant and Associate Professor of Speech and Journalism at the University of North Dakota.

MICHAEL L. RAY is Associate Professor of Marketing and Communication at Stanford University. He is a social psychologist (Northwestern University) with extensive experience in marketing and advertising. He is an Associate Editor of *Communication Research* and is on the Editorial Boards of the *Journal of Marketing Research* and *Research on Consumer Behavior.* His continuing research interest is in communication and attitude change research for policy formation.

DONALD F. ROBERTS is Assistant Professor of Communication and a Research Associate in the Institute for Communication Research at Stanford University, where he also received his Ph.D. He is co-editor of *The Process and Effects of Mass Communication,* and has conducted research on children's responses to television violence. His major research interests include processes of attitude formation and change and the role of the mass media in the socialization of children.

JANE M. RODENKIRCHEN received her M.A. in Journalism and Mass Communication at the University of Minnesota. Her interests include public opinion and community decision making as they relate to environmental issues.

LEE RUGGELS is with the Behavioral Research Department of the Stanford Research Institute. Before joining SRI in 1971 he was on the faculty of the School of Communications, University of Washington, where he was Director of the Communication Research Center. He is a communication research graduate of Stanford University.

KEITH STAMM received his Ph.D. in Mass Communications from the University of Wisconsin. He is Associate Professor and Director of the Communications Research Center in the School of Communications at the University of Washington. Before that he was Assistant Professor of Journalism at Indiana University and at the University of North Dakota.

PHILLIP J. TICHENOR is Professor of Journalism and Mass Communication at the University of Minnesota. His interests include mass communication theory and methodology, mass media and public opinion, and science journalism.

LEONARD TIPTON is Assistant Professor in the School of Communications, University of Kentucky. His Ph.D. was obtained at the University of Wisconsin. His research interests include information seeking, coorientation, and media and politics.

DANIEL B. WACKMAN is Associate Professor and Director of the Communication Research Division, School of Journalism and Mass Communication, University of Minnesota. His research has focused on the role of media and family communication in socialization and social learning, and specifically on political socialization and consumer learning.

SCOTT WARD is Associate Professor of Business Administration at Harvard University, and a Research Associate at the Marketing Science Institute in Cambridge, Mass. His research has focused on effects of television advertising on children, and his current interests are in the area of consumer socialization.

INTRODUCTION

Peter Clarke

THIS SECOND VOLUME of the Sage Annual Reviews of Communication Research presents new research into human information seeking and processing. Readers will find more than previously unpublished data, however. Each author advances a new model that has guided his research. These models can enrich others' efforts to explain why people complete or avoid communicative acts, how we select among messages, how we process information, and the structure and content of communication effects.

Carter and his colleagues have been perfecting an observational scheme for differentiating between communication act and content. The Signaled Stopping Technique (SST) has gained widespread attention at recent scholarly meetings because of its conceptual power and its instrumental simplicity. The opening chapter develops the rationale behind SST and applies the technique to a number of familiar and novel questions involving communication process variables.

Two chapters follow that deal in new imaginative ways with linkages between mass communication systems and public orientation toward government. Tichenor and his colleagues argue for a functional relationship between social conflict and informational uses of the mass media. He tests several implications of his viewpoint in a research program of great scope. Data are presented from 15 Minnesota communities; his report uses communication systems as the unit of analysis.

Edelstein points to some overlooked limitations in conventional opinion research and suggests how familiar methods may obscure an understanding of the structure of opinions about public issues, like war. His research has resulted in a comparatively unintrusive method for gauging public opinion. He reports a variety of data concerning the structure of war opinions, relationships between structure and education, and between education and communication about war.

The next two chapters illustrate the level of theoretical sophistication one can find in research on communication and consumer behavior. Ward and Wackman study levels of conceptual development among children using Piaget's stages of cognitive structure. These stages are found useful for explaining children's understanding of the purposes of television advertising, and their processing and recall of commercial messages. This chapter contains theory-based analyses of research that Ward and Wackman have previously reported to policy groups in government and business.

Ray explains the importance of examining structure in communication responses—for theory building and application of results. He presents a variety of experimental data on effects of repetition in advertising. Results are organized into a hierarchical view of advertising response that differentiates among learning, attitudinal and behavioral outcomes.

Most communication research has been guided by cross-sectional models of states. Pearce and Stamm outline a truly process model. They use it to study how the introduction of cognitive discrimination, when compared to personal expectations, leads to different communication events. They are concerned with how this process may vary as a result of the context in which expectations are formed. And, although their research has explored interpersonal communication, their concepts and results have implications for information seeking in the mass media.

The degree of cognitive selectivity in message choice is a familiar and belabored research topic. Two chapters bring fresh perspectives to bear on this question. Atkin provides a more inclusive look at functional criteria of message selection. His work helps us reconsider support utilities in light of other adaptive uses derived from information. Some of Atkin's ideas spring from European research in the "uses and gratifications" tradition—to which we are devoting volume three in the SAGE Series.

Donohew and Tipton report work that has led them to postulate a process model of message attention, evaluation, and use-or-rejection. The model may be helpful in discerning how people seek to maintain an optimum level of variety/redundancy by "managing" their communication intake.

Finally, Roberts and Maccoby isolate an intervening variable popular in research on attitude change and turn it into a response variable in its own right. Counterarguing behavior—the production of "internal" messages—seems a worthy communicative response to communication stimuli. The study of counterarguing during and after message exposure can reveal the character of information processing, as well as help predict persuasive outcomes.

The purpose of this volume will be well served if it expands the inventory of communication variables used by researchers. It seems apparent that our inquiries must go well beyond the study of channel use if we are to understand why people communicate and how we attach utility and implication to the content of messages. The work represented here provides a wealth of starting points.

Chapter 1

APPLICATION OF SIGNALED STOPPING TECHNIQUE
TO COMMUNICATION RESEARCH

Richard F. Carter, W. Lee Ruggels, Kenneth M. Jackson, and M. Beth Heffner

THE BASIC PREMISE of signaled stopping is simple enough to illustrate: A teacher is lecturing; a student holds up his hand. The student's behavior is a signaled stop. From various points of view the behavior is other things as well—but basically it is a signaled stop.

The raised hand can be seen as an interruption from the teacher's point of view. Observers of teacher-student relationships often see it that way too. Even the student may "know" that he is interrupting by holding up his hand.

The raised hand can also be seen as a "meaningful activity" by the student, if reference is made to what he does in addition to raising his hand. For example, he may ask a question or make some comment. Such activities imply some function for him or for the relationship. Information processing views often infer the function for the student—e.g., Thayer (1968); functions for the relationship are exemplified in the analyses of Newcomb (1953) and Bales (1950).

From another perspective the raised hand is just a communicative act. It suffices as a unit of behavior. Nothing need be added; the raised hand is enough. While related behaviors and points of view may add interesting information, there is something to be gained by simply observing the occurrence of raised hands. We can find out about temporal relevance, particularly:

(1) We see that the student has altered his behavior in some respect. A unit boundary has been established; he has done with something and started something else (roughly, "listening" and "interrupting").

(2) We see that regarding the teacher-student relationship there is an

identifiable content relevance condition. Something in the teacher's message has produced a functional stimulus for this student response. Thus the response gives us a unit boundary within the message to complement the one within the student.

This assumes, of course, that the observed phenomena are solely those of the teacher's message (though not necessarily just his verbal behavior) and the student's attending to that message. Students can raise their hands in response to other conditions—and are supposed to do so in the elementary grades. However, the perspective we are taking here concerns the ordinary message problem of the teacher trying to help the student get what he (the teacher) is talking about.

This is the classic communication problem not just of education but of human communication generally. Many communication effects studies are concerned with this problem. The difficulties of such studies are great, but it would seem safe to say that our task would be much easier if we were better able to handle the unit problem in communication research. The question of unit pervades content analysis, with inferences of effect contingent upon the message unit stipulated arbitrarily by the analyst (e.g., theme, sentence, paragraph, word, etc.). Laboratory studies of message effects are often predicated on responses to a total message, with no units identified within the message. The sequencing and patterning of responses is lost because there is no unit of behavior effectively observed while behavior is happening.

Thus, we do not know much about what happens during the reception of a message; what we know is what happens after the reception of a message.

Because what we think we know—i.e., a theory of behavior—is stated in units which presume within-message behavior, the lack of an observational unit within message boundaries is a serious fault. For it allows plausible explanations of behavior to persist while incomplete observation yields no conclusive tests and few new alternatives.

The construct of a communicative act, the *stop*, was designed to cope with the unit problem. It derived from a theoretical analysis of communication activities which distinguished content states from act states among observed communication phenomena.[1]

Observed Activity:	a Listening	S[b]	Interrupting
State(s):	Act & Content	Act	Act & Content

a. The vertical dotted lines represent unit boundaries.
b. This area, a unit boundary between listening and interrupting, is widened here to permit the notation of switching (S), referring to the behavior which is only act and without content—and thus not often observed (e.g., "He was listening; then he interrupted.").

Figure 1: SCHEMATIC REPRESENTATION OF OBSERVED ACTIVITIES AS COMMUN-ICATIVE ACT AND CONTENT STATES.

Figure 1 shows more formally than the teacher-student example how the signaled stop is useful for studying communication phenomena. The analysis of the switch from one activity to another (the stop), as itself a unit of behavior, allows us to better conceptualize communication possibilities. Not all communicative acts are "for" (say, expressing) something. An act can have behavioral significance without some particular content state attached which is supposed to give meaning. Further, the conceptual unit of stopping is useful for its promise in developing new communication procedures. It points to a need which is now imperfectly fulfilled by devices like punctuation. Unit definition is as important to more effective communication as it is to inferring effects of current communication behavior.

The switching of activities (e.g., from listening to interrupting) which is an act of stopping is usually inferred rather than observed. It may not even be paid much attention, for there does not seem anything "meaningful" in between. The switching behavior—if not the conceptual unit of stopping to which it pertains— is more evident in machine programming, where procedures are required for the switching itself as well as for activities analogous to listening and interrupting.

Looking at Figure 1, we can see the analytic potential of this conceptualization. For a given message stimulus, there are a minimum of two pertinent responses: (1) the stop itself; and (2) the modality by which the stop is evident. In our teaching example, for instance, we could assess any variance in the incidence of stopping per se and also the activity of interrupting relative to the message unit; there might be differences in such interrupting aspects as ardor and insistence.

Further, the interruption may be concomitant with another activity, such as voicing a question. Our teacher-student example has the interrupting activity separated from any accompanying activity; the raised hand convention accomplishes this. In less formal circumstances an interjected question or statement may be the modality of interrupting.

Thus there are responses consequent to the stopping and in addition to interrupting per se which may pertain also to an eliciting message unit. We are often interested, for instance, in whether an interruption is accompanied by a question or by a statement. In this we are closer to the kind of analysis which characterizes effects studies in much of communication research: How is the content of a message related to the content of a response made to it?

However, in coming to this correspondence somewhat round about, we have not been overly precise nor needlessly apprehensive.

If we focus on the interruption solely as indicator that a sender's message content just now provided the stimulus, for the response content which follows the interruption, we may obtain a useful adjunct to the study of message effects. One can get more evidence of, say, affective consequences from a given message. But merely focusing on what happens after the interruption misses the prior two conditions—of stopping and interrupting. These furnish us with our best approach to questions of temporal relevance, so that we get at the "how" of information processing as well as the "what."

The question of timing in message effects has long been an obstreperous one, vitiating of generalities regarding message effects. What "works" at one time may not work at another time—whether at different places in a message or for different recipients. We may say that it was not relevant the second time. That states the obvious (at least in this context).

With this conceptualization there is not only a basis for more precise observing of message units—and effects—there is also the capability for determining temporal effects within messages. The interactive effects of units within a message become available for study. There is, for example, the opportunity to see whether, given incremental notions of affective consequences, massed or distributed experimental stimulus units provide more effect. Additionally, we can see whether the unit boundaries stipulated by a message sender correspond with those established by a receiver.

We have these added capabilities because in some contexts the activity of interrupting makes evident the act of stopping, and interrupting is requisite in those contexts. "One thing at a time" implies that the receiver must halt an incoming message, in some functional sense, if he is about to do something besides attend to it. We can make use of the evidence afforded us by such interruptions.

This is an incomplete capability because the message context may not constrain the reader or listener to always interrupt in an observable modality. Various covert activities (e.g., daydreaming and thinking) can operate without such evidence. But when the evidence is there to be observed, we have a way of getting at within-message effects.

The operationalization of this approach requires that the message receiver be free to interrupt. If he is required to interrupt on schedule or not to interrupt at all until the end of the message, the approach can not be useful in determining unit boundaries. Nor can it aid the interpretation of content relevance between the responses which accompany interruptions and the message content. The act of stopping is conceptualized as unconstrained behavior; its exhibition via interrupting must be similarly free.

Although the act of stopping is conceptualized as unconstrained, this is not to say that it is uncontrolled. That is, stopping occurs relative to some antecedent condition. If that condition is not furnished by external constraint, as in some scheduling of activities (e.g., responding to questions), then whatever conditions that do control stopping must have much to do with behavioral control generally.

Some of these conditions are well known. Learned stop signals are common. They may be learned as cultural procedures, such as politely not interrupting until the message stops; they may be learned as cues, such as interrupting whenever the interrogative occurs (even though a rhetorical question is voiced). Using the signaled stopping technique, we are able to find out what some of these learned signals are.

Stopping may also be learned as a response to more general cognitive phenomena. Perceived discrepancies are a case of these phenomena. Cybernetic control mechanisms operate on the basis of stopping (switching) being contingent upon the observation of a discrepancy from a given standard.

More generally, constructs like "attitude" and "decision" pertain to the condition that a line of behavior is predicated on *singularity* of cognition; "attitude" represents a singularity of implication regarding object; "decision" represents a means for obtaining singularity of implication from alternative implications. If there is nonsingularity, no line of behavior is clearly indicated and stopping is an obvious response.[2] Thus another important contribution of the signaled stop is that it may specify conditions of nonsingularity which are functionally important for information processing.

In addition to discrepancies from given standards, there are other kinds of nonsingularity to be found. Human behavior includes discrepancies perceived after, and when, criteria are elicited by observed conditions.[3] Also, messages often contain content which does not furnish a singular implication to the receiver; there may be no implication at all or there may be multiple implication.

Further information processing relative to starting, continuing, or altering a line of behavior may ensue following a stop. Then the symbolic behavior of the receiver (as sender—just to himself) may presage further conditions of nonsingularity—and stopping.

Stopping is a critical capability in constructing pictures whether one is trying to get someone else's picture or putting together his own picture of some situation prior to taking some line of behavior. To be able to get at stopping, however incompletely and imperfectly, is to be able to come closer to comprehending some of the conditions essential to cognitive behavior.

The problem of cognition for groups of people provides some good examples. The need for stopping as a control capability is apparent in rules of order. To prevent nonsingularity, an amendment must be acted upon before the main motion; that way, singularity of implication is preserved as the collectivity proceeds. Schedules are frequent in societal controls for stopping, as in regular elections and equal time for speakers.

Stopping is functionally related to all kinds of activities because of its switching consequences. It would be erroneous to confuse it with the particular condition of "stopped"—what appears to be inactivity or covert activity. One must stop to be stopped; but, one must stop to be in any (other) condition. The condition of stopped is usually clarified when, and because, a relationship to some condition (not stopping) is adduced. Pauses and hesitations are accounted in regard to antecedents or consequences.[4] As gaps in a line of behavior, their implication is derived from prior and/or consequent behavioral content. "Stop to think" and similar phrases suggest such a derivation.

That the stopping as well as the thinking (while stopped) relates to cognitive behavior is easily overlooked if the distinction is not made between stopping and stopped.

THE TECHNIQUE

Once the conceptual basis for the technique specified what we should be doing, the general paradigm for the technique was simple. All we needed was an observational context in which the stopping acts of communicators had to occur in a context where interrupting was necessary. Conceptually this applied to message senders as well as message receivers. So we tried to simulate a computer-assisted company, in which all communication behavior was computer assisted to the point where all of it required interruptions which could be registered.

A general idea of the desired context is available from the material given our first subjects—as trainees—regarding the "Eureka Holding Company":

> ... Eureka wants its new employee to become familiar with the communication context—the use of computer and typewriter, the relevance of timing to effective communication. . . . It wants to afford the employee a personal sense of the utility of time-based procedures and complete communication practices.

The "console" of the computer was described as having eight buttons, each representing a communication activity. Their functions were described as:

> STOP INPUT & GO INPUT—for control of incoming messages relative to relevances of employee;
> NOTED IN & REFER OUT—to report that relevance of content was perceived, relative to some other employee;
> HOLD & DO—for control of message use, between thinking and action; and,
> ASK & TELL—to further identify implication of message content transmitted.

Whichever of the eight buttons was pushed, there would be evidence of an act state. By assisting him completely, the context would maximize the recording of his stopping behavior.

In the Eureka context, other persons would not be physically present. Messages had to be used. This was meant to encourage people to use their own sense of relevance, to control timing so as to increase the effectiveness of their information processing. They could respect social relations, but they were not to be affected by any constraints of interpersonal, oral conversations.

The trainee-subjects did not like that much assistance—at least not in its simulated form.

Our inquiries showed that they resented what they saw as an intrusion on their preferred mode of conduct. So much assistance—by a computer—was not welcome.

Only one student got the idea:

> The various keys are mechanisms already used by us. Eureka merely illuminates or makes a conscious factor, the process. . . . I think we are already employees of our own company, and recognition of such is EUREKA!

We have been able to make use of the widespread resentment of technological intrusion. Because we were restricted to paper and pencil research operations, total simulation or not, we drew on this resentment in subsequently urging students to practice stopping by interrupting according to *their* sense of relevance. We have been giving them different kinds of messages and urging communication initiative upon them.

None of the data reported here come from the simulation situation. We have simply emphasized the potential utility of control over incoming messages in various situations, particularly the often missing capability of interrupting the message sender at points more relevant to the receiver. The Appendix contains several examples of introductory material.

This revision in our initial effort has led to primary focus on the STOP INPUT aspect of the Eureka context. Some of the ASK & TELL aspects occur as responses subsequent to message interruptions. However, much of the observational power potentially available via such a context awaits construction of an operating—not a simulated—Eureka Holding Company.

For now, mostly, we are getting at the receiving of messages. The sending of messages is an even more exciting prospect for signaled stopping. There much of the behavior consists of individuals trying, with much difficulty, to put together something using conventional means of representation and a few construction models. The incidence of stopping is certainly very high.[5] And we need an observational capability for messages as they are being composed in print similar to that afforded by the tape recorder—from which evidences of pauses and other indications of stopping are available. Indeed, the comparison of stopping behavior and related conditions between oral and print message preparation should give some fascinating data on the nonhabitual, unconditioned but regularly occurring efforts of message senders. The combination of a typewriter and computer, as exemplified in the Eureka context, would yield this capability; we would get a temporal datum as well as a printed symbol for each stroke on the typewriter.

Meanwhile, there is much to be seen just looking at receiver interruptions of incoming messages. We gave this instruction to readers: Any time you want to stop the incoming message, mark a slash (/). Sometimes we suggested only that they record in the margin their reason for stopping. For other studies we established reporting conventions in addition to a general option. For example, we have often used this set: /A—stop to agree; /D—stop to disagree; /T—stop to think; and, /?—stop to question.

There is quite a bit about the use of this technique of which we are still ignorant, for its usage has been nonprogrammatic, and entirely due to individual initiatives in trying out the approach on matters of personal interest. That was not the projected and planned usage; it simply reflects a resources problem.

Having subjects interrupt messages—even encouraging them to—is intrusive behavior on our part. Like the experimenter who asks for an attitudinal position after presenting some stimulus, we may be getting a condition which otherwise would not occur. This seems particularly the case when we suggest to subjects some optional behaviors which they might use after stopping, such as those of asking, thinking, and giving opinions. We have noticed, for instance, that if we suggest "reread" as an option, it will occur more frequently than if we simply let it be reported in the margin (and there will be less thinking reported than if the option of reread had not been suggested).

Intrusion is not so much a problem if we are interested in stopping per se rather than in the reasons for stopping. Evidence of stopping is being obtained unobtrusively via the interruptions, in the same way that nose and finger prints against window glass index children's interests. The difference is whether the practice being indexed is encouraged (stopping) or discouraged (pressing against the glass). Intrusion is still there, but it is a common condition to the stimuli under investigation.

The general, and important, capability of showing that a stop occurred—i.e., that there was a functional stimulus unit, whatever the combination of responses to it—is there for both experimental and survey uses.

In experiments, this capability is often useful for seeing whether the experimental stimulus "works" for the subjects. If there is a hypothesis which specifies an intervening condition between the stimulus and a later response, the occurrence of that condition may be ascertained. For example, Heffner (1970) was able to show that the only inoculation effects obtained for a series of experimental conditions came for subjects who stopped during the appropriate passage in the stimulus message. Given this capability, it is more useful to put experimental stimuli into message content, rather than trying to implement them prior to the message. Source credibility would be a case in point; by implementing the difference within messages, it is possible to see not only *that* a difference is noticed but also how.

In surveys to see which stimuli are eliciting more stops (if not to ascertain the distribution of content responses for a particular stimulus) the technique is unbiased. For example, a very early study (Carter, 1969b) furnished subjects with sixteen instances of Heider triads, representing balanced and unbalanced conditions, and divided into two sets where X was, alternatively, a person and an attribute. The objective was to see if there were more stops for unbalanced than balanced triads. There was little difference. However, there were differences for some other conditions.[6] Because, as we outlined earlier, there are many control problems for an individual in which stopping is essential, this survey capability is quite useful.

Our general approach in using the technique, even for experimental studies of particular message effects, is that the subjects should regard what they are doing as *exercises*.[7] Stopping is not something over which people have good control, however facilitating of interruptions a given context may be. After an exercise we expect to examine all stimuli which produce stopping, and we try to discuss the range of such stimuli with the subjects rather than presenting a "debrief" of any focal experimental stimulus which may have been inserted in the messages.

In using the technique it should be kept in mind that systematic sources of variance accompanying its use (i.e., especially its intrusive aspects) are least likely with regard to stopping as behavior, more likely with interrupting, and most likely with responses accompanying the interruption. Therefore, survey usage should favor stopping as the focal variable. Experimental usage is less bothered by systematic aspects of intrusion. And the latter may be less of a factor as subjects practice more with the exercises. Hopefully, the degree of intrusion would approximate that of typewriter keys to the practiced typist, or the interrupting of print messages achieved by the practiced copy editor.

Comparisons afforded between or among stimuli are unbiased as long as the intrusion is similar. So experiments can be designed to see, for example, if one message stimulus draws more stops to agree than stops to disagree. And, of course, message stimuli can be compared on any one suggested option—e.g., stops to agree.

For research on communication effects, to which we shall soon turn for some examples of utilization, this consideration of intrusiveness has been a methodological necessity. But there are some other points about the technique we would also like to make. These concern the features—good and bad—of the technique as currently used, and may not apply if used in the Eureka context.

Some good features are:

(1) It is possible to conduct omnibus experimentation; we have presented as many as ten experimental stimuli in separate exercises. This capability is useful for arranging research experiences at low cost for students, who will find that there is useful data to be examined even if their experimental hunches are not supported.

(2) There are repeated observations for each person. It becomes possible to see what happened on the way to the terminal criterion measure (if the latter is used). Not only are intervening conditions more susceptible to observation, there are also possibilities of seeing if, for example, a summary change in agreement is based entirely on agreements within the message consistent with that positional change. (There might be other agreements or some disagreements that are inconsistent.) Over a number of units, the possibilities of observing behavioral changes in general and learning phenomena in particular become obvious.

(3) Repeated measures on the subjects produce a very sensitive test for those experimental conditions which can be offered several times within a given exercise. Type II errors are less likely.

(4) It is possible to employ a less constricted response repertoire. In the case where no reporting conventions are suggested, the utility of an administered experimental stimulus is obtained along with an openness of response options. When functionally equivalent responses are suspected, this may be a critical feature.

Some bad features are:

(1) The content of the reporting conventions is often ambiguous. For instance, "I agree" after a stop can signify that the subject thinks the

sender is right, that the message is correct, or that he (the receiver) is with him (the sender).

(2) For some kinds of data collected the only appropriate statistical test is whether the total distribution could have occurred by chance. Then, many possible stimuli are confounded as significant sources.

(3) There is no provision for getting at joint information processing. With listening in the presence of another a poorly controlled situation—relative to stopping—the absence of data on stopping for such situations must be counted a fault. Even the Eureka context, as it is envisioned, would not supply that capability regarding listening. However, it would give us that capability for some other modalities.

(4) There is no receiver reaction possible to consequent sender behavior if the receiver does stop, then say or ask something. An unanswered question, for example, may produce termination of information processing for a subject. This yields a biased estimate of the message's stimulus potential.

With regard to the overall status of the technique, we can say that its utility is commensurate with the state of communication research. Its heuristic value is clear. It locates behavioral units. It is at its best in surfacing data where the stimulus was not experimentally administered and where the response behavior was not anticipated. Given the state of communication research, those qualities are useful.

APPLICATIONS

Much of communication research is predicated on the message as a useful artifact. Conceptualization and observation both respect the utility of that which is transmitted, disseminated, stored, encountered—that which is sent and received, which has meaning, and which has observable corporate form. Research has focused on the effects of various messages from various senders to various receivers.

However, in presenting applications of the signaled stopping technique we are not following the paradigm of sender-message-receiver. The communicative act of stopping has many sources, many of which apply just as well to both the activities of sending and receiving. While our current research context usually imposes a receiver orientation on the subjects, the paradigm is not so restricted.

Our compilation of applications has the general character of showing the kinds of sources for stopping that we have been able to discover, along with some outcomes of stopping. These include conditions discussed in the first section: learned signals; cybernetic discrepancies; nonsingular cognitive conditions; and discrepancies which evoke criteria.

The compilation thus has a survey, not an experimental, approach. Some of the studies reported were designed to replicate, in part, experimental work on message effects. But once units were observable within the messages presented, the survey function often became more prominent, and the source-message-receiver paradigm was replaced by the more general paradigm. One consequence of this is that no statistical tests are reported for the tabled data which follow. Although some have been made, they were made only when the data were to be related to studies previously done in an experimental paradigm. Because we will not be discussing the relationships of our data to an experimental literature, the occasional statistical test would be gratuitous.

We have selected for presentation data which will not appear in other publications. These data tend to bear on the generalities of communication research, not its particulars. The latter are handled elsewhere, where appropriate to the authors' study objectives. What we have to show are some of the communication effects available once our observational capability is extended to behavior within messages.

The first data bear on learned signals for stopping. Punctuation is a primary source of cues for stopping within printed messages. But such cues are not well comprehended in that regard by readers; it is the writers who trouble over them. So, when writers want to establish a very explicit unit characteristic they may use cues other than punctuation to get the reader stopped.

A teacher often signals the unit characteristic by asking a question. In printed material a similar tactic is the blank (   ). It asks for a response, ostensibly setting up a unit characteristic. Jackson (1969) studied several such tactics for getting students to stop at appropriate points during programmed instruction. Using content from Skinner and Holland (1961), he offered 84 subjects each of four modes: sentences as separate paragraphs (Discreet Frames); sentences with blanks in them (Response Cues); both of the above; neither of the above. The sentences were put together in paragraphs. No order effect from presenting the four modes was found. Table 1 shows stopping data for programmed instruction material with and without blanks. The blanks produce more stops. Also, there is more stopping for instructional units when they are "framed" as sentences standing alone (as independent paragraphs) than when they are grouped together (in a paragraph context).

The individual must control his stopping or be acquiescent to the timing of others—to their unit characteristics. With punctuation obviously not up to such a

TABLE 1
MEAN STOPS IN PROGRAMED INSTRUCTION CONTENT
BY MODES OF CONTENT PRESENTATION

Modes of Presentation	Mean Stops
Discreet Frames (Sentences), with Response Cues (Blanks)	1.55
Discreet Frames, without Response Cues	1.29
Response Cues, without Discreet Frames	1.51
No Response Cues, No Discreet Frames	.96

sweeping challenge, content cues must be utilized. One such possible cue which seems to be used is the negative assertion (implying nonsingularity). When the reader encounters a negative assertion, he may think, "against *something*"; the negative presumes a positive while the positive may not imply a negative. A "balanced" argument is therefore a potentially unbalanced one with regard to stopping signals.

Everett (1970) conducted a study in which she presented each of 107 subjects with eight positive and eight negative assertions in a message. Each set of eight had four favorable and four unfavorable to the issue of objective vs. subjective criteria in course evaluations. Table 2 shows average stops for negative assertions to be higher than those for positive assertions. This result holds whatever the favorability of the assertion relative to the attitudinal position of the reader.

TABLE 2

MEAN STOPS FOR POSITIVE AND NEGATIVE ASSERTIONS

Type of Assertion	Mean Stops
Positive	2.8
Negative	4.2

Readers may also adopt various tactics for coping with the unit characteristic. For example, the possible contingency of future content for present content can imply a strategy of extended units—of postponing stopping. Conversations often exhibit this behavior. In reading, a similar tactic is available; the reader can return later after having read ahead. His construction of units—and thus stopping—may differ because of the better context afforded by reading further.

Table 3 shows an effect along this line. Carter (1969b) gave 37 subjects two sets of eight information triads each. The triads gave information about prospec-

TABLE 3

STOPS WITHIN AND AT END OF INFORMATION TRIADS
BY INFORMATION PROCESSING MODE

	Mode	
Stopping Place	Read Through First, Then Read Again	Just Read Through Once
Within Triad	24%[a]	39%
At End of Triad	76	61
	100%	100%
	(n=162)[b]	(n=159)[c]

a. Proportions are of total stops made in this mode.
b. Number of stops made by 19 subjects in two sets of eight triads each.
c. Number of stops made by 18 subjects in two sets of eight triads each.

tive employees. In one set the information was about relationships with present employees; in the other, the information was about potential employee attributes.

The total information did not require many lines of print. About half the subjects read through once and then started back through, stopping only the second time through. The experimenter observed the tactic and asked each subject afterwards to note down if he had used the tactic. As the table shows, subjects who read through first were more likely to follow the unit characteristic of the author, stopping at the end of triads rather than within them.

Given the necessity for some stopping control, individual differences in control mechanisms can be quite illuminating of their learning experiences. One exercise we constructed seems well-suited for discerning individual tactics and strategies. We had subjects "answer the door" for six callers. The introductory material for this exercise is reproduced in the Appendix (Exercise B). The subjects were given the verbal and nonverbal behaviors of the callers, and told to interrupt when and as they would under such circumstances. One subject left the field in four of six episodes—such as by saying, "Goodbye"; another stopped whenever the caller used the word "you"; another interrupted to make value statements about what was said to him—then stopped to think after the next statement each time; another kept asking for data to make decisions; another was concerned about statements which described some state of the caller.

Heffner (1972) found that different unit characteristics were imposed by subjects required to compose messages, according to a difference in their instructions. Some subjects were asked to compose a structural view of an issue; others were asked to compose a process view of the issue. The "structural" instruction called for subjects to describe the issue as a cross-sectional view; the "process" instruction asked for a historical view. Subjects given the same instructions were closer in their unit formation—i.e., stopping—than were those given different instructions. Subjects indicated their units by showing where their news stories should be interrupted for inclusion of an illustration for a completed point.

A very familiar theme in communication research has been the somewhat cybernetic view that individuals hold attitudinal positions which act as standards against which processed information is accounted. If there is a discrepancy, there is supposed to be an adjustive response to the discrepancy. The simplest version of this suggests that the response will be to reject any inconsistent information. This is much too simple, because it is hard to reject "information" after having obtained it. And it is difficult to establish an operational definition of "inconsistent." Some discrepancies, if not opposed to the attitudinal position, are obviously tolerated. The problems of this approach are well known; our purpose here is to introduce some evidence on stopping pertaining to selectivity.[8] It is from this class of conditions, re stopping, in which a given criterion (here, own position) is involved.

Carter and Simpson (1970) ascertained attitudinal positions for 99 subjects on four issues (in a questionnaire about student-related issues), then later presented each subject with a message on each of the issues. The four issues were selected to afford a near-equal split between arguments which would be consistent and inconsistent with the subjects' attitudes on the issues.

Table 4 shows that stops to agree or disagree with arguments presented in messages varied in accord with the consistency of the argument and the given attitudinal position.[9] Moreover, given the mean stopping to agree and disagree where the attitude was neutral, it can be inferred that the selectivity occurs for agreeing with consistent arguments and disagreeing with inconsistent arguments (the only two means on stops to agree or disagree which are not in the .70 range).

There is, however, more evidence to be considered. We also see in Table 4 that stops to ask differ by consistency of argument and attitude. There is less asking when the two are consistent; there is more asking when they are inconsistent or when the attitudinal position is neutral. Asking a question is not unreasonable as a response to inconsistency; the postulate of selectivity is too narrow for the control phenomena being evinced if it only implies stopping to disagree.

TABLE 4

MEAN STOPS FOR VARIOUS REASONS
BY CONSISTENCY OF ARGUMENT WITH ATTITUDINAL POSITION

	Mean Stops to			*Mean Total Stops*
Argument re Attitude	*Agree*	*Disagree*	*Ask*	
Consistent (n=167)	1.57	.74	1.08	3.39
Inconsistent (n=184)	.78	1.48	1.44	3.70
Neutral Attitude (n=39)	.74	.74	1.44	2.92

Further, total stopping is less for neutral attitude than for either the consistency or inconsistency situation. This recalls the question of informational utility, and how utility might overshadow any difference between consistency and inconsistency.[10] Here both effects are shown.

Selectivity in response to message content can be seen as either occurring in the exposure to content per se or as occurring consequent to content exposure. Further, the exposure question can be divided into two: exposure only to favorable content or exposure only to content pertaining to one's position (favorable or not). The signaled stopping technique gives us a way of observing both exposure and behavior consequent to exposure. The stop can be taken as an index of exposure, the reason for stopping as an index of consistency of response. (Given the anomaly of setting exposure equal to perception—because then there would be no way to achieve nonexposure regarding communication content—stopping is not an unreasonable measure for comparisons of exposure to information.)

The study by Everett (1970) gives us a good opportunity to look at all three types of selectivity because she balanced the arguments so that an equal number would be about subjects' preferences and an equal number would be favorable to the subjects' preferences. Further, the subjects' preferences were also known and their reasons for stopping (to agree or disagree) could be related to the favorability of the assertion (whether the assertion was positive or negative).

Table 5 shows that all three forms of selectivity find support in the data. The effect is much stronger for selectivity occurring consequent to the stopping—in the consistency of agreeing and disagreeing relative to subjects' attitudinal position.

TABLE 5
EVIDENCE FOR THREE TYPES OF SELECTIVITY

Type of Selectivity	Mean Stops
A. Attending Only to Content re Own Preference:	
Consistent	3.67
Inconsistent	3.34
B. Attending Only to Arguments Favoring Own Preference:	
Consistent	3.66
Inconsistent	3.35
C. Stopping to Agree or Disagree re Own Preference:	
Consistent	3.34
Inconsistent	1.88

In her study Everett also placed in the middle of her 16 arguments a paragraph in which subjects were asked their opinion on whether course evaluations should emphasize subjective or objective criteria. This midpoint question was designed to serve as a decision point. It was clear that some subjects did not treat it as such. Yet there are some fascinating data pertaining to selectivity relative to pre- and post-midpoint behavior. Table 6 shows them.

Reasons for stopping—selectivity via agreeing or disagreeing—were more consistent than not, both before and after the midpoint. The consistency was greater after the midpoint. This was also the case for selectivity as stopping for content regarding preferred alternative (favorable or not).

The greatest *difference* is in selectivity as stopping for content which is consistent with attitudinal position (favorable to preferred alternative or unfavorable to nonpreferred alternative). Before the midpoint there is more stopping for inconsistent content. After the midpoint there is more stopping for consistent content. The amount of change in selective behavior is higher for this kind of selectivity than for the others.

Perhaps the most useful aspect of Table 6 is that it makes apparent the benefits to be expected when observational capability is extended. The kind of selectivity showing the largest change from before to after the midpoint is that which most closely approximates Festinger's (1957) hypothesis about information behavior relative to decision behavior. However, it is the third kind of selectivity which most resembles operational definitions undertaken in support of that hypothesis.[11] Here it is the act itself which is observed; previously some act has been required, with an option only as to which act—i.e., its content.

TABLE 6
SELECTIVITY BEFORE AND AFTER
DECISIONAL MIDPOINT IN MESSAGE

	Mean Stops	
Type of Selectivity	Before Midpoint	After Midpoint
A. Attending Only to Content re Own Preference:		
Consistent	1.80	1.88
Inconsistent	1.76	1.58
B. Attending Only to Arguments Favoring Own Preference:		
Consistent	1.66	1.99
Inconsistent	1.91	1.44
C. Stopping to Agree or Disagree re Own Preference:		
Consistent	1.62	1.72
Inconsistent	1.11	.77

The needed singularity for cognitive pictures so that there be some, but only one, implied instruction to follow gives rise to many conditions which relate to stopping and reasons for stopping. This next section considers some of them. We shall start with the problem of nonsingularity in which the difficulty is that no implication is available. We find many such situations, often reflected in remarks like "I'm confused."

This kind of difficulty is common in dissemination questions. Mass media and educational institutions find the message artifact quite useful for mass distribution. But there is a commensurate loss of observational capability to see and respond to instances of noninstruction (Jackson, 1973).

In Table 7 we see the results in stopping behavior of two different manipulations of textbook material. Grunig prepared a simplified account and found that the amount of stopping decreased somewhat. He also prepared another simplified account in which an analogy was used to help get the picture across. This produced more stopping (perhaps because one picture had to be obtained before it could be used for the other). Another finding of some interest is that

TABLE 7

MEAN STOPS BY VERSION OF STORY
ON ECONOMICS OF NATIONAL DEBT

Story Version	Mean Stops[a]
Textbook Account (n=46)	8.48
Simplified Account (n=27)	7.96
Simplified Account, with Criterion Added[b] (n=21)	9.57

SOURCE: James F. Grunig, unpublished data from science writing study, 1971.

a. Mean stops per person per 100 lines (six words per line). Words per line were low because a large right hand margin was provided for stopping reasons.
b. The criterion added to the simplified account was an analogous household debt problem. Ss could then compare the two, for elucidation.

the simplified version increased the proportion of stops to agree or disagree relative to stops to ask or think. The simplified account with the added analogy restored the original proportions among reasons for stopping.

In the study where he looked at punctuation effects, Jackson (1969) also coded the reasons for stopping. Although he used the slant (/) convention, he did not suggest any reporting conventions. This educational use of the widely disseminable message artifact showed its difficulties. Table 8 shows the distribution of reasons given for stopping by students working with programmed instructional content from Skinner and Holland (1961).

The overriding problem of student incapability to get the picture is obvious. Without some provision for the students to obtain assistance when they want it—and need it—tactics employed in developing such materials should surface likely difficulties before the messages are distributed.

TABLE 8

REASONS GIVEN FOR STOPPING
IN PROGRAMED INSTRUCTION CONTENT

Reason for Stopping in Content	Proportion of Total Stops
To Think	23%
To Reread	20
To Express Confusion	17
To Ask Unspecified Question	13
To Seek Clarification	12
To Make Critical Comment	7
To Refer to Earlier Material	5
Other Reasons	3
	100%
	(n=449)[a]

a. The number of stops, of all kinds, made by 84 subjects.

In a later study Jackson (1971) utilized the signaled stopping technique to investigate the relationship of unit sequences within messages to learning. It was hypothesized that altered sequences would produce dysfunctional stopping—via confusion—and less learning. Early attempts at producing message sequences did not yield enough (variance in) learning to test sequence. The stopping technique allowed him to discover learner problems and correct them. But it also cut down on subsequent stopping in these exercises. And it may have removed some learning variance common to dysfunctional stopping and altered sequence. By the time the exercises were cleaned up, the results on sequence and learning were mixed.

Another common form of nonsingularity is that of multiple implication. A sender, listener, viewer, or reader is obliged to remove the multiplicity to achieve singularity. It is not unusual for a sender to assist the receiver—for whatever reason. He may draw a conclusion, give emphasis to one alternative in elaboration or placement, or otherwise suggest a preferable singularity. Many of the attitude change studies conducted as communication effects of messages are of this type; it is implicit that often messages contain implications for more than one attitude—and behavior—so their objective is to see what consequences follow from such tactics as altered source credibility and order of presentation. Attitude change does not furnish, however, a very sensitive criterion for observing all possible kinds of multiple implication in messages. It occurs but once, usually after the message has been completely processed, and is not sensitive to multiple implication per se so much as it is to any achieved singularity of implication.

A number of studies have used the signaled stopping technique to study questions of multiple implication. Some of these are being published separately, relative to substantive theoretical questions, and we shall only mention them briefly. There are several other sets of data we shall present as examples.

Heffner (1969) conducted a study of message ambiguity. This is not a condition which senders typically employ in messages, but it is a condition frequently found by receivers of messages. She found that the amount of stopping to ask was significantly greater for ambiguous content than for clear content in three of four replications. In the fourth, high subject interest in the message content produced mostly stops to assert that interest.

Allen (1973) investigated primacy and recency effects in two studies. In two-sided presentations, order of presentation could be used to suggest preferred singularity—if order effects were reliably known. He found a primacy effect for stopping to agree, and a tendency toward recency effects for all other reasons for stopping. The primacy effect for stopping to agree was greater for personality than for issue arguments.

Jacoubovitch (1972) studied the consequences of multiple signification in word pictures—the common situation where a word (or words) seems to mean several different things. Puns, for example, are well-known instances, but they depend on a sharing of the several meanings. Some instances of multiple signification may be unintended by the sender. Jacoubovitch found more stopping for multiple than for single signification word pictures. Further, he found less stopping for multiple signification pictures if the implications were additive (rather than requiring a resolution somewhere between the several implications).

The two-sided message has multiple implication that the one-sided message does not. Arguments for both of several lines of behavior are given in the two-sided message. Carter and Simpson (1970) alternated between using one- and two-sided messages in their study, so that each subject got two of each type and each issue was presented half the time by one version and half the time by the other. Table 9 shows no difference in total stopping for the two kinds of messages.

TABLE 9
MEAN STOPPING FOR VARIOUS REASONS
BY TYPE OF ARGUMENT ESPOUSED

Type of Argument	Mean Stops to			Mean Total Stops
	Agree	Disagree	Ask	
One-sided (n=195)	1.12	1.14	1.23	3.49
Two-sided (n=195)	1.12	1.03	1.35	3.50

However, there is more stopping to ask by subjects in the two-sided version and less stopping to disagree. There were very few conditions of neutral attitudinal position in this study, but for them the means on total stopping are: one-sided—2.75 (n=16); two-sided—3.34 (n=23). It would be interesting to know if educational level were correlated with one or both of the stopping to ask in two-sided messages and the stopping to disagree in one-sided messages. So far we have not used the exercises on a heterogeneous educational group.

The information triad, after Heider (1958), is another potential source of multiple implication. An unbalanced triad, formally speaking, is often that condition; two implications, not one, are derived from the relationships. (One unbalanced condition, that of three negative relationships, is nonsingular but not clearly that of double implication.) An information triad is any set of relationships of the "P-O-X" type. Heider's logic extends to unit relationships as well as to affective relationships; thus any reported triad will be of the unit type whether it meets the requirements of the affective or not. When, as in the study by Carter (1969b), from which the data in Table 10 are reported, subjects were asked to consider affective relationships between people and other objects—but were not themselves one of the triad—then the unit relationship is essentially what is being investigated.

Table 10 shows that balanced and unbalanced triads do not show any appreciable difference on stopping. However, another source does. P and O disagreeing is clearly a case of multiple implication because the disagreement is regarding X. Why P liking O should produce more stopping than P disliking O seems inexplicable.

TABLE 10
STOPS FOR INFORMATIONAL TRIADS
BY THREE CHARACTERISTICS OF TRIADS

Triad Characteristics	*Proportion of Stops[a]*
A. Balanced	50%
Unbalanced	50
	100% (n=220)[b]
B. P and O Agree	33%
P and O Disagree	67
	100% (n=220)[b]
C. P likes O	56%
P Dislikes O	44
	100% (n=220)[b]

a. The three characteristics are not distributed orthogonally over a set of eight triads, so proportions of total stops are shown for each of the three characteristics individually.
b. The number of stops at end of triad by 37 Ss for two sets of eight triads each.

The person who must construct a cognitive picture to achieve some singular implication may be either sender or receiver in the conventional sense of those terms. In either case, his constructing may be a consequence of the stopping he has engaged in, the sources of that stopping, or the reasons for the stopping.

In constructing pictures, communicators are subject to conditions affecting implication. One source of implication may differ from another in its linguistic expression. Adjectives, for example, convey implication about objects without any relating term. Thus implication via attribution can be conveyed more simply than implication via association of objects. Further, implication via attribution can be conveyed within a sentence unit which also contains implication via functional relationships (e.g., Nice P likes O; Bad P hit O). When constructing pictures, this difference in implicatory source can be important.

Table 11 shows that stopping within information triads increased when X was

TABLE 11
STOPS WITHIN AND AT END OF INFORMATION TRIADS
BY WHETHER "X" IS PERSON OR ATTRIBUTE

	"X" Was	
Stops	*Person*	*Attribute*
Within Triad	22%	42%
At end of Triad	78	58
	100%	100%
	(n=170)[a]	(n=151)[b]

a. The total number of stops made by 37 Ss to a set of eight triads in which X was a person.
b. The total number of stops made by 37 Ss to a set of eight triads in which X was an attribute.

an attribute rather than a person. Even though the attribute was being presented as a conceptual object—not as referring to either P or O—the implicatory power of attributes seems a likely source of stopping. The reader may be telling us, in effect recognizing that implication stems from any presented attribute, that he must stop to consider whether he will accept the attribute. He will not wait for the end of the informational triad and the associational implication.

Heffner (1971) conducted a study of the reporter-reader interaction using signaled stopping. She found an interesting reciprocity condition between their picture construction efforts. The reporter was asked to indicate his stops while reading through data from which he was to prepare a story. Later, the reader of the story indicated his own stops. Heffner found that when story writers used fewer stops the readers used more. It seems that a given amount of cognitive construction was to be done, and if the reporter did not do it his reader had to do it.

Taking the broadest view of attitudinal position is to include cognitive components with the affective and conative. In this view, then, there should be some functional relationship between reasons for stopping and subsequent attitudinal position. The terminal position might reflect reader constructions while reading the message, analogous to how his stops reflect his initial position.

Carter and Simpson (1970) readministered the student issues questionnaire to their subjects after the stopping exercises had been completed. For those subjects who showed a change in attitudinal position, differences in stopping behavior could be assessed. As Table 12 shows, the analogy does not extend to the data very well. There seems to be some relationship between stopping to disagree and consequent change away from the argument presented, particularly for two-sided messages. But the other relationships are small.

Two things are worth noting. The "n's" in Table 12 show that those who did

TABLE 12
ATTITUDE CHANGE FOR ONE-SIDED AND TWO-SIDED
MESSAGES BY REASONS FOR STOPPING

	Proportion Changing		
Argument Type/Reason	With the Argument	Against the Argument	
A. One-sided Messages:			
Stop to Agree	52%	48%	100% (n=62)[a]
Stop to Ask	51	49	100% (n=84)
Stop to Disagree	48	52	100% (n=65)
B. Two-sided Messages:			
Stop to Agree	49%	51%	100% (n=68)
Stop to Ask	49	51	100% (n=96)
Stop to Disagree	45	55	100% (n=80)

a. The number in parentheses is of attitude changers who gave this reason for stopping at least once while reading the message.

change attitudinal position were more likely to have stopped to ask a question than to stop to agree or disagree. And, by inference, much of the change in attitude was due to combinations of cognitive behavior (and stops), not to any simple mechanism. For instance, the "n's" are too high, given the number of subjects (99), for there to have been substantial use of only one kind of stopping even in the one-sided presentations.

For the cognitive construction which goes on while messages are being received (and sent), the attitudinal change paradigm for studying communication effects seems constraining. Like the sender-message-receiver paradigm, it points to an important constraint on behavior. Values held do affect behavior, just as transmission does define some temporal and spatial relationships. But not all behavior is so derived from values held, nor is communication just transmission.

CONCLUSION

The picture we get of how humans use communication and respond to its use by others, as reported in Klapper (1960) and later in Berelson and Steiner (1964), is conveyed by the paradigms of sender-message-receiver and of attitude change. We get a picture of incremental characteristics and of selectivity mechanisms. What is represented in such accounts is not so much summary of human communication behavior as it is summary of things observed using these paradigms.

As we increase our observational capability and look into more of the characteristics and mechanisms of information processing, the descriptive as well as the observational constraints of such paradigms can be replaced. We can focus on the explanations which were adduced to the data gathered, and pay less heed to the constructs derived from the observational paradigms. We can pursue less constrained general hypotheses. Instead of investigating selectivity as a general hypothesis, we might better postulate utility of information—then look for conditions which modify its utility. In this way we may better comprehend, for example, how people construct values as well as how they express or alter them.

Finally, there is a lesson to be learned from the history of observing communication effects. Any of our so-called information processing paradigms—decision-making, machine-processing, stopping, or whatever—is subject to the same risks. Our safeguard seems to be an analysis of the conditions *not* touched on by each paradigm, with particular attention to paradigms which make some phenomena unavailable because of consequent biases in the methodology.

After all, data produced by the attitude-change paradigm soon made the selectivity hypothesis suspect. The sender-message-receiver paradigm is more troublesome because it (still) imposes a unit feature on many observations which makes other data unavailable.

APPENDIX

The data reported in this chapter came from class exercises in which students used the signaled stopping technique while learning about situations in which stopping—and control of stopping—would be efficacious to them.

The introductory material usually included an oral presentation (by one of the authors of this chapter) which covered many of the conceptual points raised in the opening part of this chapter. Our informal observation is that this increases the total amount of stopping behavior. We would further observe that, because stopping is work, these exercises should be used carefully with subjects who have no interest in communication problems.

Generally, it is no problem to write an appropriate specific introduction to the messages used and for the reporting conventions used—as these examples indicate.

The possibility of inserting experimental stimuli in the instructions or introductory material should be considered pessimistically. It is to the observer's advantage to place any stimuli in the message content where some idea of its impact can be gained from stopping behavior. Or, if a stimulus is expected to have been present (e.g., as a personality variable) then some indication of it should be arranged in the message processing prior to the focal section where it is supposed to have causal—or some functional—significance.

For example, if involvement or commitment is considered a requisite and probable condition, find out first that it is in fact so before introducing the focal stimulus. (A direct or rhetorical question often elicits such data.)

Exercise A

Mass Media: On the Short End of a Line . . .

Sure you can write a letter. To somebody. But what about *now*? It can be very frustrating to interact with a mass medium. For example:

Suppose you are listening to the radio, to a broadcast of an interview on a topic of interest to you. You have things you would like to say. There may be things you would like to ask. *Now*. And you can't—with any answer, except maybe an echo.

The material on the following pages comes from a recent radio program, in which an interviewer talks with people about the population problem.

You may have some strong feelings on this subject. The interviewer is there. You are not there. What if you were?

Stop where you want to as you read through, marking a slash (/).

Then, we would like you to use these marks:

(A) for agreement;
(D) for disagreement;

      (?)   for question;

      (T)   for thinking.

Place them in the margin to the right of the slash to which they refer. If you feel particularly strongly about something, you can indicate it by using several marks—for example (DDD) or (AAA).

Exercise B

Time Costs . . .

One consequence of the principle of "one thing at a time" is that time literally costs something. It costs whatever is related to time that is not the "one thing" operative at any point in time. So . . . if you stop to think while someone else is talking to you, you lose whatever he says while you are thinking. On the other hand, if you continue to listen, you lose whatever profit might have come from stopping to think instead.

Similarly, if you are listening to someone describe something and you continue to listen even though you are ready to "go"—to do whatever you are going to do, there is a cost in continuing to listen. There is a cost in not continuing to listen, too; we call it politeness sometimes, but it comes down to a question of what is lost by refusing to listen. So, sometimes we interrupt—but politely, trying to heed both costs.

On the next few pages are some episodes in which you are to be a listener, on your own terms. Interrupt when you want to, for your own reasons.

We want you to imagine that these six episodes represent six people coming to your door, knocking, and starting to talk. We assume you will *not* invite them in. That represents a cost far beyond mere listening; it implies your expenditure of future time as well as present time—that you "buy" the caller if not the specific item of today's conversation.

Now, for the next few minutes, imagine that you are living alone in an apartment (bedroom, kitchenette, and bath). It is the first apartment (A) in a line of eight; you are in the one closest to the street corner. You have been there about a month and know the other residents—at least by sight. You moved from a small, single room shared with a friendly roommate, who simply wouldn't put things away (except for food and drink).

The activity of the visitor is provided here. We want you to provide the rest of the activity, whether it is to the visitor or just to yourself. To do this you will have to stop from time to time . . .

We would like you to practice making two kinds of stops:

1. Stop to *think*. Wherever you believe it would be a good idea to "interrupt" the caller to think, do so, by drawing a slash and a T (/T).
2. Stop to *say* something. Wherever you believe it would be a good idea to "interrupt" the caller to ask or tell something, do so, by drawing a slash (/) and *putting what you would say in the right hand margin*.

Exercise C

Provocative Fillers

It is a familiar practice for the mass media—and particularly the print media—to use *fillers,* those little items which fill up otherwise empty holes in the pages. Such items are typically either factual (e.g., 15,000,000 lbs. of zinc were produced by Calumet-Hecla last year in its Joplin, Missouri mines) or humorous (e.g., 15 million pounds of zinc were produced in the Joplin, Missouri mines last year by Calumet-Hecla).

There has been some move recently toward the use of provocative material in fillers. *Behavioral Science,* for example, fills up with quotes from long-neglected classics of philosophy. But what about the consumer's response to such material? It's one thing to swallow a fact or to chuckle over a funny one—you don't need someone else at hand for that. But provocative fillers may boomerang. The consumer may want to ask or say something, and there isn't someone there when mass media are the provocateurs.

The following materials deal with possible filler items; they are gleaned from many sources; they deal with various aspects of the currently important question of *quality of life,* especially topics of ecology and women's rights.

To evaluate the possible consumer reaction to such materials, we would like you to read through them, treating each as a separate item (i.e., potentially a filler item). Any time you stop, for any reason, mark a slash (/), then after the slash mark a question (?) if that was the reason for stopping, mark an (A) if you wanted to agree, mark a (D) if you wanted to disagree.

You will have four kinds of symbols then:

/?   Stopped to ask a question.
/A   Stopped to agree.
/D   Stopped to disagree.
/   Stopped (but for some other reason than above).

After you have finished, we will consider what conditions, if any, militate against the use of provocative filler materials in the mass media.

Exercise D

Practicing Stopping

The opportunity to practice stopping is not always available to us. Generally speaking, stopping usually requires us to interrupt something or someone. Such practice may not be possible because you cannot interrupt (as in viewing television) or it may not be feasible because you are penalized for interrupting if you seem to be doing it just for practice.

Printed matter, as found in books, magazines, newspapers, is one of the more accessible means for practicing stopping. So we have brought together some news story materials for you to practice on.

In the stories which follow, any time you want to stop you can. Each time that you do stop, indicate where you stopped by marking a slash (/). You might want to stop to ask a question, to say something, to think, to reread, or to do something else. In each case, tell us your reason for stopping. You can use the following conventions:

/T	Stop to think	/R	Stop to reread
/A	Stop to agree	/D	Stop to disagree
/?	Stop to question		

If you have some other reason for stopping, report it in the margin on the right.

Should you want to give additional emphasis, you can show it by this means:

/?? Really question that
/AA Agree very much

There are eight news stories for you to practice on.

Exercise E

Tell It Like It Is . . .

Why is it so hard? Why is there so often a discrepancy between *what is said* and *what is being talked about?*

Language enables us to construct pictures with words. But these pictures do not always fit very well. That is, they do not *map* things such that we can use them as helpful guides.

To some extent, languages create problems because they are both the *means* by which word pictures are built up and also the *elements* of the completed pictures. Generally, however, we simply do not know very much about the problems languages create "for getting word pictures through."

This exercise is one way in which we are trying to find out some of the difficulties which languages get us into. We want you to "receive" some word pictures and let us know what is happening as you get them.

On the following pages are a number of paragraphs, each one a word picture of something. You can show us what is happening as you receive these pictures if you will use a simple device: Anywhere you want to stop—to ask a question, to disagree, to agree, to think—mark a slash (/) at that point. Then tell us why you stopped, using abbreviations for questioning (?), disagreeing (D), agreeing (A), and thinking (T); or leave just the slash if none of these apply.

So you will have the use of five ways of telling us how the pictures are getting through:

/? Stop to ask a question
/D Stop to disagree

/A   Stop to agree
/T   Stop to think
/   Stop for some other reason

After you have done this for the set of word pictures given here, we can discuss some of the problems any language faces in trying to help you "tell it like it is."

Exercise F

Relevances for the Individual

There are some important consequences for the individual in social compacts and social institutions. Some are political, like the *quid pro quo* of freedom and responsibility. Others are important for communication, like the increased power the individual derives from having a symbol system (of words) available to him through the collective effort of the society in which he lives.

But it is rather a different story when it comes to the *timing* of communication. Off by himself, so to speak, the individual *can* control the timing of things; he can read at his own pace, for instance. But when he comes into contact with others much of the temporal sequence in which things happen *to him* is out of control. The telephone rings. Speakers drone on and on. There's no way to ask a question *now,* or to express an opinion *now.* And so on.

We know very little about the conditions which need to be studied if we are to develop ways of improving the individual's control over timing in communication. These "stopping" exercises are a way of introducing you to the problem and of furnishing a basis for discussing the problem.

We would like you here to *interrupt* what is being said, to stop whenever you want. And we would like you to say why you stopped.

On the following pages are a number of paragraphs, drawn from various sources, on the general subject of "quality of life." Any time *you* want to stop—to ask a question, to disagree, to agree, to think—mark a slash (/) at that point. And tell us why you stopped then, using these abbreviations:

/?   Stop to ask a question
/D   Stop to disagree
/A   Stop to agree
/T   Stop to think
/   Stop for some other reason

After you have done this for the set of paragraphs given here, we can discuss some of the difficulties involved in controlling timing of communication.

NOTES

1. The distinction was made primarily to get away from the "communication process" usage. The latter leads to very large units, such as compound and/or complex sequences—such as the activities of encoding and decoding, sending and receiving, etc. The theoretical discussion can be found in two earlier papers (Carter, 1969a; 1971). Much of the introductory material in this chapter is drawn from these sources and two research proposals by Carter and Ruggels (1970; 1971).

2. A preliminary discussion of singularity and its relationship to stopping can be found in a recent theoretical paper (Carter, 1972).

3. If we accept the possibility of man bringing various criteria to bear on observed conditions according to the condition observed—and not rely just on the cybernetic model, the accounting of man's behavior is less strained. This approach was used by Carter (1966) to reconceptualize psychological conflict and cognitive dissonance, and—generally—to avert a restriction that man's behavior always be consistent with a given value position.

4. Pauses and hesitations have been viewed regarding what goes on during the stopped period and for the origins of that activity in preceding speech activities. Studies have emphasized emotional and cognitive conditions; the latter are more germane to this conceptualization (for a summary, see Tannenbaum, Williams, and Hillier, 1965). Because there is variety in origin as well as in pause activity, the condition of stopping per se takes on significance. It must reconcile the differences, by explaining the multiplicity—which is inherent in the switching function of the stop itself, whatever its origin and whatever it is accompanied or followed by.

5. Mahl (1959: 13-14) notes a high frequency of pauses and hesitations (he calls them "disturbances" because of his interest in their emotional aspect) for a variety of speakers. An average of one every five seconds is just as likely for one as for another speaker. The similarity, not the expected clinical difference, is what seems striking. Together with the multiplicity factor, it suggests the general, control feature of stopping.

6. See Table 10, and pertinent discussion, in next section.

7. Examples of introductory comments used in some of our exercises are found in the Appendix.

8. Sears and Freedman (1967) provide a review of the evidence for selective exposure in which they distinguish two types: (1) selectivity of exposure, and (2) selectivity following exposure.

9. The usage "stops to agree or disagree" is conceptually repugnant, but to facilitate data presentation we shall not repeatedly distinguish between stopping, interrupting, and behavior after stopping (as in "reason for stopping").

10. Several helpful discussions of the utility factor in selectivity are: Freedman and Sears (1965); Sears and Freedman (1967); Carter, Pyszka, and Guerrero (1969); Chaffee, Stamm, Guerrero, and Tipton (1969).

11. In any case, most of these studies viewed consistent and inconsistent as mirror images, implying similar functional consequences of "supportive" information sought and of "nonsupportive" information avoided. Again, the postulate seems constraining.

REFERENCES

ALLEN, R. L. (1973) "Primacy and recency: the order of presentation." Journalism Quarterly, in press.

BALES, R. F. (1950) Interaction Process Analysis: A Method for the Study of Small Groups. Cambridge: Addison, Wesley.

BERELSON, B. and G. A. STEINER (1964) Human Behavior: An Inventory of Scientific Findings. New York: Harcourt, Brace, and World.

CARTER, R. F. (1966) Cognitive Discrepancies and Communication Behavior. Paper read at Association for Education in Journalism convention.

——— (1969a) Report of the Eureka Holding Company. Memorandum.

——— (1969b) The Alchemy of Communication. Paper read at Association for Education in Journalism convention.

——— (1971) Theoretical Development in the Use of Signaled Stopping. Paper read at Association for Education in Journalism convention.

——— (1972) A Journalistic View of Communication. Paper read at Association for Education in Journalism convention.

CARTER, R. F., R. H. PYSZKA, and J. L. GUERRERO (1969) "Dissonance and exposure to aversive information." Journalism Quarterly 46 (Spring): 37-42.

CARTER, R. F. and W. L. RUGGELS (1970) Research on Stopping: A New Approach to Research on Communication Effects. Research proposal.

——— (1971) "Educational message analysis." Research proposal.

CARTER, R. F. and R. SIMPSON (1970) Unpublished data.

CHAFFEE, S. H., K. R. STAMM, J. L. GUERRERO, and L. P. TIPTON (1969) "Experiments on cognitive discrepancies and communication." Journalism Monographs 14 (Dec.).

EVERETT, B. (1970) Communication Behavior Before and After Decision Making. Master's thesis. Seattle: University of Washington.

FESTINGER, L. (1957) A Theory of Cognitive Dissonance. New York: Row, Peterson.

FREEDMAN, J. L. and D. O. SEARS (1965) "Selective Exposure," pp. 57-97 in L. Berkowitz (ed.) Advances in Experimental Social Psychology. Volume 2. New York: Academic Press.

HEFFNER, M. B. (1969) Some Communication Effects of Message Ambiguity. Paper read at Association for Education in Journalism convention.

——— (1970) Inoculation and Stopping Behavior. Paper read at Association for Education in Journalism convention.

——— (1971) Mediated Communication and Subjective Measures of Accuracy. Paper read at Association for Education in Journalism convention.

——— (1972) The Possibility of Communicative Accuracy. Ph.D. dissertation. Seattle: University of Washington.

HEIDER, F. (1958) The Psychology of Interpersonal Relations. New York: John Wiley.

JACKSON K. M. (1969) Stipulated Stop Technique in Programed Learning Context. Paper read at Association for Education in Journalism convention.

——— (1971) A Communication Approach to Programed Instruction. Ph.D. dissertation. Seattle: University of Washington.

——— (1973) "Monitoring communication: new technique of message analysis." Journalism Quarterly, in press.

JACOUBOVITCH, M. D. (1972) Communication Consequences of Signification. Master's thesis. Seattle: University of Washington.

KLAPPER, J. T. (1960) The Effects of Mass Communication. Glencoe, Ill.: Free Press.

MAHL, G. F. (1959) "Explaining emotional states by content analysis," pp. 89-130 in I.D.S. Pool (ed.) Trends in Content Analysis. Urbana: University of Illinois Press.

NEWCOMB, T. M. (1953) "An approach to the study of communicative acts." Psychological Review 60: 393-404.

SEARS, D. O. and J. L. FREEDMAN (1967) "Selective exposure to information: a critical review," Public Opinion Quarterly 31 (Summer): 194-213.

SKINNER, B. F. and J. G. HOLLAND (1961) The Analysis of Behavior. New York: McGraw-Hill.

TANNENBAUM, P. H., F. WILLIAMS, and C. S. HILLIER (1965) "Word predictability in the environments of hesitations." Journal of Verbal Learning and Verbal Behavior 4, 2: 134-40.

THAYER, L. (1968) Communication and Communication Systems. Homewood, Ill.: Irwin.

Chapter 2

COMMUNITY ISSUES, CONFLICT, AND PUBLIC AFFAIRS KNOWLEDGE

Phillip J. Tichenor, Jane M. Rodenkirchen,
Clarice N. Olien, and George A. Donohue

CONFLICT AND INFORMATION DIFFUSION are cited frequently as basic variables in community change. The functional relationship between the two, however, is not often made explicit in empirical analyses. The need for examining the conflict-information relationship for programmatic purposes has been stressed by Marceau (1972). She contends that in modernization programs the role of mass communication needs to be re-examined in light of the fact that most developing areas are "full of conflict" and that "mass media messages become entangled in the conflicts, disputes, and disturbances" at the local level.

While writers such as Marceau tend to view conflict as a negative condition in communication, we suggest that conflict may be viewed as either positive *or* negative. However conflict may be seen as a necessary process but not a sufficient condition for mass diffusion of information—especially in situations where the goal is widespread distribution of knowledge to a general population. The perspective that conflict is not necessarily a negative factor in communication has many practical ramifications for the distribution of information through such mass media as newspapers and television.

Several scholars representing the social conflict school of thought have referred to the role of conflict in arousing and maintaining citizen participation (Coser, 1956; Dahrendorf, 1959). Coser (1967) has pointed out that the clash of values and ideas between competing interests and groups may be a sign of vitality and creativity. Conflict *within* a system can lead to revitalization of old norms or emergence of new ones; conflict with an *external* group may, in addition, strengthen internal cohesion. All of these consequences imply an increase in certain forms of communication, such as communication through mass media.

Political scientists have noted the relationship between intensities arising from political conflicts and the possession of information about political policies and objectives (Key, 1967); Hennessy, 1970). Opinion research data support the view that opinion intensity, political understanding, and political participation tend to be correlated (Almond and Verba, 1963; Lane and Sears, 1964; Key, 1967). Other social scientists have pointed up the possibility that communication may be impaired by extremely intense conflicts (Williams, 1972; Lundberg, 1939).

In most analyses of the type cited above, conflict is treated as a dichotomous condition, rather than as a variable condition. For the purposes of this analysis, conflict is defined as a varying system condition which may be treated as either a dependent or an independent variable, depending upon the nature of the analysis.

CONFLICT—A VARIABLE SYSTEM CONDITION

Social conflict, as used here, is awareness of differing public positions among interest groups or other subsystems which make up a total social system. Theoretically, the relationship between conflict and total communicative activity in a system may take on any one of a number of empirical patterns, depending on the structure of the system. Conceivably, in some systems, the relationship may be linear. In others, it may take one of several forms of curvilinearity. A point may occur in a given system, for example, where conflict reaches such an intense and rancorous level that communication changes in form and shifts from one set of actors to another. The possibility of inhibition of certain types of communication in conflict situations is alluded to by Coser (1956), Lynd (1939), and Bogardus (1920).

In a maximal conflict situation, communication through mass media may be restrained or shifted entirely from mass to interpersonal channels, leading to what is popularly called a "communication breakdown" but which may in fact be an *accommodation* to the intensity of conflict. For example, when negotiations between formal organizations become so conflict-ridden that participants cease talking to each other (and thereby cease being quoted in mass media), the negotiations frequently shift to a different set of representatives of each organization. This turning point may occur when the conflict itself becomes the focal point of concern, taking priority over the initial issue. In such cases, inhibitions to distribution, acquisition, and assimilation of information through mass media may occur as part of a new mode of adjustment to the heightened conflict condition.

Conflict, however, is not the only stimulus for communication about public affairs. A generalized feeling of pride, accomplishment, and cohesion regarding a new community project might be accompanied by high levels of both mass and interpersonal communication. Conceivably, a "whole town might talk" about a new community project which every group and individual there supports. Such communication may occur where there is minimal conflict and maximal consensus about the project.

Conflict and consensus approaches may be seen as alternative modes for resolution of tension in different social systems. In smaller, less diversified communities, for example, mass media are less likely to report certain types of controversy, particularly controversy limited to groups within the community itself. Decisions in such a community are traditionally handled on a consensus basis, or at least in a way that gives the outward appearance of consensus. In the traditional, homogeneous community, where a few individuals play multiple leadership roles, conflicts tend to be managed "behind the scenes" and are less likely to be brought to the surface.

One of the modes of accommodation—total avoidance of open conflict—apparently occurs both among governmental groups and among the mass media to a greater extent in smaller communities (Olien, Donohue, and Tichenor, 1968; Paletz, Reichert, and McIntyre, 1971). Whereas conflict in the larger, more pluralistic community may be a force for social stability, open conflict may be a negative force for maintenance and cohesion in the smaller, less pluralistic community.

Hypothetically, then, conflict should be an accelerating factor for communication until, because of the nature of the conflict and the nature of the community, tension reaches a level disruptive for that community. Beyond that inflection point, the flow of mass and other formal information is likely to dissipate. Resistance to formal, mass media communication is more likely to occur. The precise point of such inflection is an empirical question. The model used here anticipates the types of social structure in which inflection is most likely to occur, but not necessarily the precise amount of tension required for that inflection.

SOCIAL CONFLICT AND THE KNOWLEDGE GAP

One of the principal consequences of mass media coverage about national public affairs issues, particularly from the print media, appears to be an increasing "knowledge gap" between various social strata of the population. The formal statement of the hypothesis is:

> As the infusion of mass media information into a social system increases, segments of the population with higher socioeconomic status tend to acquire this information at a faster rate than the lower status segments, so that the gap in knowledge between these segments tends to increase rather than decrease. [Tichenor, Donohue and Olien, 1970]

Several factors seem to contribute to this widening gap. Persons with more formal education, for example, have higher levels of communication skills, more existing knowledge from prior exposure, and more frequent social contacts relevant to public affairs topics. Also, the mass media system itself—particularly the print media system—is geared to interests and tastes of the higher-status segment. Analyses of several sets of data, from news diffusion studies, time trends, a newspaper strike, and a field experiment, are consistent with this knowledge gap hypothesis.

Similarly, a knowledge gap appears to have been demonstrated by the first year evaluations of Sesame Street. That is, although disadvantaged viewers gained as much in basic knowledge and skills from viewing Sesame Street as did advantaged viewers, there was a pronounced tendency for higher viewing among the advantaged group (Bogatz and Ball, 1971). Therefore, there was greater gain for the total sample of advantaged children than for the total sample of disadvantaged children.

The general knowledge gap phenomenon cited above is analagous to the observed consequences of educational institutions, as described in the well-known Coleman Report (Coleman et al., 1966). Moynihan (1968), in reflecting on the Coleman Report, suggested that as socially-provided opportunities for education increase, the correlation between school achievement and such group-related characteristics as parental education tends to increase also.

The basic question here is whether social conflict in a community is likely to open the knowledge gap even further, or to close it. High levels of reporting of conflict in mass media may stimulate attention to an issue among socioeconomic strata that otherwise are less likely to become aware of the issue. The high intensity of a national election campaign, for example, has been regarded as necessary to stimulate voting among persons who are otherwise less active in political affairs (Converse, 1962).

One could argue, therefore, that certain kinds of continued conflict in a community would close the gap in knowledge. Such an outcome could occur with lengthy media coverage of a well-defined conflict situation. An illustration would be the case where, in an area of long-term concern over river pollution, a single city decides to release sewage into a river and local media give the decision heavy coverage for several weeks. In such a case, the same basic information may be repeated so frequently that it reaches into the most inactive groups of the community.

In other situations, new information may appear frequently, thus widening the gap. An example might be a running controversy over location of, say, a metropolitan airport. Different proposals, opposing views, and counter proposals might be presented through mass media sequentially, so that each time the issue appears there is a new development which is most understandable to persons and groups who know the background of the issue. In such a case, those who have prior information would be the ones most likely to learn more.

In summary, then, any number of knowledge gap patterns, involving different media coverage formats and different forms of conflict, may appear in different situations.

CONFLICT, EDUCATIONAL LEVEL, AND ATTITUDES

A variation of the knowledge gap hypothesis is the relationship, under certain community conditions, between higher socioeconomic status (as measured by level of education) and attitudinal position on social issues. At the individual level, amount of formal education has often been found to predict the position that a person takes on issues (Sears and Freedman, 1967). Variations in attitudes provide basic conditions for conflict; as the number of different attitudinal positions in a community increases, higher levels of conflict are likely to exist.

Changes in attitudinal positions over time, as the situation is defined and perhaps redefined, may frequently occur within higher educational strata themselves. In community issues such as ecology, social treatment of minorities, or drug-abuse programs, there are often socially defined positions which are accepted by various socioeconomic status groups. The initial phase in any social movement is such that information is not evenly distributed or available, but tends to be differentially possessed by persons with income and education characteristic of the upper strata.

Historically, most social movements have been introduced and supported in their initial phases by higher socioeconomic status groups. For example, "pro-environmentalist" views have been found to be more actively supported by highly educated persons (Tichenor, Donohue, Olien, and Bowers, 1971). Theoretically, this should be the nature of the initial relationship when the issue is new and persons with higher education tend to judge the issue in terms of their generalized values about ecology. A similar initial tendency might be expected for any community issue, such as school busing or urban housing.

Therefore, when the issue is relatively new and information is limited largely to one alternative, one might expect a rather strong relationship between high social status and support for that alternative. As more information is distributed throughout the system, more alternatives and arguments on various aspects of the issue may become available, and the initial relationship may well be altered. Theoretically, it would be entirely consistent to find that as publicity levels increase, the link between status and knowledge grows stronger, while the link between status and a given position may grow weaker or change entirely. But where the available information is limited largely to one view—especially of the dominant professional specialists—the relationship between status and attitudes might remain strong.

The above position holds that on any broad social issue, the initial impact of mass media inputs would be to reinforce and extend already existing gaps between social status groups. As the rate of mass media input is increased and the topic becomes more relevant, accompanied by heightened conflict, conditions are created that should lead to a closing of the gap between social status segments, in both knowledge and attitudes.[1]

HYPOTHESES UNDER STUDY

Data about communication and information distribution presented here deal with community issues as the basic unit of analysis. Several hypotheses guide our work:

(1) As the level of mass media coverage of a community issue increases, there will be a higher level of knowledge of that issue in that community.

(2) As the level of mass media coverage of a community issue increases, there will be a higher level of perception of conflict regarding that issue in that community.

(3) As the level of mass media coverage of a community issue increases, there will be an increasing gap in knowledge about that issue between persons high and low in socioeconomic status.

(4) The higher the level of perception of conflict about an issue in a community, the higher the amount of interpersonal communication about that issue within the community.

(5) The higher the level of perception of conflict regarding an issue in a community, the higher the level of knowledge about that issue in the community.

(6) The higher the level of perception of conflict regarding an issue in a community, the greater the gap in knowledge about that issue between persons high and low in socioeconomic status.

(7) The higher the level of perception of conflict regarding an issue in a community, the higher the level of perception of conflict in mass media content to which members of that community are experimentally exposed.

(8) The higher the level of perception of conflict about an issue in a community, the greater the recall from mass media content about that issue to which members of that community are experimentally exposed.

(9) The higher the level of perception of conflict regarding an issue in a community, the lower the correlation in that community between socioeconomic status and attitudes toward alternative courses of action.

While these hypotheses are stated, and will be tested, in terms of zero-order relationships, they are considered as elements of an interrelated system of relationships and the interpretation of data should be considered in light of this assumption. Ultimately, this hypothetical model should be tested in a multiple regression analysis. Because of limitations in numbers of communities and the exploratory nature of this research, the present report is limited to zero-order relationships.

DATA SOURCES, PROCEDURES, AND COMMUNITY CHARACTERISTICS

Data were taken from personal interviews conducted in 15 different community areas in Minnesota since 1969. The communities were selected in four groups, with one or more local or regional issues common to all communities in each group. Issues in three of the groups have environmental and ecological implications—nuclear radiation from a power plant, release of smoke from factories, mining in a wilderness area, pollution of rivers and lakes, and sewage control.

The principal issue in the fourth group may be viewed as a political innovation, in the form of regionalization. This issue centered around a Regional Development Act which had been passed by the Minnesota Legislature.

The major criterion for inclusion of a community in the study was the extent to which each issue had been subjected to mass media publicity, on both a local basis and on a regional or statewide basis. The communities vary in size, in social structure, and geographic location. The communities were selected so as to involve social conflict of varying levels.

In addition to involving conflict, the issues had several other elements in common. Each one contained direct implications for the future of at least one community under study. Also, each issue had arisen at least partly as a result of actions or pressures by state or federal agencies—that is from forces primarily external to the communities. Finally, each issue involved public decisions which would eventually need to be made or considered in an effort to resolve the issue.

Community Group 1: Nuclear Power Issue

Communities of St. Cloud, rural Wright county, and Osseo were studied in the spring of 1969. The issue for all three centered on the nuclear power plant which had been constructed recently at Monticello in rural Wright county. A principal question concerned the radiation emission standards under which the plant would operate, and whether ultimate control over these standards would rest with the state or with the federal government. Permissible levels of emission had been specified for the plant by the U.S. Atomic Energy Commission several months earlier.

In the two months preceding the study, media attention had focused on the power company and on the activities of a voluntary organization which opposed release of radioactive wastes from the plant. Interest in the problem heightened when, a few days before the interviewing began, the Minnesota Pollution Control Agency issued a permit which allowed for total radiation not to exceed two percent of the federal (AEC) standards.

The three community areas are roughly adjacent to each other, along the Mississippi River northwest of Minneapolis. Osseo is a metropolitan suburb and St. Cloud, one of the larger non-metropolitan communities in Minnesota, is about fifty miles northwest of Osseo. The section of rural Wright county included in the sample borders the Mississippi River in the area between Osseo and St. Cloud.

Community Group 2: Mining and Metal Industry Issues

Four communities were included in this group—Grand Rapids, Duluth, Ely, and Silver Bay, where interviewing was conducted in spring 1970. The issues were air pollution by a steel plant, taconite tailings discharge into Lake Superior, and mining exploration in the Boundary Waters Canoe Area (BWCA), a federally-designated recreation area of northeastern Minnesota.

The steel plant in Duluth was its largest employer with 2,500 persons. Pressure was being applied to the plant by state and federal pollution control agencies to meet air pollution standards. A basic issue locally was whether the company could meet these standards without reducing or discontinuing operations.

In Silver Bay the issue concerned a taconite processing plant that provides more than half of the jobs in a community of under 4,000 population, and whether taconite tailings which the plant discharges into Lake Superior have harmful effects on that body of water. There were contradictory opinions about the effect of the tailings from different research specialists, and testimony from both sides had received some publicity.

The mining issue concerned the Boundary Waters Canoe Area near Ely; the question there was whether exploratory drilling for mineral deposits should be continued in that wilderness area. The general assumption was that discovery of large mineral deposits might lead to mining in the canoe country at some future time. Environmentalist groups generally opposed both the drilling and potential mining. The opposing view was that such drilling should continue, in the hope that finding metal deposits might eventually lead to new industry and employment in the area.

Community Group 3: Political Regionalization Issue

The communities in this group included Worthington, Marshall, Thief River Falls, and Crookston. Interviewing was conducted in the fall of 1970.

The 1969 Minnesota Legislature had passed a Regional Planning Act, which laid the ground work for regional development areas without specifying precisely how such development areas would be structured politically or economically. A year later the Governor, by executive order, delineated the boundaries of eleven such regions in Minnesota; formation of regional development commissions was to be accomplished voluntarily, at the local level.

The procedure by which the law was enacted, the information used by the Legislature in preparing the law, and provisions of the act itself were sharply challenged by the daily *Worthington Globe,* circulating in that city and the surrounding trade area of southwestern Minnesota. The *Globe* published a special report, written by two specialists, which was highly critical of the Regional Development Act. The *Globe's* position, along with the special report, was publicized in Twin Cities newspapers during the two months immediately preceding the survey. The issue was germane to each of the four communities in this group in that each was a potential "regional center" economically and/or politically.

Debate tended to center around the provisions of the act, the regional boundaries, and the question of which communities (if any) might be designated as regional centers.[2] There were also debates over interpretation; at least one major newspaper in the state carried a feature article insisting that the "regional center" idea was not part of the Act at all.

Community Group 4: Water Quality Issue

This community group included Rochester, Winona-Goodview, Cosmos, and Glenwood, with the interviewing conducted in late winter and early spring 1971. The issues in this study centered around either a local sewage control question or contamination of bodies of water by mercury. In this group of communities each local issue was considered unique to the respective community area.

In Rochester the issue involved sewage control and two local levels of government, the city of Rochester itself and the Olmsted County Board of Commissioners. Prior to the study a bill authorizing the County Board to establish sewer or sewer-water districts in unincorporated areas, through local petition, had been introduced in the Minnesota Legislature. Local debate on this procedure included the question of impact on municipalities if establishment of such districts led to elimination of the need for annexation.

In the Winona area the adjoining residential village of Goodview was under instruction from the state pollution control agency either to build its own sewage treatment plant or join with the Winona system. Political leaders from both communities had voiced some support for, and some reservations about, proposals to link Goodview with the Winona treatment plant. At the time the survey was made, a proposed joint plan was under study by the respective governmental bodies of the two communities.

Cosmos, in central Minnesota, is a village with a longstanding sewage disposal problem. The village had been under state agency pressure to build a local sewage treatment system, and cost of such facilities had been a major factor in the controversy. At one point, following editorial commentary on the situation by the local newspaper, village council members had resigned. These events had occurred within a few months preceding the survey, and shortly before interviewing there began, the local newspaper announced that the sewage plan had put the village financially in the red.

Glenwood is an area in which agriculture and recreation are both major sources of employment and income. More than a fourth of the labor force of the county is employed in agriculture. Glenwood itself is situated on the shoreline of Lake Minnewaska, one of many popular recreational lakes in that area of the state.

In late fall 1970 Lake Minnewaska was mentioned in a state-federal report about mercury levels in fish taken from various bodies of water. In that initial report, state health authorities had recommended that fish from this particular lake should be eaten only in limited quantities. The lake had been put on a "mercury danger list" along with several other bodies of water around the state. This report received heavy publicity in statewide media and in the local newspaper at Glenwood, which suggested editorially that the community had been treated unfairly in the report and stood to lose its reputation as a popular resort center, and that consequently it was in danger of losing part of its seasonal business. After approximately half of the interviews had been completed in Glenwood, a new announcement from the Minnesota Department of Health indicated that the lake was being taken off the "mercury danger" list of lakes. The new report had the effect of refuting the conclusions of the earlier one.

Community Similarities and Differences

As the issues themselves might suggest, the communities vary greatly in social structure. Duluth, Rochester, and Winona are the most pluralistic and urbanized in that they have the highest division of labor, the most income and religious differentiation, and the most varied industrial mix. Duluth is the largest, with a population of slightly over 100,000 (Table 1). The communities with the highest proportions of professionally employed persons (based on samples) are Rochester, St. Cloud, and Marshall, in that order. Rochester is also the second largest community in the entire study.

At the other extreme, Cosmos is the community area with the lowest population and the lowest proportion of professional persons. Rural Wright county has the second lowest level of professional employment.

Mass Media Availability and Use

Mass media availability and use varied sharply among the community areas, as data in Table 1 indicate. The proportion of sample respondents reading two or more daily newspapers regularly varied from a low of 5 percent in Glenwood to a high of 72 percent in Crookston, with a median of about 48 percent. Proportion reporting two or more hours of television viewing daily varied from a low of 30 percent in rural Wright county to highs of 61 percent of both Ely and Silver Bay. Some of the variation in television viewing may be a product of the fact that the studies were done at different times of the year. However, variation in use of print media tends to be related to newspaper availability and community complexity.

TABLE 1

POPULATION, OCCUPATION, AND MEDIA USE DATA IN 15 MINNESOTA COMMUNITIES

Community	Month/ year of study	Population 1970 census	% in professional/ managerial positions based on sample	Reading		% watching television 2 hours or more daily
				Weekly or twice weekly	2 or more daily papers	
Nuclear Power Study	Apr.-June 1969					
St. Cloud		39,691	29%	5%	69%	35%
Rural Wright Co.		35,658	11	90	38	30
Osseo		2,908	15	70	43	31
Mining and Metal Industries Study	Apr.-June 1970					
Grand Rapids		7,247	20	67	28	49
Duluth		100,578	20	9	45	46
Ely		4,904	14	50	66	61
Silver Bay		3,504	16	42	57	61
Regional Development Study	November 1970					
Worthington		City-9,825 Nobles Co.-13,383	14	10	52	36
Marshall		City-9,886 Lyon Co.-14,387	28	97	14	37
Thief River Falls		City-8,618 Pennington Co.-13,266	18	92	27	39
Crookston		City-8,312 Polk Co.-26,123	23	28	72	41
Water Quality Study	Apr.-June 1971					
Rochester		53,766	32	6	65	45
Winona		26,438	18	20	60	47
Cosmos		570	6	84	17	45
Glenwood		2,584	22	94	5	48

Readership of weekly or twice-weekly newspapers is high in all four places which have the lowest levels of daily reading (Glenwood, Cosmos, Thief River Falls, Marshall, Grand Rapids, and Wright county). Each of these areas is served by a weekly or twice-weekly newspaper printed within the area; all daily newspapers circulating in these communities are published elsewhere. The other ten communities have daily newspapers published locally.

There is a strong negative relationship among the twelve communities for levels of daily newspaper reading and weekly or twice-weekly readership. The Spearman rank correlation is -.81 ($p < .01$), reflecting the structural differences of newspaper availability in the various community areas.

Sampling and Interviewing

In each community area, adults (aged 21 and over) were selected by probability sampling methods and were interviewed in their homes. Each community area sample is approximately half men and half women, based upon quota control.

Sampling area definitions vary for the different communities, according to the nature of the issue under study. In the mining and metal industry group each community sample was drawn from an area including the city and immediately adjoining residential areas. In the political regionalization group each sample was half city residents and half residents in the surrounding rural trade area served by the community. The Winona-Goodview sample in the water quality group included the incorporated areas of the two cities. The Rochester sample was from the city and the immediately surrounding townships, and the Glenwood and Cosmos samples were both drawn from the respective incorporated areas and the adjacent trade areas.

Interviewing in each community was done by local persons, trained specifically for this task, working under a field supervisor. The interviews were usually completed within a two-week period. Completion rates varied from highs of 100 percent in the Thief River Falls area and 98 percent in Silver Bay to lows of 88 percent in Worthington and 86 percent in Rochester.

Measures Used in the Studies

Data gathered through interviews with individuals are used as basic inputs for development of community indices, which provide the basic data for analysis. The specific operations for major variables, presented in the order in which they are mentioned in the hypotheses, are as follows:

(1) *Mass media coverage* for each issue was estimated for each community according to content in locally-circulated newspapers. This estimate, called the *newspaper coverage index,* is a weighted total of all articles about a topic appearing in newspapers that circulate in the community during the six-month period preceding the survey. The number of articles about an issue in a given

newspaper was multiplied by the proportion of persons in the sample who reported reading the newspaper in which those articles appeared. Values on this index ranged from a low of 0 for the mercury issue in Cosmos and power plant issue in Glenwood in 1971 to a high of 57.29 for the taconite issue in Silver Bay in 1970. Median value is 7.84.

(2) *Knowledge* concerning the issues was measured through a two-part, open-ended item:

Have you read or heard anything in recent months about_____?
IF YES Can you recall the most important thing you have heard about it?

One additional open probe was used with this item for each issue. Total level of knowledge was based upon the number of accurate statements which could be identified in the responses.

(3) *Perception of conflict* was defined, operationally, as the stated belief that one or both of two conditions is true. One is the belief that opposing views are held, or opposing actions are being taken by, at least two different public figures, interest groups, or population segments. The other is the belief that the issue contains tension.

Two different measures of perceived conflict was used: (a) In all communities studied, one indicator of perceived conflict was the mention, in answer to the same item upon which knowledge was based, of any type of conflict among persons or groups or of some type of tension in the situation. (b) The political regionalization and water quality studies included an additional measure, which was a direct question about the perceived tension in the issue. The item in the regionalization study, for example, was: "Would you say Regional Development is a touchy subject around here, or not?"

An indication of the validity of these measures appears in an analysis of 16 comparisons (eight communities, two issues in each) where both measures were used. The Spearman rank correlation between the two measures of perception of conflict is .65 ($p < .01$).

(4) *Interpersonal communication* about each issue was based on reported conversation with others about the topic in question. For a given community the measure was based upon the proportion of respondents answering "yes" to the question: "Have you talked with other people recently about the Regional Development issue?"

(5) *Information recall from media content* was based on responses to an actual newspaper article about the issue, which the respondent was handed near the end of the interview. The respondent was asked to read the article as he or she would "any news article." After he finished, the interviewer took the article back and asked: "What, as you recall, does this article say?" Two interviewing probes were used for each article. Information recall was defined operationally as the number of accurate statements offered by respondents about an article after reading it. The community index for information recall is the proportion of

persons who could make two or more accurate statements about a news article immediately after seeing it.

(6) *Community attitudes* toward the issues were based upon additive responses to individual items, with at least four items on each issue. On the environmentally related issues, for example (mining in the canoe country, steel and taconite plants, sewage control, and mercury pollution), the attitude items measured the extent to which the respondent would take a restrictive, pro-environmentalist position regardless of the consequences for industry, employment, taxation, or other political prerogatives.

In the case of political regionalization, for example, some of the attitude items were:

Local governments everywhere in Minnesota ought to join together for regional planning and development.

Regional development is a way to give people in the whole area a voice in what goes on, not just a favored view.

Regional development may be okay, but it never should replace city councils, county boards, or township governments.

We would all be better off if the Regional Development Act had never been passed by the Legislature.

Communication Behavior About the Issues

Attention to the issues under study varied widely in these communities (Table 2). The differing issues in the fifteen communities provide 23 comparisons for analysis. These community-issue cases are ranked from high to low in Table 2 according to the proportion having any knowledge whatsoever about the issue, as measured by responses to the open-end question.

The most widespread awareness of an issue—98 percent—was in Glenwood, where a state report had indicated that the nearby lake may have contained high levels of mercury. Lowest awareness of an issue under study was in Thief River Falls, where only one person in five was aware of the regional development issue.

In general, issues with the highest local familiarity tended to be those less abstract matters which involved specific local conditions and specific decisions which either had been made or were pending in the community. Such local specificity and low abstractness were apparent in Glenwood, where the future of the community was generally regarded as closely linked to the condition of one large body of water.

The highest awareness of the nuclear power issue was in the portion of Wright county surrounding the Monticello power plant itself. Similarly, the taconite issue centered in Silver Bay, the steel plant issue applied most directly to Duluth, and the sewage issue was most familiar in Cosmos, where a specific plan had been under study and subjected to considerable debate.

TABLE 2
COMMUNICATION BEHAVIOR REGARDING ISSUES IN
15 MINNESOTA COMMUNITIES

Community	Issue	Newspaper coverage index	% Perceiving conflict in issue	% Discussing the issue	% Rating issue as "very important"	% Having any knowledge of the issue
Glenwood	Mercury	9.61	24%	45%	32%	98%
Wright Co.	NPP	11.07	24			91
Silver Bay	Taconite	57.29	34	69		86
Duluth	Steel Plant	5.76	36	34		82
Cosmos	Sewage	2.07	13	38	50	78
Osseo	NPP	14.03	23			77
St. Cloud	NPP	13.32				76
Ely	BWCA	54.14	51	48		76
Cosmos	Mercury	0	0	21	50	63
Rochester	Sewage	8.82	7	23	57	62
Winona	Sewage	2.82	25	31	60	62
Ely	Steel Plant	15.08	34	16		61
Winona	Mercury	3.96	7	22	33	60
Rochester	Mercury	2.86	3	18	42	60
Grand Rapids	BWCA	43.56	44	14		50
Glenwood	NPP	0	11	5	25	47
Duluth	BWCA	40.32	33	11		46
Silver Bay	BWCA	50.88	27	21		45
Grand Rapids	Steel Plant	7.40	23	7		43
Worthington	RD	5.08	10	15	13	28
Crookston	RD	7.84	15	13	17	24
Marshall	RD	12.34	2	6	14	23
Thief River Falls	RD	5.94	3	5	10	19
MEDIAN VALUE		7.84	24	19.5	32.5	61

Key: BWCA = Mining in Boundary Waters Canoe Area; NPP = Nuclear Power Plant;
RD = Regional Development.

Importance of Issues in Communities

In each case where familiarity with the issue was relatively high, the issue has direct implications for *individuals* in the community. The issue need not be economic in every case but may relate to other problems, such as health, which may be based upon non-economic values. In the four communities where familiarity with issues was highest, a third or more reported discussions about the issues and nearly a fourth or more cited conflict when asked to tell what they know about the issues.[3]

Widespread familiarity with an issue tends to indicate that it will be seen as highly important in a community. Among the twelve communities where the "importance rating" question was asked directly, there does appear to be a relationship between this rating and knowledge. The rank correlation is .77 (p < .01). There is also a tendency for this relationship to be curvilinear. The highest "importance" ratings in the study were for the sewage issues in Rochester and Winona (57 percent and 60 percent, respectively, saying "very important"). Overall knowledge concerning the issues in these two places, however, was intermediate. On the other hand, the *lower* importance ratings were clearly in situations where the issues were less familiar. Among the various issues, knowledge and importance ratings were lowest for regional development, the more abstract issue which had been subjected to the least discussion and was least likely to be viewed as a matter of controversy.

The sharp differences in recognition of the regional development issue compared with the environmental topics seems to reflect both general beliefs about critical problems, abstractness of issues, and the way issues of varying abstractness are defined in the community setting. In this particular case, much of the publicity on regionalization had preceded the six-month period covered in the content analysis. Nevertheless, news articles in metropolitan newspapers, through display and tone, had clearly portrayed regionalism as a "hot issue" in some areas of Minnesota, particularly in southwestern Minnesota where Worthington is located. The Worthington newspaper had drawn more critical attention to the issue than any other newspaper in the communities studied here, to such an extent that the Worthington newspaper coverage had itself been reported in other papers. While familiarity with the issue in Worthington (28 percent aware) was somewhat higher than in the other three communities in that study group, the impressive fact is that more than two-thirds of the respondents in these communities as a whole were quite unfamiliar with the entire regional development question. Regionalization, a more abstract topic seemed to be of relatively low short-range concern to citizens at the time of the study. While community leaders may have viewed regionalization as having profound significance, the issue does not seem to have touched a highly responsive chord with the citizenry at large.

Issue Concern and Attitudes

Concern about an issue with specific meaning for a community may differ markedly from concern about the same issue in nearby communities. Furthermore, the difference extends beyond mere concern and discussion; opinions about courses of action may also vary sharply (Table 3). For example, belief in the safety of the nuclear power plant was highest in the rural Wright county closest to the nuclear power plant itself (top section of Table 3). On the other hand, opinion in the various nuclear power issue communities differed little on more general items, such as the one on industrial profits.

Similarly, there is a tendency for attitudes on the metal industry issue to vary according to the immediate local relevance of the issues. For example, residents of Ely favored mining in the canoe country to a greater extent than residents of

TABLE 3
OPINIONS ABOUT ISSUES IN 15 DIFFERENT
MINNESOTA COMMUNITIES, 1969-1971

		Percent who agree in:		
1) Nuclear power issue, 1969	*St. Cloud*	*Osseo*	*Wright County*	*Glenwood (1971)*
Since the federal government has safe standards for nuclear waste, the Monticello power plant won't endanger people.	37	43	56	45
The nuclear power plant is another case of industrial profits getting more attention than public safety.	42	45	45	37
2) Metal industry issues, 1970	*Duluth*	*Grand Rapids*	*Silver Bay*	*Ely*
The Boundary Waters Canoe Area is one area that should never be opened for mining, even in a national emergency.	42	50	41	30
The steel plant (in Duluth) should be allowed to operate and employ people, regardless of the smoke and air problem.	29	29	30	41
The taconite plant (in Silver Bay) should be allowed to operate in the way it finds necessary to maintain full employment, regardless of the lake issue.	15	18	40	36
3) Regionalization issue, 1970	*Worthington*	*Crookston*	*Marshall*	*Thief River Falls*
Local governments everywhere in Minnesota ought to join together for regional planning and government.	73	81	77	76
We would all be better off if the Regional Development Act had never been passed by the Legislature.	33	17	26	23
Regional Development may be okay but it never should replace city councils, county boards, or town governments.	80	82	78	74
4) Water quality issue, 1971	*Winona*	*Rochester*		*Cosmos*
There would really be little harm to the environment even if Cosmos didn't finish its sewage treatment plant for another 5 to 10 years. (Cosmos only)				50
Sewage disposal facilities here should be updated at any cost. (Winona-Goodview only)	66			
Either the county begins work on a suburban sewer system or the quality of our lakes, rivers, and land will continue to go downhill. (Rochester only)		60		
5) Water quality issue, 1971	*Winona*	*Rochester*	*Cosmos*	*Glenwood*
We must quit dumping waste into rivers even if it means eliminating certain residential communities.	55	53	48	70
Even though we don't know all its effects, mercury in water is clearly one of the worst biological dangers of our time.	59	40	61	45

any other community (second section of Table 3). Ely is the principal community in the canoe country, but has a long history of mining (the name of the local newspaper is Ely *Miner*) and has experienced the consequences of the recent decline in open-pit mining of iron ore. Thus, there is considerable reluctance in Ely to agree that the BWCA should "never be opened" for mining, just as there is more support for the taconite plant's current mode of operation in Silver Bay than in other communities. Again, in Silver Bay where the taconite plant is located, concern over community growth and stability seems to be an overriding factor.

In the case of the steel plant, however, Duluth residents are not unusually supportive of their local industry when compared with residents of the other communities. Size and nature of the city may be basic factors. Duluth is a metropolitan center, with more varied sources of business and employment. Although the steel plant was the city's largest employer at the time, the possibility of its cutting back or stopping operations entirely was apparently not as alarming to Duluth residents as such a potential closing might have been in a smaller, single-industry community. The differentiated social and business life of a larger, more pluralistic community may provide resilience against the loss of any particular source of employment, a resilience which may appear in attitudes among the citizenry. To the extent that a community seems able to absorb the shock of an industrial loss, its residents may be less likely to take an extremely defensive posture on the issue. Furthermore, mustering forces for action in a large city may be more difficult because of the heterogeneity and pluralism of that type of community.

Regional development is an issue with a different kind of relevance to communities. Where there are expectations that a community will become a dominant social and economic center of a region, there might be more favorable reaction toward the regional development idea. In the four communities where regionalism was studied the specific consequences for each place could not be sharply defined, although there had been some reference to the question of which community in a given area might eventually be regarded as a "regional center." In any case, the issue had not been reduced to a set of specific implications which the "regional center" designation might have for the average individual in the community.

In spite of the low initial recognition of the issue, regional development was apparently an acceptable idea to a majority of the respondents when they were asked about it directly (Table 3, third section). There is a modest tendency for residents of the Worthington area to be more opposed, which would be expected in view of the critical stance toward the Regional Development Act taken by the Worthington newspaper. Differences between these communities, however, are not great, and in general the support for regional development seems to carry with it some qualifications. While nearly three-fourths or more in all four communities *agree* that "local governments ... ought to join together for regional planning and government," similar proportions agree that such an approach should not replace existing, traditional governmental units. There are high values placed on regional cooperation in general, but these values exist alongside equally strong support for maintenance of existing community institutions.

Questions of community stability are also prominent in the communities where views on water quality were studied. Community concern was especially apparent in Cosmos, where half of the area respondents agreed that there would be little environmental harm if the sewage plant were to be delayed five to ten years (Table 3, fourth section). In both the Winona-Goodview area and in Rochester there was majority support for a proposed plan. On the mercury question, there is a tendency for the most directly affected community (Glenwood) to have *less* acceptance of the biological dangers of mercury. Here the mercury reports were clearly seen as potentially threatening to the future of the community. When asked why the issue seemed to be controversial, Glenwood respondents mentioned potential effects on tourist trade more frequently (in 35 percent of the cases) than any other single factor. Other Glenwood responses indicated a popular feeling that the entire problem had been overrated to the detriment of the community.

TESTS OF HYPOTHESES

Data at the community level are presented in terms of each of the nine hypotheses stated earlier.

> H1. As the level of mass media coverage of a community issue increases, there will be a higher level of knowledge of that issue within that community.

The data on the newspaper coverage index (the weighted total of articles) and familiarity with issues may be compared in Table 2. The rank correlation between these two community indices is not statistically significant (rank correlation = .09, n.s.). While mass media are instrumental in bringing information into a community, they clearly do not represent the only factor. Spread of information may be initiated through other channels, such as political groups, special-interest organizations, and commercial groups.

> H2. As the level of mass media coverage of a community issue increases, there will be a higher level of perception of conflict regarding that issue in that community.

The relationship between the newspaper coverage index and the proportion perceiving conflict (as measured by the open-end item) is plotted in Figure 1. The cases in the upper right of Figure 1 represent issues with statewide impact and which received frequent and wide coverage in metropolitan media. The Spearman rank correlation between these two variables for the 23 issues is .64 (p < .01). Media may not only attract attention to issues but, as these data

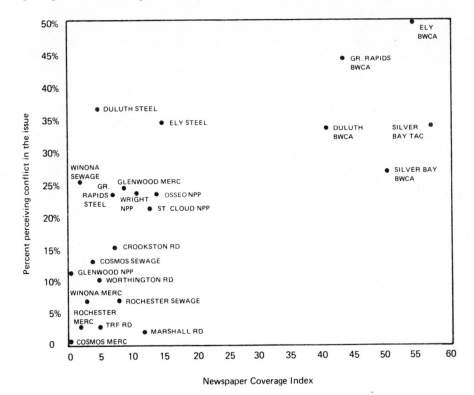

Key:
BWCA = Mining in
   Boundary Waters
   Canoe Area
TAC = Taconite issue
RD = Regional
   Development issue

NPP = Nuclear power
   plant issue
MERC = Mercury
   pollution issue
SEWAGE = Sewage
   control issue

Figure 1: NEWSPAPER COVERAGE INDEX AND PERCEIVED CONFLICT FOR 23 COMMUNITY ISSUE COMPARISONS

suggest, may sometimes be more instrumental in *defining* topics as controversial than in creating awareness alone. This hypothesis, then, receives support from the data.

> H3. As the level of mass media coverage of a community issue increases, there will be an increasing gap in knowledge about that issue between persons high and low in socioeconomic status.

In these 23 comparisons, with level of formal education used as an indicator of socioeconomic status, the knowledge gap hypothesis is not supported. In fact, the data tend to be in the opposite direction, with a rank correlation of -.29

(n.s.). The tendency indicated in Figure 2 is for the correlation between education and knowledge to be *lower* in communities where there has been extremely
heavy newspaper coverage of an issue. Instead of increasing, the size of the
knowledge gap between social status segments appears to close where there is
heavy media input.

These findings may suggest some important modifications of the knowledge-
gap hypothesis and the limits to which it may apply in specific community
situations. The earlier data (Tichenor, Donohue, and Olien, 1970) were almost
entirely based upon knowledge of issues of national concerns, such as space
research, smoking, national and world political affairs, and medical research. Is
the process and consequence of media publicity basically different in a community crisis situation?

We can ask whether the knowledge gap would appear in these communities
where non-local issues are concerned. There is one such case which may be
examined. In the four communities where regionalization was the main topic,
the question of nutritive value of breakfast cereals was used as a second topic,
for comparative purposes. This topic had been in the news in the two months
preceding that particular study. The news was directed almost entirely toward

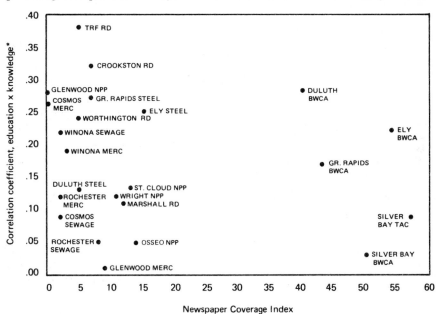

*All correlations are product-moment (Pearsonian) coefficients based on community
sample data.

**Figure 2: NEWSPAPER COVERAGE INDEX AND STRENGTH OF CORRELATION
BETWEEN EDUCATION AND KNOWLEDGE FOR 23 COMMUNITY
ISSUE COMPARISONS**

Congressional hearings and in the breakfast-food industry in general. There was virtually no implication for any individual community as such.

In the four communities where the breakfast-food issue was studied, the data are completely in line with the hypothesis of an increasing knowledge gap as media input increases (Figure 3). As newspaper attention to this issue increases, so does the correlation between education and knowledge. Furthermore, there are sharp differences in strength of the correlation coefficients, from a low of .05 in Worthington, where the topic received the least coverage, to .51 in Marshall where it received nearly three times as much newspaper coverage, according to the index used here.

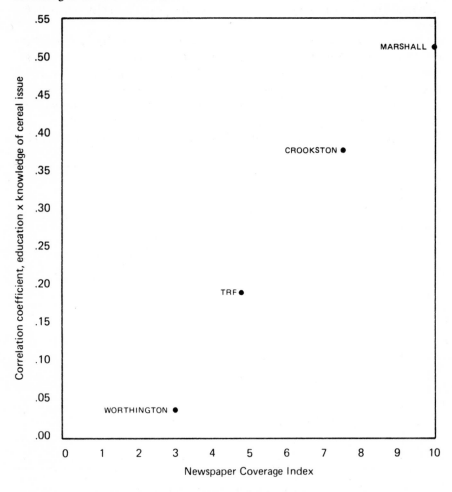

Figure 3: **NEWSPAPER COVERAGE INDEX AND STRENGTH OF CORRELATION BETWEEN EDUCATION AND KNOWLEDGE FOR THE BREAKFAST CEREAL ISSUE IN FOUR COMMUNITIES**

Under certain conditions, then, it appears that the knowledge gap may be *reduced* rather than increased as media input increases. High salience, high arousal, and concentration of attention may serve to diffuse information to a maximum extent. Further analysis suggests that interpersonal channels become a key factor. The rank order correlation between amount of discussion in the community and the knowledge gap (for 20 cases where discussion was measured) is -.59 (p < .01), higher than for the relationship between newspaper coverage and the gap. In the case of Glenwood, for example, the mercury issue was not only widely and rapidly publicized; it was also widely discussed. The "whole town was talking" about the matter in a very literal sense. Such an explosion of communicative activity may level out the knowledge gap on these salient local issues.

To what extent do such circumstances occur leading to such an equalization of information? Repeated findings that knowledge gaps occur on non-local public affairs but not on intensive community issues might have far-reaching implications for information programs. As issues go, however, such high levels of communication about a single issue may be rare. Priority for community attention to topics may be a factor, and the issues studied here may be relatively infrequent in the life of a community. However, such topics may be more likely

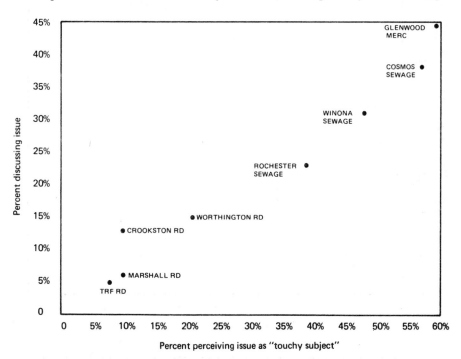

Figure 4: PERCEPTION OF ISSUE AS A "TOUCHY SUBJECT" AND INTERPERSONAL COMMUNICATION FOR EIGHT COMMUNITY COMPARISONS

to occur in an atmosphere of social controversy, as they did in these cases. Under certain conditions, levels of expectation may be such that a conflict is resolved *along with* a reduction in the knowledge gap.

> H4. The higher the level of perception of conflict about an issue in a community, the higher will be the amount of interpersonal communication about that issue within the community.

The effect of conflict may be reciprocal and cumulative. That is, media coverage may increase the level of conflict perceived in an issue as indicated above, conflict may lead to more discussion and this discussion may lead to greater awareness of a conflict. The direct test of the conflict-discussion hypothesis is taken from eight cases (all different communities) in which both the discussion question *and* the "touchy subject" question were asked. The relationship for these eight cases is strong (Figure 4); the rank correlation is .94 (p < .01).

Within the community, it seems clear that conflict at these levels is no barrier to communicative activity within the audience at large. Instead, within the limits of these issues, it is more likely an accelerating factor for informal communication.

A related finding from these data is concerned with the link between interpersonal contacts and knowledge, documented frequently in the diffusion literature in terms of a relationship among individuals. These data, at the community level, provide further support (Figure 5). For the 20 comparisons where relevant measures are available, the rank order correlation between amount of interpersonal communication and familiarity with the issue is .83 (p < .01).

> H5. The higher the level of perception of conflict regarding an issue in a community, the higher the level of knowledge about that issue within the community.

The tendency was cited earlier (Table 2) for conflict perception and familiarity with an issue to go together. The rank correlation between these two measures is .42 (p < .05) for the 23 comparisons, with perception of conflict based upon the open-end item. Where the more specific measure of conflict perception (the "touchy subject" measure) was used, the rank correlation is .52 (p < .05), for 12 cases. This hypothesis, then, is supported.

Thus far, then, these community-level data are quite consistent with the view that the existence of social tension, arising from a general perception of controversy surrounding an issue, provides a stimulus for information exchange and diffusion within a social system.

The data presented here are summary measures for communities as whole systems; it might be argued that more detailed analysis would reveal barriers to communication arising from conflict, at least at the individual level. Yet in a few communities where interpersonal communication was examined in some detail, there is little or no evidence that such blockage occurs.

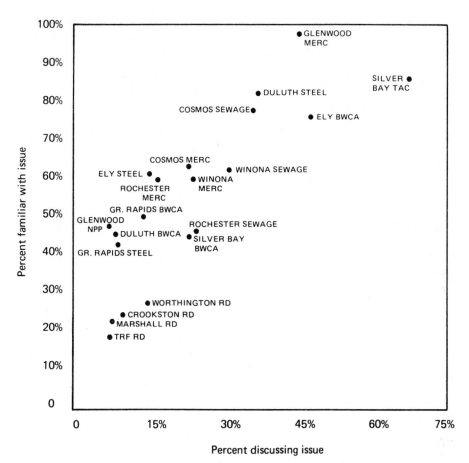

Figure 5: INTERPERSONAL COMMUNICATION AND FAMILIARITY WITH ISSUES IN 20 COMMUNITY ISSUE COMPARISONS

The most intensive such analysis was in the metal industry group of communities where people were asked *whether* they had talked about the issues, *who* they talked with, and whether any *persuasion* was attempted in the discussion. All three issues studied in these communities (steel, taconite, mining) may be treated as one general regional problem.

Figure 6 illustrates the relationship between community employment in metal industry jobs and level of discussion about any one or more of the three specific issues. As metal industry employment rises, so does interpersonal communication about this general problem.

Discussion is a community condition rather than a characteristic of individuals employed in the industry. In each community such discussion was no more likely to occur among the metal workers themselves than among persons not employed in these jobs. To the extent that a community is monolithic, one might expect a topic about the major industry to dominate local conversation.

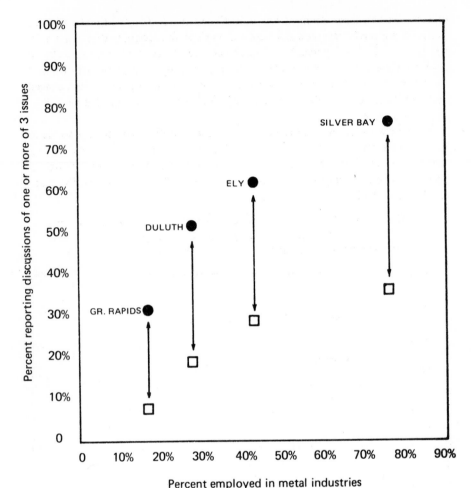

● = Percent in community who report *discussing* one or more of 3 environmental issues

□ = Percent in community who report attempts to *persuade others* on one or more of 3 issues

Figure 6: METAL INDUSTRY EMPLOYMENT AND INTERPERSONAL COMMUNICATION ABOUT ENVIRONMENT-INDUSTRY USE IN FOUR COMMUNITIES

As an illustration, both the amount of discussion *and* attempts to persuade were most frequent in Silver Bay, where the taconite industry accounts for more than 75 percent of local employment.

On the other hand, increased conversation in a volatile situation may be somewhat guarded. As percent of employment in metal industries increases, the percentage of persons talking *without recalling attempts to persuade* also increases. Furthermore, from the recipient's point of view, these attempts to persuade are rarely regarded as successful. In these four communities as a whole, nearly a fourth (24.6 percent) said they had tried to convince someone else to accept a different view, and a fifth (20.1 percent) reported persuasive attempts by others. Only 7.9 percent believed the other person's opinions had changed and only four persons admitted that their *own* views had changed as a result of these discussions.

To summarize on this point, level of controversy in this type of issue seems to be an accelerating factor in communication rather than a barrier. Persuasion, however, is another matter and appears to be a rare outcome of discussions about these issues, regardless of the conflict level. (Tichenor, Olien, Donohue and Bowers, 1971).

H6. The higher the level of perception of conflict regarding an issue in a community, the greater the gap in knowledge about that issue between persons high and low in socioeconomic status.

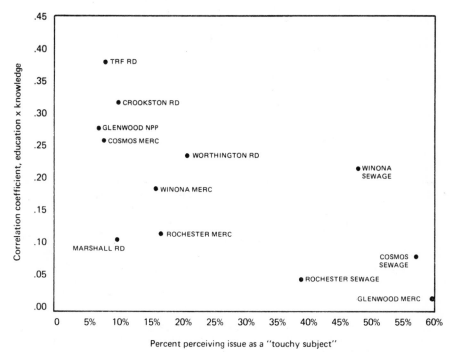

*All correlations are product-moment (Pearsonian) coefficient based on community sample data.

Figure 7: PERCEPTION OF "TOUCHINESS" AND STRENGTH OF CORRELATION BETWEEN EDUCATION AND KNOWLEDGE FOR 12 COMMUNITY ISSUE COMPARISONS

As indicated earlier, the relationship need not be linear according to our theory; it could be curvilinear. When the correlations between education and knowledge for the 23 comparisons were plotted against perception of conflict—based upon the open-end responses—the rank order correlation approached zero.

For the 12 cases where the "touchy subject" measure of perceived conflict is used, the rank correlation between such perception and the knowledge gap is -.75 (p < .01). Inspection of the specific points in the scattergram (Figure 7) suggest, however, that the effect of social conflict on the knowledge gap may vary for different issues. That is, the gap (as measured by the strength of the correlation between education and knowledge) appears clearly to decline with increasing conflict for the mercury issue. For the three communities having a sewage issue, however, that trend is not nearly as clear; Rochester has the lowest perception of conflict, among the three communities where that issue was studied, and also has the weakest correlation between education and knowledge. Winona, intermediate among the three "sewage issue" communities on conflict perception, has the highest correlation between education and knowledge.

Nevertheless, the overall pattern suggested in Figure 7 is for the knowledge gap to be *lower* where social conflict is higher. These findings, along with those presented earlier, suggest that high media attention to a local issue, accompanied by high familiarity, frequent interpersonal communication, and a conflict-laden atmosphere may jointly create the conditions under which the knowledge tends to become more equally distributed among persons higher and lower in social status.

> H7. The higher the level of perception of conflict regarding an issue in a community, the higher the level of perception of conflict in mass media content to which members of the community are experimentally exposed.

The data relevant to this hypothesis are portrayed graphically in Figure 8, which illustrates the pattern of the relationship between perceiving conflict in an *issue* and perception of conflict in news articles about the issue which respondents were asked to read. The rank correlation between these measures for the 23 comparisons is .74 (p < .01).

Although the statistical test is based upon ranks, the pattern of the scattergram is worth noting. There are a few communities in which the news articles are seen as controversial even though the issues themselves are not—at least not to a great degree. The mercury issue in Cosmos is the best example. However, the lower right corner of the scattergram is empty; there are no cases where the issue is seen as highly controversial without the news articles also being seen as containing controversy. Once an issue is recognized as a conflict, conflict may be "read into" subsequent mass media messages.

A question could be raised about message content. Does perception of conflict in news articles simply reflect the extent to which the news actually contains debates, disagreements, and disputes? Further analyses of the news

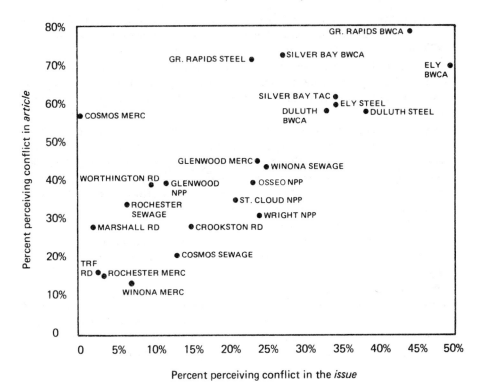

Figure 8: PERCEPTION OF CONFLICT IN ISSUE AND IN NEWS ARTICLE: 7 ISSUES IN 15 COMMUNITY COMPARISONS

articles used in the studies provides at least a partial answer to this question. The articles were analyzed for statements about *positions* on the issue, and the *direction* of these position statements was determined according to a judgmental procedure. For this analysis, a "high conflict" article is one which (a) contains a high proportion of "position" statements and (b) contains a nearly even balance between statements on two different sides of the issue. By this measure, the articles on the BWCA mining issue are high in conflict and were so perceived by residents of the four metal-industry issue communities. However, the regional development articles are *also* high on conflict but were not so perceived by the majority of respondents in the four communities where the regionalization issue was under study.

To a considerable degree, then, recognition of conflict in an article seems to be based upon prior experiences in the community. Once conflict is established, the chances increase than *any* message about the topic will be regarded as part of the conflict.

H8. The higher the level of perception of conflict about an issue in a community, the greater the recall from mass media content, about that issue, to which members of that community are experimentally exposed.

Test of this hypothesis involves responses by persons after reading news articles about the relevant issues, which were presented during the interviews. In each case, the interviewer took the article back and asked the respondent to tell "what the article says." The information recall measure for each community issue is the proportion of respondents who made two or more correct statements about the content of an article after reading it.

The data provide support for the hypothesis (Figure 9). Proportion of persons in a community able to make two or more accurate statements after reading an article tends to increase with level of perceived conflict in the community issue; the rank correlation is .55 (p < .01). Again, the evidence supports the view that perception of conflict tends to be instrumental in information seeking and reception in a community.

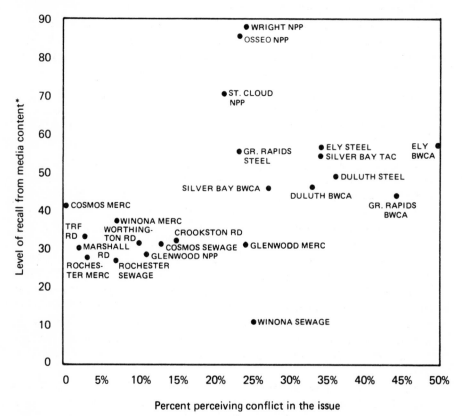

*Refers to percent of persons who gave two correct statements or more after being shown a recent newspaper article about the issue.

Figure 9: PERCEPTION OF CONFLICT IN ISSUE AND RECALL OF MEDIA CONTENT IN 12 COMMUNITY ISSUE COMPARISONS

Again, the scatter diagram in Figure 9 shows four cases (St. Cloud, Osseo, and Wright county on the nuclear power issue; Winona on sewage) that depart from the general pattern. The first three represent a statewide issue that was publicized heavily in metropolitan media, including television, and general familiarity was high. The Winona sewage issue was more local with little television coverage, general familiarity was somewhat lower, and the newspaper articles used in the study described a rather complex set of details surrounding the question of Winona-Goodview cooperation on the sewage issue.

In general, social controversy seems in most of these cases to grow in an upward spiral. Information about an issue makes people aware of a controversy, and the controversial setting seems to stimulate further information seeking. Data presented earlier indicated that the knowledge gap does not increase as *publicity* about these particular community issues increases.

At the community level, tension arising from conflict may motivate active seeking of information among the less-educated persons who are otherwise relatively inactive in public affairs. Also, such conflict may be characterized by continuing media attention to the same issue, beyond the usual amount.

> H9. The higher the level of perception of conflict regarding an issue in a community, the lower the correlation in that community between socioeconomic status and attitudes toward alternative courses of action.

Data pertinent to this hypothesis—which bears some similarities to the knowledge-gap question—need to be treated differently. Attitude measurements differ, necessarily, according to the issue under study. Scale reliabilities and variabilities will differ from one issue to another. Therefore, the only appropriate comparisons of correlations between education and attitudes are among communities in which the same measures are used.

There are two issues for which a test of the proposition is appropriate. One is the political regionalization study and the other is the water-quality study. In both cases, identical scale measures of attitudes were administered in different communities. In the regionalization study, the scale is a combined measure of the extent to which persons favor the regional development concept. In the water-quality study, it is a scale of the extent to which persons favor a pro-environmentalist position on sewage control and protection of water in rivers and lakes.

Results for both issues generally support the hypothesis (Figure 10). The regionalization issue is seen as more touchy in Worthington, where the correlation between education and support for the idea is weakest. Similarly, attitudes on the river and lakes scale are most closely tied to education in Rochester, where the mercury issue is the least controversial among the four communities where it was studied. Attitudes about mercury are least tied to education in Glenwood, where level of perceived controversy on the mercury issue is high.

While these data are based on a small number of comparisons, again they

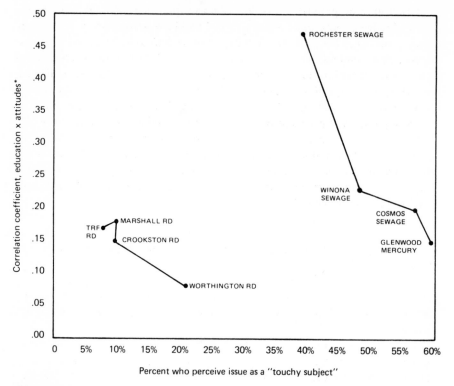

*Correlations are product-moment (Pearsonian) coefficients based on community sample data.

Figure 10: PERCEPTION OF "TOUCHINESS" AND CORRELATION BETWEEN EDUCATION AND ATTITUDES

point to some crucial aspects of intensive communication about conflict-laden issues. One consequence of high levels of communication may be greater awareness of varying and conflicting points of view among more and less educated persons alike. These findings point to the importance, in further studies, of viewing such data over time. One might expect a relatively high status-opinion relationship when an issue is introduced to the public, and a later decline as the issue receives continuing publicity *and* the subject is covered in repeated informal discussions in the community.

Such outcomes of communication may diverge sharply from the traditional expectation that "educating people about the issues" leads to greater support for particular alternatives. There is little theoretical, or empirical, reason to expect such outcomes. The more likely consequence of increased amounts of information about a community question is an increased level of social conflict and a certain amount of intense local feeling about it.

Given existing patterns of media coverage, of course, this may be a highly *controlled* level of conflict reporting kept within certain boundaries. As Hennessy puts it (1970), newspapers today tend to "air controversy and opposing views within the limits of the moderate middle." All of the controversies under study here are within the "moderate middle" in that no political radicalism, as ordinarily defined, appears in any one of them.

In polarized situations where rancorous conflict erupts between radically extreme groups and points of view, the pattern of findings in this analysis would not necessarily be expected to hold. In such cases various inhibitions and communication breakdowns might appear. There may be a point of inflection in the curve of relationship between social conflict and communication in the system. For the most part, that point of inflection seems not to have been reached in these communities.

SOCIAL CONFLICT AND COMMUNICATION: A SYNTHESIS

This analysis, while limited to single-time studies in fifteen communities, suggests a dynamic community process in which mass media input, community structure and development of social tension may be highly related and interacting factors.

Issues ordinarily are created, not in the mass media, but either in professional groups or political institutions (Tichenor, Donohue, Olien, and Bowers, 1971). Through one or more of these channels, issues become familiar in the community. The effect of mass media is ordinarily acceleration of the issue—acceleration of both awareness and of conflict dimensions.

The media are not alone in this process. In some cases they may not be the most significant factor. Depending upon the way the issue is defined in other institutions *and* in the media, awareness of an issue and perception of associated tension will be highest in precisely those communities where the issue is perceived as most relevant. Thus the canoe-country issue is highest on all counts—awareness, conflict, and discussion—in Ely rather than in Grand Rapids. The mercury issue is more salient in Glenwood rather than Rochester.

Apart from direct relevance, general community structure is an important factor in determining the course of an issue. The larger, more pluralistic community may experience less tension than a smaller, less differentiated one with the same type of issue. A public debate over ways of resolving a sewage problem may generate less conflict in the Rochester area than it might in a less diversified community.

Once an issue is created, the process seems to be cumulative—so long as information inputs continue, either from the media or other channels. A general definition of an issue as controversial leads to more learning from media content about that issue, and that content itself is regarded as controversial. This process may continue either until resolution occurs, until the flow of information from various sources diminishes, or both.

NOTES

·1. This hypothesis is stated in linear form acknowledging the possibility that conditions of heightened conflict, as discussed above, may lead to a curvilinear relationship. The simpler linear form of the hypothesis is consistent with existing data and reflects the previous state of empirical knowledge on this issue (see Tichenor, Donohue and Olien, 1970).

2. This competitive aspect of regional development was illustrated in tongue-in-cheek style by a newspaper in one of the communities which published a photograph of rioters in a European city burning an over-turned automobile as an act of political protest against a recent national announcement about regionalization. The Minnesota newspaper captioned the picture: THEY DIDN'T GET TO BE A REGIONAL CENTER.

3. Cosmos is one community in which the open-end question and the specific question about perceived conflict produced sharply different results. Whereas only 13 percent of the Cosmos area respondents mentioned conflict in answer to the general question, 57 percent said "yes" when asked if the sewage issue was a "touchy subject" in the area.

REFERENCES

ALMOND, G. and S. VERBA (1963) The Civic Culture: Political Attitudes and Democracy in Five Nations. Princeton: Princeton Univ. Press.

BLALOCK, H. M., Jr., and A. B. BLALOCK (1959) "Toward a clarification of system analysis in the social sciences," Philosophy of Science (April) 26: 84-92.

BOGARDUS, E. S. (1920) Essentials of Social Psychology. Los Angeles: University of California Press.

BOGATZ, G. A. and S. BALL (1971) The Second Year of Sesame Street: A Continuing Evaluation. Princeton: Educational Testing Service (November).

COLEMAN J. S., et al. (1966) Equality of Educational Opportunity: Summary. Washington: Government Printing Office.

COLEMAN, J. S. (1971) Resources for Social Change: Race in the United States. New York: John Wiley.

CONVERSE, P. E. (1962) "Information flow and the stability of partisan attitudes." Public Opinion Quarterly 26 (Winter): 578-599.

COSER, L. A. (1956) The Functions of Social Conflict. New York: Free Press.

——— (1967) Continuities in the Study of Social Conflict. New York: Free Press.

——— (1972) Introductory chapter in special issue on "Collective violence and civil conflict." Journal of Social Issues 28, 1: 10-11.

DAHRENDORF, R. (1959) Class and Class Conflict in Industrial Society. Stanford: Stanford Univ.

GURR, T. R. (1972) "The calculus of civil conflict." Journal of Social Issues 28, 1: 27-47.

HENNESSY, B. (1970) Public Opinion. Belmont, Calif.: Wadsworth.

KEY, V. O., Jr. (1967) Public Opinion and American Democracy. New York: Alfred A. Knopf.

LANE, R. E. and D. O. SEARS (1964) Public Opinion. Englewood Cliffs, N.J.: Prentice-Hall.

LUNDBERG, G. A. (1939) The Foundations of Sociology. New York: Macmillan.

LYND, R. S. (1939) Knowledge for What? The Place of Social Science in American Culture. Princeton: Princeton Univ. Press.

MARCEAU, F. J. (1972) "Communication and development: a reconsideration." Public Opinion Quarterly 26, 2: 235-245.

McCOMBS, M. E. and D. L. SHAW (1972) "The agenda-setting function of mass media." Public Opinion Quarterly 36, 2: 176-187.

MOYNIHAN, D. P. (1968) "Sources of resistance to the Coleman Report." Harvard Educational Review 38 (Winter): 23-35.

OLIEN, C. N., G. A. DONOHUE, and P. J. TICHENOR (1968) "The community editor's power and the reporting of conflict." Journalism Quarterly 45 (Summer): 243-252.

PALETZ, D. L., P. REICHERT and B. McINTYRE (1971) "How the media support local governmental authority." Public Opinion Quarterly 35 (Spring): 80-92.

PATCHEN, M. (1970) "Models of cooperation and conflict: a critical review." Journal of Conflict Resolution 15, 3: 389-407.

SEARS, D. O. and J. FREEDMAN (1967) "Selective exposure to information: a critical review." Public Opinion Quarterly 31 (Summer): 197-213.

TICHENOR, P. J., G. A. DONOHUE, and C. N. OLIEN (1970) "Mass media and differential growth in knowledge." Public Opinion Quarterly 34 (Summer): 158-170.

TICHENOR, P. J., G. A. DONOHUE, C. N. OLIEN, and J. K. BOWERS (1971) "Environment and public opinion." The Journal of Environmental Education 2 (Summer): 38-42.

TILLY C. and J. RULE (1965) Measuring Political Upheaval. Research Monographs, No. 19. Princeton: Center of International Studies, Princeton University.

WILLIAMS, R. M., Jr. (1972) "Conflict and social order: a research strategy for complex propositions." Journal of Social Issues 28, 1: 11-26.

Chapter 3

DECISION-MAKING AND MASS COMMUNICATION:
A CONCEPTUAL AND METHODOLOGICAL APPROACH
TO PUBLIC OPINION

Alex S. Edelstein

THE QUESTION as to whether or not the American public "supported" the war in Vietnam began to trouble academic researchers as soon as it became apparent that public policy was being carried out and/or justified on the basis of public opinion polls.

Substantial questions about survey research methodology began to be raised when poll results turned out to be "surprising" to pollsters, to the informed publics, and to media which were publishing poll findings.

Poll data had been "surprising" with regard to so-called "conflicting opinions" held by individuals about means of ending the war (Time, October 1969), about the relationships of opinion-holding and non-opinion-holding to knowledge about the war, and about the seeming lack of utility of the mass media for those who were most educated and knowledgeable about Vietnam.

Examples of so-called "surprising results" were that individuals approved of both escalation and withdrawal solutions; the usual criterion of education did not appear to correlate with "war-peace" attitudes; and those who were media

AUTHOR'S NOTE: I wish to acknowledge, with warm appreciation, the original contributions of Neil Hollander, who helped to articulate the methodology and who supervised the field work. Other colleagues included Richard F. Carter, who was an important contributor to the conceptualization; W. L. Ruggels, who participated in aspects of questionnaire formulation and data analysis; and research assistants Robert Simpson, David Pugh, and Karen Morrell. The research was funded by the Sociology and Psychology Division of the National Science Foundation, GS2053.

"fans" appeared to be no different in their war-peace attitudes or in other important respects from those who had not availed themselves of the media.[1]

These "surprising" findings were reported not only by commercial pollsters but by political scientist Sidney Verba and colleagues (1967), who had objected to the findings of the commercial pollsters as not being reflections of reality. Focusing upon what was deemed to be the major weakness of the commercial polls, Verba and colleagues proposed a methodological approach that would have as its objectives "a more fully rounded picture of *thinking* [my italics] on choices (i.e., alternative solutions) with respect to Vietnam, and the possible costs of each alternative." Their field work was conducted in late February and early March 1966 by professional interviewers of the National Opinion Research Center of Princeton University.

The preliminary data analysis was supportive of neither the way in which President Johnson had defined his policy alternatives nor the reasons he had given for following them. The report seriously questioned the degree of "support" or "opposition" that had been generated by his policies among the so-called Hawks and Doves—terms that had been coined to characterize opposing views of the war.

In fact, the researchers reported that Doves were somewhat hawkish and Hawks were similarly dovish. Each incorporated some of the values of the other. Only a small percentage of the public could be classified as *pure* Hawks or *pure* Doves. Of a total of 20 percent in the two categories, only 6 percent were *pure* Hawks and 14 percent were *pure* Doves.[2]

But to paint a more puzzling picture, the report showed that while 61 percent of the public approved of the way in which the President was handling Vietnam, there was "approval" also of seemingly contradictory *de*-escalation policies. More importantly, the academics discovered that clear majorities favored alternatives that had been suggested, not by the President, but by his critics. Members of the public were considering a greater range of alternatives than were being submitted to them in "referendum" by the President and the pollsters. And publics were accepting both "war" solutions and "peace" solutions for reasons not explained by the poll data.

The Verba study was notable methodologically because it associated "costs" or what we will call "attributes" with solutions—"focal objects." Respondents were asked if reduced aid to education, higher taxes, economic controls, reduced Medicare payments, and cutting back on the poverty program were acceptable or unacceptable to them as "costs" of maintaining the war at its present level. And they were asked if they were willing or unwilling to call up the National Guard, engage in all-out mobilization, raise the ground forces in Vietnam to a half million men, bomb cities in North Vietnam, engage in a ground war with Red China or an atomic war with Red China or the Soviet Union, as "costs" of enlarging the scope of the war. *But these "costs" or attributes were suggested to the respondents; they were not proposed by the respondents.*

The evidence that publics could agree with what the pollsters—and the President—considered conflicting alternatives raised doubts that the President and the pollsters really understood what the publics thought. What they thought the publics thought apparently was not only an inaccurate picture but an incomplete one.[3]

In their report the Verba group (1967) addressed itself to larger objectives. Two of the objectives were:

(1) To probe somewhat more deeply into public attitudes toward the war than had newspaper surveys and commercial polls, and
(2) To assess the relationships between public opinion polling, as an activity, and foreign-policy decision-making.

The researchers focused their analysis of "attitudes" on the relationship of knowledge about the war to "attitudes" toward policy alternatives, and on the relationship of various social characteristics such as political party affiliation, education, income, religion, sex, race, and "articulateness" to preferences for policy alternatives. They came to a rather pessimistic assessment as to what was happening to public opinion and an equally gloomy forecast as to what was likely to occur.

The Stanford group said it found no important relationships between level of information about the war and preferences for war or peace, nor did they find any significant relationship between education and policy preferences. They commented:

Those who expect the informed citizen to be more in favor of negotiations and de-escalation will find little comfort in our data, while those who expect the informed to favor a more militant policy will receive some—but not much—support for their position [p. 326].

The Stanford researchers went on to question television and newspaper commentators for seeming to believe that "if the public only understood situations better they would take positions quite different from the uninformed masses." The implication was plain that journalists and commentators were naive in clinging to this belief in the face of the "surprising" Stanford data that "amount of information" did not seem to make any difference in preferences as to what to do to bring the war to an end.

The researchers concluded:

The informed, in summary, cannot be said to form a particularly distinct policy public. Their preferences differ, but not substantially, from the less-informed; they are a bit more consistent, but the evidence is mixed on this; and in terms of their degree of polarization they are little different from the rest of the populace.

The scope of these inferences raised questions not only about the character of the analysis but about the validity of the data itself: Had the investigators really observed what they wished to observe?

There seemed to be at least three areas in which the Verba group might not have carried out its original purpose conceptually:

(1) By the use of formulated statements to which individuals could too easily respond. This might have obscured an essential difference between the uninformed and the informed, and the educated and the uneducated: the ability to themselves formulate problems in ways that permitted one to come to conclusions.[4]

(2) By offering a range of policy alternatives, each of which might plausibly bring the war to an end, the researchers may have confounded the desires of individuals to have *any* solution with their ability to define a *preferred* solution. By this methodological intrusiveness, the researchers had made "preferred" solutions an academic question. In the process they may also have confused ends with means.

(3) Finally, the test of knowledge that the Stanford researchers had employed might not be functionally related to the attitudes that were being tested. To illustrate, we asked ourselves how much of the following "knowledge," which made up part of the "test" administered by the Stanford research group, might bear upon a personal decision as to whether to adopt one means or another to bring the war in Vietnam to an end:

(a) The fact that Congress had not declared war.

(b) We were bombing in North Vietnam.

(c) Saigon was the capital of South Vietnam.

(d) Hanoi was the capital of North Vietnam.

(e) The number of U.S. troops in Vietnam.

(f) The number of U.S. casualties in Vietnam.

(g) Identification of the Vietcong.

(h) [We could not identify the eighth item.]

It was not demonstrable that respondents had made decisions about means of ending the war on the basis of this kind of knowledge. The information test thus did not appear to be relevant to what had been stated as the basic concern—a picture of thinking about means that had been proposed to bring the war to an end.

But the Stanford researchers had succeeded along some vital dimensions. They had called attention to the fact that individuals were considering a broader range of alternatives than had been reflected in conventional public opinion polls. They had questioned the meaning of any "public opinion" which was based upon acceptance or rejection of a limited range of alternatives. They had raised questions about the *costs* of alternatives which were being considered. And they had noted how the President, and his critics, had used the polls as "evidence" of opinion that owed its character to possibly constrictive polling practices.

Ironically, the vast publicity given to the Verba study defeated its objectives; what was emphasized in the press was that a substantial number of people did, after all, "support" the President's policies. This seeming evidence of "support" outweighed the more abundant but complex evidence that "public opinion" did not want war—they wanted an *end* to the war.

In a related effort to reassess what, and how, people thought about Vietnam, two senior researchers of the University of Michigan Survey Research Center brought together a decade of published results on the polls about Vietnam (Converse and Schuman, 1970). They concluded that it had been a mistake to apply techniques for measuring voter intentions to issues of such complexity as Vietnam.

In voting studies the alternatives are usually clear—one, two, three, or possibly more candidates—and the bases for choosing among the candidates are more narrowly defined, as well: questions of party affiliation, experience, or ability to solve a given problem. Under these circumstances it was appropriate to ask respondents to choose among limited alternatives. But about Vietnam the researchers concluded:

> The controversial aspects are almost innumerable. Each aspect requires a somewhat different question, which has its own unique meaning. Moreover, since polling agencies prefer to word their own questions, it is possible to obtain different results even when two agencies are examining essentially the same aspect of an issue. In the case of the war in Vietnam, for example, it is unusual to find instances where two questions are worded the same way.

But in reviewing the weaknesses of the methods used to assess attitudes toward Vietnam, the authors proposed correctives in *interpretation* of data rather than methodological changes. Unfortunately, the correctives carried with them additional problems of interpretation. Their proposals were to look at trends rather than at individual polls; to look at nuances in the wording of questions; and to look at different reactions to the same questions in different sectors of the population. Each of the three suggestions for "correctives" deserves discussion.

Trend analysis contains built-in problems of interpretation both with respect to the nature of the *problem* (the focal object) and the *population* which is being polled. From Time 1 to Time 2 both the nature of the problem and the nature of the individuals who are giving "opinions" may change.

With respect to the problem, the nature of the war in Vietnam changed dramatically from 1965 to late 1968, when our own study was done. The nature of the war changed further after that. The material and the human "costs" of the war, as first listed by Verba and his colleagues, also changed dramatically from Time 1 to Time 2. An individual who did not object too greatly to War 1 (the early 1965 period) might have developed a sense of opposition to War 2 (the late 1965 and 1966 periods of rapid escalation), intensified his opposition to War 3 (the war of attrition of 1966-1967-1968), but have been satisfied that some sort of a solution was in sight with respect to War 4 (Vietnamization) and War 5 (the new air and sea war).

The characteristics of the population changed as well. As War 1 merged into Wars 2, 3, 4, and 5, each engaged the attention of a different constituency. Vietnam had been on the front pages of newspapers and in the limelight of television for almost a decade. Observers were not continuous participants in the opinion-forming and opinion-holding process. Some opted out between Wars 1,

2, 3, etc. Others became newly aware; some formed opinions (on the basis of new alternatives). Many individuals changed their opinions, some from not having an opinion to having one, others from having an opinion to not having one.

Trend analysis must accept the realities of different objects, different bases for evaluating them, and different actors who are engaged in the evaluation process. These are often noncomparable.

The second "corrective" proposed by Converse and Schuman concerns nuances of question wording. Other than the semantic questions of "which war?" and "which public?" that we have raised, it is apparent that the pollsters are not sensitive to the meaning of many statements which they submit to respondents.

The problem was dramatized in October 1969 by a Louis Harris poll done expressly for *Time* magazine. In reporting the poll results, *Time* lamented the "internal inconsistencies" of the data, pointing out that respondents were "agreeing" with what were "conflicting statements." *Time* noted that some respondents were in favor of both escalation and de-escalation solutions.

The editors did not have a ready explanation for this "seeming contradiction." What had occurred was that some poll questions had asked respondents to react to means of bringing the war to an end, but the respondents were reacting in terms of ends; they were willing to accept *any* reasonable means for bringing the war to an end. If escalation, or de-escalation, or both, would bring the war to an end, the public was willing to accept these "solutions."

Further, most of the statements used by Harris contained or demanded information that the respondents did not have. Not all respondents could be aware of all the alternatives that were proposed by Harris, nor could they be aware of all the bases for adopting or rejecting these alternatives. Nor were these alternatives and their bases equally salient to all respondents. Agreement or disagreement with Harris's statements created the illusion that individuals had opinions about each of the proposals that were made for bringing the war to an end. Many of the proposals were new, and the bases for evaluating them were not widely known or well defined. Thus there were potentialities for serious errors in the assessment of opinion.

Few individuals, as an example, knew enough about the Nixon *and* the Johnson policies to answer the question, "Is Nixon following the policies of the Johnson Administration in Vietnam?"

Few respondents actually knew the "rate" of withdrawal of troops. There were mixed meanings for such terms as "immediate" and "all" in the question, "Do you favor immediate withdrawal of all troops from Vietnam?"

And there could not have been informed—or uniform—agreement among respondents as to the meaning and scope of "Vietnamization" as a policy. As "War 4" Vietnamization was still taking on additional meanings.

These were not merely semantic problems, important as they were. At issue also were questions of means and ends. Was the respondent concerned about the specific means of bringing the war to an end, as "Vietnamization," or was he willing to permit any means (within the tolerable limits suggested by Verba and his colleagues) to bring the war to an end?

In trying to learn *how* people used knowledge in making decisions, weaknesses in the structure of conventional polling questions were becoming evident. These structural errors could be formulated as of two kinds:

(1) *Solution-errors:* This occurred when the respondent was asked to agree or to disagree with or to "support" or to "reject" alternatives with which he previously was unfamiliar and which he had not evaluated previously. Examples might be "Vietnamization" or "immediate withdrawal."

(2) *Evaluation-errors:* The respondent might be familiar with the solution that had been proposed, and might have a rationale for accepting or rejecting it, but the rationale on which the respondent had based his own "opinion" was not the rationale contained in the pollster's statement. Hence the respondent would be asked to evaluate a problem on the basis of an unfamiliar criterion.

An example of the Harris survey comes readily to mind. Respondents were asked if they would approve "escalation" as a solution if it were a "last" effort and if it would "win the war." But it is possible that the respondent had not previously thought about escalation as a "last effort" or that it could "win the war." If winning by means of escalation was a possibility, it enhanced the value of the alternative. Thus the conventional methodology of "informing" respondents rather than determining what bases respondents themselves had for evaluating alternatives contributed to the illusion, rather than the reality, of public opinion with respect to such alternatives.

The third "corrective" deals with differing reactions to the same question in different sectors of the population. While age, sex, occupation, religion, and similar demographic variables had in some studies reflected differences in points of view about the war—women, for example, had been generally more anti-Vietnam war than had men, and New England has been characteristically more anti-Vietnam war than other regions—these variables "represent" social and intellectual roles. More pertinent intellectual roles might be identified. We speculated that one such variable might be the way in which the individual organized and used information to solve problems. To observe this, however, we would have to devise a method of asking questions that would permit this behavior to emerge.

When E. L. Thurstone (1929: 6-7) first developed methods of opinion measurement, he warned that the presentation to respondents of statements formulated by researchers might not describe the real behavior of the respondents, but might only describe their responses to questions propounded by the pollsters. Thurstone pointed out that at least two different behaviors might be involved:

(1) A situation in which the pollster was presenting questions to a respondent which the pollster had formulated. The respondent was

doing his best to bring his own resources to bear upon the new situation.

(2) A situation which reflected the everyday world of the respondent, in which the respondent faced neither a great number of alternatives nor felt called upon to make a decision of any kind.

The public opinion polls on Vietnam had concentrated on the first approach. They therefore encountered serious difficulties of assessment and interpretation.

We sought to develop a methodology that would permit the second condition to prevail—a situation in which the respondent defined the nature of the alternatives which he himself had been considering and the bases upon which he was considering them. And he was to be free to report to us that he had not made a decision about any alternatives, i.e., that he did not have an opinion.

A political scientist, Alden Voth of San Jose State College (1967), put it this way in confronting the same problem with respect to determining public opinion in relation to Vietnam:

> ... the fundamental difficulty of *asking questions based upon conceptualizations that were ... different from those which ... defined the issue for our respondents* [our italics]. Objective research is obviously endangered when an interviewer returns ... with information that did not exist in its crystallized form before the interview.

The essential question to be answered would be the extent to which the respondent would be asked to torture his own position to express it in the terms formulated by the pollster. This ability would vary, of course, with the competence of the respondent. The alternative approach would be to explore the potentialities for developing a less intrusive methodology.

Such a methodology should allow the respondent to define the problem in his own terms. The respondent would tell us which problems were important to him, personally. He would define, in his own words, alternatives or proposed solutions. He would describe the bases upon which he evaluated each proposed solution—reasons in favor, reasons against—and if the solution was acceptable to him personally. He would tell us if he had decided what should be done to solve the problem. We would give the respondent no information. We would suggest no alternatives nor propose any bases for evaluating them.

A theoretical approach had been suggested by the model of cognitive processes proposed by Carter (1965). In this schema, objects were things that were valued, and attributes were the bases for valuing them. The experimental literature explicating the Carter model was later summarized by Chaffee et al. (1969).

The object-attribute relationship appeared to fit in essential ways the process of opinion formation and change. One could view as an "object" any alternative proposed to bring the war in Vietnam to an end; since the alternative was that which was being "valued," it was an "object." The reasons for accepting or rejecting an alternative-object were its "attributes," that is, the means by which objects were being valued.

The Carter model pointed also to potentialities offered by other models of cognitive behavior for understanding opinion-formation and opinion-change. Respondents could be asked to provide their own objects and attributes; we could look at the extent of their relevant knowledge and at the structure of it as well. We could identify, in terms proposed by cognitive theorists, those respondents who had simple or complex cognitive structures or styles.[5] And we could observe how education and knowledge were "used by the individual to form and to maintain opinions."

The methodological approach is illustrated by a sample interview. The interview is described both in terms of the objectives and the structure of the questionnaire (in italicised comments leading into the text) and is illustrated by the text of a respondent's remarks.

The interview subject was a 50-year-old postal supervisor, a Republican who had voted for Mr. Goldwater in 1964 and who intended to vote for Mr. Nixon in 1968. He was white, earned between $10,000 and $12,000 per year, was married, and did not identify himself with any religious group. He had attended some college but had not received a degree. He had a son in the service at that time who was stationed at Norton Air Force Base in San Bernardino, California.

THE QUESTIONNAIRE ITSELF

The first two questions in the questionnaire sought to discover the salience, i.e., importance, of the problem of Vietnam to each respondent.

Q. 1: What, as you see them, are the most important problems facing the country?

Respondent: Vietnam issue, national election.

PROBE: Any others?

Respondent: Unrest in our own country.

Interviewers were required to ask each such PROBE, exactly as phrased. One PROBE per question, we learned through pre-testing, assured us of an adequate sample of the respondent's behavior.

Q. 2: Which, to you, is the most important problem?

Respondent: Unrest in our own country.

If the respondent did not mention Vietnam in response to either Question 1 *or its PROBE, he was taken to* Question 2A.

Q. 2A: What about Vietnam? Is it an important problem?

If the respondent answered "no" or "don't know" to Q. 2A, he was not interviewed. This represented 4 percent of our sample. The rationale was that individuals should not be questioned about matters that were not salient to them.

Questions 3, 4, 5, and 6 were designed to focus the attention of the respondent upon Vietnam as a social problem, that is, as a problem that was affecting the country. We were not at this point asking the individual if he himself was attempting to resolve the problem in personal terms—that is, to decide what should be done.

Answers to Questions 3, 4, 5, and 6 were a test of knowledge relevant to the causes of our involvement in Vietnam and what was presently happening there but not necessarily pertinent to a decision as to what should be done to bring the war to an end.

Q. 3: What is it about Vietnam that makes it an important problem?

Respondent: This is difficult to answer. The issue will determine if the United States is to be the police force of the world or if we will back away from commitments and return to isolationism.

PROBE: Anything else?

Respondent: It is a confrontation between the United States and Russia. We must decide if we will stop Russia's expansion.

Q. 4: Why do you think we are in Vietnam?

Respondent: Primarily because of commitments to the Asian people. Also for our own protection, that is, to contain communism.

PROBE: Any other reasons?

Respondent: Because President Johnson says to be there.

Q. 5: How did we first become involved?

Respondent: Part of the SEATO agreements that we would protect Asian nations' sovereignty. South Vietnam asked for help against infiltration of the Vietcong.

PROBE: Anything else?

Respondent: No.

Q. 6: What is happening now with respect to Vietnam?

Respondent: There is a stalemate. Our peace team is negotiating in Paris. We don't understand the Asian mind to deal with them. We should not appease them but should stand our ground.

PROBE: Anything else?

Respondent: I don't know.

The questionnaire then shifted to individual orientation toward alternative solutions "that had been proposed" and how they personally evaluated them. Question 7 asked for "proposed solutions" while a series of Question 8's asked for attributes for each solution that the respondent had mentioned.

Q. 7: We'd like to turn now to the question of what we can do to bring the war in Vietnam to an end. What solutions have been proposed?

Respondent: (1) Continue as we are now and eventually (lead to) settlement.

(2) Increase the scope of the war, such as bombing, even nuclear bombing.

PROBE: Have any other solutions been proposed? What are they?

Respondent: These are the only two I pay attention to.

The answers to the Question 8 series permitted two important modes of analysis:

(1) Cognitive structure[6] *:*

(a) We could compare individuals who had considered only war or peace solutions with those who had considered both war and peace solutions.

(b) In examining the reasons given for considering each solution, we could compare those persons who gave only positive or negative reasons for considering each solution with those who gave both positive and negative reasons for considering each solution.

We reasoned that the structure of a person's beliefs might be an effective way of categorizing groups of people in relation to decision-making and communication.

(2) Relevance of knowledge:

In asking about reasons for accepting or rejecting specific solutions, we were testing knowledge that was directly relevant to decision-making. We were not testing for general, perhaps irrelevant knowledge, the problem encountered by Verba et al.[7]

Q. 8: Now let's take the solutions you have mentioned.

(Q. A-1) What are some reasons for continuing as we are now doing?

Respondent: Some people feel that an increase in war would lead to war with Russia. Containment of war will probably prevent Russia and China from entering the war.

PROBE: Are there any other reasons for continuing as we are now?

Respondent: No.

(Q. A-2) Are there any reasons for NOT continuing as we are now?

Respondent: If we used our maximum power it would end the war.

PROBE: Are there any other reasons for NOT continuing as we are now?

Respondent: No. Force is all Asians understand.

(Q. A-3) Would "continuing as we are now" be a satisfactory solution to you?

Respondent: Definitely not. We would never end it.

The same set of questions was now asked about the second solution that the respondent had mentioned—increasing the scope of the war such as by bombing, even nuclear bombs.

(Q. B-1) What are some reasons for increasing the scope of the war effort?

Respondent: The Asiatic mind understands force only. It will accept the solution of power.

PROBE: Are there any other reasons for increasing the war effort?

Respondent: No.

(Q. B-2) Are there any reasons for NOT increasing the war effort?

Respondent: Yes.

(Q. B-2) What are some reasons for NOT increasing the war effort?

Respondent: Some people feel it would draw Russia and China into the war, increasing it to a global war.

PROBE: Any other reasons for NOT increasing the war effort?

Respondent: Political reasons. The Administration says that "we cannot do it!"

(Q. B-3) Would increasing the war effort be a satisfactory solution to you?

Respondent: Yes. The only way to solve the problem must be a maximum effort.

Having reviewed all the solutions that the respondent had proposed, and having indicated his acceptance or rejection of them, the respondent was then moved further into a personal orientation. He was asked if he personally had decided what should be done to bring the war in Vietnam to an end.

Q. 9: Have you decided what we should do to bring the war in Vietnam to an end?

Respondent: Yes.

If the respondent had not "decided," he was asked a series of questions related to his non-decisional status. If the respondent said he had "decided," he was asked a series of questions as to the nature of his decision process. This would permit us to analyze the dynamics of personal decision-making and non-decision-making. We could identify some of the difficulties experienced by individuals in the process of opinion-formation and non-opinion-formation, as well.

Q. 10: Was it difficult for you to decide?

Respondent: Yes.

(Q. 10-A) What made it difficult to decide?

Respondent: I vacillated for a long time, but I decided that we must make a stand here against communism.

PROBE: Did anything else make it difficult?

Respondent: A feeling of fear of survival—that is, a global nuclear war. We must face a nuclear war, if necessary.

The next question series was designed to learn the psychological status of each individual. For those who had "decided" what should be done and therefore had an opinion about what should be done, we tried to learn if the individual was in consonance or dissonance. If what the person said should be done was approximately what he said was being done, he was defined as being in consonance. If what the person said should be done was discrepant with what the person said was being done, he was defined as being in dissonance. As an example:

Q: What is the solution you prefer?
A: Escalate the war to a maximum effort, etc.
Q: What is being done?
A: Nothing.

If the individual had not decided what should be done, he was classified as either in conflict or non-conflict. He was in conflict if he had not decided but was trying to decide. He was in non-conflict if he had not decided and was not trying to decide.

(Q. 10-B) What do you, personally, think we should do to bring the war in Vietnam to an end? What is the solution you prefer?

Respondent: Escalate the war to a maximum effort.

PROBE: What else do you think we should do?

Respondent: Confront Russia and stop her aggression.

(Q. 10-C) What are we doing now to bring the war to an end?

Respondent: Nothing.

The next set of questions was directed at identifying how long the individual had held an opinion, if there had been any change in his point of view, and what events, if any, figured in this process. We had discovered in our pretest analyses that time of decision was related to communication behaviors. The earlier the decision, the more firmly the individual seemed to protect it by selective or by noninformational behaviors.

This series of questions also permitted us to inquire into change or non-change states of decision. We were interested in learning if a person who changed his decision from Time 1 to Time 2 engaged in different kinds and degrees of communication behaviors than those who maintained a decision or a nondecision state.

Q. 11: You said you had decided what we should do to bring the war to an end. Approximately how long have you felt this way?

Respondent: The last three or four months.

PROBE: Can you think of a particular time when you began to definitely feel this way? When was that?

Respondent: No.

Q. 12: Was there any particular event that made you feel more this way?

Respondent: Yes. The Paris peace talks. The situation there is a stalemate.

PROBE: What was the event?

Respondent: Because Asians believe we will give concessions, the talks have gone nowhere. The same thing happened in Korea.

Q. 13: Prior to this, how did you feel? That is, what did you think we should do then?

Respondent: I originally agreed with the Administration that the United States should act as a police force.

PROBE: What else did you think we should do at that time?

Respondent: Nothing.

The reader will note that, up to this time, respondents had been given no statements to evaluate. The respondents, themselves, were required to provide information.

At this point we became interested in the ability of respondents to place evaluations consistently in relation to suggested solutions. One of the assumptions of pollsters, as expressed by Voth, was that respondents were capable of fitting the pollsters' information about problems and solutions into their own personal context. We were interested in seeing if all persons could do this equally. If only the best informed, or the best educated, or the most interested persons could do this successfully, then there would be a systematic bias in any polling technique that demanded this ability.

Q. 16: Here's a card. We've placed on the card solutions that people have suggested for handling the situation in Vietnam, along with the possible results these solutions would bring. As you can see on the card (HAND PERSON A CARD), the solutions that people suggested are roughly these three:

> Escalation beyond what we are doing now;
> Or de-escalation beyond what we are doing now;
> Or continuing what we are doing now.
> (Or none of these?)

On the card were 10 statements. Opposite these statements were the proposed "solutions" and "don't know." The interviewer would ask, "What do you think would prevent a larger war . . . escalation, de-escalation, continuing what we are doing, none of these solutions, or don't you know?" "What do you think would . . . , etc.?" We looked to see if those who were most educated, most informed, most likely to have an opinion, etc., most consistently associated positive outcomes with their point of view. We did not expect complete "consistency" but we did look for "patterns" to emerge.

Our respondent had stated that the United States should engage in escalation. He was able to fit all of the values given to his "solution." Respondents sometimes stated that none of the values suited the alternatives. But our analysis showed that the best educated and informed performed this more effectively than did the less educated and informed.

The "values" were as follows:

(1) Escalation would:
> Prevent a larger war;
> End the war the soonest;
> Meet our commitments in Asia;
> Lead to a lasting solution;
> Be best for the Vietnamese people.

(2) De-escalation would:
> Lose us the most prestige.

(3) Continuing what we were doing would:
> Cost us the most money;
> Produce a higher cost of living;
> Cost the most American lives.

(4) None of these solutions would:
> Unify the country at home. (In this case the respondent stated that this value—unification—fitted none of the alternatives.)

The respondent placed nine of these values in a way that was consistent with his "decision state." Thus he was able, for the most part, to adapt our values to his object.

The questionnaire then turned to informational values: sources of information, evaluation of sources of information, and informational needs. We entertained hypotheses regarding the relationship of each of these variables to such variables as (1) structure of knowledge, (2) psychological states, (3) decisional states, (4) education, etc.

Q. 18: Where are you getting your information about Vietnam?

This respondent indicated that magazines were his most useful source of information, followed by newspapers, television and radio, and conversations with people. He read and listened to news, not mentioning any editorial or commentary other than on radio. The magazines were *Time, Life, Reader's Digest, Newsweek, Business Week,* and *Forbes.* He mentioned all the television networks and several radio stations, one of them network and two of them local stations.

(Q. 18-A) We'd like you to rank these sources of information according to how useful they are to you in learning about Vietnam.

Which source is most useful?

Which source is the next most useful?

Next most useful?

Etc.

Respondent: Magazines, daily newspaper, television, and discussion.

Q. 19: Is there any information you would like to have about what to do about Vietnam?

Respondent: Yes.

(Q. 19-A) What kind of information would you like to have?

Respondent: I don't know. I would like to see a solution proposed.

PROBE: Any other kind of information?

Respondent: If we are not getting the facts, I would like to get the actual facts.

PROBE: Where would you look for it (the information)?

Respondent: Current magazines. Reporters who have been in the area. If I knew, I wouldn't still be looking.

The next questions were designed to test information selectivity; we hypothesized that individuals who were the most informed and best educated would be most likely to find the content of information "not useful." We reasoned that those who had the most information would be most likely to encounter information in the mass media that was redundant or not useful in, presumably, the decision-making process in which the individual was engaged. Similarly, there should be awareness in this way as to which sources of information contained the most relevant and useful information. This respondent, it should be noted, was characterized by "some college" as a level of education and was not one of our "best informed" members of the sample. Hence, he was not selective. As our aggregate analysis indicates, our expectations were largely confirmed.

Q. 20: Is there any information about what to do about Vietnam that you do not find particularly useful?

Respondent: No.

If the respondent had answered "yes," he would have been asked in Question 20A about the kind of information that he did not find "useful."

(Q. 20-B) Are there any sources of information that you would not use with respect to Vietnam?

Respondent: I don't know. (The interviewer noted that the respondent did not wish to answer this question or the question that followed, Q. 20-C: "What are the sources you would not use?" and "Why would you not use these sources?")

The next set of questions asked about interpersonal discussion. We entertained a set of hypotheses centering upon interaction by "cognitive peers." In this conceptualization we would expect deciders to talk to other deciders rather than deciders to talk to nondeciders, as might be formulated in an "opinion-leader" construct. While this respondent did report a change in decision as a result of interpersonal communication, this was not often the case; what was more evident was that deciders (as in this case) tended to perceive that they had talked to other deciders, and nondeciders perceived that they were talking primarily to other nondeciders. In our view, the opinion leader model too easily rejected the functional value of nondecision for the nondecider.

Q. 21: Have you discussed Vietnam with anyone?

Respondent: Yes.

(Q. 21-B) What was the most recent conversation you have had about Vietnam? Who was the person—a friend, relative, co-worker, or who?

Respondent: Three weeks ago with co-workers.

(Q. 21-C) Had they decided what should be done about Vietnam?

Respondent: Yes.

(Q. 21-D) What solutions did they propose?

Respondent: Increase the war effort!

(Q. 21-E) What reasons did they give for adopting this solution?

Respondent: They feel it is the only thing that North Vietnam understands. Force will bring them sooner to acquiescence.

(Q. 21-F) Did you propose a solution?

Respondent: No.

It should be noted that the respondent reported that what his peers had said was consistent with what he reported in the interview as his own views. As will be seen later, we apparently caught this respondent just after he had shifted conclusions. Interpersonal communication in this case apparently had shown him how his values would be more consistent with another policy alternative. The questions that follow were designed to get at these effects.

(Q. 21-K) How would you characterize the discussion? Were you more of a listener, more of an opinion-giver, or did each of you express about the same number of opinions?

Respondent: Each of us expressed about the same number of opinions.

(Q. 21-L) Were there any points on which you had different views?

Respondent: Yes.

(Q. 21-M) What were the differences?

Respondent: Until three or four months ago I had believed in containment. They have convinced me that escalation is the right answer.

(Q. 21-N) Were you able to resolve any of the differences?

Respondent: Yes.

(Q. 21-O) How were you able to resolve them?

Respondent: I changed my opinion to agree with theirs.

We then turned specifically to conversations with servicemen. We were curious about any tendency for those who were attracted to military solutions to have personal contact with the military, particularly military who had some personal knowledge about Vietnam. Since the questions are similar to those asked about the earlier discussion, they are not repeated here. We entertained the hypothesis that the more knowledgeable persons would be more likely to have conversations with servicemen, and this hypothesis was confirmed.

The interview was concluded with a demographic inventory.

METHODOLOGICAL AND CONCEPTUAL BASES FOR DATA ANALYSIS

The methodology that we have outlined was, in our terms, unobtrusive in content although structured in form; to state it another way, our methodology was open-ended in terms of content but closed-ended in terms of structure.

Because we were permitting the idividual to define his own cognitive orientation to the war, rather than imposing alternatives upon him, we could permit a number of new variables and perspectives to emerge. These included how many solutions were proposed, and the nature of those solutions (warfare or peacefare), i.e., military as compared to nonmilitary means of problem-solving.

The method also made clear the bases upon which the solutions were valued—number of attributes, and the complexity of attribute structure, i.e., positive and negative attributes, or only positive or negative attributes. We also assessed acceptance, rejection, or inability to decide about attributes. And we measured policy preferences, i.e., the ability to decide which, among alternatives, was the individual's own policy preference. The nature of this policy preference (warfare or peacefare) was also included.

The methodology incorporated a test of relevant knowledge as well. By counting the number of attributes the respondent provided for each object that was proposed, we were in possession of a quantitative test of knowledge that the respondent was using to judge alternatives. By observing the *structure* of those attributes, i.e., if the respondent cited positive and negative values as compared to only positive or negative values, we could assess a *qualitative* test of relevant knowledge. Given also measures of use of information sources and communication, we could ask what kinds of people engaged in what kinds of cognitive and communications behavior.

We could test the inferences that there were no substantial differences in policy preferences between the best educated and the less educated. If policy differences existed, as seemed more likely to us, we could ask what kinds of behavior underlay such differences.

We employed a multi-stage sampling design for the city of Seattle. The city was gridded into areas, enumerated and sampled. Blocks then were enumerated and sampled within these areas. Dwelling units then were enumerated within the block clusters. Interviewers were given lists of dwelling units and instructed to interview adult residents, defined as 21 years of age and older. Male and female respondents were specified; no variations could be made without approval by the director of field work. Approximately forty interviewers were used; incorporated in this number were five field supervisors, three of whom were doctoral students. Interviews were carried out in October 1968, prior to President Johnson's "resignation" speech.

Stated as a paradigm of behavior, we would test the following propositions. The more educated person would:

| 1. Acquire greater knowledge (quantitative and qualitative) that was relevant to a greater range of policy alternatives. | 2. Engage in more effective and different decisional processes. | 3. Produce different war-peace orientations. | 4. Use and evaluate more critically mass and interpersonal communication relating to those decisions. |

Our "test of education" was number of years in school. We divided our educational groupings into those who had attended college and those who had not attended college.

Part I. Amount and Quality of Knowledge Relevant to Policy Alternatives

Our first group of variables was designed to assess quantitative and qualitative dimensions of knowledge held by our two educational groupings.

We developed seven measures of relevant quantitative and qualitative knowledge:

Number of Reasons (Attributes) for Vietnam Being "Important"

As can be seen in Table 1, those of higher education were able to state more reasons why Vietnam was an important problem.

TABLE 1
EDUCATION AND SALIENCE ATTRIBUTES

	Education[a]	
Number of reasons why Vietnam is important problem	Lo N=348	Hi N=249
0	1%	0%
1	18	11
2	55	55
3 or more	26	34
Total	100%	100%

a. Chi-square = 9.2; 3 df.; p < .03.

It should be noted that this did not constitute a relevant test of knowledge about solutions, i.e., alternatives that were proposed as a means of bringing the war in Vietnam to an end. While it was possible that attributes describing the importance of a problem might be invoked as attributes for a proposed solution, this need not necessarily be the case. One might use—and respondents frequently did use—an entirely different set of attributes to evaluate (1) the importance of the problem as compared to (2) reasons why one solution or another should be adopted.[8]

Number of Solutions Proposed

Individuals then were asked, "What solutions have been proposed?" Any reference to continuing the existing level of war activity or increasing the scope of war activities was coded as "warfare." It was reasoned that proposed solutions for bringing the war to an end constituted relevant knowledge, as compared—as we have stated—to information that only described the "importance" of the war as a problem. As indicated in Table 2, the more educated persons named a significantly greater number of proposed "warfare" solutions.

TABLE 2
EDUCATION AND AWARENESS OF PROPOSED
WARFARE SOLUTIONS

	Education[a]	
Number of warfare solutions	Lo N=348	Hi N=297
0	57%	38%
1	37	48
2 or more	6	14
Total	100%	100%

a. Chi-square = 26.2; 2 df.; p < .01.

If the respondent proposed political or diplomatic solutions, or any reduction in the existing level of warfare, the response was coded as "peacefare." As can be seen in Table 3, the more educated persons also were significantly more able to name proposed peacefare solutions. The differences were greater in ability to name "peacefare" than with respect to naming "warfare" solutions, although in each case the more educated were more informed.

We have, in these data, an early intimation of probable differences in policy orientations of the more educated and less educated groupings. One implication of this finding would appear to be that more knowledge of peacefare alternatives would bring greater acceptance of those alternatives, a question treated in PART II of our findings.

TABLE 3

EDUCATION AND AWARENESS OF PROPOSED
PEACEFARE SOLUTIONS

	Education[a]	
	Lo	Hi
Number of Peacefare solutions	*N=348*	*N=297*
0	22%	10%
1	47	30
2 or more	32	61
Total	101%	101%

a. Chi-square = 56.0; 2 df.; p $<$ .01.

As can be seen in Table 4, which provides a somewhat different analysis than is incorporated in Tables 2 and 3, those of higher education proposed a significantly greater number of solutions of all kinds, thus demonstrating greater relevant knowledge as to "What should be done to bring the war in Vietnam to an end?" As suggested earlier, this test of relevant knowledge is different from tests of substantive but not necessarily relevant knowledge employed in other studies.

TABLE 4

EDUCATION AND TOTAL NUMBER OF
PROPOSED SOLUTIONS

	Education[a]	
	Lo	Hi
Total number of proposed solutions	*N=348*	*N=297*
0	14%	6%
1	30	14
2	52	58
3 or more	4	22
Total	100%	100%

a. Chi-square = 71.9; 3 df.; p $<$ .01.

Number of Attributes (Values Assigned) to Those Solutions

This is an additional test of relevant knowledge. In this case, the knowledge is relevant to an evaluation of each proposed solution. This measure included all the reasons an individual could give both for accepting the proposed alternatives and for rejecting them. As is shown in Table 5, those of higher education were able to propose a significantly greater number of reasons why proposed solutions should be accepted.

TABLE 5
EDUCATION AND NUMBER OF ATTRIBUTES
FOR PROPOSED SOLUTIONS

	Education[a]	
Number of attributes	Hi [b]$N=291$	Lo [c]$N=277$
0	16%	7%
1	8	4
2	22	11
3 or more	54	79
Total	100%	101%

a. Chi-square = 44.7; 3 df.; p < .01.   c. 20 missing observations (no solutions).
b. 57 missing observations (no solutions).

Relative Complexity of Knowledge Possessed by Individuals About Proposed Solutions

A "simple structure" was defined as a situation where the individual could propose only positive or negative reasons for the evaluation of an alternative. A "complex structure" was defined as having both positive and negative values for alternatives. Those of higher education, as shown in Table 6, demonstrated a more complex structure of attributes for evaluating proposed solutions.

TABLE 6
EDUCATION AND COMPLEXITY OF ATTRIBUTE
STRUCTURE FOR PROPOSED SOLUTIONS

	Education[a]	
Complexity of structure of attributes	Lo [b]$N=291$	Hi [c]$N=277$
Simple	33%	20%
Non-Complex	42	25
Complex	25	56
Total	100%	101%

a. Chi-square = 55.1; 2 df.; p < .01.
b. 57 missing observations (no solutions).
c. 20 missing observations (no solutions).

TABLE 7

EDUCATION AND COMPLEXITY OF STRUCTURE
OF PROPOSED ALTERNATIVES

Complexity of structure of alternatives	*Education[a]*	
	Lo [b]$_{N=273}$	*Hi* [c]$_{N=268}$
Simple	54%	35%
Complex	46	65
Total	100%	100%

a. Chi-square = 17.8; 1 df.; p <.01.
b. 75 missing observations (omitted "non-complex" category).
c. 29 missing observations (omitted "non-complex" category).

A related structural analysis was suggested by the range of objects-alternatives that different educational groupings might be considering. Were they considering only warfare solutions or only peacefare solutions, or were they giving consideration to both warfare and peacefare solutions? Data of this kind would provide additional qualitative evidence that individuals of higher education were considering a more complex range of solutions, as well as considering a greater number of proposed solutions. As Table 7 shows, those of higher education did consider a broader range of solutions.[9]

While our findings in Part I of our analysis corroborated those of Verba, there were important differences:

Our test of knowledge required the respondent to propose alternatives and values to be assigned to these alternatives. Verba and colleagues supplied the alternatives and the means for valuing them.

Our tests of knowledge were relevant to decision-making about alternatives that had been proposed. Verba's test of knowledge did not demand knowledge relevant to decision-making.

Finally, our test of knowledge was qualitative (structurally defined) as well as quantitative. Verba's test of knowledge was only quantitative.

Part II. Analysis of Decisional Processes and Decision-Making

We reasoned that the more educated respondent would engage in more complex decisional processes and in more effective decision-making about those alternatives. By "complex" we meant cognitive and psychological states; by "effective" we meant the ability to make a decision. We also anticipated differences in policy preferences, to be treated in Part III.

Our reasoning was that greater and more differentiated knowledge, coupled with educational skills, would facilitate decision-making. Implicit in a greater and more differentiated knowledge would be a corresponding tendency to accept solutions that were more demanding. Our assumption was that peacefare solutions, requiring the individual to abstract *beyond* what was observable as policy and practice, would be more considered by those of greater education. (This reasoning would assume that more educated persons might be more likely to give consideration to *war* alternatives in time of *peace.*)[10]

Several variables gave us insight into the ability to cope with solutions proposed by others as well as to cope with solutions proposed by the respondents themselves. We were interested, as well, in difficulties experienced by the individual as reflected by the cognitive and psychological states that functioned in his decisional processes. Such psychological states as conflict, dissonance, consonance, and leaving the psychological field appeared to us to be indications of processes of decision-making at work in the individual.

Acceptance of Proposed Solutions

We assumed that those of greater education would be able to cope more effectively with solutions proposed by others. The rationale lay in the demand placed on the individual to bring one's own information to bear upon problems formulated by others; this would not imply agreement with points of view formulated by others, but rather an ability to understand the points of view espoused by others. Given normal potentialities for agreement, those of higher education would be more capable of "accepting" solutions proposed by others than would those of lower education. However, the great number of warfare solutions in this instance mitigated against a straightforward hypothesis.

Table 8 shows that those of higher education were actually less accepting of solutions than were those of lower education. The evidence of almost equal latitudes of acceptance affirmed that the educated person, no less than the less-educated one, was willing to work within "tolerable" limits of policy alternatives. Our findings did not suggest, supportive of the findings of Verba, a large ideological or educational elite that would accept only a narrow range of solutions.

TABLE 8
EDUCATION AND ACCEPTANCE OF SOLUTIONS PROPOSED BY OTHERS

Solutions	*Education*[a]	
	Lo [b]*N=438*	*Hi* [b]*N=470*
One or more solutions accepted	48%	44%
One or more solutions not accepted	37	47
One or more solutions "don't know"	15	9
Total	100%	100%

a. Chi-square = 13.6; 2 df.; p $<$ .01.
b. Multiple responses. (Single response N=653.)

The distinction that appeared to be the most interesting was the tendency on the part of the better educated to reject more solutions and to be more able to cope with any proposed solution. The tendency to reject would be part of a capacity to make more discriminations; this might be more demanding cognitively than to be accepting.

We expected that those of lesser education would be more likely to say that they "did not know" if the solution that was proposed by someone else was acceptable or not acceptable to them personally. There was only a small difference, but it was in the expected direction. Some 15 percent of the less educated, compared with 9 percent of the better educated persons, were unable to decide whether or not to accept a solution.

Ability to Decide What Should Be Done

Greater levels of education were presumed to represent greater ability to make decisions; this would be one way in which the educated would differ from the less educated. This variable was unspecified by Verba and colleagues and is seldom permitted to emerge as a distinguishing variable in conventional opinion-research methodologies. As can be seen in Table 9, those of higher education were significantly more able to make decisions as to what should be done to bring the war to an end. This is consistent with our earlier findings that those of higher education not only had more relevant information but that it was qualitatively different, as well.

TABLE 9
EDUCATION AND DECISION-MAKING

	Education[a]	
	Lo	Hi
Ability to decide	N=348	N=297
Yes	36%	51%
No	64	49
Total	100%	100%

a. Chi-square = 15.9; 1 df.; p < .01.

Difficulty in Decision-Making

Our assumption was that if individuals of greater education were processing more information about more alternatives, and if the structure of that knowledge was complex both with respect to alternatives and to the means of evaluating them, we should expect those individuals to encounter difficulties in decision-making as a function of that increased activity.

As Table 10 indicates, however, those of higher education were not more likely to report significantly more difficulty. The reason was that knowledge and structure of knowledge were diffused across educational groups to some con-

TABLE 10
EDUCATION AND DIFFICULTY IN DECIDING

| | Education[a] | |
	Lo [b]N=117	Hi [b]N=171
Difficulty deciding		
No	67%	64%
Yes, Don't Know	33	36
Total	100%	100%

a. Chi-square = .2; 1 df.; p $<$ .70.
b. Non-deciders excluded.

siderable extent. When, however, education and complexity of knowledge were treated together (as in Edelstein and Hollander, 1969), the expected findings emerged.

More interestingly, when we asked respondents why it was difficult for them to decide, they referred to such reasons as information overload and lack of discriminating information. Those who were unable to make decisions said more often that "It is not up to me to decide," "I am unable to make decisions of that kind," rather than expressing a concern about the value of information.

Four Kinds of Psychological States

The kinds of difficulties experienced in decision-making seemed to be of two kinds—lack of information, and inability to cope with information or with the decision-making role. This led us to postulate that an important part of decisional processes were the psychological states either precedent to or a consequence of decision-making. Four states were postulated.

Conflict vs. Leaving the Psychological Field: Conflict was operationalized as a pre-decisional situation where individuals were trying to decide. Presumably,

TABLE 11
EDUCATION AND PRE-DECISIONAL
PSYCHOLOGICAL STATES

| | Education[a] | |
	Lo [b]N=224	Hi [b]N=142
Pre-decisional state		
Opting Out	47%	35%
Conflict	50	63
Uncodable	4	1
Total	101%	99%

a. Chi-square = 7.3; 2 df.; p $<$ .03.
b. Post-decisional persons are excluded from table.

those of higher education would more likely be trying to make a decision; they had merely been caught by our interviewers at a point in time where the decision had not yet been made. Those of higher education thus should be more likely to be in conflict than would those of lower education (who were not trying to decide and thus were not in conflict). Table 11 indicates the extent to which this occurred.

Dissonance vs. Consonance: These were defined as post-decisional states. Dissonance represented a discrepancy between what the individual wanted to be done and what he observed was being done, while consonance represented the lack of a discrepancy. We hypothesized that more of those of higher education would suffer dissonance because of a greater complexity of knowledge. We evidently encountered a temporal dimension where we were not catching dissonance as it occurred but at a time when it had been resolved. As seen in Table 12, there was no difference between our two educational groups. Table 13 shows that more of those of higher education were able to find events that were consonant with their "decision," although differences were not highly significant.

TABLE 12
EDUCATION AND DISSONANCE

| | $Education^a$ | |
	Lo $^bN=129$	Hi $^bN=162$
Dissonant		
Yes	15%	19%
No	85	81
Total	100%	100%

a. Chi-square = 1.0; 1 df.; p $<$.4.
b. Pre-decision persons excluded from table.

TABLE 13
EDUCATION AND CONSONANCE

| | $Education^a$ | |
	Lo $^bN=129$	Hi $^bN=162$
Consonant		
Yes	89%	82%
No	11	19
Total	100%	101%

a. Chi-square = 2.7; 1 df.; p $<$.10.
b. Pre-decision persons excluded from table.

Part III. Policy Orientations Toward Warfare and Peacefare Solutions

Verba and colleagues had expressed surprise that those of higher education did not differ appreciably from those of lower education in their orientations to warfare and peacefare solutions. And Harris, it will be remembered, expressed surprise that individuals could be so "inconsistent" in their orientations to warfare and peacefare solutions.

Tables 2 and 3 showed earlier that those of higher education were likely to be aware of more proposed peacefare solutions. We examined three variables to note relationships among level of education and acceptance or rejection of warfare and peacefare solutions as well as expressed preferences for solutions.

Acceptance and Preference for Solutions

As implied earlier, the tendency of those of higher education to accept a range of alternative solutions is demonstrated in Table 14; here it is evident that those of higher education were as likely to accept a warfare solution as were those of lower education.

TABLE 14
EDUCATION AND ACCEPTANCE OF
PROPOSED WARFARE SOLUTIONS

	Education[a]	
	Lo	*Hi*
Accept warfare solutions	*N=348*	*N=297*
0	79%	80%
1	20	19
2 or more	1	2
Total	100%	101%

a. Chi-square = 1.1; 2 df.; $p < .59$.

TABLE 15
EDUCATION AND ACCEPTANCE OF PROPOSED
PEACEFARE SOLUTIONS

	Education[a]	
	Hi	*Lo*
Accept peacefare solutions	*N=348*	*N=297*
0	54%	43%
1	38	40
2 or more	8	18
Total	100%	101%

a. Chi-square = 14.6; 2 df.; $p < .01$.

As also suggested, those of higher education were more likely than those of lower education to accept peacefare solutions; this proposed that those of higher education were equally accepting of war but that they were more accepting of peace. We speculated earlier that peace represented the unknown value. This was demonstrated in Table 15.

Those who said they had decided what should be done to bring the war in Vietnam to an end were asked, "What solution do you prefer?"

As shown in Table 16, those of higher education tended more to express a preference for peacefare solutions. The earlier evidence of awareness of more peaceful solutions, being more accepting of peacefare solutions, and themselves expressing a preference for peaceful solutions, appear to give assurance that the policy preference of those who are better educated did, indeed, differ from the policy preferences of those who were less educated. Thus, we differed dramatically across several variables from the findings reported by other investigators.[11]

TABLE 16
EDUCATION AND PREFERENCE FOR SOLUTION

	Education[a]	
Prefer	*Lo* [b]*N=127*	*Hi* [b]*N=161*
Warfare	44%	29%
Peacefare	47	64
Warfare/Peacefare	9	8
Total	100%	101%

a. Chi-square = 9.0; 2 df.; p $<$ .02.
b. Excludes those who did not express a preference.

Part IV. Use and Evaluation of Mass and Interpersonal Communication

We entertained relatively complex hypotheses about mass media use and evaluation. Our assumptions were that individuals who were trying to solve problems probably were more similar than different in their *use* of media but were more different than similar in their *evaluation of the utility* of media.

We asked respondents how they were learning about the war and which of the media were providing most of their information about the war. Overall, newspapers were cited most often (33 percent), followed by television (32 percent), magazines (17 percent), people (10 percent), and radio (7 percent).

Preference for Media

The significant differences in preferences for media existed only at the level of magazines (more preferred by those of higher education) and television (more preferred by those of lower education). But with respect to newspapers, radio, and people as sources of information, there were few differences observable. This can be seen in Table 17.

TABLE 17
EDUCATION AND USE OF MEDIA

	Education[a]		
Most used source of information	Lo N=373	Hi N=316	All [b]N=689
Newspapers	35%	31%	33%
Television	32	26	33
Magazines	10	26	17
People	10	10	10
Radio	8	6	7
Total	100%	99%	100%

a. Chi-square = 35.2; 4 df.; p < .01.
b. Multiple responses (Single response N=653).

Evaluation of Sources of Information

The most significant differences were observed in the use and evaluation of content and sources of information. The higher educated persons were more critical of information sources and information content. In response to the question, "Was any information *not* useful to you?" those of higher education were much more likely to answer "yes" than were those of lower education; this is seen in Table 18.

TABLE 18
EDUCATION AND EVALUATION OF CONTENT
OF INFORMATION

	Education[a]	
Content not useful	Lo [b]N=346	Hi [c]N=292
No	80%	61%
Yes	20	39
Total	100%	100%

a. Chi-square = 9.1; 1 df.; p < .01.
b. 2 missing observations.
c. 5 missing observations

Similarly, when asked "Are there any sources of information that have *not* been useful to you? those of higher education were significantly more likely again to answer "yes," as reflected in Table 19.

Thus those of higher education used more information but they were more critical of the information and the sources of that information. It was difficult in the face of this evidence to accept the proposition set forth by Verba and colleagues that there was no basis for believing that those of higher education used media differently than did those of lower education.

TABLE 19

EDUCATION AND EVALUATION OF SOURCE
OF INFORMATION

	Education[a]	
	Lo	Hi
Source not useful	[b]N=318	[c]N=285
No	66%	54%
Yes	34	46
Total	100%	100%

a. Chi-square = 9.1; 1 df.; p < .01.
b. 30 non-source references.
c. 12 non-source references.

TABLE 20

EDUCATION AND WANTING MORE INFORMATION

	Education[a]	
	Lo	Hi
Wants information	[b]N=346	[b]N=295
No	67%	51%
Yes	33	49
Total	100%	100%

a. Chi-square = 16.3; 1 df.; p < .01.
b. 2 missing observations.

Continued Belief in Efficacy of Information

Finally, we assumed that individuals of higher education, to whom information was a means to an end, would wish to maintain the utility of their decision making by a continued belief in the efficacy of information. This concept was operationalized by the question,

"Would you like any more information?"

Those of higher education, as indicated in Table 20, were more likely to answer "yes" to this question.

Finally, we permitted individuals to describe the nature of interpersonal communication; if the data that we had developed was to be validated, we should expect cognitive behavior to evidence itself in interpersonal relations as well as in media use.

Interpersonal Communication

We would expect those of higher education to engage more in interpersonal discussion and to use it differently. The use of interpersonal discussion would be consistent with having a range of knowledge about what to do about the war, skill and confidence in decision-making, and confidence in one's ability to use interpersonal discussion in an efficacious manner. As expected, although levels of interpersonal communication were high for both groups, our more educated group engaged in more discussion, as indicated in Table 21.

TABLE 21
EDUCATION AND INTERPERSONAL DISCUSSION

	Education[a]	
	Lo	*Hi*
Interpersonal discussion	*N=348*	*N=297*
No	29%	11%
Yes	71	89
Total	100%	100%

a. Chi-square = 30.2; 1 df.; p $<$ .01.

We expected that a communication situation permitted a number of potentialities that were relevant to a discussion of what to do to bring the war in Vietnam to an end. Each person, if he had personally decided what should be done to bring the war to an end, could propose a solution.

We expected that those of higher education, not merely because they were more likely to have made a decision, but because of their information-processing capabilities and stronger sense of social competence, would be more likely to perceive that they had introduced their own views into the discussion and that this behavior had been engaged in also by their partners.

Contrary to the implications of the two-step flow hypothesis and opinion leadership constructs, we expected "cognitive" peers to *exchange* information

TABLE 22
EDUCATION AND RESPONDENT PROPOSING
A SOLUTION TO OTHERS

	Education[a]	
	Lo	*Hi*
Respondent proposed solution	[b]*N=342*	[b]*N=255*
No	74%	68%
Yes	26	32
Total	100%	100%

a. Chi-square = 2.0; 1 df.; p $<$ .16.
b. Excludes those who did not report interpersonal discussion.

TABLE 23
EDUCATION AND OTHER PERSON
PROPOSING A SOLUTION

| | Education[a] | |
	Lo [b]N=342	Hi [b]N=255
Other person suggested solution		
No	63%	49%
Yes	37	51
Total	100%	100%

a. Chi-square = 10.1; 1 df.; p $<$.01.
b. Excludes those who did not report interpersonal discussions.

and advice. Thus, those who had made decisions would be more likely to perceive that they had discussed decisions with others and that others had discussed *their* decisions with them. Table 22 is weakly supportive, but Table 23 confirms our expectations.

An implication of the sharing of knowledge about solutions was that differences in point of view would be encountered by the parties to the discussion. We hypothesized that those of higher education not only would engage in more exchanges of points of view but would more likely *perceive* differences in points of view. As indicated in Table 24, this expectation was confirmed.

An inevitable correlative question occurred: Was there any accommodation of the differences in point of view? These differences could be resolved, our respondents suggested, by minimizing differences, by agreeing to disagree, or by one or the other accepting the other person's point of view. All these responses required adaptation of one's own behavior to that of another. We hypothesized, therefore, that the more educated persons would perceive themselves as having been more successful in this behavior. As Table 25 indicates, our expectations again were confirmed.

TABLE 24
EDUCATION AND PERCEPTION OF
DIFFERENCES IN POINT OF VIEW

| | Education[a] | |
	Lo [b]N=341	Hi [b]N=252
Encountered different viewpoint		
No	69%	59%
Yes	31	41
Total	100%	100%

a. Chi-square = 5.1; 1 df.; p $<$.03.
b. Excludes those who did not report interpersonal discussions.

TABLE 25
EDUCATION AND RESOLUTION OF
DIFFERENCES IN POINT OF VIEW

	Education[a]	
Resolved differences in viewpoints	*Lo* [b]*N=95*	*Hi* [b]*N=104*
No	93%	81%
Yes	7	19
Total	100%	100%

a. Chi-square = 4.8; 1 df.; p < .03.
b. Includes only those who reported difference in point of view.

CONCLUSIONS

In general, our expectations were confirmed. There were few "surprises."

Contrary to the findings of Verba: those of higher education expressed different policy preferences; not only were they more knowledgeable but the structure of their knowledge differed, as did their decisional processes and psychological states; they did not *use* media so differently as they evaluated its utility differently, indicating that the faith by columnists and commentators in a relevant readership was not misplaced; they demonstrated not only more use of information but a greater belief in the efficacy of information for use in problem-solving. Our conceptual and methodological assumptions appeared to be validated.

A number of questions were raised, nonetheless, by our methodological approach. These were matters of the amenability of the methodology to administration. We are able to make a number of assertions based upon this and subsequent research employing the methodology (in cross-cultural as well as in the Seattle context):

- Training of interviewers: In Seattle we have effectively used Gallup, Roper, Harris and University of Michigan Survey Research Center interviewers. We have also been able to train students. Training time is actually minimal. In Yugoslavia and in Finland we have used graduate students who are trained interviewers.
- Time of interviews was surprisingly short. The reason was that respondents were talking about problems that were important to them personally and thus were able to discuss the problems in their own terms.
- Interviewers experienced some difficulties in recording everything that a respondent said, as they were instructed to do. We have made progress toward permitting abbreviation techniques. (A danger is that interviewers will translate and summarize rather than use the words of the respondent.)

- Interviewers expressed satisfaction with the interview situation because each interview was different.
- Respondents expressed satisfaction with the interview because it asked for more information than it gave; there was nonetheless a tendency for those of the least information to perceive more redundancies in questions, particularly with respect to probes. This is a "cost" implicit in the methodological approach.
- A more serious implication was the frequent statement by respondents that they liked the questionnaire because it helped them to "realize" what they were thinking; we viewed this as a problem but as less of a problem than if we were giving information or doing their thinking for them.
- Coding of "open-ended" responses was not as difficult as we had anticipated; we set a 95 percent reliability of coding standard and achieved it with little difficulty once we gained familiarity with modal kinds of responses. Thus, all qualitative variables are reliable at 95 or better among two or more coders.
- The cost of administration of the methodology was low, not only because the time of interview was reduced but because costs of coding are less than costs of data collection.
- The productivity of the data exceeded that yielded by conventional methodology, which restricts responses and hence reduces the amount of information that can be obtained from a respondent.
- Differences by levels of education actually were reduced by the methodological approach; the reason was that those of lower education were able to talk about matters that were salient to them personally. One implication of this outcome was that those of lower education were able to report more media use than might be the case if the problem were not salient to them personally; i.e., their incidental media learning would be less than for those of higher education for most problems.
- One important implication of the approach is to permit an inductive although systematic and quantifiable approach to the development of knowledge about the uses and evaluation of mass communication for the individual; the less constricted approach permits us to build theory on the basis of observation rather than to test theory in a constricted setting.

NOTES

1. V. O. Key (1961) asserted that few persons shared a media content-attitudinal relationship; we are not dealing, however, so much with content as with the *structure* of content. Nor have we conceptualized knowledge or decision as "attitudinal." Key takes an essentially sociological approach to the utility of mass communication for the individual, stressing the values for communication content that are rooted in social groups. Our approach is essentially cognitive, in that it says that individuals may be problem-centered and that the group as a value may or may not be a relevant attribute in a particular situation. See Chapter 14, "Media: Spectre and Reality."

2. The Gallup studies reported that in all surveys since 1965, about 20 percent were classified as Super Hawks and 20 percent were classified as Super Doves. These figures differ significantly from those assessed by Verba. Like Verba we found much less "super" sentiment, and even when we did, we found that it was heavily qualified. We consider the inflated nature of such responses to be a direct function of methodological intrusiveness. See Gallup Report No. 52, pp. 2-3.

3. Insight into the real significance of questions that ask individuals whether or not they approve of the policies of the President is provided by Frankel (1969): "Thus it may be the case . . . that a majority of Americans are on President Nixon's side with regard to his policy in Vietnam. But it is hard to say what this proves. Simply out of loyalty to their President, many Americans would no doubt support Mr. Nixon if he followed a course diametrically opposed to his present one. A President, by posing issues in one way or another, makes and unmakes majorities." The point here is that it is not the policy that may be supported but the fact of a policy; it is not a substantive but an institutional gesture under many circumstances. Somehow, it would seem, the public opinion polls should at some time address themselves to more difficult problems than predicting outcomes, as great an art as that might be.

4. Some of the implications of "observer orientation" are revealed in a letter to the editor of the *American Political Science Review,* in which the writer, Michael Parenti of Sarah Lawrence College, objects to the use by Verba and colleagues of the terms "responsible" and "irresponsible" to characterize responses of the "American public" to items in their study. Parenti noted that unless "responsible" and "irresponsible" were conceptualized operationally, no empirical validity was possible. In their reply Verba and colleagues conceded the point but stated that they had not presented these evaluations as scientific findings but rather as "policy oriented" statements. What was significant to this writer was the conviction articulated here that responses by individuals to constricted alternatives devised by an observer might be considered, with no other test applied, as sufficient basis for policy-oriented conclusions. Our objection to intrusive methodology is that it lends itself to the too-facile formulation of policy statements. See "Communications," *American Political Science Review,* pp. 1103-1104. Converse (1964) noted that the fact that ideational worlds differ greatly in character posed problems of adequate representation and measurement in conventional public opinion studies. However, in dealing with political objects broad enough to be characterized as ideologies, or belief systems, Converse deals at a macro level with problems that we approach in a highly situational context. Converse concedes that the actor himself must in any situation perceive a meaningful link between values held in the abstract and a judgment about some policy alternative.

5. Readers who are interested in cognitive processing as an heuristic construct will see the relationship of these formulations with the work of Carter (1966) and Chaffee (1969; also Chaffee et al., 1969). Taken at the level of structure rather than a sequence (or process) of discriminations, our work also is compatible with that of Schroder et al. (1967), Schroder (1971), Bieri (1966, 1968) and Scott (1962, 1963).

6. What we are proposing, in asking reasons for and reasons for not adopting given alternatives, is in the same genre and no more difficult to "code" than examples given in the *Fortune* 500-Yankelovich Survey which asked which proposals of the Nixon Administration were having the greatest success and the least success (Diamond, 1970).

7. As an indication of the need to learn the bases for individual opinions as expressed in a conventional sample survey, Frankel (1969) comments: "Opinion on a particular issue may not in fact express opinion on *that* specific issue. It may express a general party loyalty; it may express the individual's sense that he should go along with a coalition of interests with which he is broadly sympathetic even if he disagrees with the particular policy at issue; it may reflect simply his judgment that he does not know enough to have a reliable opinion on the specific question he has been asked, and his decision, therefore, to accept the opinion of people in authority."

8. Clarke and Jackson (1968) asked what solutions respondents "favored" with respect to a test of information. Their questions were not conceived, however, as tests of information but as a measure of "attitudes" toward escalation and de-escalation. Clarke and Jackson employed the same rationale as did Verba earlier, stating: "We judged that a person would be better equipped to interpret changes in the war situation and political events at home if he knew what the Gulf of Tonkin Resolution meant, understood some of the content of the Geneva Accords of 1954, could identify the Viet Cong, was aware of the levels of U.S. troop commitments and losses, and could specify the roles of newsmakers closely identified with the conflict." It was of interest to us, however, that consistent with what Lipset (1966) has asserted, much of the basis of the decision-making of our Seattle sample as to what to do about Vietnam was centered on containment of communism and upon situational costs and presumed benefits. The Gulf of Tonkin Resolution and the Geneva Accords were not often cited as attributes, nor were the names of "newsmakers." Knowledge about the Viet Cong and levels of U.S. troop commitments and losses might, on the other hand, more easily be translated into relevant data about what to do to bring the war to an end.

9. The formulation of structural variables such as "attribute structure" and "object structure" made it possible for us to link cognitive structure with media variables as well as with education. This analysis is provided in Edelstein and Hollander (1969). There was evidence in these analyses that a more complex object structure (proposing both war *and* peace alternatives, as compared with proposing only war *or* peace alternatives) was associated with more preference for newspapers and less preference for radio and television, the latter being a more pronounced finding. A slight preference for magazines also was demonstrated. Those with more complex object structures also were more likely to want more information and were more critical of mass media content. Interestingly, however, those with complex object structure did not experience more difficulty in decision-making than those who had a simple object structure.

The answer to that seeming puzzle was found in the analysis of attribute structure. A complex attribute structure was defined as having both positive and negative alternatives for an alternative as contrasted with having only positive or negative attributes for an alternative. In the case of complex attribute structure, as contrasted with complex object structure, the individual did experience more difficulty in making a decision. In this and in other ways, attribute structure was a more effective predictor and produced more complex media and communication behavior than did object structure.

As examples, complex attribute structure produced more variance with respect to (1) acceptance and rejection of proposed solutions, (2) psychological states, (3) less use of television, (4) more preference for magazines, (5) more criticism of the media, (6) more discussion, and (7) higher levels of education.

10. Gamson and Modigliani (1966) cite Korean war data that supports the inference. This is cited in partial refutation of the "enlightenment" model. The authors also cite a "mainstream model" and a "cognitive consistency" model. Neither, however, is equivalent to a decision-making model which permits the individual to provide his own definition of the situation and to define the relevant elements in it.

11. It is unfortunate that we were unable to undertake several waves of interviews over time so that we might provide more directly comparable data on the temporal dimensions. We encounter the problem of "Which war?" to which we alluded earlier.

REFERENCES

ARMOR, D. J., J. B. CIACQUINTA, R. G. McINTOSH, and D. E. H. RUSSELL (1967) "Professors' attitudes toward the Vietnam war." Public Opinion Quarterly 31: 159-175.

BIERI, JAMES (1966) "Cognitive complexity and personality development," in O. J. Harvey (ed.) Experience, Structure and Adaptability. New York: Springer.

——— (1968) "Cognitive complexity and judgment of inconsistent information," in Robert P. Abelson et al., Theories of Cognitive Consistency: A Sourcebook. Chicago: Rand McNally.

———, et al. (1966) Clinical and Social Judgment: The Discrimination of Behavioral Information. New York: John Wiley.

CARTER, R. F. (1965) "Communication and affective relations." Journalism Quarterly 42: 203-212.

——— (1966) Cognitive Discrepancies and Communication Behavior. Paper read at Association for Education in Journalism convention, Theory and Methodology division.

CHAFFEE, S. (1967) "Salience and pertinence as sources of value change." Journal of Communication 17: 25-38.

——— (1969) "Experiments in cognitive discrepancies and communication." Journalism Monographs 14 (December): 4-8.

CHAFFEE, S., K. R. STAMM, J. L. GUERRERO, and L. P. TIPTON (1969) "Experiments on cognitive discrepancies and communication." Journalism Monographs 14 (December).

CLARKE, P. and K. JACKSON (1968) Media Use, Information-seeking, and Knowledge about the War in Vietnam. Paper presented to the Association for Education in Journalism convention, Lawrence, Kan.

CONVERSE, P. E. (1964) "The nature of belief systems in mass publics," in D. E. Apter (ed.) International Yearbook of Political Behavior Research 5: Ideology and Discontent. Glencoe, Ill.: Free Press.

CONVERSE, P. E. and H. SCHUMAN (1970) "Silent majorities and the Vietnam war." Scientific American 222 (June): 17-24.

DIAMOND, R. S. (1970) "The Fortune 500-Yankelovich survey: shaken faith in Nixon." Fortune (June): 60-62.

EDELSTEIN, A. S. (1969) "Communication and international conflict." Mass Media and International Understanding. Ljubljana, Yugoslavia: Higher School of Political Science and Sociology.

———, W. L. RUGGELS, N. HOLLANDER and R. SIMPSON (1969) "Communication and international conflict: an interim report." Napa, Calif.: Pacific Association for Public Opinion Research (February).

EDELSTEIN, A. S. and N. HOLLANDER (1969) Perceptions of Social Conflict, Education and Communication with Respect to Vietnam. Paper read at Association for Education in Journalism convention, Berkeley, Calif.

——— (1969) The Public Opinion Polls as a Source of Distortion in the International Flow of News." XVII International Symposium, International Centre for Higher Education, Strasbourg, France (December).

FRANKEL, C. (1969) "The silenced majority." Saturday Review (December 13): 22/51.

GAMSON, W. A. and A. MODIGLIANI (1966) "Knowledge and foreign policy opinions: some models for consideration." Public Opinion Quarterly 30: 187-199.

Gallup International, Inc. (1969) "Public opinion on the Vietnam war, 1964-1969." The Gallup Opinion Index 52 (October).

HAHN, H. (1970) "Correlates of public sentiments about war: local referenda on the Vietnam issue." American Political Science Review 64: 1186-94.

KEY, V. O. (1961) Public Opinion and American Democracy. New York: Alfred A. Knopf.

LIPSET, S. M. (1966) "Doves, hawks, and polls." Encounter 27: 38-45. See also "The President, the polls, and Vietnam," Trans-action 3, 6 (September/October): 19-24.

POLSBY, N. W. (1969) "Political science and the press: notes on coverage of a public opinion survey on the Vietnam war." Western Political Quarterly 22 (March): 47-59.

ROBINSON, J. P., J. G. RUSK, and K. B. HEAD (1968) Measures of Political Attitudes. Institute for Social Research (September): 366-371. Ann Arbor: University of Michigan.

SCHRODER, H. M. (1971) "Cognitive complexity," in Schroder et al., Personality Theory and Information Processing. New York: Ronald Press.

SCHRODER, H. M., M. J. DRIVER and S. STREUFERT (1967) Human Information Processing. New York: Holt, Rinehart, Winston.

SCOTT, W. A. (1962) "Cognitive complexity and cognitive flexibility." Sociometry 25, 4 (December): 405-414.

SCOTT, W. A. (1963) "Cognitive complexity and cognitive balance." Sociometry 26, 1 (March): 66-74.

THURSTONE, L. L. and E. J. CHAVE (1929) The Measurement of Attitude. Chicago: University of Chicago.

Time-Louis Harris Poll (1969) "Americans on the war: divided, glum, unwilling to quit." Time [magazine] (October 31): 13-16.

VERBA, S., G. BLACK, R. A. BRODY, P. EKMAN, H. H. NIE, E. B. PARKER, N. W. POLSBY, P. H. ROSSI, and P. SHEATSLEY (undated) Public Opinion and the War in Vietnam. Advance copy.

VERBA, S., R. A. BRODY, E. B. PARKER, N. H. NIE, N. W. POLSBY, P. EKMAN, and G. S. BLACK (1967) "Public opinion and the war in Vietnam," American Political Science Review 61 (June): 317-333.

VOTH, A. (1967) "Vietnam—studying a major controversy," Journal of Conflict Resolution 2 (December): 431-443.

Chapter 4

CHILDREN'S INFORMATION PROCESSING OF TELEVISION ADVERTISING

Scott Ward and Daniel B. Wackman

THE GENERAL FOCUS of this article is on information processing of children as a developmental phenomenon. Our basic theoretical orientation relies heavily upon Piaget's theory of cognitive development, a theoretical orientation which has only recently gained prominence in studies of children's communication behavior (Flavell, 1968) and information processing (Farnham-Diggory, 1972).

Aspects of Piaget's theory were applied in the design of studies which examined two aspects of children's information processing of television commercials—selection of information and cognitive processing of information. Children's selection of information was indexed in terms of patterns of attention to television commercials in the natural environment of the home. Children's cognitive processing of information was indexed in terms of responses to a variety of questions concerning TV commercials and programs.[1]

PIAGET'S THEORY OF COGNITIVE DEVELOPMENT

In recent years, child development research has been characterized by concern with socialization processes, i.e., interaction between individual characteristics and environmental factors in shaping children's attitudes, knowledge, and behavior. Several theoretical traditions have stimulated research in socialization processes—most notably, social anthropology, psychoanalysis, learning theory, and cognitive-developmental theories. Historically, the majority position

AUTHOR'S NOTE: Research reported here was supported by grants from the National Institute of Mental Health, The Marketing Science Institute, and the American Association of Advertising Agencies.

of developmental theorists has been learning theory, although increasing attention has been devoted to cognitive developmental theories, as a result of Piaget's heuristic work. His theoretical essays and empirical research on development of basic cognitive skills in children have stimulated more recent socialization research in such areas as dependency, morality, and sex-role identification (Kohlberg, 1963; Kohlberg and Zigler, 1967; Turiel, 1966; Zigler, 1963).

There are several reasons for the emerging importance of cognitive-developmental theories. A primary reason is that the latter focus on the interaction of personal and environmental factors, while learning theorists characteristically view behavior as a function of forces applied to the child. Psychoanalytic theorists, on the other hand, focus primarily on affective dimensions of parent-child relationships; in any case, both social anthropological and psychoanalytic systematic positions are not developed to the point at which clearly testable propositions can be derived, and both approaches are incomplete in that they do not deal with many aspects of social behavior which are of interest to socialization researchers. (For a more complete discussion, see Zigler and Child, 1969.)

In Piaget's theory, development is a function of "equilibration," which is influenced by environmental and personal factors. The concept refers to processes by which children experience latent contradictions in mental structure, which in turn serve to stimulate inner reorganization (Zigler and Child, 1969). These qualitative changes over the course of development are posited to occur in four major cognitive stages as children develop from infancy to adulthood. These stages are the sensorimotor stage (up to about two years old), preoperational stage (from two to about seven), concrete operational stage (seven to about eleven), and formal operations stage (eleven through adulthood).

Stages are defined in terms of the formal systems—primarily cognitive structures—that the child is able to use in perceiving and dealing with the environment at different ages.

For Piaget a cognitive structure is a pattern of action, not necessarily overt, which displays coherence and order. This definition has two important aspects. First, it implies that the child is an *active* agent, i.e., a cognitive structure is used to describe classes of children's psychological and behavioral activities. Second, it refers to the basic cognitive structure underlying the child's overt behavior, the bases of his behavior. Although Piaget's stages provide concepts for roughly describing children's cognitive functioning, the various structures he identifies provide much more explicit theoretical bases for understanding children's thought processes and behavior than earlier, atheoretical normative studies (viz., normative and longitudinal research traditions).

In Piaget's theory, a number of structures are used to differentiate one stage from another, but certain structures appear to be more important than others. Two structures are of particular significance for distinguishing the preoperational stage from the concrete operational stages, the two stages characterizing most children in our study. The first is perceptual boundedness, the tendency for children to focus on and respond primarily to aspects of their immediate perceived environment. Perceptual boundedness particularly characterizes preoperational children: Piaget characterizes the mental processes of children at this stage as a "mental experiment": the child duplicates in mental imagery representations of the visual stimuli he receives. By contrast, the concrete operational child may not only duplicate what he sees, but also can manipulate mentally the elements in his perception. Thus, he is able to examine a number of possibilities in concrete situations, not simply accept what he perceives as the only reality [2].

The second structure of special significance for differentiating the preoperational and concrete operational stages is centration, the tendency to focus on a limited amount of the information available. The preoperational child tends to focus on one dimension of a situation, failing to make use of other dimensions which may be of equal relevance. Consequently, he has difficulty in appreciating the relations between two dimensions and in handling situations which require that two dimensions be dealt with simultaneously. The concrete operational child, on the other hand, is capable of decentration, i.e., he is able to focus on several dimensions of a situation or problem at the same time and to relate the dimensions.

Several other structures which are intimately related to perceptual boundedness and centration are also used by Piaget to differentiate the preoperational and concrete operational stages. These other structures include the following: (1) egocentric communication, i.e., the inability to take the role of others in communicating to them; (2) syncretism, i.e., a tendency to link ideas and images into a confused whole; and (3) juxtaposition, i.e., a tendency to link events, one after the other, without seeing clear relationships among them, and an inability to understand either part-whole or ordinal relations. The thought of the preoperational child is characterized by each of these structures, but the concrete operational child has developed beyond them. Thus, for example, the concrete operational child is able to reverse his thought processes and discover inconsistencies in his logic, something the preoperational child with the structure of juxtaposition is not able to do.

That various structures characterizing each stage in Piaget's theory are intimately related is not surprising, since an important concept in the theory is organization, the tendency of the child to integrate structures into coherent and stable patterns. However, Piaget does not assume that the child's organization constitutes a *stable* equilibrium. Rather, he assumes that the child's ways of thinking tend toward a certain balance, but as new events occur which cannot be dealt with in terms of his available structures, the child will develop new structures to fit the requirements of the new situation. With increasing experience, the child acquires more and more structures, and therefore adapts more easily to an increasing number of situations.

Piaget's assumption of a dynamic equilibrium implies that growth is continuous and gradual. The child does not abandon a structure one day and replace it with a more advanced one the next. The assumption of dynamic equilibrium also implies that various structures characterizing a stage are not all learned at the same time, and, recalling the additional assumption that the child is an active agent, it implies that the structures which are learned, and the age at which the structures are learned, is dependent upon experience as well as maturation. This point requires some elaboration.

Maturation and inheritance are central explanatory concepts in Piaget's theory. The central role these concepts play in the theory is indicated by Piaget's assumption that the order of stages is invariant, an assumption supported by a great deal of data collected in a number of cultures. But the central role of experience in cognitive development is also supported by these same data, which indicate that various structures are learned at different ages in different cultures and within different subcultures in a single culture.[3]

To summarize briefly, Piaget's theory proposes that children develop through four major stages between infancy and adults. Each stage is characterized by a number of cognitive structures. Two stages of primary concern in this study, preoperational and concrete operational stages, are differentiated principally in terms of changes of two important cognitive structures—perceptual boundedness and centration.

The changes in cognitive structures from the preoperational stage to the concrete operational stage have a number of implications for children's information processing behavior. For example, in differentiating two stimuli, such as a television program and a television commercial, we would expect the preoperational child to focus on only a few dimensions (centration). Furthermore, young children's perceptual boundedness would lead us to expect them to focus on visual aspects of message stimuli rather than on message content. On the other hand, the concrete operational child should be able to focus on a larger number of dimensions (decentration), and he should be able to focus on the meaning of the stimulus messages, not simply on perceptual aspects.

As another example, in describing a complex stimulus such as a television commercial, we would expect the preoperational child to recall several images from the commercial but have difficulty in relating the images in the proper sequence (syncretism and juxtaposition). But we would expect the concrete operational child, who has progressed beyond these structures, to describe the stimulus in an appropriate sequence.

The structural changes have implications not only for how children process information but also for how children select information. We would expect that the preoperational child will exhibit less differentiation in his responses to a sequence of visual and auditory stimuli, such as a television program-commercial sequence, than a concrete operational child, since there should be decreasing perceptual boundedness and a shift from centration to decentration.

These general hypotheses regarding processing of information and selection of information guided the design of the studies reported here.

DESIGN OF THE STUDIES

Three types of data were collected in this project from sets of mother-child pairs. Initially, a random sample of fifteen women's service clubs in the Boston area was contacted. From each of these clubs approximately equal numbers of mothers of 5-12 year olds were randomly selected to participate in the study. The sample is skewed slightly toward the upper-middle class compared to SMSA data for Boston. This is largely a result of the socioeconomic status distribution of membership in this type of club. The median age of mothers was 33 years, and the median number of children per household was 3.

Of 108 mothers initially contacted, 90 finally agreed to participate. The first study focused on children's attention to television programing and advertising. The data consisted of the mothers' unobtrusive observation of their children watching television in the home during normal viewing periods. A donation of $10 was made to the women's club for each observation record completed by a club member. The observational procedures used will be described in detail when data relevant to children's selection of information are presented.

The mothers were later interviewed concerning purchase influence attempts by children, and yielding to these attempts, providing the second type of data in the project. These findings are reported elsewhere (Ward and Wackman, 1972).

Approximately four months after the mothers were interviewed, they were again contacted for the purpose of arranging interviews with the child whose television behavior had been observed. All but two mothers cooperated in making their child available for the interview; children were paid $5 for their participation.

These personal interviews provide the third kind of data collected in the project and include data relevant to children's processing of information from commercials.

The final sample, for which all three kinds of data are available, numbered 67. Table 1 indicates that approximately equal numbers of children from each age group are included in the sample, but somewhat more boys than girls are included.

TABLE 1
CHARACTERISTICS OF THE SAMPLE

Age	N	%	Sex	N	%
5-6	17	25			
7-8	17	25	Male	39	58
9-10	13	20			
11-12	20	30	Female	28	42
Total	67	100%	Total	67	100%

Children's Processing of Information from Commercials

In collecting data concerning how children process information from commercials, two interviewers were employed; one conducted the interview while the other transcribed the child's responses. Pretesting indicated that tape recorders inhibited children's responses, so written transcriptions were made. Efforts were made to be alone with the child, although this was often not possible, especially with younger children. The interviewers were successful, however, in minimizing interruptions and intrusions by other family members. The interviews lasted an average of one hour. Interview transcripts were coded independently by two research assistants and a small number of discrepancies were reconciled.

The initial questions in the interview attempted to determine the child's level of understanding of commercials. Respondents were asked, "What is a commercial?" and "What is the difference between a TV commercial and a TV program?" Children differ substantially in their level of understanding of commercials as indicated by responses to both questions.

We expected the youngest children to exhibit characteristics of preoperational thought in answering the question, "What is a commercial?" That is, these children should rely primarily on perceptual cues in television stimuli and rely on few attributes or dimensions in responding. Such responses constitute the "low level" category, e.g., "it's part of a show," "it interrupts the show," "they show things," or a specific advertisement was identified. Children with a medium level of understanding appear to have the beginnings of a concept of advertising, saying "it tells people about things to buy," "it says good things about the thing they're showing," "it advertises things," etc. Finally, children with a high level of understanding rely less on perceptual cues and identify commercials in terms of more complex and abstract dimensions, e.g., the persuasion motive, and in some cases, the concept of sponsorship.

As Table 2[4] indicates, nearly two-thirds of the 5-8 year olds exhibit a low level understanding of commercials, compared to only one in six of the 9-12 year olds, most of whom exhibit a medium-level understanding, i.e., some notion

TABLE 2
AWARENESS OF "WHAT A COMMERCIAL IS" BY AGE

Level of Awareness	Age		
	5-8	9-12	Total
Low	63%	16%	39%
Medium	34	75	55
High	3	9	6
	100%	100%	100%
N	(32)	(32)	(64)

Chi-square = 12.9; 1 df.; p < .001.

of the concept "advertising." Only a few respondents indicate a high level of understanding of commercials in response to this direct question.

Two levels of understanding of commercials are distinguishable from responses to the question concerning children's differentiation between commercials and programs. Low-level differentiation responses are often based on recognition of different perceptual cues, e.g., "commercials are short and programs are long," "commercials usually come before or after the show," "programs are better," "lots of things happen in a program," "programs have more people than commercials." In contrast, children exhibiting a high level of differentiation indicate some understanding of the meaning of the message, giving responses such as: "shows have a story or moral," "commercials show products," "programs are supposed to entertain," "they get you to watch programs so you'll see commercials," "commercials try to sell things." Again, 5-8 year olds generally exhibit a low level of understanding, as Table 3 indicates. Nearly four of five younger children exhibit a low level of differentiation. In contrast, three-fourths of the older children exhibit a high level of differentiation.

TABLE 3
PROGRAM-COMMERCIAL DIFFERENTIATION BY AGE

Level of Differentiation	Age		Total
	5-8	9-12	
Low	79%	27%	54%
High	21	73	46
	100%	100%	100%
N	(34)	(33)	(67)

Chi-Square = 16.3; 1 df.; p $<$ .001.

In examining responses to questions concerning understanding of commercials and program-commercial differentiation, low-level responses to both questions clearly indicate characteristics of preoperational stage thought—reliance on perceptual cues in particular and, to a lesser extent, centration. On the other hand, the higher-level responses indicate less dependency on perceptual cues and greater understanding of the meaning of the message—characteristics of concrete operational thought. As expected, level of understanding is related to age.

For the remainder of the analyses, a scale of cognitive level was constructed from responses to the two questions discussed above. The index was constructed since chronological age is simply a presumed correlate of cognitive level, which is the primary independent variable in Piaget's theory. While our index is a crude one at best, the questions were assumed to tap fundamental structural dimensions which would be associated with different cognitive levels. More direct tests of our general hypotheses could be obtained via analysis by cognitive level, rather than simply by age.

Three cognitive levels were distinguished. *Low cognitive-level* children gave low-level responses to both questions—understanding of commercials and program-commercial differentiation. *Medium cognitive-level* children gave a medium- or high-level response to the first question and a high-level response to the second. Twenty of the children were classified as low cognitive-level, 22 as medium, and 25 as high cognitive-level.

Table 4 indicates a substantial relationship between age and cognitive-level. However, over 50 percent of the younger children (5-8) are not categorized in the lowest cognitive-level, the level most related to preoperational stage thought. On the other hand, only two of the 34 younger children are at the high cognitive-level, which presumably is highly related to concrete operational thought. In terms of our measure, 30 percent of the older children (9-12) have not yet reached high cognitive-level in their understanding of commercials. Thus, although age is a very good predictor of cognitive level, not all of the younger children are preoperational in their thinking about commercials (indeed, a majority are not), and a substantial minority of the older children do not exhibit responses characteristic of the concrete operational stage. Fully one-third of the children are at a level between the two stages.[5]

TABLE 4
COGNITIVE LEVEL BY AGE

Cognitive Level	Age				Total
	5-6	7-8	9-10	11-12	
Low	53%	41%	23%	5%	30%
Medium	41	53	23	15	33
High	6	6	54	80	37
	100%	100%	100%	100%	100%
N	(17)	(17)	(13)	(20)	(67)

Chi-square = 29.8; 2 df.; p < .001.

Following the questions designed to measure children's understanding of what a commercial is, we attempted to gauge children's understanding of the purpose of commercials ("Why are commercials shown on TV?").

Again, we expected low cognitive-level children to lack the ability to "take the role" of the advertiser and to discuss profit and selling motives in commercials. This is due to lack of information concerning the nature of advertising and the "egocentric communication" characteristic of preoperational children. The three-level distribution of responses to the question appears to confirm our expectations.

Children exhibiting a low level of understanding have little awareness of selling motives of commercials and no understanding of profit motives. They give answers such as: "to show you things," "to let people know things they can buy," "to help people," "to tell you where you can buy things," "so actors can make money." Children exhibiting medium understanding indicate recognition of the selling motive but little awareness of profit motives; e.g., "to make people buy things," "to sell products." Children with high understanding are aware of both selling and profit motives, and some appear to be aware of the sponsorship concept: e.g., "to make money," "to get you to buy one product and not others," "they pay for the show."

Nearly one-half of the children exhibit little understanding of the purpose of commercials, including three-fourths of the low cognitive-level children compared to only one in five of the high cognitive-level children (Table 5). On the other hand, over one-fourth of the high cognitive-level children understand the selling and profit motives, whereas none of the low cognitive-level children understand these concepts. Apparently, the low cognitive-level children are not able to understand the motives behind commercials very well, but medium and high cognitive-level children are more aware of these motives.

TABLE 5
UNDERSTANDING OF THE PURPOSE OF
COMMERCIALS BY COGNITIVE LEVEL

Understanding of Purpose	*Cognitive Level*			*Total*
	Low	*Medium*	*High*	
Low	75%	50%	20%	47%
Medium	25	41	52	40
High	0	9	28	13
	100%	100%	100%	100%
N	(20)	(22)	(25)	(67)

Chi-square = 13.8; 2df.; p $<$ .005.

This finding is in line with Flavell's (1968) results which indicate that young children were unable to take the role of the other in a series of role-taking tasks. In Flavell's experiments, young children showed little ability in taking the perspective of the experimenter on tasks ranging from describing designs from the experimenter's position (which differed from the child's), to describing how to move from one point to another on a map, to assessing another's intentions in a situation. While young children may simply lack information about the nature of television advertising, or fail to comprehend this information, it may be that low cognitive-level children cannot abandon their own perspective and take the perspective of the advertiser when viewing commercials.

The next set of questions was designed to measure children's ability to process a complex stimulus, a TV commercial. We asked them to indicate their favorite commercial, and also to describe the one that they "really don't like—the one you don't like the most." After they had identified a liked or disliked commercial, we asked them two questions. First, "Tell me what happens in this commercial?"; second, "Why do (don't) you like it?"

Three levels of complexity of recall of the commercial are distinguishable, following closely Piaget's description of changes in cognitive structures from the preoperational to concrete operational stage. Low-complexity children recall one or two images but their responses indicate no unified recall of the commercial message e.g., "there was a man on a horse," "there were two hands covered with gook." Medium-complexity children recall several images but the images are randomly related. Their answers indicate no unified recall of the message; the sequence and conclusion of the ad are not clearly stated. High-complexity children recall multiple images, too, but describe the sequence of images in a coherent fashion and clearly state the conclusion.

Again, level of complexity of recall is strongly related to cognitive level, as Table 6 indicates.[6] Over one-half of the high cognitive-level children exhibit high complexity of recall, compared to only one-fifth of the low cognitive level, and two-fifths of the medium cognitive-level children. Responses to this question perhaps provide a more direct test of implications of Piaget's theory for understanding children's information processing than did the question concerning children's understanding of the purpose of commercials. But in both instances, the data strongly support the general hypothesis derived from the theory.[7]

TABLE 6
COMPLEXITY OF RECALL OF LIKED AND
DISLIKED COMMERCIALS BY COGNITIVE LEVEL

Level of Complexity	Cognitive Level			Total
	Low	Medium	High	
Low	23%	22%	7%	16%
Medium	58	39	39	44
High	19	39	54	40
	100%	100%	100%	100%
N	(26)	(28)	(41)	(95)

Regarding reasons for liking and disliking particular commercials, we expected that some preoperational children are unable to process meaningfully the sequence of images constituting the message and instead focus on the product displayed in the commercial, which is usually the single image of most relevance perceptually. This expectation is also consistent with other research which indicates that as age increases, the impact of affective responses toward an object on the child's perception of the object decreases (Solley, 1966).

Responses to the question concerning reasons for liking and disliking particular commercials were analyzed in terms of dimensions used in evaluation. The distribution of responses revealed four dimensions. *Entertainment* reasons include references to music, humor, amusing characters, animals in the commercial, repetitiveness, and summary comments such as "dull," "boring," "stupid," and so forth. *Technical-taste* reasons include statements about characters (pretty, good actors, scary, rude), originality (clever), bragging about the product, incoherence, ineffectiveness of the explanation. *Product* reasons include liking or disliking the product, and ownership of the product. *Other* reasons include "just (don't) like it," interrupts favorite program, free offer, etc.

Entertainment reasons are the modal response for children of each cognitive level, as Table 7 indicates, although this response was most frequent for high cognitive-level children. However, as we expected, nearly one-third of both low and medium cognitive-level children based their liking or disliking of the commercial on their response to the product advertised, compared to only five percent of the high cognitive-level children. This may indicate that the lower cognitive-level children have a more difficult time making a distinction between the product itself and the symbol for the product—the commercial.

TABLE 7
REASON FOR LIKING/DISLIKING COMMERCIALS
BY COGNITIVE LEVEL

| | Cognitive Level | | | |
Reason	Low	Medium	High	Total
Entertainment	38%	42%	57%	47%
Technical-Taste	19	13	24	19
Product	31	32	5	21
Other	12	13	14	13
	100%	100%	100%	100%
N	(32)	(31)	(42)	(105)

Finally, to further examine children's understanding of commercials and their purpose we asked the following set of questions: "Do TV commercials always tell the truth?", "How do you know they (don't) tell the truth?", "Why do (don't) they tell the truth?"

A majority of the children think commercials definitely do not always tell the truth, as Table 8 indicates, and a third think commercials "sometimes" don't tell the truth. Only among high cognitive-level children is there a clear majority (80 percent) who think commercials definitely do not always tell the truth. Approximately two-fifths of both the low and medium cognitive-level children think commercials "sometimes" don't tell the truth, and nearly a third of the low cognitive-level children think commercials *do* tell the truth all the time.

Responses to the follow-up questions are more interesting for theoretical purposes. We would expect low cognitive-level children to focus on perceptual aspects of message stimuli as the basis for their reasoning, while higher cognitive-level children would be expected to explain their reasoning in terms of more complex criteria, which may go beyond the cues actually perceived in commercial messages. Analysis of the data support these expectations. Answers to the question, "How do you know commercials (don't) tell the truth?", fall into two categories. *Perceptual* reasons focus upon things the child could see in the

TABLE 8

PERCEIVED TRUTHFULNESS OF COMMERCIALS
BY COGNITIVE LEVEL

Do commercials always tell the truth?	Cognitive Level			Total
	Low	*Medium*	*High*	*Total*
Yes	30%	18%	8%	18%
Sometimes	40	46	12	31
No	30	36	80	51
	100%	100%	100%	100%
N	(20)	(22)	(25)	(67)

Chi-square = 13.9; 2 df.; p $<$ .001.

commercial in relation to aspects of the message of the product. For example, children who don't think commercials always tell the truth and who give perceptual reasons to justify their answer say such things as, "people in commercials aren't real," "people don't really walk out of walls," "I don't see things in the store." And children who think commercials do tell the truth and give perceptual reasons express reasons such as: "I know they're true because I see these things in the store," "sometimes I see things I wanted." *Reality-test* reasons focus upon several different ways the child may have tested the truth of commercials, e.g., "things don't always work the way they do on TV," "I bought the car and it didn't work right," "I asked my Mom and she told me so," "they just want you to buy the product."

Nearly three of five low cognitive-level children give perceptual responses as a basis for judging the truthfulness of commercials, compared to 30 percent of the medium-level and 12 percent of the high cognitive-level children. On the other hand, 50 percent of the medium and 84 percent of the high cognitive-level children give reality-test responses. Nearly a fifth of both low and medium

TABLE 9

BASIS FOR JUDGING TRUTHFULNESS OF
COMMERCIALS BY COGNITIVE LEVEL

Basis for Judging Truthfulness	Cognitive Level			Total
	Low	*Medium*	*High*	*Total*
Perceptual	59%	30%	12%	31%
Reality-test	23	50	84	56
Don't know	18	20	4	13
	100%	100%	100%	100%
N	(17)	(20)	(25)	(62)

Chi-square = 13.2; 2 df.; p $<$ .005.

cognitive-level children don't know how to tell if commercials tell the truth. This result is clearly consistent with Piaget's theoretical description of the perceptual "literalness" of the preoperational child, who is similar to the low cognitive-level child in the present study. According to Piaget, what the preoperational child perceives is what is true for him, and this tendency is reflected in the reasons low cognitive-level children give for judging commercials' truthfulness.

Differences between preoperational children and concrete operational children can also be seen in responses to a question about "Why do (don't) TV commercials tell the truth?" Preoperational children would be expected to have difficulty assuming the advertiser's role, while concrete operational children should be able to identify selling motives as a basis for their reasoning.

Consistent with these expectations, two categories of responses were distinguished: *Trusting* responses indicate the child does not question the motives of commercials. Examples of these responses are "they don't know if it works," "they are trying to be funny," "it's a mistake," "they want to help people," "they don't want to lie." *Selling motive* responses indicate understanding of this motive of commercials, although several children who thought commercials always tell the truth also acknowledged the selling motive in their response, e.g., "they want you to buy their product, so they wouldn't lie to you." Examples of distrusting responses are, "they want you to think their product is good," "they want you to buy their product," "so they can make money," "to make you buy one brand and not others."

As Table 10 indicates, about one-third of the low and medium cognitive-level children give trusting responses, but only 19 percent of the low cognitive-level children give selling motive responses compared to 47 percent of the medium cognitive-level children. All of the high cognitive-level children give selling motive responses. The extremely large differences in responses to this question are clearly consistent with Piaget's discussion of differences between preoperational and concrete operational children's cognitive structures, and with Flavell's (1968) experiments on development of role-taking skills, noted above.

TABLE 10
REASON WHY COMMERCIALS DO (DON'T) TELL THE TRUTH BY COGNITIVE LEVEL

Reason Why True/Untrue	Cognitive Level			Total
	Low	Medium	High	
Trusting	38%	32%	0%	20%
Selling Motive	19	47	100	61
Don't Know	43	21	0	19
	100%	100%	100%	100%
N	(16)	(19)	(24)	(59)

Chi-square = 36.9; 4 df.; p < .001.

Summary of Information Processing Study

Responses to the questions in the interview are highly consistent with Piaget's theoretical discussion regarding differences in the cognitive structures of preoperational and concrete operational children. In general, low cognitive-level children, who are similar to Piaget's preoperational child, give responses which clearly indicate the operation of tendencies to focus on only a few dimensions (centration)—dimensions which are largely perceptual in nature (high perceptual boundedness). On the other hand, high cognitive-level children, who are most similar to Piaget's concrete operational child, respond in terms of more dimensions (decentration), and the dimensions they focus on tend to be less perceptual and more symbolic in nature (low perceptual boundedness).

Responses of children classified as medium cognitive-level are most interesting in some respects. Their responses to some questions indicate a greater similarity to low than to high cognitive-level children, e.g., "Why do you like (dislike) this commercial?" (Table 7), "Why do (don't) commercials tell the truth?" (Table 10). But their answers to other questions indicate just the reverse—a greater similarity to high cognitive-level children, e.g., "Why are commercials shown on TV?" (Table 5), "How do you know they (don't) tell the truth?" (Table 9). These results are consistent with Piaget's theoretical position in two ways. First, Piaget emphasizes that development is continuous, i.e., children don't jump from one stage to another but rather their development is gradual as they learn new structures. Second, Piaget emphasizes that in moving to a higher stage of cognitive development, the child does not learn all the structures at the same time. Thus, for example, a medium-level child may decrease in perceptual boundedness but still maintain the centration structure.

The results in this study, then, are highly consistent with a number of aspects of Piaget's theoretical position. On the other hand, an alternative explanation for at least some of the data is simply that children of a higher cognitive level are more familiar with TV commercials since they tend to be older and thus have had more exposure to commercials.[8] However, cognitive level predicts a number of the children's responses better than age, providing some support for the validity of Piaget's theoretical position.

Children's Selection of Information

The design of the study of children's selection of information was also guided by Piaget's theory—in particular by the general hypothesis noted previously: The preoperational child will exhibit less differentiation in his responses to varied visual and auditory stimuli than the concrete operational child, since the latter should be less perceptually bound and should be capable of relating several dimensions involved in the stimuli (decentration).

Our index of information selection is the attention behavior of the child.

Attention to a stimulus is a necessary condition for selecting information from the stimulus and for subsequent processing of the information. However, simply measuring a child's attention to a stimulus indicates little concerning what information he selects from the stimulus.

Much research on children's attention has focused on stimulus selection—what aspects of stimuli are attended to and what aspects are ignored. Berlyne (1960) suggests that stimulus novelty, complexity, and surprisingness are important stimulus properties influencing attention. More recent research suggests that children's attention is particularly influenced by stimulus complexity (Munsinger and Kessen, 1964), though the "optimal" complexity level depends upon the child's information-processing abilities. Repetition, size, and contrast of stimuli have also been related to children's attention (Kagan and Kogan, 1970).

In these studies, stimulus selection is most often measured in the laboratory in terms of pupil dilation and eye movements. Little research has examined children's responses to complex audio-visual stimuli, such as television programs or commercials, although research used in designing *Sesame Street* did examine children's attention to television in laboratory situations, and related attention behavior to learning outcomes (Lesser, 1972). However, measurement of stimulus selection in the natural home environment is very difficult.

While gross measures of attention behavior provide little precise data concerning the exact stimulus cues children select, these measures can provide useful data concerning children's selection of gross segments of audio-visual information. By observing changes in children's *pattern* of attention, we are at least able to draw inferences about discrimination of different cues in the stimulus and in the viewing context.

There have been two types of measures used in studies of attention to television among children and adults in the home environment. Steiner (1966), Ward, Robertson, and Wackman (1971), and Murray (1972) used in-home observers to unobtrusively record attention to commercial and programing sequences among adults or children. Allen (1965) and Bechtel, Achelpohl, and Akers (1972) used mechanical devices (cameras adjacent or attached to the TV set) to provide continuous surveillance of audience behavior during viewing in the home environment.

In general, these studies show that both adults and children exhibit a decrease in attention from programing to commercials (Bechtel et al, 1972; Ward et al, 1971). Basing his data on time sequence photographs of in-home audiences, moreover, Allen (1965) found that no audience was present or the audience was "inattentive," during 48 percent of recorded commercials minutes during one week (n=224 observed commercial minutes).

Bechtel et al. used a camera attached to the set to video-tape audience behavior continuously among 93 persons in 20 families during a six-day period. Attention behavior was coded during replay of these video tapes, one observation for every two and a half minutes of viewing time. Commercials were ranked last in a list of eleven "program types" in terms of percentage of time watched while the program type was aired. Commercials were watched 55 percent of the time they were on, compared to first-ranked movies (76 percent). Bechtel and his colleagues found that children (ages 1-10) are less likely to watch commercials than older people. Unfortunately, small sample sizes apparently precluded examination of watching behavior among more narrowly defined age groups.

Most previous research has not focused on patterns of children's attention to commercials. Consequently, the objective of the present study was to examine children's attention to commercial sequences (i.e., "blocks" of up to six commercials which occur sequentially either during programing or between programs).

Piaget's theory leads us to expect preoperational children will exhibit less differentiation in responses to varied stimuli than will concrete operational children. Consequently, our working hypothesis was that low cognitive-level children would exhibit more stability in their attention to television stimuli than other children, and high cognitive-level children would exhibit the most differentiation. We also expected, based on previous research, that children would attend less to commercials than to programs but that low cognitive-level children would "tune out" least. Finally, we expected that attention would decrease throughout commercial sequences.

To measure attention behavior in the present study, mothers were rigorously trained in the use of observation sheets in small group meetings. The mothers observed research assistants role-playing children's television watching in ways that permitted illustration of all various coding categories. The mothers practiced coding, and their coding was checked.

The various coding categories were operationally defined as follows:

I. Behavior Before Commercial Onset

This rating concerns your child's level of attention to television immediately before the onset of the commercial being rated, on the following three-point scale:
1. Watching-full attention; eyes on set;
2. Watching-partial attention; eyes on and off set;
3. Not watching TV

II. Behavior During Commercial

The degree of attention to the message itself, according to the following three-point scale:
1. Full attention—stays in viewing position and watches all or almost all; eyes on set;
2. Partial attention—stays in viewing position but does not pay full attention (turns around, talks, etc.); eyes on and off set;
3. No attention—stays in room but completely occupied with other activities; leaves room; not in room at onset.

In a departure from previous studies, times during which mothers would actually observe their child watching television were controlled. Mothers completed viewing logs for the child to be observed which indicated programs and times when the child was likely to watch in a given week. Specific times for observation and coding were sampled from these logs in order to represent the child's normal viewing times during the week in which observations would take place. Mothers were instructed to code a minimum of three viewing hours to a maximum of six, depending on the amount of TV watching by the particular child. Assigning times for observation enabled us to approximate the normal viewing behavior of the child as well as to avoid selection of observation times by mothers.

Mothers were instructed to practice unobtrusive observation and coding at home for at least a half-hour before actual observations began, and a "hot line" was established for questions or problems which arose. Then they observed the child for one week; days during which observations were to begin were randomized.

Every tenth commercial sequence that the child watched was coded and keypunched, resulting in a sample of 526 commercial sequences watched by the 67 children, an average of 8 sequences per child (Table 11). Of the total sequences coded, one-fifth consisted of only one commercial, 36 percent consisted of two commercials, and 24 percent consisted of three commercials.

For the first commercial in a sequence full attention occurred about half the time, but full attention decreased for later commercials, as Table 12 indicates, falling to a level of 29 percent full attention for the fourth commercial. One-fifth of the children paid partial attention to each commercial position in the sequence. Inattention increased from 30 percent for the first commercial in the sequence to over 50 percent for commercials in the fourth position in the sequence. As expected, attention decreased throughout the commercial sequence.

To test the general hypothesis based on Piaget's theory—that preoperational children will exhibit less differentiation in their responses to varied stimuli than will concrete operational children—a variety of comparisons of *changes* in

TABLE 11
DESCRIPTIVE DATA: SAMPLE OF COMMERCIAL SEQUENCES

Number of Commercials in Sequence	N	%	Position of Commercial in Sequence	N	%
1	109	21%	1st	526	41%
2	187	36	2nd	417	33
3	128	24	3rd	230	18
4	102	19	4th	102	8
	526	100%		1,275	100%

TABLE 12
ATTENTION LEVEL TO COMMERCIALS AT
EACH POSITION IN THE SEQUENCE

Attention	*Position in Sequence*			
Level	*1st*	*2nd*	*3rd*	*4th*
Full	49%	41%	35%	19%
Partial	21%	21	17	20
None	30	38	48	51
	100%	100%	100%	100%
N	(526)	(417	(230)	(102)

attention behavior were made.[9] In each of these comparisons the expectation was that the percentage of full-attention responses by low cognitive-level children would be more stable than the percentage for medium or high cognitive-level children. We also expected that high cognitive-level children would have the least stable percentage of full attention.

The first comparison, shown in Figure 1, is between full attention to program and that to the first commercial in a sequence. The percentage of full attention to the program is 58 percent among low cognitive-level children, and this decreases by 2 percent for the first commercial. Medium cognitive-level children's percentage decreased 18 percent from 62 percent full attention to the program to 44 percent full attention to the first commercial; high cognitive-level children's percentage decreased 23 percent from 70 percent for the program to 47 percent for the first commercial. Thus, as predicted, low cognitive-level children's responses to the program-commercial transition are more stable than either medium or high cognitive-level children; the latter group shows the greatest differentiation between attention to the program and first commercial.

This result parallels the finding reported earlier (Table 3) concerning the level of differentiation between program and commercial of children of different ages. This measure, it will be recalled, was used in constructing the index of cognitive level for the analysis. Thus, the data in Figure 1 appear to provide behavioral validation for using responses to the question, "What is the difference between a TV commercial and a TV program?", as a measure of cognitive level and more specifically as an indicator of centration, the tendency to focus on a limited amount of the available information and to make fewer discriminations between stimuli.

The next comparison, shown in Figure 2, is between full attention to commercials which occur in the middle of programs and those at the beginning or end.[10] Our purpose in this comparison was to see if commercial placement relative to programing differentially affects attention responses of various cognitive-level children. Percentage full attention to commercials at the beginning or end of the program is 38 percent among low cognitive-level children compared to 47 percent full attention for commercials in the middle of the

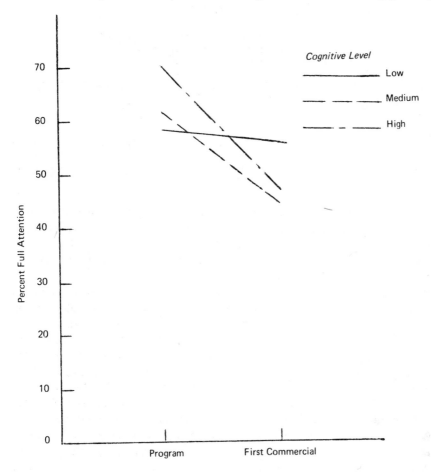

Figure 1: FULL ATTENTION TO PROGRAM AND FIRST COMMERCIAL BY COGNITIVE LEVEL

program, a difference of 9 percent. The difference for medium cognitive-level children is 11 percent (34 percent for beginning or end commercials and 45 percent for middle commercials), and 21 percent for high cognitive-level children (60 percent for beginning or end commercials compared to 39 percent for middle commercials). Again, low cognitive-level children exhibit the most stability in their attention behavior, and high cognitive-level children exhibit the greatest differentiation.

The third comparison concerns full attention to commercials for different types of products—toys or games, food or soft drinks, personal products such as toothpaste and cosmetics, and all other products. As Figure 3 indicates, except for toy and game commercials, percentage full attention for low cognitive-level

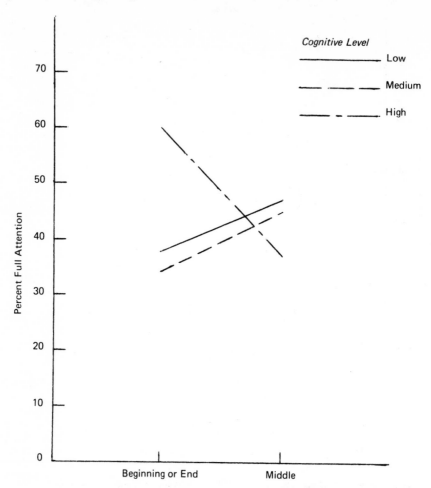

Figure 2: FULL ATTENTION TO COMMERCIALS AT DIFFERENT POSITIONS IN THE PROGRAM BY COGNITIVE LEVEL

children is quite stable, ranging from 47 percent for food and soft drink commercials to 37 percent for commercials about other products, a range of 10 percent. The range among medium cognitive-level children is 18 percent from a high of 56 percent to a low of 38 percent. Among high cognitive-level children, the range is 23 percent with a high of 51 percent and a low of 28 percent. Again, the results indicate the greater attention behavior stability of the low cognitive-level children compared to the medium and high cognitive-level children.

Low cognitive-level children do deviate considerably from their average attention behavior when toy or game commercials come on the air. This indicates that their attention behavior is not entirely stable, as the other data discussed so far suggest. However, it may be that low cognitive-level children

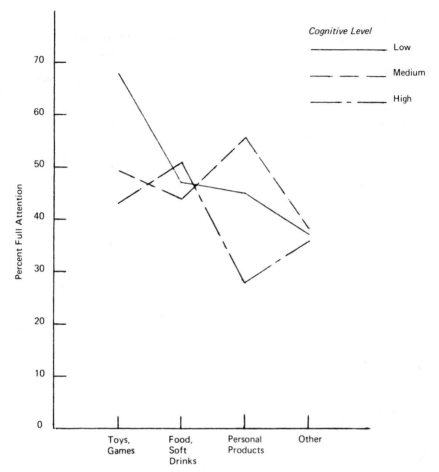

Figure 3: FULL ATTENTION TO COMMERCIALS FOR DIFFERENT PRODUCT TYPES BY COGNITIVE LEVEL

increase attention only when highly salient stimulus cues (such as toys or games) are included in the commercial.

The comparisons so far have involved attentional differences among television stimuli, i.e., program-commercial, position in program, or type of product advertised in the commercial. The next comparison involves differences in the context of viewing, i.e., the time of the week when the commercial occurs. Three viewing times were distinguished for analytic purposes, early weekday evenings, Saturday mornings, and other times. Generally, our data indicate that the social context of viewing differs at these different times. Early evenings are characteristically a total family viewing time, whereas Saturday morning is generally restricted to child viewing; viewing at other times shows no single characteristic pattern.

Figure 4 indicates that the differentiation of attention behavior in terms of contextual cues is greatest among high cognitive-level children; their full attention to commercials ranges from 75 percent on Saturday mornings to a low of 27 percent full attention to early weekday evening commercials. The range for medium cognitive-level children is 17 percent; for low cognitive-level children the range is only 4 percent. Thus, low cognitive-level children exhibit a high degree of stability when contextual cues vary, just as they do when stimulus cues vary.

The final comparison controlled the stimulus cues (to some extent) and varied the contextual cues. This was done by comparing children's attention to food or soft drink commercials at two different times—Saturday mornings and

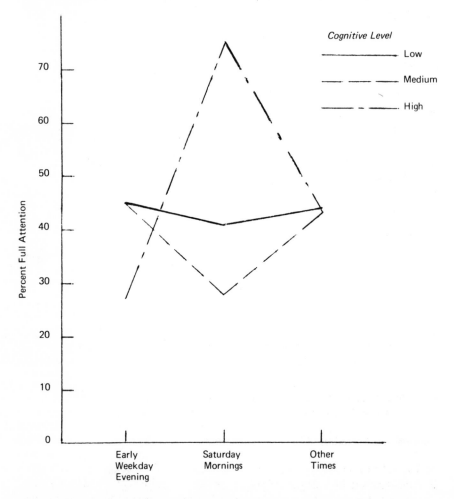

Figure 4: FULL ATTENTION TO COMMERCIALS AT DIFFERENT TIMES IN THE WEEK BY COGNITIVE LEVEL

other times. Low cognitive-level children again exhibit a high degree of stability in their attention behavior, with a range of only 8 percent (Figure 5). The range of full attention for medium-cognitive children is 31 percent, and high cognitive-level children have a range of 40 percent.

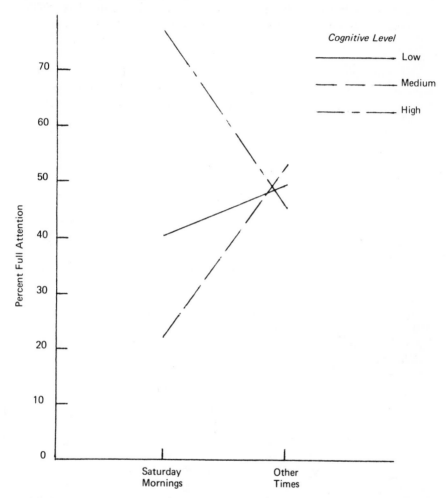

Figure 5: **FULL ATTENTION TO FOOD OR SOFT DRINK COMMERCIALS ON SATURDAY MORNINGS AND AT OTHER TIMES BY COGNITIVE LEVEL**

Summary of Selection of Information Study

The set of comparisons of attention to different stimuli are highly consistent in indicating the high degree of stability of low cognitive-level children in their attention behavior, and the high degree of differentiation in attention behavior of high cognitive-level children. Medium cognitive-level children fall between low and high cognitive level in every comparison, although generally, their range is closer to that of the high cognitive-level children.

These data provide impressive and relatively direct support for the general hypothesis derived from Piaget—that low cognitive-level children will exhibit less differentiation in their responses to varied stimuli than will concrete operational children. Several comparisons were made in which stimulus cues were varied in a number of different ways, and in each case the hypothesis was borne out—low cognitive-level children had more similar full attention percentages to the varied stimuli than did medium or high cognitive-level children. Also, in each case high cognitive-level children exhibited the greatest difference in their full attention behavior. Similar support for the hypothesis was obtained when context of viewing was varied. Thus, Piaget's developmental theory has implications for the analysis of children's selection of information. Apparently differences in cognitive structures of children at different stages of cognitive development have an impact on how they attend to stimuli.

DISCUSSION

Although the data consistently support the general hypotheses guiding the studies reported here, there are two important limitations. First, the measure of cognitive level used in the present study was based upon answers to questions about commercials. A better procedure would be to measure the levels more directly in terms of tasks similar to the ones Piaget used in describing the structures which differentiate the various stages. As noted above, however, data in the selection of information study do provide some confirmation of the validity of our measure of cognitive level with a very different kind of data.

Second, the sample size in the present studies was very small and it was somewhat non-random in nature, although attempts were made to randomize in the selection of women's service clubs in the Boston area and in the random selection of mothers within these clubs. Nevertheless, the sample was skewed toward the upper middle class.

The small sample limitation, however, is mitigated somewhat by the high degree of consistency in the results. Data in the information processing study uniformly supported the hypotheses, and in each case the result was highly significant in a statistical sense. Data in the information selection study also was uniformly consistent in supporting the hypothesis, and differences among the three cognitive levels were large, although statistical tests were not performed because of the dependencies in the data. The high degree of consistency of the results is, however, a major strength of the studies.

The second major strength of the studies is that two very different kinds of data, collected with two different methodologies, were used to test the hypotheses, and the two sources of data were consistently supportive. While the studies are not a precise application of the multi-trait, multi-method research

(Campbell and Fiske, 1959), they nevertheless represent an application of the general principle of using multiple methods to test the same proposition. In this case, the broad theoretical proposition was that children's information selection and processing is influenced by their cognitive development.

The third major strength is that in several instances the same specific hypothesis was tested in several different ways. For example, in the information selection study five comparisons were made to test the same proposition. As Stinchcombe (1968) points out, such a procedure increases our confidence in the validity of the proposition *if* the results are consistent, as they are in the present studies.

Thus, although the sample size and measurement of cognitive level in the present studies impose important limitations, the consistency of results, the use of different methodologies, and the multiple tests of specific hypotheses are major strengths of the studies.

Also of significance is the fact that the two studies are based upon a comprehensive theoretical position concerning psychological development—Piaget's theory. Some may argue that the results in the present studies simply reflect age differences. In part, this is true, since 23 of 25 high cognitive-level children in our sample are in the 9-12 year range. However, among children in the 5-8 year range, stage and age are not related (see Table 4); furthermore, a number of 9-12 year olds are either low or medium cognitive level. Also, stage is a better predictor than age for a number of the comparisons in the study, though in a number of other instances age and stage are equally good predictors.

Finally, the theory and data presented here are intended to illustrate the utility of theoretical explanation for research which is also highly important for immediate social policy decisions. These data have been useful in formulating policy decisions regarding advertising practices affecting children (Ward, 1971). The theoretical bases of the data are useful in order to link the particular results with a much broader area of research; in this case, the results fit into a much larger pattern of research generated within the cognitive-developmental tradition. Secondly, the theory provides *explanation* of why differences occur in children's processing and selection of information. This explanation, of course, is based on the changes in cognitive structure which occur as the child develops. The concept of age, on the other hand, provides no theoretical explanation for the results.

Piaget's theory has a number of further implications for communication and mass communication researchers. Some of these implications have been tested by Flavell (1968) in his studies of the development of children's role-taking skills and communication skills. However, for the most part Piaget's theory has not played an important role in research concerning children's mass communication behavior. Yet a number of specific hypotheses can be derived concerning children's mass communication behavior.

For example, Piaget's theory can be used to predict that young children's attention to a TV program is more dependent upon visual style than upon the content of the program. Which particular elements of style are most important is not suggested by the theory, but the general prediction is based upon the young child's high perceptual boundedness and centration structures. Linking this prediction to other mass communication research, we might predict that Watt and Krull's (1972) visual and auditory style analysis of TV programs would correlate more highly with low cognitive-level young children's program preferences than with either adolescents' or adults' program choices. Another prediction relevant to mass communication research would be that the low cognitive-level child can learn violent behaviors from a model on television but that he cannot learn the concept of justice. Again, this prediction is based on the structural concepts of perceptual boundedness and centration, but also on Flavell's (1968) research indicating that young children have difficulty taking the role of the other, a skill necessary for learning the concept of justice.

In future research, we plan to build on the results reported here and examine the processes involved in children's acquiring skills, attitudes, and knowledge relevant to their developing patterns of consumer behavior.

Our general interest is in relating television advertising's effects to such variables as knowledge of economic concepts, intra-family purchase influence patterns, and so forth. Again, Piaget's theory should be useful in deriving hypotheses regarding such "consumer learning" among children at various developmental stages.

NOTES

1. See Flavell (1963) and Ginsberg and Opper (1969) for extensive reviews of Piaget's theory and the data supporting it.

2. The concrete operational child is not able to function cognitively entirely outside the perceptual world, however; this does not occur until the formal operations stage. Only in this stage is a child able to perform mental operations on purely abstract concepts. We must hasten to add, however, that the formal operations child doesn't deal *only* with abstractions. Rather, he has the ability to do so when he wants to, unlike the concrete operational child who cannot think in pure abstraction.

3. See Flavell (1963) for a summary of a number of studies concerning the invariance of stages and cultural differences in the age at which various structures are learned.

4. In this table, and in a number of others, rows of the table are collapsed for purposes of statistical testing. This was done because of the small cell sizes in certain rows in these tables. In Tables 2, 3, 5, and 6, only the first response of the child was used as a basis for categorization. Only one out of five children gave multiple responses, and visual inspection indicated these were usually consistent with first answer.

5. Sex of the child is not related to cognitive level.

6. Differences in complexity of recall may be partially dependent on differences in memory of children of various ages. However, it should be noted that many information processing theorists (e.g., Simon, 1972; Inhelder, 1972; Hagen, 1972) conceptualize long-term memory as a set of strategies or structures for processing information, i.e., precisely the structures Piaget's theory is concerned with. Thus, according to these theorists, if an older child can recall more facts and can relate them more cogently, it is not simply because he can store more information, but rather it is because he possesses better structures for storing and recalling information.

7. In Tables 6 and 7, most respondents are represented twice because they answered the same question twice, once concerning their favorite commercial and the second time concerning their most disliked commercial. Responses to the favorite and most disliked commercial formed essentially the same pattern; therefore, including the two sets of responses in the same table is justified.

8. In terms of the children's present behavior, analysis of current TV viewing indicates no difference among children of the three cognitive levels in the amount of time spent watching TV.

9. Statistical tests were not performed on any of the attention behavior (Table 12 and Figures 1 through 5) due to dependencies in the data.

10. Commercials at the beginning and end of the program were grouped because of small sample size.

REFERENCES

ALLEN, L. (1965) "Photographing the TV audience." Journal of Advertising Research.

BECHTEL, R. B., C. ACHELPOHL, and R. AKERS (1972) "Correlates between observed behavior and questionnaire responses on television viewing," in E. A. Rubinstein et al., (eds.), Television and Social Behavior. Volume 4. Washington: U. S. Dept. of Health, Education and Welfare.

BERLYNE, D. E. (1960) Conflict, Arousal and Curiosity. New York: McGraw-Hill.

CAMPBELL, D. T. and D. W. FISKE (1959) "Convergent and discriminant validation by the multitrait-multimethod matrix." Psychological Bulletin 56: 81-105.

FARNHAM-DIGGORY, S. (1972) Information Processing in Children. New York: Academic Press.

FLAVELL, J. H. (1963) The Developmental Psychology of Jean Piaget. Princeton: Van Nostrand.

——— (1968) The Development of Role-Taking and Communication Skills in Children. New York: John Wiley.

GINSBERG, H. and S. OPPER (1969) Piaget's Theory of Intellectual Development. Englewood Cliffs, N.J.: Prentice-Hall.

HAGEN, J. W. (1972) "Information processing tendencies in recent experiments in cognitive learning—empirical studies," pp. 103-114 in Farnham-Diggory (1972).

KAGAN, J. and N. KOGAN (1970) "Individual variation in cognitive processes," in Paul Mussen (ed.), Manual of Child Psychology. Volume 1. New York: John Wiley.

KOHLBERG, L. (1963) "The Development of children's orientations toward a moral order: I. Sequence in the Development of Moral Thought." Vita Humana 6: 11-33.

KOHLBERG, L., and E. ZIGLER (1967) "The Impact of cognitive maturity on the development of sex-role attitudes in the years four to eight." Genetic Psychology Monographs 75: 89-165.

LESSER, G. S. (1972) "Learning, teaching and television production for children: The experience of Sesame Street." Harvard Educational Review 42: 232-72.

MUNSINGER, H. and K. W. KESSEN (1964) "Uncertainty, structure, and preference." Psychological Monographs 78, 586.

MURRAY, J. P. (1972) "Television in inner-city homes: Viewing behavior of young boys," in E. A. Rubinstein et al. (eds.) Television and Social Behavior. Volume 4. Washington: U. S. Dept. of Health, Education and Welfare.

SIMON, H. A. (1972) "On the Development of the Processor," pp. 3-22 in Farnham-Diggory (1972).

SOLLEY, C. M. (1966) "Affective processes in perceptual development," pp. 275-304 in A. H. Kidd and J. L. Rivoire (eds.) Perceptual Development in Children. New York: International Universities Press.

STEINER, G., (1966) "The People look at commercials: A study of audience behavior." Journal of Business 9: 272-304.

STINCHCOMBE, A. (1968) Constructing Social Theories. New York: Harcourt, Brace, World.

TURIEL, E. (1966) "An experimental test of the sequentiality of developmental stages in the child's moral judgments." Journal of Personality and Social Psychology 3: 611-618.

WATT, J. and R. KRULL (1972) An Information Theory Measure of Television Content." Presented at Association for Education in Journalism, Carbondale, Ill.

WARD, S., T. S. ROBERTSON and D. B. WACKMAN (1971) "Children's attention to television advertising." Proceedings: Association for Consumer Research, 1971 Conference, College Park, Md.

WARD, S. and D. B. WACKMAN (1972) "Children's purchase influence attempts and parental yielding." Journal of Marketing Research 9: 316-319.

WARD, S. (1971) Testimony Before the Federal Trade Commission, Hearings on Modern Advertising Practices (November).

ZIGLER, E. (1963) "Social reinforcement, environment, and the child." American Journal of Orthopsychiatry 33: 614-623.

ZIGLER, E. and J. L. CHILD (1969) "Socialization," pp. 450-590 in G. Lindzey and E. Aronson (eds.) Handbook of Social Psychology III.

Chapter 5

MARKETING COMMUNICATION AND
THE HIERARCHY-OF-EFFECTS

Michael L. Ray
In collaboration with Alan G. Sawyer, Michael L. Rothschild,
Roger M. Heeler, Edward C. Strong, and Jerome B. Reed

IN COMMUNICATION RESEARCH the barriers between basic and applied study are often blurred. Nowhere is this truer than in the area of marketing communication; particularly in research involving the "hierarchy-of-effects," which constitutes both the key basic theoretical construct and the main planning tool in the field.

This chapter presents results from a program of applied research based on a hierarchy model of marketing communication effect. The research emphasizes laboratory experiments but has also involved computer simulation and field experimentation. The model is a conditional one which assumes that while communication always has effect in terms of levels of a response hierarchy, there actually are three patterns of response depending on conditions of involvement, communication sources, and differentiation of alternatives. The following sections describe marketing communication, the hierarchy model, a laboratory design for research on the hierarchy, findings relative to the model, and implications.

AUTHOR'S NOTE: This research was supported by a grant from the American Association of Advertising Agencies Educational Foundation, which is gratefully acknowledged.

MARKETING COMMUNICATION

Marketing communication is a subfield of marketing which involves personal selling, advertising, publicity, public relations, reseller support—merchandising, product sampling, and packaging changes. These are all communication tools, and the subfield is really an attempt to bring together several diverse parts of the marketing mix under one conceptual framework based on communication research and theory.

"Marketing" implies selling and a goal of economic benefit for the communicator. But marketing communication techniques can be used for a variety of other purposes, such as for political campaigns, improvement of health practices, changes in societal beliefs, etc. The great recent interest in social applications of marketing have all focused on the possible non-profit uses of marketing communication (Kotler and Zaltman, 1971). Thus much of what follows applies to persuasive mass media campaigns of all types.

Use of the hierarchy-of-effects idea can best be understood in context of the total flow of marketing communication decisions. After a marketing manager has decided upon his overall sales goal and the part communication will play in achieving that goal, he and his co-workers must determine how each element of communication will be used. Three key decisions are made separately for selling, advertising, etc.:

(1) Communication goals—While the overall purpose of the campaign may be to increase sales, votes, blood donations, or summer job offers, the goal of each communication element is typically something more modest. Goals are set in terms of some communication response. And these responses are thought of in terms of a hierarchy-of-effects, including awareness, comprehension, conviction and action. For example, the communication goal for publicity might be to create awareness, for advertising to develop comprehension and conviction, and for personal selling to affect action.

In this way each component of the mix is assigned a task. It is important to note, however, that these assignments can be made only by making certain hierarchy-of-effects assumptions, which are examined in this chapter.

(2) Message strategy—Given a particular goal for each element of the mix, the manager must decide how these goals are to be achieved. He must decide what to say (appeal) and how to say it (format). It is at this point the management team gets into issues that are normally found in the study of communication and persuasion. Examples include one- versus two-sided messages, order effect, fear appeals, implicit versus explicit recommendation, effects of visual devices, refutational and supportive appeals, source credibility, and extremity of message position.

The interesting difference between marketing communication consideration and basic research on these issues is that in marketing communication the entire hierarchy and several research methods are taken into account. In this paper message issues will be considered in terms of the implications of the hierarchy model.

(3) Message distribution—Once goals and message strategy are established, the marketing communication manager must determine how the messages will be distributed. Since marketing communication is paid communication, the communicator typically has more control over distribution than do other mass media people such as journalists. Thus many of the key issues of communication and persuasion research become quite relevant. In the message distribution questions of advertising, for instance, there is a concern with media scheduling. Repetition, selective exposure, audience differences, forgetting, primacy versus recency, media characteristics, audio versus video presentation—all these become quite vital. Again, as with the message issues, media and distribution questions will be considered here in terms of the full hierarchy-of-effects. This is especially possible in marketing because of the availability of computer simulation and field experimental facilities.

Considered in terms of the three decision stages, marketing communication is really an applied manifestation of the old Lasswellian communication research paradigm of "Who says What to Whom through which Channels with what Effect." The valuable aspect of marketing communication is that it presents both the need and the resources to examine the Lasswell linkage in its entirety instead of in terms of disconnected pieces.

A THREE-ORDERS HIERARCHY MODEL

The basic hierarchy-of-effects model consists of a sequence of mental stages or levels which an audience member is supposed to experience during a communication campaign. The typical sequence is from simple to more complex response stages. For instance, one mentioned above includes the levels of awareness, comprehension, conviction, and action. These are the levels used in a prominent aid to advertising planners (Colley, 1960). Also in advertising, the hierarchy appeared in the form of the acronym AIDA, standing for awareness-interest-desire-action. Another hierarchy example is the innovation-adoption process which was conceptualized as consisting of the steps of awareness-interest-evaluation-trial-adoption.

Although each of these and many other hierarchy classifications undoubtedly offer interesting alternatives, they all have three major levels corresponding to the typical attitude structure components of *cognitive, affective,* and *conative*.

The cognitive component includes such variables as attention, awareness, comprehension, and learning. While there is revolutionary development in this area of research (Hintzman, 1971; Kintsch, 1970; Greeno and Bjork, 1973), it is convenient to think, for present purposes, in terms of all of these variables as falling under the cognitive heading. Similarly, there is exciting study going on in terms of the affective variables of interest, evaluation, attitude, feeling, conviction, and yielding, but here they will all be covered under the one heading. And, finally, the issues of this chapter which relate to intention, behavior, and action are grouped under the heading of "conative."

Virtually no one doubts the existence of the cognitive, affective, and conative reactions to communication. But there are two serious quarrels with the hierarchy viewpoint. One is really almost extinct and will not be considered here. That is the so-called "black box" approach espoused by both quantitative management scientists and Skinnerian behaviorists. They have often argued that it is unnecessary to consider anything more than inputs and outputs, stimuli and responses. In marketing communication this could mean going as far as ignoring the hierarchy of individual mental states in favor of gross dollar media expenditures (input) and dollar sales or profits (output). But, increasingly—even in business—planning and research are governed by the intermediate response levels.

The more important question for the present purposes involves relationships within the hierarchy, i.e., whether cognitive reactions must precede affective which must precede conative. The original students of the hierarchy in marketing communication (Lavidge and Steiner, 1961) posited that the levels of the hierarchy were linked in this stairstep fashion, learning before attitude change before behavior change. It is this stairstep hypothesis that has so often branded the hierarchy-of-effects ideas as a "learning theory" or behavioristic approach, since "learning" is posited to be essential to subsequent responses. For instance, William McGuire's (1968, 1974) "information processing" approach is based essentially on a hierarchy, and he characterizes his approach as a learning one.

Both empirical evidence and theory indicate that the stairstep hierarchy notion is, at the very least, too simple. Many studies both in psychology and in marketing communication indicate that learning or cognitive response is often not a measurable precedent to either affect or conation (Greenwald, 1968; Haskins, 1964; Wright, 1972). Similarly, the affective-conative link is questioned by studies of the attitude-behavior relationship that have been done over the last forty years (Campbell, 1963; Day, 1970; Festinger, 1964; Fishbein and Ajzen, 1972; La Piere, 1934).

These deviations from the stairstep hierarchy can be due to either theoretical or methodological shortcomings. Clearly there are some hypothetical conditions and measurements under which the stairstep hierarchy will occur and others in which it will not.

Consider, for instance, the three major levels of response: cognitive, affective, and conative. If we knew nothing about them, it would be reasonable to assume that they could be ordered in all six possible permutations of three things. In fact, there is a great deal of research which indicates that the majority of communication response situations are represented by just three of the orders: (1) The Learning hierarchy: cognitive-affective-conative; (2) the Dissonance-Attribution hierarchy: conative-affective-cognitive; and (3) the Low-Involvement hierarchy: cognitive-conative-affective.

Because each of these three hypothesized orders of response is related to a particular research tradition, each is supported by theory and empirical evidence on the conditions under which it is elicited. A major thesis of this paper is that much will be gained by using the theory and results of all three approaches, rather than considering them as competitors. In fact, the Three-Orders hierarchy model of this paper is a specification and exploration of the conditions under which each is found.

The Learning Hierarchy

The Learning hierarchy is the equivalent of the stairstep one discussed above. While it has been posited as a basic progression of reactions to communication, even those individuals who examine the Learning hierarchy most thoroughly will caution that it exists only under special conditions. McGuire (1968, 1974), for one, mentions several other approaches to attitude research, and then points out that he would lose all credibility as an attitude researcher if he claimed that the Learning hierarchy (he does not use this particular term) existed for a majority of communication situations.

Under what conditions does it exist? Research by McGuire and others seems to indicate that it typically occurs when the audience is *involved* in the topic of the campaign and when there are *clear differences between alternatives.* Research on the diffusion of new products and innovation provides the best illustration of such conditions. Those audiences that are most interested in new ideas are involved, and new products or ideas offer clear alternatives. It is under such conditions that audience members first become aware, then develop interest, make evaluations, try, and adopt—the adoption process hierarchy.

Of course, there are exceptions to the Learning hierarchy even in the adoption situation (Robertson, 1971; Rogers and Shoemaker, 1971), and these usually occur when there is varying availability of mass media sources of information. Marketing communication is more concerned with mass media messages. In the adoption process it is sometimes true that personal sources of information and persuasion cause a behavior change before attitude change and learning from mass media can take place. It is such situations that are covered by the second type of hierarchy.

The Dissonance-Attribution Hierarchy

The "Dissonance-Attribution" hierarchy is the exact reverse of the standard Learning one. That is, both dissonance (Aronson, 1969) and attribution (Bem,

1972; Kelley, 1973) theorists have posited and examined situations in which behavior occurs first, then attitude change, and finally learning: a conative-affective-cognitive relationship. These have typically been situations in which the audience has been *involved* but the *alternatives have been almost indistinguishable.* The consumer or pseudo-consumer is forced to make a choice or behavior on the basis of some *non-media or non-marketing communication source.* Then he or she changes attitude in order to bolster that choice—often on the basis of experience with the chosen alternative. Finally, learning itself occurs on a selective basis, in order to bolster the original choice by response to messages that are supportive of it.

Obviously, the mass media can have an effect in promoting the original choice behavior and attitude change, but both dissonance and attribution theorists argue that the main mass media effect is in terms of reducing dissonance or providing information for attribution or self-perception—*after* behavior and attitude change have occurred.

In the third type of hierarchy, on the other hand, mass media learning is the key initial step.

The Low-Involvement Hierarchy

Herbert E. Krugman (1965) is most responsible for recognizing what is here called the Low-Involvement hierarchy. Krugman was interested in determining why television advertising seems to have such a strong aggregate effect, although laboratory research often indicates little effect of TV ads on individual attitude change.

He concluded that most television viewers are *not involved* with either the advertising or its topics. This means that there is very little perceptual defense against the messages. Although television ads may not directly change attitude, they might, after overwhelming repetition, make possible a shift in cognitive structure. Consumers may be better able to recall the name or idea of a product. Then the next time they are in a purchasing situation, that name comes to mind, they buy, and attitude is subsequently changed as a result of experience with the product. Thus the Low-Involvement hierarchy is a cognitive-conative-affective one.

The Low-Involvement hierarchy most often occurs when there are *minimal differences between alternatives* or when low involvement makes actual differences unimportant to the audience. This does not mean, however, that it is restricted to broadcast communication about low-priced consumer goods. In fact the Low-Involvement situation can hold for a variety of social acts, including voting, as a study discussed below makes clear.

Model Predictions and Testing Alternatives

The Three-Orders model posits the existence and importance of three separate hierarchies, each depending on a particular combination of involvement, differentiation of alternatives, and communication source.

This model could be tested by either the correlation-regression or the experimental approach. The correlation-regression approach would establish the sequence of responses for each of a number of audience members over the course of a communication campaign. This requires panel research or repetitive surveys, with measurement taken at several points in time from each panel member or from audience groups. Then it is possible to make comparisons from one measurement period to another to see which responses tend to occur first. The search for sequences can be done with cross-lag correlation (O'Brien, 1971), recursive regression models (Claycamp and Liddy, 1969), distributed lag models (Palda, 1964, 1966) and various other econometric techniques (Aaker, 1971).

Despite the fact that this correlation-regression approach has provided valuable information, it is rejected here because of difficulties of measurement. Measurement during a process of change can alter the process itself. During panel research especially, it is possible that measurement at one point in time can lead to particular patterns of response in the next period—whether the relevant communication stimuli occurred or not.

A more important problem with the correlation-regression approach is that measurement is made on such a gross basis that it becomes nearly impossible to attribute any particular response sequence to any particular communication situation. This is a serious flaw in regard to the Three-Orders model, because it is a conditional one (Birnbaum, 1973). If the correlation-regression approach provides little indication of the particular involvement-differention-source combination that led to a response sequence, it cannot really be used to test the Three-Orders model.

Thus, experimentation—the second broad method of testing the model—is necessary. Respondents must be specifically and differentially exposed to communication stimuli with experimental control. Each differentially exposed group would be measured once after exposure and comparisons across groups could be made to establish the curve of response for the cognitive, affective, and conative variables.

In Figure 1 predictions from the Three-Orders model are recast in terms of the curves of response expected for different degrees of message exposure in such an experimental test. The basic assumption here is that the underlying repetition function is a sigmoidal or S-shaped one. In general, repetition first has little effect, then there is a period of great effect, followed by a leveling-off or even a negative-returns period. But the S-shaped function is seldom observed in total for any particular measure. The hierarchy predictions are based on the assumption that those responses that are easiest to affect, which are supposed to

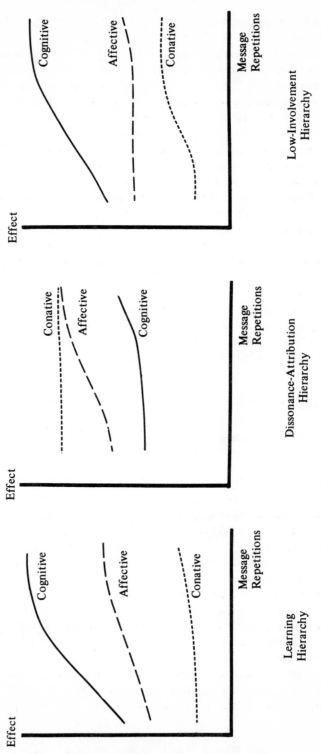

Figure 1: THREE-ORDERS MODEL PREDICTIONS FOR REPETITION EFFECT

occur earlier in the sequence for any particular hierarchy, will show only the later parts of the underlying S-shaped function.

In the Learning hierarchy prediction of Figure 1, for instance, cognitive responses, which are supposed to come first, are affected most (higher intercept and slope) and exhibit the late part of S-shape function (great growth and leveling). The affect response is supposed to be influenced next, and accordingly, it is lower and sloped less than the cognitive one. An earlier part of the S-shaped function is shown. The conative response is predicted to be most difficult to change in the Learning hierarchy situation, and, as shown in Figure 1, the conative curve shows the flat early part of the S-shaped function, with a slight upturn at the end—among a relatively small proportion of the audience.

The Dissonance-Attribution hierarchy assumes a situation in which the conative response, a choice among undifferentiated alternatives, is made through some non-mass media source. Then attitude and cognitive responses are supposed to follow, in that order. This is shown in Figure 1 in terms of a flat high conative function and lower affect and cognitive curves, each exhibiting an earlier part of the underlying S-shaped function.

The Low-Involvement hierarchy is based on the notion of almost unlimited effect on the cognitive variable because audience members don't care or are not involved. This is shown in Figure 1 with a high, sharply rising cognitive function. This eventually leads to conative change on the basis of almost blind choices and, much later, some change in the affective function.

LABORATORY DESIGN FOR RESEARCH ON HIERARCHY-OF-EFFECTS

The Three-Orders predictions shown in Figure 1 demand laboratory research because of the need for economical and strict control of the marketing communication situations which are predicted to lead to various hierarchies.

Laboratory research on the hierarchy presents a dilemma, however. On the one hand it is necessary to do some very unnatural things in the lab, such as presenting messages repetitively and measuring extensively on several response levels. On the other hand, the presentation and measurement must be natural enough so that results are valid, that is, relate to those found from the field.

The results reported in this chapter are from a series of studies all based on one general laboratory technique. This technique is an attempt to balance the horns of the unnatural-natural dilemma in order to produce valid results. This is done by use of a cover story which produces seemingly unbiased attention to a series of product advertisements. Ads are short enough to be presented repetitively but complex enough to be used as representations of communication research variables.

Respondents are asked to participate in a study of one method of "Shopping of the Future." As they enter the testing area they are given a reasonably involving one-page description of such a method, a cable television, telephone, and on-line computer system which would allow highly individualistic in-home shopping.

The description prepares respondents to view a crude approximation of the future shopping system. Then a stream of product advertisements are shown one after another on a television screen. A variety of print and broadcast advertising displays have been shown in the series of studies. In one study, for example, there were 9 test advertisements exposed from 1 to 6 times in a stream of 52 exposures which included 20 filler advertisements. The total showing time per respondent in that study was under 10 minutes.

In all studies measurement is made immediately after exposure. In some of the research, physiological or interest measurements are made during exposure, and delayed measurement is sometimes added. But measurement relative to the communication has been avoided before exposure so that respondents will not be sensitized to the purpose of the research.

After-exposure measures follow the cognitive-affective-conative order. The first measures consist of a page of questions relating to the shopping method; these provide further support for the cover story while constituting an interlude that avoids abnormally high levels of recall. Cognitive recall measurement follows and consists of an open-end request to play back information about the advertisements in any order desired. This part of the technique is directly analogous to the free recall paradigm of verbal learning (Kintsch, 1970), with the exception that the stimuli are not nonsense syllables but ads which represent communication variables.

Following recall, general attitude or evaluation is measured for the brands, services, candidates, or ideas in the test advertising. Then respondents are put into a shopping role and asked what their purchase intention would be for the products of interest. Note that both attitude and intention measures for the test products are embedded in a series of other product stimuli in order to avoid undue biasing emphasis on the test materials. The questionnaire usually closes with classification questions such as those on demographics and general shopping patterns. On occasion we add a variety of supplementary measures of cognitive response, attitude, and behaviors.

Our general technique is flexible. It has been conducted in mobile units, in store fronts in shopping centers, in central business locations, in schools and churches, and in a management science laboratory. Respondents have come from all age groups from 10 to 65, from all marital and family life-cycle groupings, from all but the most extreme social class, education, and income groupings, from both sexes, and from target audiences for a wide variety of messages.

By making changes in the cover story (e.g., to "Home Information Center of the Future Project" or to "Television Humor-Violence Project"), it is possible to use the technique for a wide variety of message types covering both commercial and non-commercial topics. In all the research done thus far with the technique there has been only one study (on political advertising) in which there was any serious question about the efficacy of the cover story.

The technique allows manipulation of nearly all communication research variables as well as some that are normally not found in communication research. That is, it is possible to manipulate not only appeal, repetition, and format but also the proportion and nature of competitive messages, the types of surrounding program or editorial material, the media and media mix, and, to a lesser extent, the schedule.

The laboratory technique provides optimal arrangements for examining the Three-Orders model because the technique has multiple measurement, repetitive exposure, and the opportunity to vary conditions enough to observe the various hierarchy patterns. At the same time, the materials are viewed in as unbiased a way as possible by use of a cover story and other procedures which disguise the purpose of the experiments until debriefing. In addition, the conditions of viewing are quite natural for a laboratory experiment; the viewing room is made into an "in-home" environment, several people are viewing at any given time, and there are noises and distractions common to ordinary viewing. Instructions also discourage respondents from paying any more than ordinary attention to the advertisements and commercials.

REPETITION RESEARCH ON THE HIERARCHY

The laboratory repetition technique provides exactly the kind of situation in which the predictions of Figure 1 might be observed. It has been used in ten experiments involving over 2,300 respondents. Field experimentation with another 5,000 respondents has provided support for the laboratory findings. But no one has looked across these studies and considered their meaning for the hierarchy question. That is the purpose of this section.

Nature of the Laboratory Data

The laboratory data present certain biases and characteristics that should be examined before an overall consideration of the Three-Orders predictions.

In the first place, it may not be possible to observe all three conditions in a marketing communication laboratory which uses products and advertisements that have already been exposed in the mass media and otherwise. The Three-Orders model is based on the assumption that in some situations the choices are quite equal and sources other than mass media advertising push one toward decision. Such are the conditions of most dissonance or attribution studies. But in the repetition laboratory research the audience may have made decisions about products long before seeing advertising in the lab. It will be hard to observe Dissonance-Attribution curves such as those that are shown in the hypothesized relationships in Figure 1.

In contrast, it is clear that the laboratory is biased toward finding the

Learning hierarchy. The measures are typically all taken in one session with cognitive questions asked first, then affective, and finally conative. Just based on forgetting, that is, less effect as time and interpolated tasks occur between exposure and measurement, it is clear that cognitive measures should be affected most, then affect measures, and finally conative—as shown for the Learning hierarchy in Figure 1.

In fact, if one were to look just at correlations across measures, the studies show strong support for the Learning hierarchy. For instance, in two experiments by Roger Heeler (1972: 83) ad recall, brand rating, and brand preference measurements were taken in the experimental setting from nearly 300 respondents, and a mail survey was done three weeks later to determine subsequent purchase.

The correlations of the lab measures with purchase, while understandably low, are in the exact order predicted by the Learning hierarchy. Reported purchasing was related most to preference (Kendall rank order correlation = .165, $p < .01$), next to brand rating (.090, $p < .10$), next to ad recall (.028, N.S.). The same general kind of correlational support for the Learning hierarchy was found in studies by Sawyer (1971), Strong (1972), Reed (1974), and Rothschild (1974).

But it would be possible to have such covariation and still get repetition function relationships like the Dissonance-Attribution and Low-Involvement ones in Figure 1. The relative size of correlations provides some support, but it is a much weaker indication than that which might be provided by repetition curves (Birnbaum, 1973). Low-Involvement and Dissonance-Attribution curves may exist even when measures are sequentially related.

Predominance of the Low-Involvement Hierarchy

Actually, when the curves of all the studies are examined, it is clear that the Low-Involvement hierarchy occurs somewhat more often than the Learning one. The Dissonance-Attribution curves simply do not occur in the repetition laboratory setting. Despite a myriad of definitions and redefinitions of variables, it was nearly impossible to find a set of curves with the conative highest and flat or even one with affect curves rising faster than cognitive at any point (Heeler, 1972; Reed, 1973; Rothschild, 1974; Sawyer, 1971).

Figure 2 shows an example of the Low-Involvement hierarchy result that predominated those from the laboratory. This particular one was developed by Sawyer (1971, p. 165) in a study involving two test advertisements and a competitive ad from each of five product classes. The laboratory procedure was similar to that explained earlier with test ads exposed from one to six times and a competitive one always at a two-exposure level. The cognitive, affective, and conative measures are defined competitively. "Top Recall" indicates the percentage of respondents recalling the test ad before the competitive, "Top Attitude"

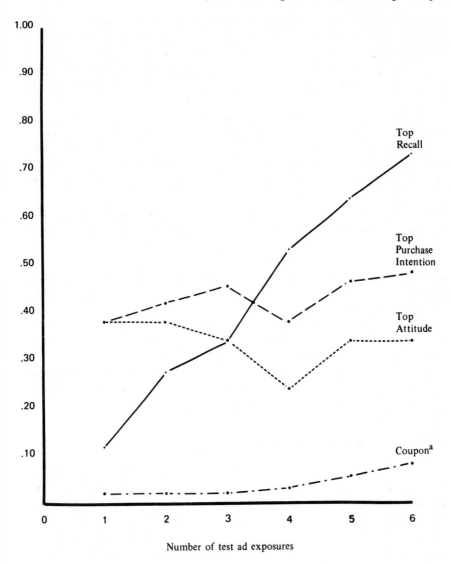

Number of test ad exposures

[a]120 observations per exposure condition

SOURCE: Sawyer, 1971, p. 165.

**Figure 2: EFFECTS OF REPETITION ON COMPARATIVE MEASURES
(200 observations per exposure condition)**

is the proportion rating the test brand higher than competition, and "Top Purchase Intention" is the proportion saying they are more likely to purchase the test brand than the competitive one.

As can be seen, the result is even more in favor of the Low-Involvement hierarchy than the hypothesized curves shown in Figure 1. The cognitive measure of Top Recall is affected more $(p < .001)$, followed by the conative Top Purchase Intention $(p < .05)$. The affective Top Attitude is not just unchanged by repetition; there seems to be a slight negative effect. Even the coupon measure (coupons cashed in for test brands) was positively affected by repetition although the effect was slight (linear trend $F = 3.96$, 1 and 10 df, $p < .10$).

Figure 2 is typical of Low-Involvement results often found in the repetition studies. Whether scores are considered competitively or not, recall and purchase intention are significantly affected by repetition but attitude-evaluation-rating-affect is typically not. It should be pointed out such a finding is not unique in marketing communication research. Krugman (1965) implied a lesser effect on attitude in his original formulation of the Low-Involvement hypothesis, and Silk and Vavra (1972), in reviewing the literature on the effects of pleasant and unpleasant advertising format, point out that significant findings less often result with evaluation measures than with recall or action.

Before dismissing the Dissonance-Attribution hierarchy in the laboratory, it is instructive to examine one field experimental repetition result to see the research conditions under which this kind of result might occur. Strong (1972) did a field study in which print advertisements were repetitively mailed under various scheduling conditions to housewives. His results were based on 2,784 observations over a thirteen-week period. To some extent they show the Dissonance-Attribution effect in that a conative measure, reported brand usage (Strong, 1972: 341), is relatively high and not affected by repetition; while an affective measure, brand rated best, rises more over repetitions than a cognitive measure, agreement with beliefs expressed in the advertising (Strong, 1972: 204, 423-28). This is similar to the Dissonance-Attribution hypothesis shown in Figure 1: conative flat and relatively high, affective rising faster than cognitive.

Three factors seem to explain this isolated Dissonance-Attribution result. One is the possibility that communication sources other than the test advertising could intervene in a field study with at least a week between exposures, thus leading to the behavior-attitude-learning result. Secondly, the products involved in the Strong study were rather popular ones in markets in which there is low differentiation, and this is almost a definition of the conditions under which the Dissonance-Attribution hierarchy is expected to occur. Third and most important, the cognitive measure was a rather difficult one involving both comprehension and belief. The less difficult cognitive response of gross awareness was affected more than brand rating in Strong's study, as it was in all the repetition studies, lab or field. In order to observe the Dissonance-Attribution hierarchy, then, it seems there must first be a physical behavior with commitment (Kiesler,

1968) followed by general evaluation change which then must lead to complex cognitive changes. The laboratory studies reviewed here did not provide such conditions, but this does not mean that they cannot provide them.

The point here is not that the Low-Involvement hypothesis has been "proved" by the laboratory results. In fact, in some conditions in the studies reviewed here the Learning hierarchy occurs (Heeler, 1972: 117, 146) instead of the Low-Involvement one (Heeler, 1972: 147). The key question, given those findings, is to determine if the variables that explain different hierarchy results are those which are posited in the Three-Orders model.

Explanatory Variables I: Involvement

The key explanatory variable in the Three-Orders model is involvement in the communication and its topic. This variable can be operationalized in many ways, but the main hypothesis is that under high involvement the Learning hierarchy should occur; otherwise, as the name indicates, there will be a Low-Involvement hierarchy result.

One rather direct way to detect lack of involvement is by observing (1) the number of times respondents indicate they "don't know" when they are evaluating a series of brands, or (2) the extent to which they do not use many points on a brand rating scale. Both of these measures of involvement were used by Sawyer (1971), and he found evidence for their validity in their correlations with advertising recall and with favorable evaluations of the shopping method used in the cover story.

Figure 3 shows how attitude and purchase intention curves differ for those low-involved individuals who use the "don't know" category often (63 percent of the sample in this study) as opposed to the more involved respondents. As can be seen, the Three-Orders model receives support. With low-involvement respondents, only purchase intention is affected by repetition. With high-involved respondents, both attitude and purchase intention are affected by repetition as would be expected for the Learning hierarchy.

Results were similar when respondents were divided on the basis of the extent to which they used points on a scale. The reader should be cautioned, however, that the analysis was post hoc. Also the Learning hypothesis would predict somewhat less effect for the purchase intention measure than is shown in Figure 3. But in general there is a clear, predicted effect of involvement here.

Another way to vary involvement is across topics rather than across individuals. Such variation produced predicted hierarchy differences for convenience versus shopping goods in two studies (Ray and Sawyer, 1971a; Ray, Sawyer, and Strong, 1971; Strong, 1972), and these results will be examined more thoroughly below under communication sources and differentiation.

Clear differences in involvement are also found across political races. Michael L. Rothschild (1972, 1974; Rothschild and Ray, 1973) performed a laboratory experiment in which test advertisements were repetitively exposed

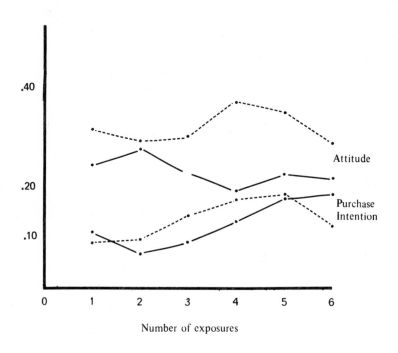

Number of exposures

——————— Respondents using "Don't Know" scale point in at least four
out of five ratings in a product category

--------------- Respondents using "Don't Know" scale point less than four times

SOURCE: Sawyer, 1971, p. 104.

**Figure 3: ATTITUDE AND PURCHASE INTENTION SCORES FOR RESPONDENTS
WHO VARIED ON THEIR USAGE OF "DON'T KNOW" POINT ON
ATTITUDE SCALE**

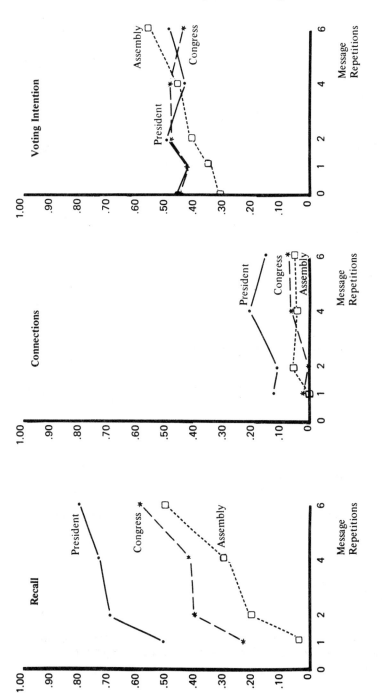

SOURCE: Rothschild and Ray, 1973. N per message-exposure condition ranged from 25-31.

Figure 4: HIERARCHY EFFECTS ACROSS VARIOUS POLITICAL CONTESTS

for candidates in the Presidential, Congressional, and California State Assembly races in 1972. As shown in Figure 4, he found strong across-races differences, which are supportive of the involvement prediction of the Three-Orders model.

First, while it may be generally agreed that voters are more involved in the Presidential race than the Congressional or State Assembly one, Rothschild provided a measure of this through the "connections" response. Krugman (1966) indicated that connections or verbatim comments linking the personal life of the respondent to the message can be used to show involvement. As can be seen from Figure 4, the connections responses, although low, were in the exact order from President (average of 15 percent per group) to State Assembly (average of 3.9 percent per group).

The results for the three races were also in that order. The Presidential race produced some slope in recall, a moderate slope in connections (also an affect measure, see Greenwald, 1968; Wright, 1972), and almost a flat voting intention curve—a good representation of the Learning hierarchy. The State Assembly race produced dramatic recall and intention curves and minimal effects in connections after two exposures—a good Low-Involvement hierarchy. The Congressional race fell in between the other two.

In all, the involvement variable seems to explain hierarchy effects more clearly than does any other single mediating variable.

Explanatory Variables II: Communication Sources and Differentiation

The definition of marketing communication given earlier in this chapter listed seven types of impersonal and personal commercial communications. In addition to these, individuals can learn from a variety of other totally personal sources. If they do, their reaction to mass media communication is likely to be less dramatic than when personal sources are not involved. This diminution would not necessarily be due to a difference in involvement but merely to the way consumers use the media in the context of their total information search.

These differences in communication sources and differentiation of alternatives can cause differences in hierarchy effect. One such effect is shown in Figure 5 which gives both recall and purchase intention results from a set of convenience goods (soaps, soups, and mouth washes) and of shopping goods (portable televisions, foundation garments, and washing machines). Nine advertisements were repeated for each set of products. Convenience and shopping goods differ in both sources and differentiation. Consumers tend to depend more on personal sources to purchase the somewhat more different and complex shopping goods.

The result is that messages about convenience goods produce what might be called a Low-Involvement hierarchy (attitude was not affected for either class), while those about shopping goods produce less effect overall and something like a Learning hierarchy. The linear interaction of product type and repetition was

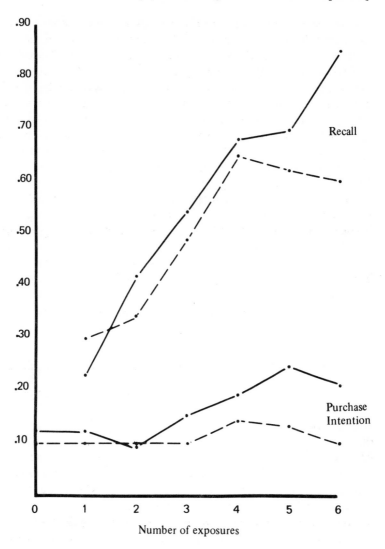

Recall

Purchase
Intention

Number of exposures

―――――― = Convenience goods ads

― ― ― ― ― = Shopping goods ads

SOURCE: Sawyer, 1971, p. 114.

**Figure 5: EFFECTS OF REPETITION ON CONVENIENCE AND SHOPPING GOODS
ADS**
(126 observations per exposure condition)

significant at the .05 level for both recall and purchase intention (Ray and Sawyer, 1971a).

Product class differences in sources and differentiation tended to produce effects equivalent to those above throughout the repetition studies. These results were not as consistent as those for involvement, however, because there seldom was a large enough sample of messages for each class.

In general, the laboratory shows different communication sources and differentiation to have an effect on the form of the hierarchy that would be predicted from the Three-Orders model. Because these results come from a laboratory, however, it is harder to observe the effects of consumer communication and search patterns in other than a static way. The lack of Dissonance-Attribution hierarchy results is some evidence of this. The Dissonance-Attribution hierarchy requires a choice that is effected primarily through non-mass media means. This can be created in the laboratory through elaborate contrivances (Aronson and Carl-smith, 1968). But these procedures raise questions of external validity which are crucial to communication planning.

The answer seems to be the use of field experimentation. This is the only research setting that produced anything like Dissonance-Attribution results in this research program. Perhaps the laboratory is appropriate for examining only those situations which depend mainly on mass media communication. Or the laboratory might be used to examine one part of the information-search process, with computer simulation converting these results into a total prediction.

Explanatory Variables III: McGuire's Compensation Principle

In developing his Learning-hierarchy information-processing approach to communication, McGuire had the insight that any communication variable that had a strong effect on one level of the hierarchy would tend to have an opposite effect on some other (1968, 1974). He called this idea the "compensation principle" and used it to explain such phenomena as a nonmonotonic effect of increasing levels of fear appeals.

Stated in compensation-principle terms, the effect of great fear in a message may be to *increase* attention and awareness but correspondingly to *decrease* attitudinal effects—because the audience may reject such high fear as being unreasonable. The interaction of these two effects leads to a nonmonotonic effect with moderate levels of fear being most effective (Ray and Wilkie, 1970).

It could be that compensation, operating within a Learning hierarchy, caused what were previously called Low-Involvement hierarchy results in the laboratory. It would not be the first time that compensation was confused with poor attitude-behavior relationships (Achenbaum, 1966; Festinger, 1964).

Unfortunately, compensation is somewhat confounded with involvement and communication sources in the present studies, which were not designed expressly to test for their interactions. Further studies may determine whether involvement is related to compensation in producing particular patterns of results. What is apparent, however, is that compensation does occur and can be demonstrated quite clearly in a repetition laboratory setting.

One example of such compensation relates to two message types: refutational and supportive appeals. These are discussed quite thoroughly in Chapter 9 of this volume by Roberts and Maccoby. Supportive appeals are one-sided and present only arguments in favor of a particular position. Refutational appeals first briefly present counterarguments to a position and then refute those in a way favorable to the position.

These message types are posited to have different effects across hierarchy levels (McGuire, 1964; Ray, 1968). In addition, refutational messages have been reported to work best in a situation with competition, which is key in the compensation results discussed here.

In a study by Heeler (1972) experimental groups were given either refutational or supportive versions of advertisements for Bayer aspirin and Parker pens. These experimental groups were each further divided into those who received none, two, or four exposures of competitive advertisements. There was one cognitive variable, recall of the test advertisement. The affect measure was a simple seven-point rating scale, from "best" to "one of the worst." One conative measure "preference," was taken right after advertising exposure, and it consisted of the number of times respondents indicated either Bayer or Parker was their first choice in preference in a mock supermarket environment. The second conative measure, "purchase," was a postcard report received from respondents three weeks after the experiment.

The results, shown in Figure 6, show that as competition increased, the advantage of the refutational appeal increased over the supportive for both the cognitive and the conative variables. But for the affective rating variable there was a decrease with greater competition. The effect of the supportive messages on general brand evaluation seems to increase slightly in the face of competition. The refutational advantage in competition is shown most clearly for recall and the conative variables of preference and purchase.

This was only one of many compensation results found in the repetition studies. Other examples include:

- In a pattern which underlies most compensation results, a set of "grabber" ads (judged to be visually outstanding in a way that would produce strong one-exposure effects) gave a slightly greater recall repetition slope than did non-grabber ads. Conversely, however, the non-grabbers lead in both level and slope for purchase intention (Ray and Sawyer, 1971a).
- A set of one-color canned food advertisements produced a greater repetition slope for recall and purchase intention than did an equivalent set of advertisements without the color. Conversely, the black-and-white versions of the same ads produced greater repetition slope for a

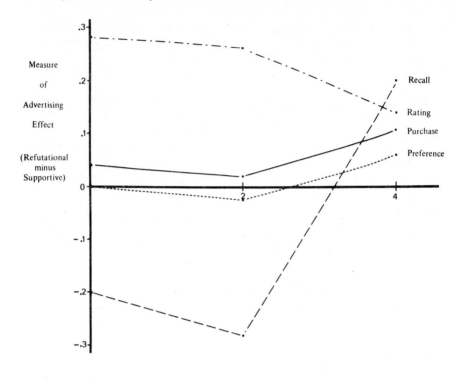

Average n per appeal per level of competitive advertising = 35 responses
(Zero test brand repetition condition excluded).

SOURCE: Heeler, 1972, p. 127.

**Figure 6: THE RELATIVE EFFECTIVENESS OF REFUTATIONAL VERSUS
SUPPORTIVE ADVERTISING AT THREE LEVELS OF COMPETITIVE
ADVERTISING REPETITION**

measure of verbal quality of the recall (Ray, Sawyer, and Strong,
1971). Apparently the color was successful in gaining attention but
those who paid attention to the black-and-white versions seemed to
recall more of their verbal content.

● A "grabber" ad for a new product, Phase III toilet soap, produced a
sharp effect of repetition on recall when compared to the recall effect
from a non-grabber ad for the well-known Ivory soap. For brand rating
and purchase intention, the results were reversed. Ivory produced a
higher, steeper slope (Ray and Sawyer, 1971a).

● A nude model in a print advertisement for Bali foundation garments
produced significantly greater effects for recall than did more ordinary

ads for its competitor Vassarette. On brand rating, however, the results were reversed (purchase intention response was too low for analysis). Apparently the nude helped the housewife respondents to recall the Bali ad but the effect was somewhat negative on attitude (Sawyer, 1971: 131-133).

- An ad for Whirlpool washers contained an unusual illustration showing a working-class mother and the T-shirted male members of her family standing around a washing machine. The ad quoted the mother as saying that the new Whirlpool helped her to get the men to change their underwear every day. This ad, when compared to a competitive one for G.E., produced positive effects on recall and slightly negative on brand rating.

- Roger Heeler examined the old question of the effects of variety in advertising on repetition effects. He hypothesized and found that the outcome depends on the level of the hierarchy. Mixed schedules, with two ads repeated, did better than the average of two single-ad schedules, for only the recall measure. For brand rating, preferences, and reported purchase the reverse was true (Heeler, 1972: 113-117).

- The compensation principle can apply to competitive messages as well. Heeler (1972: 121-122) found that increases in the level of competitive messages produced corresponding *increases* in recall of test advertising and *decreases* in rating, preference, and reported purchase.

- A final compensation result involved no variation in repetition; both test messages were repeated twice. But there was variation in distraction, which provided evidence relevant to the issues covered by Roberts and Maccoby in this volume, as well as to the hierarchy issue itself.

Senior high school students saw one of two anti-drug abuse commercials embedded in an eighteen-minute television program. One message was directed at them and another was directed at parents. As audio distraction increased, recall of student-oriented commercial decreased and the parent-oriented one increased; there was little difference in attitude results.

By contrast, interest in receiving an anti-drug information booklet showed findings opposite to those for recall. The student commercial produced increasing booklet interest as distraction increased, the parent commercial decreasing interest.

Some explanation for the differential distraction result may have to do, as Roberts and Maccoby suggest, with differential counterarguing under distraction. Counterarguing dropped to zero in the high distraction condition among those high schoolers who received and recalled the high-school oriented commercial. Counterarguing actually increased slightly in high distraction among those who received and recalled the less relevant parent-oriented message. (Ray, Reed, and Ward, 1973; Reed, 1974).

The compensation principle most often operates to produce something equivalent to Krugman's Low-Involvement hierarchy with significant effects on cognitive and conative responses and less on affective. But, as shown above, there are other patterns of compensation within the hierarchy. Researchers must be concerned with these interactions in terms of the effect of any particular communication variable. Marketing communication planners would be advised to develop message and communication distribution strategies that take compensation into account. It may be possible to use each communication tool to affect a different level of the hierarchy in a positively compensating way.

IMPLICATIONS

This chapter has reviewed results relative to a Three-Orders model of marketing communication effect. In this particular laboratory repetition setting that was used, only two of the orders, the Learning hierarchy and the Low-Involvement hierarchy, were found. There was good evidence that these two hierarchies are likely to be explained by varying conditions of involvement. Evidence was less strong for the effect of varying communication sources and differentiation of alternatives, two other variables posited by the model to have effect. Part of the reason for this may be the constrained time period of the laboratory. For instance, the other predicted order, the Dissonance-Attribution hierarchy, was found only in a field experiment where the communication sources and differentiation may have operated.

Hierarchy Research System

Clearly there is need for hierarchy research in settings other than the laboratory one discussed most often in this chapter. Perhaps by combining several settings in single research programs, it will be possible to balance the control of the laboratory against the natural environment of the field.

Such a "research system" approach might involve, in order: problem definition, model development, laboratory studies, computer simulation, field experiments, and campaign monitoring. The basic assumption would be that various kinds of communication research offer complementary characteristics for getting at any particular communication phenomenon. Once a problem has been identified and a model developed to deal with it, the laboratory can be used to examine alternatives inexpensively in a controlled setting. Then the results can be utilized in a computer simulation which represents aspects of the natural environment that cannot be represented in a laboratory. Those alternatives surviving both the lab and the simulation can be further examined in field experimentation which provides some control along with more natural exposure. Finally, those campaigns which are actually run can be monitored for hierarchy effects by the use of consumer panels or repetitive surveys.

Such a research system would move from stages in which the researcher has great control to those in which the researcher has very little control over exposure or extraneous elements. As control decreases, the expense of doing research increases correspondingly. Thus it is much more expensive to run a campaign and make measurements for the field experimental and campaign monitoring stages than it is to do laboratory experimentation. The general strategy of the research system is to pare the communication alternatives in the early stages and then use the more natural but higher-cost later stages on just those alternatives which promise to show important hierarchy differences.

Hierarchy Research Potential in Marketing Communication

This type of research system has seldom been suggested, much less implemented, in communication research. Typically, those writing on behavioral science methodology emphasize *one* type of research—labs, simulation, field experimentation, panel, or survey—as superior to others (Campbell, 1969; Haskins, 1968; Nicosia, 1968; Sawyer, 1972). Those writing about several research levels usually bemoan the lack of comparable results and then suggest more frequent use of natural settings for experiments (Hovland, 1959; McGuire, 1969; Weick, 1967).

Marketing communication, however, provides both a need and resources for a research system approach. The need arises from the fact that, at early planning stages, a great number of alternatives must be economically eliminated. This calls for laboratory experiments. But the experiments must be valid in the sense that they will predict what will happen in the field. This calls for simulation and field experimentation. Finally, because marketing communication managers must have up-to-date information on progress, it is common to institute tracking or campaign-monitoring systems, which can include measures of the hierarchy of effects. At every step in the planning process, therefore, marketing communicators need information on communication goals, and this has led to a corresponding need for research procedures to measure goal achievement in hierarchy terms.

Even more fortunate for the communication researcher, the marketing communication field has had the resources to provide the necessary research facilities. A wide variety of laboratory testing facilities are available (ARF, 1972; Robinson, 1968). Computer simulation is the basis for several planning models and consumer behavior models (Amstutz, 1967; Gensch, 1970; Little and Lodish, 1969; Little, 1972; Nicosia, 1966). These models are often founded on large up-to-date data bases, which make them even more valuable for the communication researcher. Field experimental facilities are also quite frequent in, say, advertising where split runs in both print and television, while costly, offer the possibilities of perfect experimental designs (Adler and Kuehn, 1969; Ule, 1966). And more and more marketers are developing information systems which provide opportunities to do campaign monitoring and panel research of a very sophisticated type.

Communication researchers should pay particular attention to the fact that the advertising part of marketing communication provides an especially good representation of basic communication variables. Advertisements are short, are well-produced, are run continuously, and have clear-cut audiences and objectives. While much communication research is done with rather ponderous or amateurish materials, the advertising setting offers a vital area in which to do basic research.

Assessment: The Three-Orders Model

Before considering the advantages of the Three-Orders model, several cautions should be observed. First, each of these orders or separate hierarchies represents a tremendous amount of research which is only suggested in this chapter. Each order represents a whole middle-range theory (Robertson and Ward, 1973). It is not correct to assume that all the studies within these theories are represented here. Nor are all their terms, measures, or detailed linkages between measures of concern. Much sophistication has been sacrificed here in order to take an overview of three major structures in communication response.

One example of this simplification involves the term "conative." It normally signifies an intervening variable relating to *propensity* to behave, not necessarily behavior itself. In this chapter these two types of response are grouped together under one heading; the issues of intention-behavior relations have been ignored, as well as has the fact that all variables are measured by "behavior" of one sort or another. Similar issues are implicit throughout the Three-Orders model. They were ignored in this chapter, however, in order to demonstrate the advantages of considering the possibility of all three orders in any particular decision or research situation.

The Three-Orders model offers solutions to both applied and basic problems in communication research. In the applied area of marketing communication, the simple hierarchy-of-effects has been used as a planning tool but has often created problems because the relationships among communication responses have not held. The Three-Orders model offers explanation for divergent results and an outline which can be used to analyze each marketing communication situation. Basic theory and research in communication has often suffered from a surfeit of competing views, more or less represented by the three hierarchy orders. The model suggests that the alternative views in the field are not competing; instead, each deals with a different situation. Involvement, differentiation, and communication sources can be analyzed to determine which view is most likely to be operative for each communication situation.

The question of whether man thinks before acting or acts before thinking is as old as Plato and as new as Skinner, attribution theory, humanistic psychology, and mathematical learning theory. This chapter examined that question in one very small, well-controlled, and specific laboratory setting. Even in that setting there is much to be learned, and it is clear that even much more can be learned by taking the more textured view of the Three-Orders model into a variety of other settings.

REFERENCES

AAKER, D. A. (1971) Multivariate Analysis in Marketing: Theory and Application. Belmont, Calif.: Wadsworth.

ACHENBAUM, A. A. (1966) "An answer to one of the unanswered questions about the measurement of advertising effectiveness," pp. 24-32 in Proceedings of the 12th Annual Meeting of the Advertising Research Foundation. New York: Advertising Research Foundation.

ADLER, J. and A. KUEHN (1969) "How advertising works in market experiments," pp. 63-70 in Proceedings of the 15th Annual Meeting of the Advertising Research Foundation. New York: Advertising Research Foundation.

AMSTUTZ, A. E. (1967) Computer Simulation of Competitive Market Response. Cambridge: M.I.T. Press.

ARF (1972) Copy Testing: An Annotated Bibliography, 1960-1972. New York: Advertising Research Foundation.

ARONSON, E. (1969) "The theory of cognitive dissonance." Chapter 1 in L. Berkowitz (ed.) Advances in Experimental Social Psychology. Volume 4. New York: Academic Press.

ARONSON E. and J. M. CARLSMITH (1968) "Experimentation in social psychology," in G. Lindzey and E. Aronson (eds.) The Handbook of Social Psychology (rev. ed.). Volume 2. Reading, Mass.: Addison-Wesley.

BEM, D. J. (1972) "Self Perception Theory." Chapter 1 in L. Berkowitz (ed.) Advances in Experimental Social Psychology. Volume 6. New York: Academic Press.

BIRNBAUM, M. H. (1973) "The Devil rides again: Correlation as an index of fit." Psychological Bulletin 79: 239-242.

CAMPBELL, D. T. (1963) "Social attitudes and other acquired behavioral dispositions," pp. 94-172 in S. Koch (ed.) Psychology: A Study of a Science. Volume 6. New York: McGraw-Hill.

––– (1969) "Reforms as experiments." American Psychologist 24: 409-429.

CLAYCAMP, H. J. and L. E. LIDDY (1969) "Prediction of new product performance: An analytical approach." Journal of Marketing Research 6: 414-420.

COLLEY, R. (1961) Defining Goals for Measured Advertising Results. New York: Association of National Advertisers.

DAY, G. S. (1970) Buyer Attitudes and Brand Choice Behavior. New York: Free Press.

FESTINGER, L. (1964) "Behavioral support for opinion change." Public Opinion Q. 28 (Fall): 404-417.

FISHBEIN, M. and I. AJZEN (1972) "Attitudes and opinions." Annual Review of Psychology 23: 487-554.

GENSCH, D. H. (1970) "Media factors: A review article." Journal of Marketing Research 7: 216-225.

GREENWALD, A. G. (1968) "Cognitive learning, cognitive response to persuasion, and attitude change," pp. 147-170 in A. G. Greenwald, T. C. Brock, and T. M. Ostrom (eds.) Psychological Foundations of Attitudes. New York: Academic Press.

GREENO, J. G. and R. A. BJORK (1973) "Mathematical learning theory and the new 'mental forestry'." Annual Review of Psychology 24: 81-116.

HASKINS, J. B. (1964) "Factual recall as a measure of advertising effectiveness." Journal of Advertising Research 4: 2-28.

––– (1968) How to Evaluate Mass Communication. New York: Advertising Research Foundation.

HEELER, R. M. (1972) "The effects of mixed media, multiple copy, repetition, and competition in advertising: A laboratory investigation." Ph.D. dissertation. Stanford: Graduate School of Business, Stanford University.

HINTZMAN, D. L. (1971) "Markov excellence." Contemporary Psychology 16: 337-339.
HOVLAND, C. I. (1959) "Reconciling conflicting results derived from experimental and survey studies of attitude change." American Psychologist 14: 8-17.
KELLEY, H. H. (1973) "The processes of causal attribution." American Psychologist 28: 107-128.
KIESLER, C. A. (1968) "Commitment," pp. 448-456 in R. P. Abelson et al. (eds.) Theories of Cognitive Consistency: A Sourcebook. Chicago: Rand-McNally.
KINTSCH, W. (1970) Learning, Memory and Conceptual Processes. New York: John Wiley.
KOTLER, P. and G. ZALTMAN (1971) "Social marketing: An approach to planned social change." Journal of Marketing 35: 3-12.
KRUGMAN, H. E. (1965) "The impact of television advertising: Learning without involvement. Public Opinion Q. 29: 349-356.
––– (1966) "The measuring of advertising involvement." Public Opinion Q. 30: 583-596.
LA PIERE, R. T. (1934) "Attitudes versus actions." Social Forces 13: 230-237.
LAVIDGE, R. and G. A. STEINER (1961) "A model for predictive measurements of advertising effectiveness." Journal of Marketing 25: 59-62.
LITTLE, J. D. C. (1972) BRANDAID: An On-Line Marketing Model. Working paper 586-72, Sloan School of Management, Massachusetts Institute of Technology.
LITTLE, J. D. C. and L. M. LODISH (1969) "A media planning calculus." Operations Research 17: 1-35.
McGUIRE, W. J. (1964) "Inducing resistance to persuasion: Some contemporary approaches," pp. 191-229 in L. Berkowitz (ed.) Advances in Experimental Social Psychology. Volume 1. New York: Academic Press.
––– (1968) "Personality and attitude change: An information-processing theory," pp. 171-196 in A. G. Greenwald, T. C. Brock, and T. M. Ostrom (eds.) Psychological Foundations of Attitudes. New York: Academic Press.
––– (1969) "Theory-oriented research in natural settings: The best of both worlds for social psychology," pp. 21-51 in M. Sherif and C. W. Sherif (eds.) Inter-disciplinary Relationships in the Social Sciences. Chicago: Aldine.
––– (forthcoming 1974) "An information-processing approach to advertising effectiveness," in H. Davis and A. J. Silk (eds.) The Behavioral and Management Sciences in Marketing. New York: Ronald Press.
NICOSIA, F. M. (1966) Consumer Decision Processes: Marketing and Advertising Implications. Englewood Cliffs, N.J.: Prentice-Hall.
––– (1968) "Advertising management, consumer behavior and simulation." Journal of Advertising Research 8: 29-38.
O'BRIEN, T. (1971) "Stages of consumer decisionmaking." Journal of Marketing Research. 8: 283-289.
PALDA, K. S. (1964) "The measurement of cumulative advertising effects. Englewood Cliffs, N.J.: Prentice-Hall.
––– (1966) "The hypothesis of a hierarchy of effects: A partial evaluation." Journal of Marketing Research 8: 283-289.
RAY, M. L. (1968) "Biases in selection of messages designed to induce resistance to persuasion." Journal of Personality and Social Psychology 9: 335-339.
RAY, M. L., J. B. REED and S. WARD (1973) Pretesting Techniques for Social Advertising. Working paper, Marketing Science Institute, Cambridge, Mass.
RAY, M. L. and A. G. SAWYER (1971a) "Repetition in media models: A laboratory technique." Journal of Marketing Research 8: 20-30.
––– (1971b) "Behavioral measurement for marketing models." Management Science 18 (Dec., Part II): 73-89.
RAY, M. L., A. G. SAWYER, and E. C. STRONG (1971) "Frequency effects revisited." Journal of Advertising Research 11: 14-20.

RAY, M. L. and W. L. WILKIE (1970) "Fear: the potential of an appeal neglected by marketing." Journal of Marketing 34: 54-62.

REED, J. B. (1974) Planned Social Advertising: Testing for Effects of Appeals, Distraction, Involvement, and Competition. Ph.D. dissertation. Graduate School of Business, Stanford University.

ROBERTSON, T. S. (1971) Innovative Behavior and Communication. New York: Holt, Rinehart, Winston.

ROBERTSON, T. S. and S. WARD (1973) "Introduction," in S. Ward and T. S. Robertson (eds.) Consumer Behavior: Theoretical Sourcebook. Englewood Cliffs, N.J.: Prentice-Hall.

ROBINSON, P. J. (1968) Advertising Measurement and Decision Making. New York: Allyn, Bacon.

ROGERS, E. M. with F. F. SHOEMAKER (1971) Communication of Innovations: A Cross-Cultural Approach. New York: Free Press.

ROTHSCHILD, M. L. (1972) Two Types of Involvement: A Microtheoretical Notion. Unpublished paper. Graduate School of Business, Stanford University.

––– (1974) The Effects of Political Advertising upon the Voting Behavior of a Low Involvement Electorate. Ph.D. dissertation. Graduate School of Business, Stanford University.

ROTHSCHILD, M. L. and M. L. RAY (1973) Involvement and Political Advertising Effectiveness. Paper presented to the 1973 Conference of the American Association for Public Opinion Research, Asheville, N.C.

SAWYER, A. G. (1971) A Laboratory Experimental Investigation of the Effects of Repetition of Advertising. Ph.D. dissertation. Graduate School of Business, Stanford University.

––– (1972) The Effects of Repetition: Conclusions and Suggestions about Experimental Laboratory Research. Paper presented at the Association for Consumer Research/American Marketing Association Workshop on Consumer Information Processing, Chicago.

––– (1972) "The effect of repetition of refutational and supportive advertising appeals." Journal of Marketing Research 10: 23-33.

SILK, A. J. and T. VAVRA (1972) The Influence of Advertising's Affective Qualities on Consumer Response. Paper presented at the Association for Consumer Research/American Marketing Association Workshop on Consumer Information Processing, Chicago.

STRONG, E. C. (1972) The Effects of Repetition in Advertising: A Field Experiment. Ph.D. dissertation. Graduate School of Business, Stanford University.

ULE, G. M. (1966) "The Milwaukee Advertising Laboratory–Its Second Year." Proceedings of the 12th Annual Meeting of the Advertising Research Foundation. New York: Advertising Research Foundation.

WEICK, K. (1967) "Promise and limitations of laboratory experiments in the development of attitude change theory," in C. W. Sherif and M. Sherif (eds.) Attitude, Ego-Involvement and Change. New York: John Wiley.

WRIGHT, P. L. (1972) On The Direct Monitoring of Cognitive Response to Advertising. Paper presented at the Association for Consumer Research/American Marketing Association Workshop on Consumer Information Processing, Chicago.

Chapter 6

COORIENTATIONAL STATES AND INTERPERSONAL
COMMUNICATION

W. Barnett Pearce and Keith R. Stamm

WIENER'S (1954) DICTUM "to live effectively is to live with adequate information" focuses attention on the processes by which information moves to and from people. Some social structures are better than others at supplying contexts in which individuals obtain appropriate information, and certain persons in almost any organization are more adequately informed than others. Particularly in loosely structured relationships, interpersonal communication is an important source of information.

Exchanges of information between persons, however, are constrained by several factors. People do not address an equal number of messages to those equally accessible to them, nor is the type of messages the same in all communication relationships. These decisions about to whom and what to communicate may have important consequences both for individuals and their societies.

Jourard (1971) reported a tendency for people to conceal information about themselves, particularly information they perceive as making them vulnerable to exploitation by the other. Kelley (1951) and Cohen (1958) observed that upward communication in hierarchically-structured organizations contains disproportionately many positively evaluated messages (e.g., "everything is fine, I'm doing my job well") and few negatively evaluated messages (e.g., "I can't handle my job").

In a recent study of a campus strike, Pearce, Stamm, and Strentz (1971) found that both participants' and non-participants' choices of students with whom to talk about the strike brought them information disproportionately supportive of their own positions. As a result, the strikers and the "target population" of their persuasive and educational efforts (the non-strikers) differed drastically in their assessment of the success of the strike. Most of the strikers believed that they had effectively informed other students and the community about the issues of Vietnam and national priorities, but 60 percent of the non-participants reported that their group had not changed in knowledge or opinion, and an additional 14 percent felt that there had been a "backlash" against the strikers.

This paper reports our efforts to identify some of the conditions in which individuals decide whether and in what form to exchange information with others. Our focus is on communication acts per se—i.e., the seeking and giving of information—and their cognitive antecedents. The paradigm explicated in this article defines four cognitive states immediately preceding communication behavior. These states involve ways in which each person in a dyad perceives the similarity between himself and the other in their orientation toward the topic of their communication.

As we see it, the coorientational states identified by our model describe some of the cognitive processes involved in decisions about communication behavior in specific situations. But communication between members of a dyad may serve several purposes. We distinguish between communication by means of which the dyad accomplishes purposes external to their relationship.[1] We describe the former as "relationship" communication, and the latter as "task" communication.[2] Relatively pure forms of "relationship" communication occur in dyads whose continuation is based on factors unrelated to the individuals' current activities. For example, strangers in adjacent seats on a jet communicate differently from strangers who find themselves on a jury. Relatively pure forms of "task" communication are found in temporary dyads which exist only as long as the individuals are involved in interdependent activities, such as teacher-student, reporter-source, and doctor-patient dyads. This paper reports studies of communication behavior by persons in different coorientational states—some in situations involving "relationship" communication, and others "task" communication.

Based on our conceptualization of coorientation, we expect communication behavior to differ in the four coorientational states identified by our model. Further, we expect sequences of cognitive states to produce different forms of communication behavior in "relationship" and "task" situations.

Before presenting a detailed description of our model, we will discuss several types of models employed in the study of interpersonal communication. In this discussion, we hope to clarify how our model differs from other models of dyadic communication. This explication and the studies reported later demonstrate the unique appropriateness of a process model in answering the types of questions about communication behavior with which we are concerned.

MODELS OF INTERPERSONAL COMMUNICATION

Bergman (1966) differentiated three types of scientific theories: cross-sectional, equilibrium, and process. Each of these may be depicted by a model, and all three types have been employed in studies of interpersonal communication. It is important to note that there are inherent limitations in research based on any of these models.

Cross-sectional models are distinguished by the absence of a time order—either among the various states of the system described, or among the variables defined. If the phenomenon modeled is a process, as communication is generally conceived, cross-sectional models produce "snapshots" of process. They allow the observer to describe relations among a set of variables at a particular time. Thus, if the value of one variable is known, the value of all other variables at that time can be determined if the cross-sectional law connecting them is known.

Equilibrium models define the state of the variables in the system and specify an equilibrium rule connecting them. The equilibrium rule generally refers to some intervening drive (e.g., an aversion to dissonance or a strain toward symmetry) that explains the relationship. Thus, the equilibrium model makes predictions about states of the system at subsequent points in time (e.g., balanced or imbalanced), but attempts no temporal description of the processes of change.

A process model describes as well as predicts temporal change within a system. Such a model defines states of a system that are both necessary and sufficient for any other state of the system, which means that a causal state can be inferred from its effect and vice versa.

The Chaffee-McLeod (1968) coorientation model (from which we draw heavily) is a cross-sectional model. As shown in Figure 1, it defines an interpersonal state in terms of three general relations among the elements of the model: agreement, congruency, and accuracy. Computing these relations affords some diagnostic "snapshots" of the dyad, particularly when several observations made over a time interval are compared.

Selecting agreement as a criterion, an observer might conclude that "persuasion" has occurred if agreement increases from $time_1$ to $time_2$. (This is, as Chaffee, McLeod, and Guerrerro [1969] noted, a dubious but common inference.) Increases in accuracy may be used as evidence that communication between members of a dyad has occurred.

The utility of cross-sectional models of dyadic communication is limited, however. Comparing successive measures may locate changes in the state of the system, but the observer does not know how communication occurred in the intervals between measurements. This procedure results in a "black box" artifact in which changes are observed, and intervening conditions are inferred. As a result, the model may predict but cannot describe changes.

For example, we may predict that accuracy will change (become greater) when people who have high congruency and high agreement talk. The model, however, does not provide for observations of the talking (other than to say it occurred between $time_1$ and $time_2$), nor does it describe the processes by which talking led to change in accuracy.

The function of equilibrium models can best be seen by contrasting their explanatory power with that of cross-sectional models. Explanatory power is

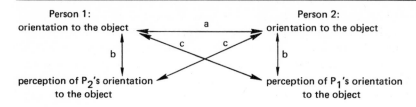

where agreement ("a") = comparison between P_1 and P_2's orientation toward the object;
congruency ("b") = comparison between P_1's orientation and his perception of P_2's orientation;
accuracy ("c") = comparison between P_1's perception of P_2's orientation and P_2's actual orientation

a. adapted from Chaffee and McLeod, 1968.

Figure 1: CHAFFEE AND MCLEOD'S CROSS-SECTIONAL MODEL OF COORIENTATION.[a]

gained by invoking an equilibrium rule—e.g., a "strain toward symmetry" (Newcomb, 1953)—which connects several states of the system. If a state of equilibrium (balance, homeostasis, congruency, etc.) does not exist at a given time, such rules predict that some change will occur to restore the system to equilibrium. Based on the forms which non-equilibrium takes, several states may be defined in a model (e.g., Heider, 1958).

While equilibrium rules represent an advance beyond cross-sectional models in accounting for the relationship between various states of the system, they do not specify any defined states in terms of temporal order. It may be argued that rules such as "strain for symmetry" or "dissonance-reduction" explain the connection between imbalanced and balanced states. However, the processes which occur between an imbalanced state and a balanced one still challenge both observation and theory.

An example of the distinction between an equilibrium model and a process model may be obtained by comparing Festinger's (1957) theory of cognitive dissonance with Carter's (1966) process model of cognitive discrepancies. Festinger's model postulates a drive state which connects all balanced (consonant) and unbalanced (dissonant) cognitions.[3] The inability of dissonance theory to cope with process is evidenced by the difficulty its proponents have had in distinguishing between conflict and dissonance. Festinger (1964) finally invoked a temporal sequence to serve as a distinguishing characteristic. He defines conflict as pre-decisional imbalance and dissonance as post-decisional imbalance.

By introducing the temporal orientation, Festinger made his original equilibrium model approximate a process model. Unfortunately, the distinction he suggested is wrong; Carter and Sweigert (1964) found that having made a decision is neither a necessary nor a sufficient condition for dissonance.

The process model of cognitive discrepancies (Carter, 1966), conversely, distinguishes between conflict and dissonance in terms of the temporal sequence of cognitive events in the system. Such a process model makes equilibrium rules superfluous. Instead of accounting for changes by invoking hypothesized drive states, the model describes the sequence of cognitive acts that generate the two specified states (conflict and dissonance). In addition, it leads one to observe what communication behaviors occur subsequent to cognitive discrepancies, rather than to search for forms of dissonance-reducing activity.

The Stamm-Pearce process model follows Carter's (1966) procedure of describing sequences of cognitive events as descriptors of coorientational states. Further, it suggests a paradigm in which the observed behavior, interpersonal communication, is a part of the process of coorientation.

COORIENTATIONAL STATES:
ANTECEDENTS OF COMMUNICATION BEHAVIOR

As recently expressed by Newcomb (1968), the coorientational approach in describing interpersonal behavior involves three factors: (1) the individual's desires, beliefs, and values; (2) his orientations toward objects in his environment; and (3) his relationships with other people. Further, for a dyad to be cooriented requires that a number of conditions be met. Chaffee (1971) concludes that cooriented dyads are rare—the exception rather than the norm.

However, meaningful applications of the coorientational approach may be made without assuming that all of the conditions specified by Chaffee are met (see, e.g., McLeod, 1971). Our model focuses on the individual, rather than the dyad, as the unit of analysis. By examining each person's behavior separately, usable data may be collected even from what Chaffee calls asymmetrically oriented dyads.[4]

We stipulate that an individual is in a *coorientational state* if he has an orientation which includes an object and a relevant other. "Orientation" may refer to cognitive (belief) and/or affective (liking) relationships—similar to Heider's (1958) distinction between unit and sentiment relations. Usually an orientation includes both. There are a number of conditions under which the other individual may be perceived as "relevant" to a person's orientations toward an object. The other may be perceived as facilitating or hindering the person's goals with respect to the object; as supporting or not supporting the individual's construction of reality; or as sharing a norm about a class of phenomena including the object.

In theorizing about interpersonal communication behavior, we make several assumptions.

First, we assume the basic premise of Newcomb's (1953) analysis of communication acts: that communication exchanges are determined by the individual's orientation to the object *and* by his relationship with the person to whom messages (if any) are addressed.

Second, we assume that two forms of relations between persons may be distinguished. On the one hand, each individual perceives the similarity or dissimilarity between his and the other's orientation toward the object. In addition, we are sometimes interested in relationships between the individuals exclusive of their orientations toward the object. For example, they may be employer-employee, peers working at a task requiring unanimous judgment, parent and child, or members of polarized groups. They may love, trust, feel superior to, or pity each other. As previously noted, the studies reported here are particularly concerned with differences between "relationship" and "task" communication.

Finally, we assume that a key process in dyadic behavior consists of juxtaposing current and past experience. This process is widely represented in the literature, including Carter's process model of cognitive discrepancies, the "hypothesis testing" in Miller, Galanter, and Pribrim's TOTE model (1960), the experiential factors in perception (Forgus, 1966), and concept formation (Bruner, Goodnow, and Austin, 1956). Although these processes often have been described, they have not been systematically employed in building a model of interpersonal communication.

The coorientation approach is broader than any particular model or study of coorientation—a fact pointed up by the diversity of papers appearing in a recent issue of *American Behavioral Scientist* (Chaffee and McLeod, eds., 1973).

The Stamm-Pearce model (see Figure 2) assumes measurement of three events in a specifiable context of person-to-person relations: the individual's orientation to the object (P_1 :0); the individual's perception of the other's orientation to the object (P_1 :[P_2 :0]); and the individual's discrimination of the other's actual orientation toward the object (P_2 :0).

Two derived variables are included in the model, congruency and accuracy. *Congruency* defines the *individual's judgment of the similarity between his and the other's orientation* toward the object. Accuracy occurs subsequent to and "includes" congruency. After receiving a message from the other, an individual makes a judgment about the other's orientation toward the object and compares this discrimination with his expectation of similar (or dissimilar) orientations.

These discriminations may represent considerable inferential leaps, and the juxtapositions may be surprising, of course. For example, longstanding political opponents may hear each other making casual remarks about pending legislation and infer, "Why, he *is* interested in environmental quality!" Juxtaposing this discrimination and their expectancies, they may conclude that they are much more similar in orientation to this issue, at least, than either previously believed. Our model suggests that we anticipate different forms of communication behavior in this case than if each discriminates a confirmation of his expectancy. *Accuracy* is thus defined as the *juxtaposition of a discrimination and an expectancy.*

Time:	1	2	3

Person 1's orienta-
tion to an object
$(P_1:0)$

Person 1's discrimi-
nation of person 2's
"actual" orientation
toward the object
$(P_2:0)$

a ⟶ c ⟶ b

↑
a
↓

Person 1's expecta-
tion of person 2's
orientation to the
object $P_1:(P_2:0)$

b

Where: a = congruency, or expected similarity. This may take the form of predicted agreement (PA) or predicted disagreement (PD);

b = discrimination of P_2's actual orientation;

c = accuracy, a justaposition of expected similarity and the discrimination. This may confirm (C) or disconfirm (D) the expectancy.

Example: P_1, who likes orchestra concerts, believes that P_2 does not enjoy concerts,
which produces a congruency state of predicted disagreement (PD). P_1
overhears P_2, however, discussing a recent concert with considerable exper-
tise and appreciation. P_1 discriminates from this that P_2 in fact does enjoy
concerts. Juxtaposing this discrimination against his expectancy, his accuracy state is predicted disagreement disconfirmed (PDD).

Possible Coorientational States:

Expectancy:	*Discrimination:*	*Coorientational State:*
agreement	agreement	PAC (predicted agree-ment confirmed)
agreement	disagreement	PAD (predicted agree-ment disconfirmed)
disagreement	disagreement	PDC (predicted disa-greement confirmed)
disagreement	agreement	PDD (predicted disa-greement disconfirmed)

Figure 2: CONGRUENCY AND ACCURACY IN THE PROCESS MODEL OF COORIENTATION.

For convenience, we have reduced congruency to a dichotomy: the individual
predicts agreement (PA) or disagreement (PD). Similarly, discriminations are
expressed as either confirming (C) or disconfirming (D) the expectation of
similarity. In the discussion of our studies, we will refer to the coorientational
states by the labels PAC, PAD, PDC, and PDD.

Fuller explanation of the model involves clarifying its differences from the
Chaffee-McLeod (1968) cross-sectional model. In addition to the differences

inherent in a process model (the inclusion of temporal sequence and the description as well as prediction of changes in the system), our model differs in perspective. Chaffee and McLeod describe a series of dyadic relations as they might appear to a third party, presumably a dispassionate observer (see Figure 1). While this perspective lends itself to use in diagnostic research designed to locate absence of communication, it confounds two of the relationships (see Figure 3).

Point of View:

Coorientational Relation	Observor	Actor
Agreement	dyadic	—
Congruency	monadic	dyadic
Accuracy	dyadic	monadic

Figure 3: AN EXPLICATION OF COORIENTATIONAL RELATIONS FROM TWO PERSPECTIVES.

Agreement (the comparison between P_1 and P_2's orientations) cannot be functional for the individual, since only the observer knows the orientations of both individuals. Similarly, accuracy as defined by Chaffee and McLeod is an observer's construct. It compares each person's perception of the other with the observer's measure of the other's "actual" orientation.

Only congruency describes a relation which represents a viewpoint experienced by the participants. Chaffee and McLeod minimized the importance of congruency, arguing (from their observer's viewpoint) that it is an intrapersonal—not a dyadic—relation.

For some purposes, viewing dyads from the perspective of an observer is useful (see Pearce, Stamm, and Strenz, 1971), but not for our present purpose, which is to specify the antecedent states of communication behavior. Our perspective is that of one member of a dyad cooriented with the other. Choosing this point of view necessitates redefining the coorientational relations identified by Chaffee and McLeod.

First, agreement is dropped: as a member of an interacting dyad, the individual can only know his own perceptions. He cannot know how the other "really" is oriented, although his perceptions may, happily, approach complete overlap with those of the other under some conditions (e.g., trust, unambiguity, and concurrent validation).

Second, congruency is strongly emphasized. In the process model, congruency is the criterion of expected similarity against which discriminations are juxtaposed.

Finally, accuracy becomes a relation which contains all of the information within the model. Defined from the participant's perspective, accuracy consists of the juxtaposition of a discrimination against a criterion.

An illustration may help. Consider a woman who thinks San Francisco might be a nice place to live, and also thinks her spouse would also enjoy moving there (congruency: predicted agreement re San Francisco). One day she hears her husband lamenting the ills of urban living, citing San Francisco as a case in point (discrimination: he doesn't view San Francisco as a good place to live).

By juxtaposing the criterion and the discrimination ("I guess I have been wrong about our agreeing that San Francisco is a nice place to live"), she arrives at an accuracy state of predicted agreement disconfirmed (PAD). Her subsequent behavior—both toward her husband and the San Francisco Chamber of Commerce—may be partly explained by these cognitive events.

SOCIAL RELATIONSHIPS: CONTEXT OF COMMUNICATION BEHAVIOR

While communication behavior is in part a function of the coorientational states defined by our model, it also differs in various social relationships between sources and receivers of messages. There is some evidence that people with different status, affiliation, and control relations generate messages with different frequency and form.

Watzlawick, Beavin, and Jackson (1967) note that both linguistic and non-verbal cues express speakers' perceptions of the relationship between themselves and the person addressed. Hulett (1966) describes ways in which unacceptable relational cues can disrupt communication.

In a previous paper (Pearce and Stamm, 1971), we attempted to incorporate social relationships in our process model of coorientation. Although we are not prepared to disavow that effort, we have not yet been able to operationalize those concepts.

However, we have deliberately designed studies which include a variety of social relationships between the members of cooriented dyads. Three of the studies reported here involve communication between peers, some in relatively pure "relationship" situations, some in relatively pure "task" situations, and some in a situation not well described by either. We also report two studies of communication in a "task" situation in which there is status incongruity.

COMMUNICATION BEHAVIOR IN COORIENTATIONAL STATES: SOME STUDIES

Our primary expectation in each of these studies is that communication behavior will differ when individuals are in different coorientational states. Since we are using a process model, we are able to observe and describe sequences of cognitive states and communication behavior. Because we have no a priori equilibrium rule, we neither can nor need to make specific "directional" hypotheses.

In addition, we expect that communication behavior in each coorientational state will differ when individuals are in different social relationships. Again, we refrain from making intuitive "directional" hypotheses in favor of predicting that there will be differences and letting the data describe the nature of the differences.

The procedures in each study are similar to those described in Stamm and Pearce (1971). Social relations were induced either by selection of subjects or by assigning them tasks. To operationalize our model of coorientational relations required (1) measuring each person's orientation toward the object; (2) measuring the person's perception of the other's orientation; (3) providing the person with unambiguous evidence of the other's actual orientation toward the object; and (4) monitoring the individual's communication behavior.

Communication Between Peers About Topics of Mutual Interest

The initial studies of information exchanging as a function of coorientational states involved peers (students in speech and journalism classes at the University of North Dakota) discussing topics of mutual interest, but about which the dyad had no assigned responsibilities. Topics were reading interests, selection of conversation topics, and preferred places to live. Dyads were formed by randomly pairing members of classes. These procedures created a social situation in which "relationship" communication could be assumed to occur.[5] These data, reported by Stamm and Pearce (1971), demonstrated that communication behavior was most frequent subsequent to the coorientational states in which expectancies were disconfirmed. Subjects in these studies were more likely to seek information than to give it. The most frequent type of message was a request for information about the other's orientation toward the topic. It occurred with greatest relative frequency when individuals inaccurately perceived agreement with the other member of the dyad (PAD).

The preference for questions in PAD may be interpreted as an attempt by subjects to determine why their expectations were wrong and to establish grounds for further discussion. Messages which gave the other information about the subject's own orientation toward the topic were most frequent when perceived agreement was confirmed (PAC) and least frequent when perceived disagreement was disconfirmed (PDD).

The disproportionately high number of comments in the PDD condition may relate to the unique nature of this state: the subject had failed to detect an area of agreement between himself and the other. The resulting embarrassment prompts him to offer reasons for his error.

The results of these studies support distinctions among coorientational states made by our model (but not those made by other approaches to dyadic relations). We are prepared to generalize that communication behavior among peers about topics similar to those used in these studies varies according to coorientational states (Stamm and Pearce, 1971). We wanted, however, to test the model in contexts other than the classroom and with social relations other than peers engaging in casual conversation.

We replicated our procedures using a natural status relationship (instructors and students) and a mutually relevant topic about which at least one member of the dyad must make decisions (an examination).[6] These procedures created a social situation with status variance in which task-oriented communication is likely.

In this study, we monitored the communication behavior of 83 students concerning a test their instructors had supposedly prepared and administered to them. It was designed to be a genuinely bad test with items that were ambiguous, "picky," or to which there was no correct answer.

During the class period subsequent to the one in which they took the test, the students were asked to list as many as six adjectives which they thought appropriately described the test, then to indicate whether they thought their instructor (ostensibly the author of the exam) would agree that each adjective was appropriate. After collecting these forms, the instructors wrote whether they agreed or disagreed with the student's judgment about the appropriateness of each adjective and returned the form to the student. Finally, we provided an opportunity for the students to address comments to their instructors.

Unlike the subjects in the studies of peer groups, students were considerably more likely to give information than to request it. Table 1 shows that 61 percent of the subjects made a comment, compared with only 23 percent of those in the earlier study. However, only 5 percent of these students asked their instructor a question, compared with 30 percent in the peer-dyads. As in the peer studies, however, comments occurred most frequently (92 percent) in the PDD condition and questions (18 percent) in the PAD state.

TABLE 1

COMMUNICATION BY STUDENTS IN COORIENTATIONAL STATES
TO THEIR INSTRUCTORS ABOUT AN EXAM[a]

Communication Behavior	Coorientational state								Σ	
	PAC		PAD		PDC		PDD			
	%	(f)	%	(f)	%	(f)	%	(f)	%	(f)
Questions	0	(0)	18	(3)	0	(0)	8	(1)	5	(4)
Comments	53	(23)	59	(10)	64	(7)	92	(11)	61	(51)
N	43		17		11		12		66	(83)

a. Statistical tests were not performed on these data because of the low cell frequencies for questions in all four conditions.

The data for the teacher-student dyads demonstrated an interaction between social relationship and coorientational states. The status difference between the subjects and/or the task-oriented nature of the communication somehow inhibited questions. Although this study cannot be directly compared with the earlier study, it demonstrated at least that information exchanges in various coorientational states do not always follow the pattern of the peer dyads.

A second study of status-incongruent coorientation was conducted by Schmidt (1972). It differed from the previous studies in three ways: (1) it was a field study rather than an experiment using "captive" subject pools in classrooms; (2) it measured the communication behavior of the "higher" status (parents) members rather than the "lows" (high school students); and (3) only some of the coorientational states were induced.

In the context of a major study of drug usage in the Grand Forks, North Dakota, high schools, Schmidt found evidence that considerable discrepancy existed between the percentage of students actually using drugs and the percentage which many parents believed were users. A questionnaire mailed to a randomly selected sample of parents of high school students asked parents to estimate the percentage of local high school students they believed used drugs. After recording their estimate, they were told the actual figure (31.4 percent) and asked what, if anything, they would like to ask or tell the students.

This procedure only approximated our model of coorientation because the object of the parent's orientation was the same as the group to whom they communicated—the students. Operationally, the congruency and accuracy states are defined uniquely in this study. Congruency was defined as P_1's feeling that his orientation toward P_2 was correct. Accuracy denoted a revised estimate of P_2's behavior, rather than a juxtaposition of two judgments of similarity.

Assuming that the parents began with the perception of correctly estimating student drug use, their estimates could either be confirmed as accurate (PAC) or inaccurate (PAD). Two types of inaccuracy were kept separate in the analysis— overestimation and underestimation of the extent of drug use among local high school students.

About 33 percent of the questionnairs were returned.[7] Of these, 31 declined to estimate the percentage of drug use. Table 2 shows the estimates made by the remaining 107 parents. Thirty-eight percent of the parents underestimated the extent of drug use. When told the actual percentage (one form of PAD), 73 percent made a comment and 93 percent asked a question. The bulk of the comments were advice-giving, while questions included general inquiries about the reasons why students use drugs and specific questions about the users' knowledge of the legal, emotional, moral, and physical aspects of drug use.

Forty-one percent of the parents correctly identified the range (25-50 percent) in which the actual percentage of users fell. When informed that they were correct (PAC), 77 percent made a comment (predominately advice-giving) and 89 percent asked a question. The most frequent questions were a general inquiry about why drugs were used; queries about the users' knowledge of legal, emotional, physical, and moral implications; and requests for information concerning drugs and drug usage.

Finally, 21 percent of the parents overestimated the extent of drug use (another form of PAD). When informed of the correct percentage 95 percent

TABLE 2

COMMUNICATION BY PATENTS IN COORIENTATIONAL STATES TO STUDENTS ABOUT DRUG USE[a]

Communication Behavior After Receiving Actual Figure (31.4%)	Parent's Prediction of Percent of Students Using Drugs						
	0%-5% % (f)	*5%-15%* % (f)	*15%-25%* % (f)	*25%-50%* % (f)	*50%-75%* % (f)	*75%-100%* % (f)	*don't know* % (f)
Comments	60 (3)	69 (9)	78 (18)	77 (34)	95 (18)	100 (3)	68 (21)
Questions	80 (4)	92 (12)	96 (22)	89 (39)	89 (17)	100 (3)	84 (26)
N	5	13	23	44	19	3	31

Communication Behavior	Coorientational States			
	PAD (underestimated) % (f)	*PAC* % (f)	*PAD (overestimated)* % (f)	
Comments	73 (30)	77 (34)	95 (21)	$x^2=4.21$[b]
Questions	93 (38)	89 (39)	91 (20)	$x^2=0.41$[c]
N	41	44	22	

a. Source: Schmidt, 1972.
b. $p < .20$, 2 df.
c. $p < .60$, 2 df.

made a comment (mostly advice) and 91 percent asked questions (mostly general inquiries about why students used drugs and requests for information about drugs and drug use).

Comparing the communication behavior in these three states reveals that equal proportions asked questions in each, but that comments were made more frequently when the expected level of drug use was greater than the actual drug use.

Because of the low return of the questionnaires and the difficulty of operationalizing coorientational states in a field study, it is difficult to compare these results with those in the previous studies. The most interesting and least risky comparison is with the teacher-student dyads which also involved status-incongruent relations. The latter study monitored the communication behavior of the "lows" and found a relative absence of questions, while Schmidt monitored "highs" and found a higher percentage of subjects exchanging messages and a tendency for more subjects to ask questions (91 percent) than to make comments (79 percent).

The behavior of subjects communicating to a different-status person supports our belief that communication is a function both of the person's coorientational state as defined by our model and of his social relationship with the other. On the basis of these studies, we conclude that the disconfirmatory states (PAD and PDD) are those most probable to induce an exchange of messages, but that the status relation and/or task orientation of the individuals are primary factors in determining whether they will offer or request information. These data also suggest the applicability of coorientational analysis to studies of information flow in complex organizations (see Mulder, 1960; Cohen, 1958; and Kelley, 1951).

Communication Between Polarized Groups

The above studies have been limited to social relations in which the members of dyads may be assumed to like each other or have a positive task orientation. Students obviously have a vested interest in helping their instructor write better tests; parents responding to a questionnaire are likely to be concerned about their children's use of drugs; and randomly assigned pairs of classmates probably have no reason not to cooperate with each other.

A study by Nightingale (1972) induced coorientational states and observed delegates to the Democratic and Republican (North Dakota) state conventions as they communicated with members of the John Birch Society. Recent political history in the locality (a strong bid for power which resulted in a virtual secession by the Society from the Republican's 18th District) and responses in the interviews indicated that the subjects disliked the John Birch Society and did not want it to succeed in its political activities. These data allowed us to examine types of communication behavior which occur in negative or non-supportive social relationships.

Polarization is a type of relationship which has important implications for social interaction. In the study of a campus strike, Pearce, Stamm, and Strentz (1971) defined polarization as one type of perceptual inaccuracy: exaggerating the differences between one's own orientations and those of another person or group. Nightingale (1972) was able to operationalize polarization in terms of the process model. The process is that the individual predicts that he and the other group disagree, but discovers that they in fact agree.[8] Based on this process definition, a group in which the member's perceptual errors are predominately PDD rather than PAD may be described as a polarized group.

Some features of Nightingale's procedure deserve further comment. The six political topics were ones on which the Society held varying positions: two with which they agreed, two about which they were neutral, and two with which they disagreed. Interviews with local leaders of the Society enabled Nightingale to describe their positions on a seven-point Likert-type scale.

Fifteen delegates from each party were randomly selected from the District 18 delegate list and were asked to describe (on seven-point Likert-type scales) their orientation toward each topic, including (1) their own belief, (2) those positions which they found unacceptable,[9] and (3) the position which they believed the John Birch Society endorsed. The respondents were then shown the "actual" John Birch Society position and given an opportunity to write questions or comments which would be delivered to the Society.

The spaces which the subjects had marked "unacceptable" became the basis for determining coorientational states. If a delegate estimated that the Society's position was represented by a response he marked "unacceptable," predicted disagreement (PD) was said to occur. If the Society's position was not described on a scale marked "unacceptable," predicted agreement (PA) was assumed. Confirmatory discriminations were identified on the basis of whether the Society's actual position was included or not included in the range of responses marked unacceptable.

As shown in Table 3, the predictions of both Democrats and Republicans about the John Birch Society's position on the topics were more often confirmed than disconfirmed, a result of both the accuracy with which the subjects perceived the Society's views and the rather stringent criterion for disconfirmation. Republicans' predictions were confirmed almost four times as often as disconfirmed. The Democrats were a little less accurate; their predictions were disconfirmed 27 percent of the time.

Some directional differences are important: Democrats whose predictions were disconfirmed were four times as likely to err by exaggerating the difference between themselves and the John Birch Society. This pattern of errors led Nightingale to describe the Democrats as more polarized with respect to the John Birch Society than the Republicans.

Significant differences were observed between the two groups in their communication behavior. Fewer Republicans asked questions (29 percent compared to 40 percent), but more made comments (65 percent compared to 47 percent)

TABLE 3

COMMUNICATION IN COORIENTATIONAL STATES BY
REPUBLICAN AND DEMOCRATIC CONVENTION DELEGATES
TO THE JOHN BIRCH SOCIETY ABOUT POLITICAL ISSUES[a]

Communication Behavior	*Coorientation State*								
	PAC		*PAD*		*PDC*		*PDD*		
	%	*(f)*	%	*(f)*	%	*(f)*	%	*(f)*	
Republicans									
Comments	70	(26)	71	(5)	48	(13)	60	(6)	$x^2=.95^b$
Questions	32	(12)	29	(2)	26	(7)	30	(3)	$x^2=.35^c$
N	37		7		27		10		
Democrats									
Comments	50	(5)	40	(2)	51	(26)	41	(7)	$x^2=.90^b$
Questions	20	(2)	20	(1)	43	(22)	47	(8)	$x^2=3.08^d$
N	10		5		51		17		

a. Source: Nightingale, 1972.
b. $p < .70$, 3 df.
c. $p < .90$, 3 df.
d. $p < .50$, 3 df.

than did Democrats. Republicans were more likely to make comments than to ask questions in any coorientational state except PDC. On the other hand, Democrats were more likely to ask questions than to make comments in any coorientational state other than PAD. Coorientational states per se, however, did not differentiate between frequencies of communication behavior.

An analysis of the content of the messages addressed to the Society revealed several differences in communication behavior. Although Democrats asked more questions than Republicans, both asked for information about the Birch Society (its attitudes on related subjects or specific reasoning processes) with about the same frequency as they asked about the topic. By far the most frequent form of behavior by Republicans consisted of telling the Society about the topic (42 percent), while Democrats told the Society about the topic with about the same frequency (29 percent) as they asked about the topic (26 percent) or about the Society (23 percent).

These data are not interpretable in terms of our model of coorientational states. Several factors may account for this. The most parsimonious interpretation of this study is in terms of the relative importance of social relations regardless of coorientational states. Given an intense relationship such as polarization or extreme dislike, surprising confirmations of agreement about specific topics might be less important than maintaining the relationship itself. Assuming that many of these subjects perceived Society members as politically influential in affecting the success of their own party's goals, delegates may have decided to seek or give information primarily as a persuasive device or as a means of discovering how much cooperation might be expected from the Society.

As a result of these studies, we had good reason to believe that social relationships affect types of communication behavior which occur in each coorientational state. Unfortunately, studies of status, incongruous dyads, and polarized groups inevitably confounded a number of variables in the social relationship. The primary purpose of our most recent study was to replicate our procedure while controlling the nature of the social relationship.

Communication and Coorientation Between Peers Required to Make a Unilateral or Mutual Decision

In our original test of the process model of coorientation (Stamm and Pearce, 1971), we used as subjects peers randomly assigned to dyads. The social situation required them to describe their own orientation and perception of the other's orientation toward some interesting but not immediately important topics. Subjects then exchanged descriptions of their respective orientations. Following the exchange of orientations, subjects were allowed (but not required) to exchange further messages related to *any* of the orientation situations in the experiment. The dependent variable was communication behavior. We interpreted their messages seeking or giving information as "relationship" communication because they had no immediate task which required coordinated activity.

This type of situation sometimes occurs, as do situations in which either the dyad or each individual separately has to make a decision about the topic of conversation. On the basis of our previous studies, we believed that introducing the constraint of having to make a decision (with the understanding that it would later be judged for correctness) would affect the pattern of information exchanges in various coorientational states.

This expectation is supported by results from other lines of research. Festinger (1950) and Vinokur (1971) reported that individuals who are forced to make decisions about ambiguous problems frequently compare information and judgments with others in their group.

In this study, we created two types of task-oriented situations, both requiring that subjects make a decision about the topic of communication, but differing on the basis of whether the decision was to be made unilaterally (by each person separately) or mutually (by both members of a dyad).

We interpret the resulting social relations as differing on the basis of "joint movement." Where each made his own decision, we expected subjects to use each other as information sources in an attempt to verify that they had made the correct decision. On the other hand, when the dyad had to achieve a mutual decision, we expected communication to serve an educational/persuasive function in the case of disagreement, or a socializing/expressive function in the case of agreement.

The interaction of coorientational states and these two movement conditions (unilateral or joint decision) have some implications for the behavior of the

	Coorientational States							
	PAC		PAD		PDC		PDD	
Factors:	Mutual	Unilateral	Mutual	Unilateral	Mutual	Unilateral	Mutual	Unilateral
Joint Movement Possible	Yes	Irrelevant	No	Irrelevant	No	Irrelevant	Yes	Irrelevant
Social Support for the Individual's Decision	Yes	Yes	No	No	No	No	Yes	Yes
Confirmation of Expectation About the Other's Orientation	Yes	Yes	No	No	Yes	Yes	No	No

Figure 4: THE IMPLICATIONS OF COORIENTATIONAL STATES IN TWO TYPES OF DECISION-MAKING SITUATIONS.

individual. The interactions are summarized in Figure 4. We turn now to explicating the implications of these interactions more fully.

In PAC, the individual discovers not only that he and the other agree about the topic but that he is correct in his perceptions of the other. In the unilateral decision condition, where the individuals are concerned about their own correctness, this is supportive. Similarly, the mutual decision subjects find that they both agree with and understand the other; there is no problem in joint movement toward a decision.

The PDD state is like PAC in that the individuals discover that they agree, but unlike PAC, the PDD discrimination is surprising and implies that the individual has inaccurately perceived the other's orientation. In the unilateral decision condition, this discrimination confers unexpected support for the individual's view. In the mutual decision condition, an anticipated problem in achieving unanimity is suddenly resolved. This coorientational state is quite different from PAC, although both involve dyads whose members "actually" agree.

In the PDC state, the individual discriminates that his perception of disagreement is correct. In the unilateral decision condition, the PDC state implies a lack of support for the individual's decision. In the mutual decision condition, the expected obstacle to joint movement is perceived as existing.

In the PAD state, the individual discriminates that his perception of the other was inaccurate and that the other disagrees with him. In the mutual decision treatment, this poses an unexpected barrier to joint movement and in both treatments is a surprising absence of support for the individual's own position.

Our hypothesis states that communication behavior will differ in the various coorientational states, and that behavior in each coorientational state will differ between subjects required to make mutual or unilateral decisions about the topic.

To test the hypothesis, we developed a protocol containing seven summaries of cases concerning some aspect of communication law.[10] Subjects developed a basis for predicting the other's decisions by comparing their "verdicts" on three "warm-up" cases. The next four cases comprised the experimental conditions. Subjects read each case, recorded their own decision and the decision they expected the other to make. Each subject was then shown the other's actual decision, given two minutes in which to communicate with the other (if he chose to), and then asked to record his final decision and his confidence in that decision.

Some subjects were told that they were required to reach a mutual decision. Others were instructed to reach the decision they personally thought best.

Subjects were 70 students in Communication 200 at Indiana University (36 in the mutual decision and 34 in the individual decision condition) and 52 students in Speech 101 at the University of North Dakota (38 in the mutual-decision and 14 in the individual decision condition).[11] All subjects were told that the exercise constituted a review of judicial decisions that would appear on an exam later in the course. We believe that all subjects perceived achieving a correct verdict as highly desirable.

As in the 1971 study, dyads were formed by randomly assigning members of classes together. To control the available channels of communication, subjects were seated back-to-back and told not to speak to each other. Messages were limited to exchanges of written notes.

North Dakota dyads tended to exchange more messages than the Indiana subjects, but the pattern of behavior was very similar. After this was determined, all analyses were based on combined data from both samples. The results show that communication behavior was significantly different in various coorientational states, and that patterns of communication behavior in various coorientational states differed depending on the social relationship within the dyad.

Both "task" oriented groups engaged in more information-giving than seeking. Sixty-two percent of the subjects in the mutual decision treatment made a comment, while 27 percent asked a question. Although subjects making a unilateral decision communicated less frequently, the pattern of communication behavior was the same: 52 percent made a comment and 19 percent asked a question. These data are quite unlike those from our previous study (Stamm and Pearce, 1971), in which subjects not required to make a decision sought information more frequently (57 percent) than they offered it (43 percent).

Comments were made most frequently in the PAD and PDC states (conditions in which there is disagreement between the members of the dyad), in both the mutual and unilateral decision treatments (see Table 4). Information-giving was more frequent in the mutual decision treatment (where it approached 100 percent) than in the unilateral decision treatment. There was also a large

TABLE 4
RELATIVE FREQUENCY OF COMMUNICATION
BEHAVIOR IN COORIENTATIONAL STATES

	PAC % (f)[a]	PAD % (f)	PDC % (f)	PDD % (f)	
Comments					
Mutual Decision	47 (75)	91 (78)	95 (20)	38 (11)	x^2=62.10[b]
N	159	86	21	29	
Unilateral Decision	47 (56)	59 (22)	72 (13)	47 (8)	x^2= 4.81[c]
N	118	37	18	17	
No Decision	20 (89)	25 (20)	22 (10)	51 (20)	x^2=14.99[b]
N	438	81	45	39	
Questions					
Mutual Decision	18 (29)	41 (35)	38 (8)	24 (7)	x^2=15.33[b]
N	159	86	21	29	
Individual Decision	16 (19)	14 (5)	44 (8)	29 (5)	x^2= 9.90[b]
N	118	37	18	17	
No Decision	22 (97)	73 (59)	29 (13)	33 (13)	x^2=58.38[b]
N	438	81	45	39	

a. Frequency denotes the number of persons in a particular coorientational state who engaged in the specified form of behavior, not necessarily the total number of messages sent. If one person wrote 5 comments and 1 question and four others wrote nothing, **both** comments and questions would be scored % = 20, f = 1, N = 5.
b. $p < .05$.
c. $.20 > p > .0$.

difference between frequency of comments in the PDC (72 percent) and PAD (59 percent) states in the unilateral treatment which did not appear among mutually-deciding subjects. Differentiating among coorientational states did explain the differences in the frequency of information-giving in the mutual decision ($p < .05$) but not in the unilateral decision ($.20 < p < .10$) condition.

In the unilateral condition, questions were asked most frequently (44 percent) in the PDC state and least frequently (16 percent and 14 percent) in PAC and PAD. In the mutual decision treatment, most questions were asked in the PAD and PDC states (41 percent and 38 percent, respectively). In both decision conditions, the number of questions asked varied across coorientational states ($p < .05$).

Neither of these patterns of behavior approximated that by subjects in the no-decision treatment. These subjects made disproportionately many comments in the PDD state and asked disproportionately many questions in PAD.

As shown in Table 5, the proportion of questions to comments was about the same in each coorientational state in both the unilateral and mutual decision conditions. This was not true of the no-decision study.

It is not difficult to understand why subjects required to make a decision communicated most frequently in the PAD and PDC states. Since it implies disagreement, the discrimination does not provide consensual support for the

TABLE 5
RELATIVE FREQUENCY OF QUESTIONS AND
COMMENTS IN COORIENTATIONAL STATES

	PAC		PAD		PDC		PDD		
	%	(f)	%	(f)	%	(f)	%	(f)	
Mutual Decision									
Questions	28	(29)	31	(35)	29	(8)	39	(7)	$x^2 = .87^a$
Comments	72	(75)	69	(78)	71	(20)	61	(11)	
N	104		113		28		18		
Unilateral Decision									
Questions	25	(19)	19	(5)	38	(8)	38	(5)	$x^2 = 3.26^a$
Comments	75	(56)	81	(22)	62	(13)	62	(8)	
N	75		27		21		13		
No Decision									
Questions	52	(97)	75	(59)	57	(13)	39	(13)	$x^2 = 16.00^b$
Comments	48	(89)	25	(20)	43	(10)	61	(20)	
N	186		79		23		33		

a. $p > .05$, n.s.
b. $p < .05$.

individual's judgment about the case and—in the mutual-decision treatment—poses a barrier to joint movement. It is likely that the bulk of this communication is instrumental in persuading/educating the other, while in PAC and PDD it is largely socializing/expressive. If subjects took our social setting seriously, the former may well have been perceived as mandatory but the latter optional.

The data do pose two problems for interpretation. First, it is not clear why the preferred communication behavior in PAD differed between mutual and unilateral decision conditions. Second, we wonder why the patterns of communication in these task-oriented social settings differed in the ways they did from the no-decision treatment. In both mutual and unilateral decision treatments, comments were preferred to questions, but mutually-deciding subjects made about the same number of comments and questions in PDC as in PAD.

Unilaterally-deciding subjects, however, made considerably fewer comments and asked more questions in PAD than in PDC. In the no-decision treatment, questions occurred most frequently in PAD, which is similar to the mutual but unlike the unilateral decision condition. Comments in the no-decision condition occurred most frequently in PDD. In contrast, both mutually- and unilaterally-deciding subjects made fewest comments in this same condition.

To account for these results—strictly on a post hoc basis—we turn to some recent theorizing by Carter. Based on a principle of singularity (which posits that actions by an entity occur one at a time), Carter (1972a) describes "pictures" (cognitive orientations) as they are held by individuals and groups. The process of decision-making, Carter says, is an invented procedure designed to produce a shared picture with a single implication. Concerted action by a group cannot occur unless the members have a similar picture, and the picture must neither lack an implication nor imply more than one course of action for the same time and place.

Applied to our research, these concepts suggest that where the members of a dyad combine pictures, then discover more than one implication for action (e.g., inaccuracy or disagreement), we may expect communication behaviors designed to achieve the singularity needed for individual or mutual movement. Two points in particular are relevant to our research. First, the communication procedures which are useful in producing a cognitive orientation with singular implication for an individual in a unilateral decision situation may not be the same as those most useful for a collectivity in a mutual decision situation. Second, the accuracy states defined by our model have different implications for decision behavior depending upon whether the individual is acting autonomously or as part of a group (in this case, a dyad).

Consider the inaccuracy state of perceived agreement disconfirmed (PAD). Based on our analysis of the implication of coorientational states (summarized in Figure 4), we assume that the communication behavior in PAD reflects some combination of (1) socialization/expressive communication, (2) reactions to the disconfirmation of expectations about the other's orientation, (3) the lack of support for the individual's position and—in the mutual decision treatment—(4) attempts to achieve joint movement. Apparently, some factor inhibits communication behavior in PAD for unilaterally-deciding subjects in comparison with mutually-deciding subjects. As shown in Figure 4, PAD is most similar to PDC in terms of its implications for the subjects, and, as we expected, communication behavior in these states was more alike than if either were compared to PAC or PDD. By contrasting the implications of these states, it may be possible to account for the observed differences in communication behavior.

Assuming that the need to discover why the other disagrees and to achieve consensual support by persuasion/education is comparable in PAD and PDC, the difference in communication behavior for unilaterally-deciding subjects involves socialization/expressive communication. Apparently, the disconfirmation of expected agreement inhibits both information-seeking and information-giving when subjects are required to make a unilateral decision about the topic.

Perhaps the best explanation of this phenomenon is that subjects avoid messages which might create a picture with multiple implications; to retain confidence in their decision, many subjects refrain from communicating with the other. (This is not the most rational behavior, of course, but people often do not follow optimum strategies. See, for example, Vinacke, 1969.)

This explanation is tentative at best, but gains some support from the analysis of the subjects' confidence in their decisions (Table 6). Subjects[12] in the mutual decision treatment, where communication in PAD and PDC was very similar, differed only slightly in confidence. The means were 2.13 for PAD and 2.18 for PDC (where 1 = very confident and 5 = very unconfident). However, in the

TABLE 6

CONFIDENCE IN VERDICTS BY COORIENTATIONAL STATE

Treatment	PAC	PAD	PDC	PDD
Mutual Decision[a]	1.31[b]	2.13	2.18	1.92
Unilateral Decision	1.93	2.00	3.00	1.50

a. Subjects included the University of North Dakota sample only.
b. Cell values are means. Raw scores ranged from 1 to 5, where 1 = very confident, and 5 = very unconfident.

unilateral decision condition (where less communication occurred in PAD than PDC), subjects in PAD were more confident (2.00) than those in PDC (3.00). Perhaps subjects in the unilateral decision condition believed that communicating with the other—who surprisingly disagreed—would threaten their own confidence. This would account for their less frequent communication behavior, particularly the low incidence of questions.

The inhibition of communication in the PAD state for subjects in the unilateral decision condition is surprising when compared to the no-decision condition, in which questions occurred most frequently (73 percent) in the PAD state. This suggests that questions are a preferred behavior in the PAD state when communication serves a relational function for the dyad. But questions are avoided when each member of the dyad is communicating to reach his own individual decision.

In the no-decision treatment, a disproportionate number of comments were made in the PDD condition. Subjects who had to make a decision, however, made about the same number of comments in PDD and PAC—many fewer than in either PAD or PDC. These data may indicate that comments are a preferred behavior in the PDD state when communication serves a relational function for the dyad, but not when the dyad communicates in order to achieve joint movement.

Earlier studies have documented the importance of inaccuracy (PAD; PDD) as an antecedent of communication behavior (Stamm and Pearce, 1971). The social conditions created by our manipulations of decision requirements altered this effect somewhat. In this study, communication varied primarily as a function of disagreement (PAD; PDC) with the other—a phenomenon understandable on the basis of the task assignment. But disagreement did not explain all the findings. Communication behavior in disagreement conditions was inhibited by inaccuracy (PAD) in the unilateral decision condition.

CONCLUSION

The initial purpose of the research program we have described has been to determine whether the coorientational states distinguished by our model can reveal previously undetected patterns of communication behavior. Against this criterion, the model has proved satisfactory in a variety of contexts. While it is true that coorientational states interact with social relationships in still unexplained ways, the model has yielded a new body of findings which has extended our knowledge of dyadic communication.

The findings we have reported indicate subtle differences in the processes of information exchange between peers as a function of coorientational states. Messages between peers are most likely when inaccuracy is discovered (either misperceived agreement or disagreement), provided that the subjects do not have to make a decision about the topic.

When decisions are required, the type and frequency of communication behavior changes. Information giving is the most frequent means employed to resolve interpersonal disagreement, particularly in the presence of a constraint for joint movement. Discovering inaccuracy—particularly that perceived agreement does not exist between persons required to make unilateral decisions—seems to inhibit communication. Information-giving rather than information-seeking is the preferred mode of communication in task-oriented situations. In situations in which peers have no task, information-seeking and giving are roughly proportional.

Our data show the inapplicability of cross-sectional or equilibrium models in accounting for communication behavior. Our model combines an analysis of intrapersonal cognitive states (following Carter, 1966) and interpersonal similarity (following Newcomb, 1953, and Chaffee and McLeod, 1968). It structures these variables in terms of process, which allows us to describe cognitive states and communication behavior in temporal sequence.

NOTES

1. We do not mean to imply that these are discrete categories. Some messages serve both functions. For example, if a task-oriented message between co-workers implies an unacceptable definition of their relationship, (e.g., "No, stupid, the answer is number 2"), the dyad may suddenly switch from communication which is primarily instrumental in reaching external goals to communication concerning the nature of their relationship. Extreme types of each are identifiable, and these differ in important respects.

2. Granted, the "task" of a dyad in some situations is to establish a workable relationship. However, these labels serve our purpose if "relationship" is understood to denote factors intrinsic, and "task," factors extrinsic, to the dyad.

3. Festinger defined an imbalanced state and then reified it in the form of a drive state. The stipulation of a drive to reduce dissonance cannot be considered an analytic statement since the drive is viewed as a potentially observable phenomenon. However, most attempts to observe directly the aversion to dissonance have been unsuccessful (see Cronkhite, 1966).

4. As Chaffee (1971) noted, this approach generates a kind of theory different from his. We believe that it has the advantage of being generalizable to asymmetrical dyads, which Chaffee concedes to be the predominant type.

5. These procedures will later be called the "no decision" treatment.

6. The subjects were students in several sections of Speech 101 (Fundamentals of Public Speaking) at the University of North Dakota. The instructors were Mr. Stewart Michael Sharp (now at Clinical Research Department, Sandoz Pharmaceutical Company, Hanover, New Jersey) and Mr. Tom Haller (now at Purdue University).

7. The low return rate was not critical in this study, since a test of the relationships involved does not require a random sample. There is no intent to say that the views expressed by these parents are representative of the population. A more serious question is whether people who respond to mailed questionnaires communicate differently from those who do not. It seems likely that they do—at least in terms of total communication. The specific question in this study is whether those parents who did return the questionnaire communicated differently depending on the coorientational state they were in.

8. Polarization has been defined in a number of ways. Our definition is unlike some common uses. Note that it is the person making the perceptual mistake, not the group which he is perceiving, who is said to be polarized. Note also that absolute magnitude of the difference between groups is unrelated to polarization. The subject who correctly perceived a difference (PDC) is *not* considered polarized. The criterion is a directional error in perception.

9. Following Sherif and Hovland's (1961) analysis, and procedures described by Sherif, Sherif, and Nebergall (1965).

10. Although these studies are directly comparable in terms of subject population and general procedures, one important aspect of the "decision" treatments deserves comment. We asked subjects to make judgments about legal cases, a situation in which there might be strong pressures to be correct. Carter (1972b) suggested that evidence of disagreement about a point of law may prompt more communication behavior (in an attempt to insure that one's opinion is correct) than a disagreement about topics such as those we used in the earlier study (reading interests, characteristics of good places to live, interesting communication topics). His observation suggests two possible explanations for differences between these studies: the necessity to make a decision, and the strength of the need to be correct (as evaluated by some external criterion) about the topic. The effect of either or both of these factors, however, enables us to describe the social conditions as different along the lines indicated by our discussion of "task" and "relationship" communication.

11. The number of subjects in the four conditions is not balanced. An adequate test of the hypothesis did not require a balanced design. This allowed the economy of using intact

classes as experimental groups. The classes were randomly assigned to unilateral and joint-decision conditions. Also, individuals were randomly assigned to dyads as a means of randomizing the assignment to coorientational states.

12. These data were gathered from the University of North Dakota sample only.

REFERENCES

BERGMAN, G. (1966) The Philosophy of Science. Madison: University of Wisconsin Press.

BRUNER, J., J. GOODNOW, and G. AUSTIN (1956) A Study of Thinking. New York: John Wiley.

BYRNE, D. (1971) The Attraction Paradigm. New York: Academic Press.

CARTER, R. (1966) Cognitive Discrepancies and Communication Behavior. Paper presented to the Association for Education in Journalism convention, Iowa City.

——— (1971) Theoretic Developments in the Use of Signaled Stopping. Paper presented to the Association for Education in Journalism convention, Columbia, S.C.

——— (1972a) A Journalistic View of Communication. Paper presented to the Association for Education in Journalism convention, Carbondale, Ill.

——— (1972b) Personal Communication.

CARTER, R., and R. SWEIGERT (1964) "Rehearsal dissonance and selective information seeking," in W. A. Danielson (ed.) Paul J. Deutschmann Memorial Papers in Mass Communication Research. Cincinnati: Scripps-Howard Research.

CHAFFEE, S. (1971) Pseudo-data in Communication Research. Paper presented to the Association for Education in Journalism convention, Columbia, S.C.

CHAFFEE, S., and J. McLEOD (1968) "Sensitization in panel design: a coorientational experiment." Journalism Quarterly 45: 661-669.

——— (eds.) (1973) Communication and Interpersonal Perception, special issue of the American Behavioral Scientist.

CHAFFEE, S., J. McLEOD, and J. GUERRERO (1969) Origins and Implications of the Coorientational Approach in Communication Research. Paper presented to the Association for Education in Journalism convention, Berkeley.

COHEN, A. (1958) "Upward communication in experimentally created hierarchies." Human Relations 11: 41-53.

CRONKHITE, G. (1966) "Toward a real test of dissonance theory." Quarterly Journal of Speech 52: 172-178.

FESTINGER, L. (1950) "Informal social communication." Psychological Review 17: 271-282.

——— (1957) A Theory of Cognitive Dissonance. Palo Alto: Stanford University Press.

——— (1964) Conflict, Decision and Dissonance. Palo Alto: Stanford University Press.

FORGUS, R. (1966) Perception. New York: McGraw-Hill.

HEIDER, F. (1958) The Psychology of Interpersonal Relations. New York: John Wiley.

HULETT, E. J., Jr. (1966) "A symbolic interactionist model of human communication, Part two: The receiver's function; Pathology of communication; Noncommunication." Audio-Visual Communication Review 14: 203-220.

JOURARD, S. (1971) The Transparent Self. 2nd ed. New York: Van Nostrand.

KELLEY, H. (1951) "Communication in experimentally created hierarchies." Human Relations 4: 39-56.

McLEOD, J. (1971) Issues and Strategies in Coorientation Research. Paper presented to the Association for Education in Journalism convention, Columbia, S.C.

MILLER, G., E. GALANTER, and K. PRIBRIM (1960) Plans and the Structure of Behavior. New York: Holt.

MULDER, M. (1960) "The power variable in communication experiments." Human Relations 13: 241-256.

NEWCOMB, T. (1947) "Autistic hostility and social reality." Human Relations 1: 69-86.

——— (1953) "An approach to the study of communicative acts." Psychological Review 60: 393-404.

——— (1968) "Interpersonal balance," pp. 28-51 in R. Abelson et al. (eds.) Theories of Cognitive Consistency. Chicago: Rand McNally.

NIGHTINGALE, J. (1972) Polarization and Communication: An Analysis of Coorientational States as Antecedent Conditions of Communication Behavior with the John Birch Society. Unpublished M.A. thesis, University of North Dakota.

PEARCE, W. B., and K. STAMM (1971) Coorientation States as Antecedents to Communication Behavior: A Process Model of Person-Object and Person-Person Relations. Paper presented to the Association for Education in Journalism convention, Columbia, S.C.

PEARCE, W. B., K. STAMM, and H. STRENTZ (1971) "Communication and polarization during a campus strike." Public Opinion Quarterly 35: 228-234.

ROKEACH, M. (1960) The Open and Closed Mind. New York: Basic Books.

SCHMIDT, K. (1972) Attitudes, Beliefs and Communication About Drugs: A Coorientation Analysis. Unpublished paper, University of North Dakota.

SHERIF, M., and C. HOVLAND (1961) Social Judgment: Assimilation and Contrast Effects in Communication and Attitude Change. New Haven: Yale University Press.

SHERIF, M., C. SHERIF, and R. NEBERGALL (1965) Attitude and Attitude Change. Philadelphia: Saunders.

STAMM, L., and W. B. PEARCE (1971) "Communication behavior and coorientational relations." Journal of Communication 21: 208-220.

SULLIVAN, H. S. (1953) The Interpersonal Theory of Psychiatry. New York: Norton.

VINACKE, W. E. (1969) "Variables in experimental games." Psychological Bulletin 71: 293-318.

VINOKUR, A. (1971) "Review and theoretical analysis of the effects of group processes upon individual and group decisions involving risk." Psychological Bulletin 76: 231-250.

WATZLAWICK, P., J. BEAVIN, and D. JACKSON (1967) Pragmatics of Human Communication. New York: Norton.

WIENER, N. (1954) The Human Use of Human Beings. 2nd ed. Garden City, N.Y.: Anchor Books.

Chapter 7

INSTRUMENTAL UTILITIES AND INFORMATION SEEKING

Charles Atkin

A SIMPLE ACT of mass media exposure can be traced to a complex set of determinants involving the needs of the receiver and attributes of the message. This paper examines information seeking for utilitarian purposes, where an individual acquires message content as a means toward solving his practical problems.

A message has instrumental utility for the receiver when it provides him with a helpful input for responding to everyday environmental stimuli or for defending personal predispositions. He may need information to keep abreast of governmental actions, to guide his consumer decision-making, or to reinforce his political preferences. These types of informational needs generate extrinsic motivation to seek messages from mass media sources.

Message selection may also be based on non-instrumental considerations, such as personal interest in the subject matter or entertainment value of the material. In these cases, the individual derives consummatory gratifications in the form of intrinsic satisfaction during exposure, but he does not directly apply the content to problem-solving. Analysis of exposure for this purpose is beyond the scope of the present paper.

This report presents evidence regarding several extrinsic determinants of information seeking, focusing on the needs for reinforcing information. In a detailed examination of the selective exposure issue, preference for supportive messages is assessed in the context of other instrumental information seeking strategies.

BASIC CONCEPTS IN INSTRUMENTAL INFORMATION SEEKING

Before considering the research evidence, several key concepts must be described. A general model of the overall message selection process will be presented at the end of the chapter. Briefly, this model predicts that an individual will select a mass media message when he estimates that the message reward value exceeds the expenditures incurred in obtaining it. Instrumental utility is one major component of reward value.

Figure 1 outlines the basic factors contributing to the instrumental utility of a message. Most of the conceptualization will focus on the antecedents of the individual's informational needs. This will be followed by a discussion of message content attributes and the expenditure concept.

The *need for information* is a function of extrinsic uncertainty produced by a perceived discrepancy between the individual's current level of certainty about important environmental objects and a criterion state he seeks to achieve.

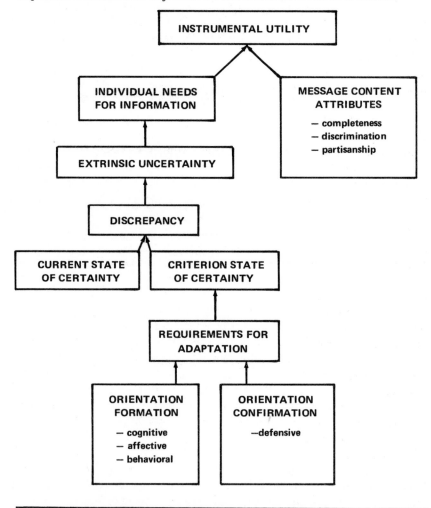

Figure 1: CONTRIBUTIONS TO INSTRUMENTAL UTILITY.

Information is defined in terms of cognitive uncertainty; it represents something that the receiver does not already know. An environmental object is a concept, event, thing, or person that exists psychologically for the individual, and an attribute is any quality that the object can possess to some degree.

Uncertainty is the key concept in this paradigm. For a given object, the individual's level of knowledge varies along a continuum from total uncertainty to total certainty. The basic building blocks contributing to increased certainty are cognitions. These are discrete pieces of knowledge about the existence of an object, the nature of its attributes, or its relations with other objects.

A primitive cognitive uncertainty arises when the individual perceives an insufficient level of knowledge about an object after reprocessing stored cognitions from previous experience. Acquisition of external information from a message automatically reduces the individual's knowledge gap, following the technical information theory approach (Shannon and Weaver, 1949).

Most types of practical problem-solving involve more complex cognitive processes than a simple gain in knowledge about an object. The individual usually wants to combine cognitions to form an attitude or to direct behavior. He is "uncertain" in the conventional sense of being unsure about making a decision or performing an act. Or, he may be doubtful about the appropriateness of a particular attitude.

A complex cognitive uncertainty occurs when existing cognitions are inadequate for responding to these situations that require orientations, decisions, or performances involving one or more objects. This higher-order uncertainty then generates primitive cognitive uncertainty, and it may be reduced by acquiring information.

Although complex uncertainty roughly parallels the more mechanical uncertainty concept, there is one important difference. Informational inputs that reduce primitive uncertainty may occasionally increase complex uncertainty, as when new knowledge about object attributes makes it more difficult to discriminate between objects in a choice situation.

Extrinsic uncertainty encompasses those primitive and complex uncertainty states generated by a lack of knowledge concerning anticipated adaptive responses or psychological adjustments to previous behavioral, affective, or cognitive activities. The magnitude of this uncertainty depends on the extent to which current knowledge falls short of optimum certainty.

Since the individual's range of knowledge is severely limited, there is a wide variety of uncertainties that he can perceive. His extrinsic uncertainties are channeled toward particular objects by requirements for adaptation to everyday environmental and psychological problems.

The importance of an adaptive requirement to the individual's satisfaction serves to define his *criterion level of certainty*. This combines with his current level of certainty to determine a discrepancy state. The discrepancy then produces extrinsic uncertainty, which is expressed in terms of implicit or explicit "questions" about environmental objects. The individual may ask himself,

"Which product is best?", or, "Am I supporting the right candidate?" These questions may be activated by a message cue encountered during routine mass media scanning activity, or may be due to prior internal or external instigation or problem-solving.

Types of Adaptation

In this tentative conceptualization, there are four basic types of adaptation requirements that impel the individual toward extrinsic uncertainty. These progress along a cognitive-affective-behavioral continuum, and they involve both formation and confirmation requirements. In each category, two or three specific kinds of uncertainty will be identified. In later sections of the paper, most of these uncertainty states are discussed and assessed with empirical evidence.

Cognitive adaptation. To the extent that an individual perceives that environmental objects may personally affect him, he will want to achieve a criterion level of awareness and understanding of them. (He may also want to interpret internal responses of varying significance to him.) Basically, the individual desires to formulate precise cognitive orientations toward those stimuli that potentially or currently impinge on his well-being. This type of goal helps define specific states of awareness uncertainty or understanding uncertainty that produce the need for surveillance information.

Affective adaptation. The individual may feel it is important to form an affective disposition toward an object, such as an attitude, value, opinion, emotion, or formal decision. When he is faced with an object and wants to be sure how to relate to it in a correct or socially appropriate manner, evaluative uncertainty arises. In a choice situation, decisional uncertainty varies to the extent that a choice between objects is crucial to the individual and he is unable to distinguish satisfactorily between various alternatives. These uncertainties generate a need for guidance information.

Behavioral adaptation. In terms of overt behavior, the individual may lack the knowledge to accomplish a particular action sequence successfully. As the importance of the anticipated behavior increases, he desires a more certain idea of how to implement the action. Several specific types of goal states can be identified, and these define communicatory uncertainty, enactment uncertainty, and task uncertainty, when considered relative to his current level of knowledge. In each case, the uncertainty creates a need for performance information.

Defensive adaptation. When the individual is committed to a particular cognitive orientation, he may want to be certain that it is valid. Post-cognitive uncertainty depends on the magnitude of the desire to verify cognitions currently in storage or recently learned. Similarly, the individual may not be confident that his firmly held attitudes or decisions are correct or appropriate. Here, his perceived requirements for adaptation vary with the centrality of the affect and contribute to post-affective uncertainty. In some instances, he may be eager to learn how well he performed a behavior, defining a goal state of knowledge that helps to determine post-performance uncertainty. Each of these uncertainties resulting from self-doubt produces a need for reinforcement information.

In order to reduce extrinsic uncertainty, the individual obtains and processes messages in the mass media. A message is a shared-meaning symbolic abstraction referring to environmental objects which is transmitted into a channel. Mass media messages may have informational value for the individual, depending on such qualities as object-attribute completeness, multi-object discriminability, and partisanship of object valuation, along with veracity and refutability. Most research has focused exclusively on the object valence dimension, assessing the relationship between audience predispositions toward an object and the partisanship of the message presentation.

These message content attributes combine with the individual's informational needs to define the instrumental utility of the message. When he estimates that a message will be helpful in resolving his extrinsic uncertainty, this contributes to the overall reward value of the message. However, reward value must be balanced against the expenditures involved in message handling activity.

The expenditure concept relates the cost attributes of the message to the resources of the individual. His resources can be delineated in terms of money, time, energy, and mental ability; cost attributes include monetary expense, length, comprehensibility, signal clarity, prominance, and accessibility.

These factors determine the seeking expenditures incurred both in obtaining and in processing the message. In cases where an unrewarding message is highly available and obtrusive, however, an expenditure of resources may be necessary to avoid obtaining it.

All of these determinants contribute to both the amount and the nature of message selection. Most of the research presented here deals with amount of exposure, defined simply as the number of messages and the length of exposure to each message. The nature of exposure patterns is examined only along the qualitative dimension of supportiveness. This is the degree to which the object valence of a message is consonant or discrepant with existing attitudes, decisions, and behaviors.

This report presents empirical evidence regarding several extrinsic determinants of information seeking, and explores the extent and conditions of supportive information preferences. The data base includes new findings from recent research investigations, secondary analyses of previously collected data, and compilations of relevant results from a number of published studies examining mass media consumption.

SOURCES OF EMPIRICAL EVIDENCE

Most of the research data is derived from nine studies conducted by the author at Michigan State University and the University of Wisconsin. Occasionally, there are extended references to data collected by other researchers.

Rather than describe the background of a particular study each time it is mentioned in the report, the key investigations are briefly outlined here.

Political Panel Study. In-class questionnaires were administered to 319 available underclassmen at Michigan State University and Colorado State University in two waves during October and November 1972. The investigation focused on the role of mass communication in the political socialization of college students. The study is described in Atkin, Galloway, and Nayman (1973).

Democratic Convention Study. (This study is fully reported in Atkin, Galloway, and Nayman [1973].) Telephone interviews were conducted with a systematic sample of 213 adult voters drawn from the Lansing telephone directory during July 1972. The study dealt with the determinants and effects of television exposure to the Democratic National Convention.

Political Advertising Study. During the 1970 gubernatorial campaigns in Wisconsin and Colorado, telephone interviews were conducted with 512 voters systematically selected from the Madison, Wisconsin, area telephone directory and the Larimar County, Colorado, voter registration list. This investigation of the determinants and effects of exposure to televised spot advertising is reported in Atkin, Bowen, Nayman, and Sheinkopf (1973), and Sheinkopf, Atkin and Bowen (1973).

Presidential Primary Study. Telephone interviews were conducted with 342 Michigan State student voters systematically drawn from the list of registered students. The study basically assessed mass media exposure and voting behavior during the 1972 Presidential preference primary election campaign in Michigan and is described in Atkin, Crouch, and Troldahl (1973).

City Council Study. In November 1971, 165 Michigan State student voters sampled systematically from university registration lists were interviewed by telephone concerning their mass media exposure and voting behavior in a local city council election. This examination of the initial exercise of the 18-year-old vote is presented in Atkin, Crouch, and Troldahl (1973).

Party Worker Study. Mail questionnaires were completed by 160 Republican and Democratic party activists during the 1970 gubernatorial contest in Wisconsin. County chairmen and subordinates from across the state were asked about the role of political advertising in their campaign activities. Data from this investigation appear in Sheinkopf, Atkin, and Bowen (1972, 1973).

Abortion Information Study. A total of 285 female students from a systematically drawn sample of Michigan State females returned mail questionnaires during a May 1972 survey. This pilot study by Rogers and Atkin (1972) primarily measured knowledge, attitudes, experiences, and information sources on the topic of abortion.

Four-day Work-week. Two-waves of self-administered questionnaires were obtained from 100 manufacturing workers in a Denver plant in 1971 and 1972. Changes in patterns of mass media usage and leisure pursuits after conversion to a four-day work-week were examined in this survey, presented in Nayman, Atkin, and Gillette (1973).

Message Availability Study. Interviewers telephoned 122 Madison voters selected systematically from the fourth ward city directory during the 1970 city council election campaign. The survey focused on the rate of selective exposure under varying conditions of partisan information availability in newspapers read by each respondent. It is reported in Atkin (1971).

Republican Convention Study. During the 1968 presidential campaign, 1,293 parents of junior and senior high school students in five Wisconsin cities were personally interviewed in a study of mass media use, political socialization, and family communication directed by McLeod and Chaffee. Secondary analyses were performed on these data, as described in Atkin (1970, 1972).

Newspaper Motivation Study. A probability sample of 167 Madison adults was personally interviewed in 1963 by McLeod, Ward, and Tancill (1965-66). Data on reasons for and correlates of newspaper reading were subjected to secondary analysis.

Lazarsfeld, Berelson, and Gaudet Study. Seven waves of personal interviews were conducted with 600 Erie County voters during the 1940 Presidential campaign between Roosevelt and Willkie. Some mass media findings were re-analyzed from the report by Lazarsfeld, Berelson, and Gaudet (1948).

Blumler and McQuail Study. A secondary analysis was carried out with several results obtained by Blumler and McQuail (1969) in their survey of 677 British voters during the 1964 general election. In this research, three waves of personal interviews were conducted to investigate the basic relationship between voting behavior and exposure to televised campaign coverage.

Butler and Stokes Study. Personal interviews with 2,009 British voters provided findings for a secondary analysis in this survey of mass media and electoral behavior, which was originally reported in Butler and Stokes (1969).

Data from these sources are initially presented under the four separate categories of instrumental utility and under the expenditure heading. In each section, the role of the various need and expenditure factors is empirically assessed to determine how each contributes to general message exposure patterns. The first objective of the data exposition is to demonstrate the importance of each element considered in isolation.

The second objective is to show how utilities and expenditures apply to selective exposure behavior. Thus, certain evidence from these studies are integrated into an analysis of the viability of the classic selectivity proposition in the final data section.

COGNITIVE ADAPTATION: NEED FOR SURVEILLANCE INFORMATION

If people cannot master their environment, at least they can attempt to attain an awareness and understanding of the latest developments that may affect their well-being. The individual seeks to keep abreast of relevant events in the world around him, and to interpret his internal feelings in response to environmental stimuli. He maintains surveillance over potential changes that may require adaptive adjustments, monitoring threats or opportunities and forming cognitive orientations such as comprehension, expectations, and beliefs.

Although the individual may not be particularly interested or favorably disposed toward certain public figures, he may feel a pragmatic necessity to become knowledgeable due to possible personal consequences resulting from their activities.

The role of *awareness uncertainty* and *understanding uncertainty* is illustrated with data from several surveys of manifest motivations for exposure to news content in the mass media. There is also correlational evidence from one survey investigation, followed by a discussion of studies examining individual differences in cognitive adaptation.

In the Newspaper Motivation survey probing the "generally important" reasons for newspaper reading, 88 percent of the respondents identified "to help me keep up with things" and 67 percent said "for interpretation of important events." These factors were cited much more often than those associated with reading pleasure, vicarious interaction, escape, and excitement.

In the political realm, Blumler and McQuail explored the reasons for watching British party broadcasts. Open-ended pretesting indicated that surveillance of the political environment was the most frequently mentioned factor, as voters generally sought to follow the flow of current affairs and specifically wanted to ascertain what might be in store for them. Of the structured items used in the main survey, the two most prominently cited reasons were "to see what some party will do if it gets into power" (55 percent) and "to keep up with the main issues of the day" (52 percent). In addition, a moderately endorsed item was "to judge who is likely to win the election" (31 percent). The authors conclude: "Many citizens recognize that political developments impinge upon their personal circumstances, and they wish to acquire information that might help them to grasp how they are likely to be affected by that connection." (Blumler and McQuail, 1969: 85).

Among eight possible reasons for watching the national political nominating convention in the Democratic Convention survey, the data in Table 1 indicate that 31 percent of all viewers cited "because you wanted to see the candidate in case he might be President some day." However, reference to this reason was not correlated with amount of attention to the convention coverage.

Correlation evidence suggesting a surveillance information need was obtained in the Abortion Information survey. It was hypothesized that college women contemplating the possibility of an abortion would acquire more material about abortion from mass media and interpersonal sources. Table 2 shows somewhat higher exposure levels for those responding affirmatively when asked, "If you had an unwanted pregnancy, would you ever seek an abortion?" Averaging across the top thirteen sources, 32 percent of the "yes" respondents and 25 percent of the "no" respondents sought information, with those who said "it depends on circumstances" midway at 28 percent. When exposure to print

TABLE 1

REASONS FOR VIEWING DEMOCRATIC CONVENTION BY
CANDIDATE PREFERENCE, AND CORRELATIONS WITH
ATTENTION TO TELEVISED CONVENTION COVERAGE

Reason: Did you watch because. . . .	*Candidate Preference*			*Biserial r with Attention*
	McGovern	*Nixon*	*Undecided*	
you are interested in political affairs	85%	66%	64%	+.37
you wanted to obtain information to help in deciding whether to support the man who was nominated	49	64	33	+.16
there was nothing else to watch on television	42	55	60	−.32
you wanted to make sure you were supporting the right man	46	55	38	+.10
you wanted to see if your candidate would do well	71	22	29	+.31
you wanted to see the candidate in case he might be President some day	37	39	26	−.03
you like the excitement of conventions	43	36	21	+.24
you wanted to hear good things about your party	20	12	12	+.14
(Number of cases)	(65)	(67)	(42)	(174)

NOTE: These statistics were computed on 174 of the 224 voters contacted; the others did not report viewing the convention.

media alone is considered, the differences are stronger, rising from 33 percent to 39 percent to 48 percent with likelihood of usefulness. Differential seeking by source will be discussed in the Expenditures section.

There are probably individual differences in surveillance information seeking. Buss (1967) measured the personality attribute "need for cognition" with Rosen's (1964) instrument and found a strong correlation with magazine exposure and a mild association with newspaper reading. Anxiety has been suggested as another factor influencing this type of information acquisition (Maslow, 1963), and a study by Kay (1954) supported the expectation that low-anxiety individuals would choose to read more news stories than those with greater anxiety. To the extent that formal education expands students' recognition of environmental forces that have a potential impact on their lives, the cognitive

TABLE 2
EXPOSURE TO ABORTION INFORMATION SOURCES BY
EXPECTATION OF SEEKING AN ABORTION

Source of Information About Abortion	Might Abort Unwanted Pregancy		
	Yes	Depends on Circumstances	No
Sex education books	46%	36%	33%
Pamphlets	54	35	33
Medical personnel	34	16	15
Magazines	61	57	45
Newspapers	46	47	39
Medical column in paper	21	20	15
Friends	58	56	58
Boyfriend/husband	22	11	12
Roommate	18	24	27
Acquaintances	15	21	18
Mother	12	14	9
Television	13	17	12
Radio	6	10	12
(Number of cases)	(114)	(133)	(33)

NOTE: Table entries are percentage citing exposure to abortion information from each source during past year. Respondents are sorted according to response to this item: "If you had an unwanted pregancy, would you ever seek an abortion?"

adjustment factor may be a partial explanation for the well-documented relationship between years of schooling and news information exposure.

Although the data presented in this section are limited primarily to self-report assessments, it is clear that surveillance information needs are a significant contributor to exposure acts. Since this type of information seeking is not linked to immediate decisional or behavioral requirements, it seems reasonable to categorize this factor separately in a cognitive classification.

Subsequent research is needed to measure the relative importance of cognitive adaptation for message selection behavior. Investigators should attempt to identify how much news seeking is directly tied to awareness and understanding uncertainties. It is likely that much of this exposure is due to intrinsic interest in news topics, or a function of process gratifications from habitual reading or viewing patterns developed throughout one's lifetime.

AFFECTIVE ADAPTATION: NEED FOR GUIDANCE INFORMATION

Uncertainty is also generated by needs for affective orientations toward environmental objects, such as attitude formation and decision-making. This uncertainty produces guidance information seeking.

In response to encounters with novel objects or situations, the individual may need a basis for forming an evaluative disposition. The need for guidance information becomes even more salient when he is faced with a formal decision among various alternatives and his current cognitive and affective orientations do not afford an adequate discrimination. In these ubiquitous conflict states, external information may provide both new alternatives and clarification of the relative merits of each possibility.

Research described in this section examines the significance of *decisional uncertainty*. This is one of the most active areas of information-seeking research, with extensive research traditions in psychology, marketing, and political science. The findings presented here were gathered in voting studies focusing on the candidate selection process.

Numerous decision-making experiments have demonstrated that information search increases systematically with degree of uncertainty, operationalized as the number and relative strengths of alternatives in the choice situation (Lanzetta and Driscoll, 1968). These studies also show that importance of the decision adds to the amount of search behavior.

The average person most frequently experiences pre-decisional uncertainty in the marketplace, and the relationship between decision-making and information handling has been intensively studied by consumer behavior experts. Cox (1967) edited a volume of investigations based on the premise that the nature and amount of a consumer's "perceived risk" (Bauer, 1960) determines the sources, types, and amounts of information acquisition.

Bauer notes that any decision entails consequences that cannot be completely anticipated, and that the individual often tries to calculate the implications of purchasing or not purchasing a product. The risk-taking process involves pre-decisional discriminations of products along attributes relating to post-purchase performance goals and psychosocial goals. These two sub-types of uncertainty may lead to information-seeking to determine whether the product will work well and how it will affect self-esteem and the opinion of others. Empirical evidence indicates greater information acquisition under increased perception of risk.

Voting studies have also pointed to pre-decisional uncertainty as a prime factor stimulating information-seeking. Among the reasons for watching party broadcasts in the Blumler-McQuail study, 51 percent of the respondents cited "to judge what political leaders are like" and 26 percent chose the more specific response, "to help me make up my mind how to vote." In addition, the most prominantly mentioned reason for avoiding party programs was "because my mind is already made up."

An important contribution of the Blumler-McQuail study is the isolation of a subgroup of "pure vote-guidance seekers" who endorsed the help-make-up-mind item but not a reinforcement-seeking item. Analyses show that they were the most heavily exposed to all types of party broadcasts of any set of respondents, despite personal and social characteristics that might dampen exposure behavior.

In the Democratic Convention investigation, 51 percent of the viewers said they watched "because you wanted to obtain information to help in deciding whether to support the man who was nominated." Reference to this reason correlates + .16 with attention to the convention coverage on television (see Table 1).

Several studies in the literature suggest a widespread reliance on newspaper editorial endorsements for electoral guidance. Vinyard and Sigel (1971) asked 250 Detroit residents, "How much do you depend on the newspaper in helping you decide how to vote in a non-partisan election, such as for Detroit councilman?" Surprisingly, 36 percent said a lot, 25 percent said quite a bit, and 18 percent depended a little. For a Presidential election, the percentages were slightly lower, with 51 percent indicating a lot or quite a bit. Rarick (1970) found that 43 percent of 402 Oregon voters replied affirmatively to the question, "If you were not sure how to vote on a local bond issue, would you take the advice of the *Register-Guard* on how to vote?" Finally, a survey of 383 Toledo voters by Blume and Lyons (1968) showed that 26 percent said "yes" when asked, "Do you consider the endorsement of the *Blade* when deciding for whom to vote?"

In the City Council election study, where candidates were generally unfamiliar to student voters, 55 percent reported reading the editorial endorsement in the campus newspaper. The exposure rate was 62 percent among the large number of students who were still undecided on the day of the endorsement. On the other hand, few students remained undecided in the Michigan Primary election stury, and only 25 percent of the overall sample referred to the editorial recommendation.

Indecision also prompts attention to campaign advertising. Voters in the Political Advertising study who reported making their final decision late in the campaign were asked whether each candidate's TV ads "helped you in making your decision to vote" for or against the candidate. Advertisements for the chosen candidate were cited by 59 percent of the late-deciders, while 50 percent also said that the non-chosen candidate's ads affected their choice. Those who mentioned the usefulness of TV advertising paid substantially more attention to these messages.

There is some evidence indicating that Political Panel voters who were undecided a month before the election subsequently sought more candidate information than committed voters. In Michigan there was a zero correlation between political media exposure and decisional state, ranging from "undecided" to "slightly favor" to "strongly favor." When interest in the campaign was controlled, the partial correlation dropped to - .12. However, the Colorado findings showed a slight positive relationship between these variables, even with interest controlled.

Most of this research on pre-decisional exposure patterns documents the obvious role of decisional uncertainty in determining information seeking. When people face an important decision, such as the choice between political candidates, they are motivated to seek out mass media content to help them decide. More research is needed to examine how information seeking is affected by less immediate requirements for affective adaptation, such as general attitude and opinion formation.

In addition, researchers should attempt to identify the range of everyday situations necessitating the development of affective dispositions, and relate these to the types of content presented in the mass media. This would provide an indication of the relative importance of the affective adaptation factor in accounting for information-seeking patterns.

BEHAVIORAL ADAPTATION:
NEED FOR PERFORMANCE INFORMATION

When the individual is unsure how to execute some obligatory task or undertake a voluntary action sequence, he will need information that is useful for directing such anticipated behavior. Extrinsic uncertainty arises when a subsequent activity cannot be satisfactorily accomplished without a more complete understanding of relevant objects and attributes.

Three subsets of performance information needs are assessed in this section. A distinction is made between performances that fulfill an assigned duty (task uncertainty), implement a voluntary activity (enactment uncertainty), or merely entail routine informal communication (communicatory uncertainty).

Atkin (1972) defines communicatory uncertainty as a cognitive state of incomplete familiarity with a potential conversation topic. Information that the individual acquires from mass media sources may be useful in a variety of subsequent communicatory situations, including informal interaction with friends and relatives or casual interaction during special occasions such as meetings or social affairs. Messages from the media can be re-transmitted as raw material in direct exchange, or can be combined with previous cognitions to yield new conversational material. Both correlational and experimental evidence presented by Atkin indicated that the anticipated discussion or current news topics significantly affected message selections.

Manifest motivation to acquire messages for communicatory utility appears to be limited, since conscious movement toward mass media content is reported relatively infrequently. A secondary analysis of the Newspaper Motivation data shows that reading newspapers explicitly "to give me something to talk about with others" was cited as an important reason by 50 percent of the respondents, ranking behind several other reasons for reading; only 10 percent of the voters in the Blumler-McQuail study said they watched party TV broadcasts in order to gain information "to use as ammunition in arguments with others."

Nevertheless, correlational evidence from several political investigations reaffirms the clear relationship between topical discussion frequency and amount of relevant media exposure. In the City Council survey, the amount of campaign discussion (along a four-step scale of frequency) correlates moderately with readership of campaign articles in the campus newspaper. Since intrinsic interest in the election might account for such a relationship, campaign interest was controlled, yielding a partial correlation of + .22. In the Presidential Primary study, the same measures show a zero-order correlation of + .26 and a partial of + .16. Secondary analysis of data from the Republican Convention study during the 1968 campaign shows considerably stronger associations. The frequency of talking about the fall campaign correlates + .49 with print media exposure, and the partial correlation controlling for campaign interest is + .30.

These three investigations also indicate that electronic media exposure is not as closely related to communicatory activities. The partial correlation with viewing of TV news and public affairs programing is only + .15 in the Republican Convention survey. For voters in the Presidential Primary sample, the association between campaign discussion and TV news exposure is only + .03 when interest is partialed out. Apparently television is a less useful source of specifically relevant conversation material. This observation is supported by results from the Television Advertising study, where the frequency of campaign discussion is more closely related to newspaper advertising attention (r = + .25, partial r = + .16) than to television advertising attention (r = + .19, partial r = + .10).

Evidence bearing on communicatory utility is also available in the Party Workers investigation. The campaign workers were asked how often they talked with co-workers about their candidate's television advertising and about the opposition candidate's TV ads. Frequency of discussing the former correlates + .26 with attention to their candidate's advertisements, and discussion of the opponent's political spots correlates + .21 with attention to them.

A comparison between advertising attention levels of party workers versus ordinary voters in the same Wisconsin gubernatorial campaign illustrates the role of *task uncertainty* in producing performance information seeking. Results on identical questions in the Political Advertising and Party Workers surveys show that twice as many party activists as general public paid close attention to television ads, and three times as many read newspaper ads closely (Sheinkopf, Atkin, and Bowen, 1973). Furthermore, the campaign workers, who had greater practical need for the material, much more often cited informational reasons for viewing the political spots.

One key reason for this heavier consumption involves the workers' routine efforts to sway voters. Almost two-thirds agreed that TV ads for their candidate "provide you with ideas and arguments to use when you try to persuade the public to vote for him," and three-quarters felt that the opponent's ads "provide you with information to use when trying to persuade hesitant voters to vote for your candidate." Those who reported the greatest persuasive use for the content of the advertising messages are most closely exposed, with a correlation of + .20 for their candidate's ads and + .21 for the opponent's spots.

For the average citizen, the major voluntary action sequence of a political nature involves the formal casting of his vote on election day. Numerous studies demonstrate that individuals who turn out in elections are more heavily exposed to mass media campaign content than non-voters, who have less need for performance information (Lazarsfeld, Berelson and Gaudet, 1948; Berelson, Lazarsfeld and McPhee, 1954; Campbell, Gurin and Miller, 1954; Glaser, 1965).

In the three studies of student voting behavior, enactment uncertainty was operationalized in terms of likelihood of turnout along a seven-step scale. In each case, print exposure to campaign news is substantially more closely related to expectation of turnout than is electronic media exposure. For the Presidential Primary sample, there is a correlation of $+.25$ with frequency of newspaper reading (index of exposure to campus and local newspaper coverage) and $+.19$ with electronic exposure (index of viewing national news broadcasts and campaign specials, and listening to radio newscasts). When interest in the campaign in controlled, the partial correlations drop to $+.13$ and $+.09$, respectively. Similar exposure measures are associated slightly more strongly with turnout in the Political Panel study (newspaper $r = +.19$, partial $r = +.08$; broadcast $r = +.13$, partial $r = +.02$).

Finally, the City Council correlation is $+.31$ with reading of the campus newspaper, dropping to a partial of $+.18$. Among the half of the sample who claimed to be very likely to vote, 36 percent read "most" of the articles about the city council, while only 7 percent of the less-likely voters read this much. Radio exposure is unrelated to turnout in this study.

The role of *enactment uncertainty* is illuminated by data on changes in mass media content preferences accompanying restructured working patterns in the Four-day Work-week investigation. Conversion to the four-day week provided manufacturing workers with an opportunity to spend more time in active leisure pursuits on the long weekends. Results indicate a seeking of specific types of content for direct application to activities such as outdoor recreation, hobbies, or creative cookery. A number of workers began watching or increased exposure to an outdoor sports program (14 percent), gourmet cooking programs (15 percent), a show dealing with pets (12 percent), and another dealing with sewing (5 percent). Between the first and second waves of the study, a substantial proportion of workers began reading sports and hobby magazines (17 percent), homemaking periodicals (19 percent), and men's magazines (11 percent). On the other hand, there was only a slight increase in readership of general-interest magazines (4 percent).

Additional evidence of the utilitarian nature of the new exposure patterns is derived from an analysis of the relationship between the change in outdoor recreational activity and the change in relevant mass media usage after the on-set of the four-day week. An index based on the gain in viewing of the fish-and-game report and reading of outdoor sports magazines correlates $+.37$ with an index combining separate increases in the frequency of hunting, fishing, camping, boating, climbing, skiing, and snowmobiling.

Recent trends in magazine circulation suggest the significance of the need for performance information. While general-interest magazines such as *Life, Look,* and *Saturday Evening Post* have folded, there has been a strong increase in readership of specialized periodicals catering to pragmatic problems and leisure-time avocations of narrow audiences. For instance, Helen Gurley Brown revived the fortunes of *Cosmopolitan* magazine by re-orienting the content to the practical needs of the young working woman, "offering advice on careers, self-improvement, entertainment, health, fashions, and how to cope in the man-woman relationship—from sex to conversation" (*Journalism Educator,* 1972: 5).

From this evidence, it appears that performance uncertainty is also a significant factor stimulating information seeking. People who plan to discuss a topic, carry out a task, or undertake a new activity often obtain relevant messages as an aid to performing these behaviors. A casual content analysis of mass media features will provide numerous examples of "how to" articles and programs designed to reduce enactment and task uncertainty. Simple readership and viewership surveys should produce valuable evidence concerning the specific needs that are satisfied by the media and the frequency of this type of information seeking.

Communicatory uncertainty is a rather unique concept in the information-seeking process. While most exposure acts are motivated by purely intrapersonal needs, the communicatory utility findings illustrate the role of social factors in message selection. In addition, communicatory differs qualitatively from the other performance uncertainties. It is not such an obvious manifest motivation for information seeking, and the media do not manifestly cater to this type of need. Nevertheless, the data suggest that communicatory uncertainty makes a significant contribution to exposure patterns.

DEFENSIVE ADAPTATION:
NEED FOR REINFORCEMENT INFORMATION

After the individual has formed a cognitive or affective orientation, he may have doubts about whether he holds the right view. In these post-orientational states, the need for information is usually biased in nature. In many cases, the individual wants to know that his orientations are right, not *if* they are right. He is looking for confirmation and reassurance of beliefs and attitudes, rather than objectively assessing their soundness. This is particularly the case in post-decisional and post-performance situations, where a behavioral commitment often precludes a change in the choice or action sequence already executed. He is in a defensive posture, striving to allay his doubts that the most rewarding alternative was chosen. This is the classic case of cognitive dissonance where the bad features of the chosen alternative and the good points of the unchosen possibilities are in an inconsistent relationship with the decision act (Festinger, 1957, 1964).

Thus, the need for information is really a need for consistent information that reinforces prior dispositions or behaviors. Under these conditions, the individual is likely to select supportive rather than discrepant messages, in an attempt to increase his confidence that he thinks, feels, or has done the correct thing. In addition to a heightened amount of information seeking, he should exhibit selective exposure patterns.

Social scientists have engaged in an extensive controversy over the viability of the selective exposure proposition since Freedman and Sears (1965) severely questioned the existance of a general psychological preference for supportive versus discrepant information. Until their critical examination of the research literature, most scholars had accepted the basic principle that people are motivated to expose themselves selectively to mass communication messages, seeking out information that reinforces their attitudes and practices and avoiding inconsistent material.

After assessing data from a number of social psychological experiments, Freedman and Sears argued that laboratory research offers no convincing evidence of selective exposure. In this and subsequent reviews (Sears and Freedman, 1967; Sears, 1968; Sears and Abeles, 1969), they did acknowledge that de facto selectivity was generally obtained in field studies, but offered more parsimonious explanations for these voluntary exposure patterns. In response to these renewed attacks, Mills (1968) and Katz (1968) joined the battle with vigorous defenses of the venerable proposition, while citing limitations of applicability.

Since data presented in this section come from non-laboratory research, most relationships are of course open to alternative explanations. Thus, the findings basically deal with de facto selective exposure; the case for motivated selectivity will be discussed in a subsequent section.

The empirical evidence is primarily concerned with *post-affective uncertainty*. After a description of self-report findings, data on selective exposure to individual message units will be presented. Individual differences in message selectivity will then be examined, followed by an assessment of selective exposure at the molar level of overall source preferences.

First, self-reports of respondents in political surveys suggest the existence of a need for reinforcement information among a large proportion of the electorate. Results from the Blumler-McQuail study show that 36 percent of the voters watched party broadcasts "to remind me of my party's strong points." This was the fourth most frequently cited reason for viewing.

In the Democratic Convention survey, 48 percent of the viewers said they watched "to make sure you were supporting the right man" and 42 percent viewed "to see if your candidate would do well." (Since the only candidate likely to do well was McGovern, the 71 percent figure among his partisans is more indicative of the importance of this reason.) Only 15 percent admitted that they watched expressly "to hear good things about your party." (The low percentage may be due to the poorly worded item or the propensity for

Democratic Convention-goers not to display good things about their party.) Across these three reasons there is a modest tendency for those mentioning reinforcement reasons to pay close attention to the television coverage (see Table 1).

Numerous voting studies have shown that partisans read, listen, and see more campaign messages favorable to their candidate than for the opposition candidate. As long ago as 1940, the Lazarsfeld, Berelson and Gaudet study presented data indicating a selective exposure rate of 75 percent among voters holding a consistent preference throughout the campaign. This figure, based on calculations drawn from three tables in *The People's Choice* (Lazarsfeld, Berelson, and Gaudet, 1948: 90, 164, 167) directly contradicts the computations of Freedman and Sears (1965), which were based on marginals from an inappropriate table.

While Freedman and Sears estimated that only 70 percent of the Republicans and 50 percent of the Democrats were selectly exposed, Atkin (1970) demonstrated that the correct proportions were 76 percent for Republicans and 74 percent for Democrats. In addition, Atkin's re-analysis showed that 72 percent of the late-deciding respondents with Democratic characteristics were primarily exposed to Democratic material, and 61 percent of the Republican late-deciders chose predominantly Republican content.

During the 1948 Presidential campaign, Berelson, Lazarsfeld, and McPhee (1954) found that Democratic voters were exposed to Truman items by a 57 to 43 percent ratio and Republicans chose Dewey content by a margin of 54 to 46 percent. In a controlled field study, Stempel (1961) discovered that 31 percent of student respondents who preferred a candidate read more information about him, 1 percent read more about the opponent, and the others were exposed equally to both candidates. Freedman and Sears (1963) offered voters a choice between candidate pamphlets during the California gubernatorial campaign, and found that 58 percent of the partisan respondents first selected supportive material.

Atkin (1971) described secondary analyses of two studies of Madison voters conducted by Chaffee and McLeod. During the 1966 Congressional and gubernatorial races, interviewers gave voters three pamphlet titles (one supporting each candidate and a third presenting impartial material about both candidates) and offered to mail the campaign information to their homes. While most respondents first selected the neutral booklet, in 84 percent of the cases where one partisan title was chosen, voters wanted to receive material supporting their candidate. In a 1968 campaign survey, another sample of voters was asked which presidential candidate pamphlets they would select if they had the opportunity to receive them. With bipartisan and third party material excluded from analysis, there was an 87 percent rate of selective exposure.

In the Blumler-McQuail study, British voters watched more broadcasts for their own party than for either of the other parties. Re-analysis of the data indicates that on the average, partisans saw 1.92 programs for their party and

1.33 for each of the other two parties. However, the combined exposure to other-party broadcasts outdistances own-party viewing.

Additional evidence of selectivity is provided in three studies of exposure to a single partisan message. Schramm and Carter (1959) found that 22 percent of the Republicans and 10 percent of the Democrats in a California sample watched a political telethon of Republican Senator Knowland. McGinnies and Rosenbaum (1965) discovered that those who were more favorable toward existing foreign policy were more exposed to a TV appearance by President Johnson concerning the Vietnam war situation. A secondary analysis of some Blumler-McQuail findings shows that 34 percent of the Labour supporters and 19 percent of the Conservatives watched a particular Labour campaign broadcast.

The primary source of new data is the Political Panel study. Table 3 shows that messages about McGovern on television and in newspapers were attended significantly more closely by McGovern supporters than Nixon partisans ($p < .01$, t-test), while the opposite finding is obtained for Nixon messages. McGovern backers paid substantially more attention to content about their candidate, Nixon supporters preferred Nixon materials by a slight margin, and the undecided students were in between. Strongest selectivity is found for televised speeches and advertising, while news content attention is less biased.

TABLE 3
ATTENTION TO MASS MEDIA POLITICAL TOPICS BY CANDIDATE PREFERENCE

Late-Campaign Attention		*Mid-Campaign Preference*		
		McGovern	*Nixon*	*Undecided*
Newscast stories:	McGovern	1.32	1.07	.72
	Nixon	1.04	1.07	.90
Television speeches:	McGovern	1.06	.79	.81
	Nixon	.66	.80	.73
TV advertisements:	McGovern	1.36	1.11	1.03
	Nixon	1.04	1.14	.88
Newspaper articles:	McGovern	1.03	.71	.60
	Nixon	.65	.62	.43
Total attention:	McGovern	4.77	3.64	3.25
	Nixon	3.39	3.68	3.00
(Number of cases)		(142)	(140)	(39)

NOTE: Cell entries are means, ranging from 0 ("Haven't watched" or "haven't read") to 2 ("close attention"). Significant differences between McGovern and Nixon supporters were obtained separately for each sample by t-tests; for total attention to McGovern content ($p < .01$ Michigan and $p < .05$ Colorado), and for total attention to Nixon content ($p < .05$ Colorado).

Since candidate preference was identified in the first wave of the panel and exposure was measured for subsequent mass media messages, any flow of causality is from preference to exposure in this study.

In the Political Advertising study, selectivity of advertising reception patterns was examined at two levels: frequency of exposure, and closeness of attention. Atkin, Bowen, Nayman, and Sheinkopf (1973) reported that partisan respondents were generally unselective in relative *exposure,* as 31 percent saw more ads for their candidate, 26 percent saw more for the opposition candidate, and the remainder said they viewed the same number of ads for each. The selective *attention* rate was very high among those paying differential attention, with 20 percent giving closer attention to the ads of their candidate and only 3 percent attending the opponent's ads more closely; the others paid approximately equal attention to each set of ads. Among the small minority who reported avoidance of one candidate's ads but not the other's ads, 87 percent selectively avoided the discrepant messages. Respondents in the Wisconsin portion of the sample also described their newspaper attention patterns. Although most paid about equal attention to each candidate's advertising, 26 percent read selectively and 3 percent read the opposition ads more closely.

These relationships were also assessed with the same measures in the Party Workers survey. At the raw exposure level, Sheinkopf, Atkin, and Bowen (1973) found evidence of non-selectivity: 38 percent of the activists saw more ads for the opposing candidate; only 19 percent viewed more of their candidates ads, and the others watched equal amounts for each. This pattern was reversed at the attention level, as 15 percent watched their candidate's ads more closely and 2 percent more closely attended the ads of the opposition.

There was a selective avoidance rate of 89 percent among the few who tried to avoid one set of ads but not the other. Newspaper attention was also selective, with 18 percent paying closer attention to their candidate's print advertisements and 9 percent reading the opposition ads more closely. As with the general public, most workers paid about equal attention to each set of ads on television and in newspapers.

Although almost all party workers were exposed to the opposition's advertising, they did erect defenses at the level of message acceptance. In response to the question, "When you are watching the opposition candidate's TV ads, do you find yourself arguing against the claims that are presented?", 53 percent of the viewers marked "quite a lot" and 7 percent answered "not at all," with the remaining respondents in intermediate categories.

Suggestive findings are also available from the two political convention investigations. During the 1968 Republican Convention, 36 percent of the Republicans versus 25 percent of the Democrats watched "most" of the proceedings, and the overall difference is highly significant ($p < .001$, chi-square test). Among Democratic Convention viewers in 1972, 42 percent of the McGovern partisans versus 28 percent of the pro-Nixon voters paid "close" attention ($p < .05$, chi-square test). The difference is much more pronounced for viewership of the McGovern acceptance speech, with 48 percent of the McGovern backers watching and only 9 percent of the Nixon supporters in the audience.

Attention to the Convention and the McGovern speech is consistently greater for McGovern partisans who cited reinforcement reasons for viewing. For instance, 57 percent of those who "wanted to see if your candidate would do well" watched the acceptance speech, compared to 26 percent among McGovern supporters who did not mention this reason; the difference between these two groups for overall Convention attention is 46 versus 32 percent. Viewership of the speech decreases steadily from 85 percent for those citing all three reinforcement motivations to 33 percent among McGovernites who mentioned none.

Several likely individual difference variables were tested as correlates of selectivity. Clarke and James (1967) found that dogmatism, a personality style characterized by rigid thought and intolerance for inconsistency (Rokeach, 1960), was moderately associated with selective information preferences in a private information processing experimental condition. In the Political Panel investigation, dogmatism (measured on a six-item instrument) is mildly related to selective attention (indexed by relative attention to own candidate's versus opponent's messages). Averaging across the two sets of partisans in Michigan and Colorado, the correlation is $+.18$ with newspaper selectivity and $+.06$ with television selectivity.

Parental emphasis on a free and open awareness of contrasting viewpoints and concepts might be expected to produce less selectivity. The degree of concept-orientation experienced during adolescence (measured on six items employed by McLeod, Atkin, and Chaffee, 1972) correlates slightly in the predicted direction with TV selective attention ($r = -.08$) but positively with print selectivity ($r = +.08$) in the Political Panel study.

Another plausible factor is amount of formal education, which may lead to a greater confidence and a wider tolerance for divergent ideas. In the Political Advertising survey, years of education does not correlate with the selective attention index for television or newspaper advertising. For the generally elite Party Workers sample, education does correlate $-.18$ with selective attention.

Education was held constant in the two political convention investigations. In the Republican Convention study, there is a very slight tendency for those with at least some college to attend less selectively (biserial $r = +.10$ between amount of exposure and party preference) than the less educated respondents ($+.13$). On the other hand, there is a slight difference in the opposite direction among Democratic Convention viewers (biserial $r = +.15$ for high school graduate or less, compared to $+.17$ for college educated).

The analyses for these individual difference variables are generally disappointing. With the exception of dogmatism and print selectivity, these factors relate inconsistently or negligibly with biased information reception.

The overall selectivity evidence shows a definite preference for supportive messages but little exclusion of discrepant materials. In each study examined, partisans pay greater attention to mass media content about their favored political candidate than to opposition messages, while absolute avoidance is quite rare. Where only a crude two- or three-level gradation of attention is measured, most respondents are equally exposed to both sides. Although the relative preference for reinforcing information is clear and consistent, the magnitude of bias is not impressive for selection of individual messages.

Perhaps selectivity is more evident in the habitual patterns of exposure to multi-message mass media sources. If the individual regularly reads a partisan newspaper reflecting his political outlook, he efficiently avoids repeated message selection decisions and possible dissonance arousal from awareness of contrary articles. A number of investigations indicate that selective exposure is much stronger at the level of overall source preferences.

McLeod, Wackman, Hurt, and Payne (1965) found an overwhelming bias in choice of newspaper by 137 partisan voters in Madison, Wisconsin. Among Democrats, 70 percent read the liberal *Capital Times* and 43 percent were exposed to the conservative *State Journal*. On the other hand, 90 percent of the Republicans read the Republican newspaper, with only 19 percent reading the Democratic paper.

A secondary analysis of newspaper reading data collected by Butler and Stokes during a recent British campaign also shows clear selectivity. Among the vast majority of respondents reading one newspaper, 83 percent of the Conservatives read a Conservative newspaper (*Daily Express, Daily Mail, Daily Telegraph, Daily Sketch*), 64 percent of the Labourites preferred a Labour paper (*Daily Mirror, Daily Sun*), and other respondents chose Conservative dailies by a 59 to 41 percent margin.

This same pattern was found for magazine preferences in a survey of 1,420 political activists by Grupp (1969). John Birch Society members preferred conservative opinion magazines such as *National Review* and *Human Events,* while members of the Americans for Democratic Action subscribed to *New Republic, Reporter,* and similar liberal periodicals. There was no overlap in readership patterns. Selectivity extended to news magazines, as more ADA than Birch members read *Time* (20 versus 6 percent) and *Newsweek* (18 versus 4 percent), while fewer read the conservative *U.S. News and World Report* (3 versus 31 percent).

Shifting to radio preferences, a survey reported by Davison (1959) showed that 80 percent of the West Berlin radio audience primarily listened to the United States-sponsored station in Berlin during the 1948 blockade. Only 15 percent attended most often to the Communist-operated radio station. In addition, almost all of the West Berlin newspaper readers regularly read non-communist papers.

In a study of partisan newspaper and radio preferences of 260 Arab college students, Diab (1965) found that most respondents who opposed Arab unity were exposed to media outlets rated by judges as anti-Arab-unity. Students favoring Arab unity exhibited the opposite pattern. Excluding preferences for outlets judged as "mixed" in partisanship, 71 percent of the partisans read supportive newspapers and 89 percent listened to supportive radio stations.

Finally, Lazarsfeld, Berelson, and Gaudet discovered that Erie County Democrats were primarily exposed to radio coverage of the campaign while Republicans tended to read newspapers—holding education constant. The authors pointed out that the predominantly Republican partisanship of the newspapers and Roosevelt's orientation toward the airwaves provided "a medium for each party."

These habitual media source preferences strongly suggest that readers and listeners are seeking information to satisfy reinforcement needs. The findings at the individual message level offer less impressive evidence, but do consistently show an unbalanced pattern of exposure favoring supportive messages.

While these correlational data appear to support the selective exposure proposition, a definitive conclusion cannot be reached without considering other factors that might account for the observed association. This will be attempted in the final data section.

Nevertheless, the findings do offer clear evidence of the existence of de facto selectivity. The research presented in this section provides exhaustive documentation of the tendency for people to be exposed to consonant mass media material. The major shortcoming of the evidence is the narrow focus of most investigations, which have examined only political attitudes and exposure patterns. More diversified research is needed to study selectivity for other types of subject matter, and for other reinforcement needs.

CONTRIBUTION OF ORIGINAL CERTAINTY LEVEL

This presentation has concentrated on the various requirements for adaptation that determine the criterion level of certainty to which the individual aspires. It must be kept in mind that uncertainty is also dependent on his current state of knowledge; a well-informed individual has less need for information than an ignorant counterpart striving for the same degree of certainty in a given situation.

This general point is illustrated with data reported in the classic Star and Hughes (1950) study of the Cincinnati Plan for the United Nations. In a survey preceding the mass communication educational campaign, they found that 62 percent of respondents with high interest in international events expressed a desire for more information about the UN, compared to 53 percent of the less interested. This would be expected, since interested people should have a higher need for intrinsically gratifying information.

The proposed paradigm also predicts that less-informed individuals would have a greater need for information. When this second factor is also considered, the greatest discrepancy should occur for those with high interest and low knowledge about the UN, while the smallest discrepancy should arise for those with low interest and high knowledge. When the investigators asked 745 respondents whether they wanted to obtain more UN information, the information-seeking data are consistent with twin-determinant prediction: 68 percent among poorly informed and interested, 61 percent among poorly informed and uninterested, 58 percent among better informed and interested, and 42 percent among better informed and uninterested (Star and Hughes, 1950: 387).

Similar findings were obtained in the Presidential Primary study. While the correlation between campaign interest and overall campaign exposure is predictably sizable (r = + .36), the relationship is far weaker among respondents who were knowledgeable about the campaign (indexed by the sum of responses to items asking about the leading issues and the names, offices, and home states of various Presidential candidates). For respondents ranking in the lowest third on the knowledge scale, the correlation is + .45. This compares with an association of + .17 among those with moderate knowledge, and + .11 for the most knowledgeable third of the respondents.

In the case of extrinsic uncertainties, data from the Presidential Primary investigation also indicate the contribution of original level of certainty. Expectation of turning out in the election correlates + .29 with overall exposure to campaign coverage, as those who were sure that they would vote sought information for behavioral enactment purposes. However, turnout expectation is not related to exposure among those with high political knowledge (r = - .04), presumably because they already possessed sufficient knowledge to enact this behavior. On the other hand, the moderately well informed respondents show a slight positive relationship (r = + .12), and the low knowledge group yields the strongest association (r = + .36).

The findings are less supportive for the communicatory uncertainty factor in this study. As expected, those scoring lowest in knowledge tend to be much more exposed as frequency of discussing the campaign increases (r = + .41). This is stronger than the relationship among the better-informed voters, although the moderately knowledgeable group shows a lower correlation (- .06) than is found in the high knowledge group (+ .27).

The analogous situation for defensive post-performance uncertainty can be assessed in the Party Workers research. Those workers who are unsure of the prospects for electoral success or doubtful of the value of their labor have a larger discrepancy from the high criterion level of certainty that campaign workers generally require. Thus, they should seek information selectively to bolster their outlook.

An index of selective exposure was calculated by subtracting the closeness of attention to opposition advertising from attention to own candidate advertising. There is a tendency for those with lower morale to choose supportive ads more than those high in esprit de corps, as this variable correlates - .30 with the selectivity index. Confidence that their candidate will do well in the election correlates - .32 with selectivity, indicating that the less certain workers particularly prefer newspaper and TV ads for the candidate they work for.

These sets of data offer preliminary support for the role of original certainty level in affecting the magnitude of uncertainty. Although the findings are somewhat marginal and limited to a few studies, the evidence suggests that both current and criterion certainty states should be considered in determining discrepancy. Of course, additional research will be required to assess whether this factor makes a relatively major or minor contribution to overall uncertainty.

THE ROLE OF EXPENDITURES

The individual must consider more than content attributes in selecting messages. The cost of a message relative to the resources of the consumer is also a vital factor affecting exposure patterns. Most of the research here deals with the cost attributes of obtaining the message, particularly prominence.

One of the longstanding principles of mass communication research holds that "the major countering factor to self-selection is sheer accessibility: people tend to see and hear communications to the degree that they are readily available" (Berelson and Steiner, 1964). In studies of political television broadcasts in Britain, from 40 to 70 percent of the viewers tuned in almost incidentally for nonpolitical purposes, primarily due to high availability (Trenaman and McQuail, 1961; Blumler and McQuail, 1969). Berelson, Lazarsfeld, and McPhee (1948) found that voters who paid more general attention to the mass media tended to "run across" and attend more political content than low media users, controlling interest.

Atkin (1971) showed that neutral newspaper items were chosen in proportion to their relative availability in terms of amount of space and prominence of placement in the newspaper. In an experiment, subjects received a set of dummy composite front pages that featured seven headlines representing news items. Stories in the high availability news slot were given a substantial advantage over less available items in number of column inches, favorability of page position, and headline column width and type size. Subjects chose to read highly available items in almost two-thirds of the cases.

In the Democratic Convention study, 51 percent of the viewers said they were exposed to the Convention because "there was nothing else to watch on TV," as all three networks carried the proceedings. This proportion of unmotivated viewing is similar to the Blumler-McQuail findings.

Many types of mass media presentations are expressly designed to minimize the cost attributes to such an extent that a receiver must expend almost no resources to obtain and process the message. In fact, advertisements and headline stories may be so obtrusive that more effort must be expended to avoid than obtain them. In the Political Advertising survey, voters were offered three possible reasons for viewing televised advertisements. Half of the respondents said they watched because they "can't avoid them," while the others watched for information or enjoyment rewards.

In addition, the Political Advertising respondents tended to view more spot ads for the candidate who advertised most often in each state. The correlation between perceived relative availability of each candidate's advertising and relative exposure frequency was + .40 in Wisconsin and + .59 in Colorado. Indeed, the relative availability factor overcame partisan selectivity at the raw exposure level, although it did not affect relative closeness of attention.

Data from the Abortion Information investigation in Table 2 illustrate how accessibility affects the surveillance information seeking. Examining exposure to sources requiring low expenditures (the last seven listed, primarily interpersonal and electronic media sources), there is no difference by expectation of ever obtaining an abortion. For women who did not anticipate an abortion, an average of 21 percent had received information from these easily accessible sources, compared to 20 percent among the respondents who said they would seek the operation.

For three sources involving somewhat greater effort (magazines and newspapers), the difference by respondent condition is 33 to 43 percent. Sources that require the most effort (books, magazines, and medical personnel) yield a strong 27 percent to 45 percent difference. Thus, the need for surveillance information is not related to exposure when expenditures are negligible, since unmotivated women may run across these messages and become exposed almost incidentally. Costlier sources are sought much more often by those who need the information provided in the content.

Aside from message characteristics, the resources of the individual also contribute to expenditures. If he has little available time, amount of media exposure is likely to be restricted. For instance, Samuelson, Carter, and Ruggels (1963) found that number of job-connected hours per week correlated - .28 with television exposure time and - .27 with time reading daily newspapers.

The obviously important role of expenditures in message selection does not require lengthy documentation. It is surprising how little research has been devoted to this factor. Subsequent investigations should assess how the various components of expenditure affect exposure patterns. The data presented here have only dealt with the dimension of message prominence, while other message attributes and receiver characteristics are not well understood. In addition, the present analysis has concentrated on costs and resources involved in obtaining messages. This emphasis ignores the question of how information exposure is affected by expenditures associated with message decoding.

SELECTIVITY IN THE CONTEXT OF OTHER EXPOSURE DETERMINANTS

The need for reinforcement information is only one of many factors that might contribute to biased patterns of message selection. This section examines how these other determinants may explain or obscure instances of selective exposure.

McGuire observed that "the enemies of the selective exposure postulate find it easy to attribute the occasional confirmations to spurious factors" (1968: 799). Freedman and Sears (1965) argued that apparent evidence of reinforcement seeking could be accounted for either by lower expenditures or higher utilities associated with supportive messages. According to Sears (1968), the predominant availability of supportive information in the environment is one of the most probable reasons for de facto selective exposure; evidence of motivated selectivity may be due to an unbalanced proportion of favorable and unfavorable information that corresponds to respondent preferences.

Freedman and Sears contended that selectivity must be defined in terms of deviations from an information availability baseline, and argued that apparent selective exposure in the Lazarsfeld, Berelson, and Gaudet study was largely due to the 2-to-1 Republican availability advantage in the local media. However, the re-analysis of these data discussed earlier showed that the Freedman-Sears computations underestimated the selective exposure rate, and that partisans of each party were selective to the same degree despite the relative prominence of Republican messages. Furthermore, selectivity evidence in studies by Stempel (1961), Freedman and Sears (1963), Atkin (1971), and Blumler and McQuail was gathered under conditions of explicitly equal availability.

Many demonstrations of de facto selective exposure come from survey investigations of information campaigns or public affairs presentations in the mass media. Freedman and Sears claimed that education is the most powerful predictor of attention to this type of content, and that this might artifactually produce apparent selectivity on issues where highly educated individuals tend to have a common set of political or social attitudes. In particular, they cautioned against inferring reinforcement seeking in the Schramm and Carter (1959) study showing Republicans twice as likely as Democrats to view a Republican telethon: "We must remember that Republicans are generally better educated than Democrats, and thus more likely to be in any public affairs audience" (1965: 81).

While Republicans are more heavily exposed to the informational print media, there is no empirical support for the contention that this is the case for comparable electronic programing (Lazarsfeld, Berelson, and Gaudet, 1948; Katz and Feldman, 1962). Analyzing general exposure data from the Republican Convention study, Atkin (1970) demonstrated that there was little difference by party: 50 percent of the Democrats watched national news broadcasts "very often," compared to 43 percent of the Republicans; for television news specials, 32 percent of the Democrats versus 30 percent of the Republicans watched "very often"; and 46 percent of the Republicans versus 43 percent of the Democrats watched network interview programs at least "sometimes."

Thus, the assumption that better-educated Republicans are more likely to be in any television public affairs audience seems unwarranted. As indicated previously, the Republican Convention data yield clear but modest evidence of selectivity, even when education is held constant.

The argument that non-reinforcement utilities can explain de facto selective exposure also appears to be unsubstantiated beyond several isolated cases cited by Freedman and Sears. In the research reported in this paper, utilitarian rewards would not seem to be linked to supportive rather than discrepant materials. It is possible that voters plan to participate in interpersonal discussions about their preferred candidate more often than conversing about his opponent, and this one-sided communicatory uncertainty could account for some selectivity. This factor was measured only in the Party Worker study, where frequency of talking about own candidate correlates + .14 with the index of selective attention to TV advertising. During the 1972 presidential campaign, Nixon supporters might have exposed themselves mostly to Nixon messages in order to keep surveillance over the activities of the obvious winning candidate, but the Political Panel data show little absolute selectivity for pro-Nixon respondents.

Another determinant not mentioned by Freedman and Sears is intrinsic interest in the chosen object. Since people tend to be more familiar with their preferred candidate and usually develop greater interest with increased familiarity, they may read and view more content about their favorite contender. There are no data available on this point, however.

Selective exposure behavior may also be disguised by certain factors that contribute to the reward value or lower the costs of discrepant messages. For instance, Democratic voters may have attended messages about Nixon during the 1972 Presidential campaign for surveillance information seeking, or unconvinced partisans of either party may have exposed themselves to discrepant content in preparation for a reversal of affective orientation. Or, exposure to opposition propaganda might be traced to unusually high message availability from saturation news coverage during the final weeks of the campaign.

There are some data indicating that respondents in the Party Worker study monitored the opposition messages for performance information. There is a + .21 association between attention to the other candidate's TV advertising and interpersonal discussion of his commercials. This discussion variable correlates - .03 with the selectivity index, and the part correlation drops to - .14 controlling for discussion of own candidate's ads. In addition, there is a + .21 correlation between reporting that opposition ads "provide you with information to use when trying to persuade hesitant voters" and attention to these ads, and this produces a slight negative rate of selectivity ($r = - .04$). Thus, discrepant messages may be sought for task utility.

The communicatory utility of contrary messages may also suppress selective exposure. In the Political Advertising survey, frequency of discussing the campaign correlated + .07 with attention to opposition advertising.

Aside from such utilitarian motives, there is evidence of expenditures obscuring selectivity in the Political Advertising study. The relative availability factor clearly produced greater exposure to discrepant television advertisements where they were more prominently featured. In both Wisconsin and Colorado, supporters of the candidate with the smaller advertising budget reported seeing a greater number of opposition than supportive commercials.

Thus, the Freedman and Sears argument that relative availability can account for selective exposure findings can be turned around to show how it can also suppress selectivity evidence. It should be noted that data reported by Atkin (1971) indicate that the need for reinforcement information overshadows most typical availability advantages. It is only for unusually obtrusive messages that availability will affect the rate of selective exposure.

Interest in a particular topic, a powerful correlate of general exposure, may stimulate voters to seek out many discrepant as well as supportive messages. In the Democratic Convention survey, close attention was paid by 33 percent of the pro-Nixon voters who reported watching the proceedings because they were interested in the political campaign, compared to 21 percent of the uninterested Nixon supporters. Degree of interest is correlated + .31 with attention to contrary messages in the Political Panel study, and + .17 in the Political Advertising study. In both cases, however, interest correlates even more strongly with attention to supportive content, and this produces a mild positive association with the selectivity index ($r = + .10$ and $ + .07$, respectively). Thus interest appears to contribute to absolute reception of discrepant information, but does not inhibit the selectivity rate.

Content attributes of the discrepant messages is another likely factor limiting selective exposure. Lowin (1967) found that easily refutable discrepant material was preferred over consonant material offered in a field experiment. The Political Advertising respondents who felt that the opposing candidate's ads were entertaining attended much more closely than those who thought the ads were boring ($r = + .22$). On the other hand, only 25 percent of the Nixon supporters who watched the Democratic Convention because of the excitement of conventions paid close attention, while 30 percent of Nixonites not citing this reason attended closely.

Finally, the original level of certainty variable may lead to low selectivity. An individual who is self-assured in his orientation may have little need for reinforcing information and seek out the opposite side for variety. For many specific supportive messages, a partisan may be well acquainted with the content due to previous exposure experiences, thus limiting the uncertainty reduction value of the material.

In sum, non-experimental demonstrations of de facto selective exposure in past and present research seem to be most parsimoniously explained by reinforcement information seeking rather than other utilitarian or expenditure factors. Several alternative explanations offered by Freedman and Sears to account for supportive message selection can be applied as well to account for cases when discrepant messages are selected. Their specific criticism of two early selective exposure studies does not appear to be well founded. A close examination of the data and context of the Erie County and Knowland telethon investigations indicates that neither can be challenged on the grounds proposed by Freedman and Sears.

Nevertheless, the issue raised by these observers serves a valuable function in directing attention away from the assessment of selective exposure in isolation. The research presented in this chapter outlines a number of significant exposure determinants that must also be considered in examining the viability of the selectivity proposition.

DISCUSSION

We have reviewed a wide variety of correlational evidence indicating the important role of extrinsic uncertainty in determining information-seeking patterns. The data consistently show that people attend messages that provide instrumental utility for adapting to practical environmental and psychological problems. It is clear that message exposure is frequently affected by informational needs associated with the formation of orientations and behaviors.

Throughout most of the discussion, various types of needs for information have been treated separately to identify how each contributes to message selection (although an attempt was made to examine how several variables combine to produce certain selective exposure behaviors). It should be pointed out that the individual may often be in more than one state of specific uncertainty—which may be conflicting, complementary, or redundant. It is the precise combination of these forces that determines the individual's information acquisition activity.

Although data reviewed here primarily involve exposure to public affairs messages in the mass media, information seeking need not be restricted to the manifest "informational" content. Such disparate types of content as soap operas, situation comedies, and advice columns may be sought out for relevant adjustive inputs for all types of uncertainty (Herzog, 1944; Wolf and Fiske, 1949; and Riley and Riley, 1951).

For example, Dervin and Greenberg (1972) discovered that 69 percent of a sample of low-income blacks agreed that people watch television because "they can learn from the mistakes of others," and 61 percent because "it shows how other people solve the same problems they have."

Selective Exposure Issue

It was proposed that defensive adaptation to post-affective and post-performance doubts would stimulate a need for reinforcement information. Extensive evidence from field studies demonstrates that partisans tend to pay more attention to supportive than discrepant messages.

The task of isolating the actual causes of apparent selectivity has challenged mass communication researchers for years. As outlined by Katz (1968: 788):

> The question is whether there is a motivated choice involved, one that is specifically associated with the quest for reinforcement, as distinct from the expression of "interest" or the search for utility and the like, and as distinct from de facto selectivity whereby circumstances rather than motives conspire to expose people to congenial communications.

Findings from several studies suggest that the alternative explanations offered by Freedman and Sears cannot account for disproportionate exposure and attention to consonant messages. Reinforcement seeking remains the most likely candidate for explaining the impressive array of selective exposure data that has accrued since 1940. Indeed, new evidence presented here indicates that these other determinants may obscure selectivity in some instances.

If people are predispositionally selective, the preference for supportive material seems to be relative rather than absolute. Only in rare cases do receivers exhibit total avoidance of discrepant messages. They typically choose a relatively greater number of reinforcing messages, or pay closer attention to these items, while exposing themselves to some inconsistent information.

The evidence also indicates that selectivity is much stronger for habitual source preferences than for selection of individual messages. The data clearly show that people characteristically attend particular magazines, newspapers, and broadcast stations that reflect their ideological views.

Future research must specify the conditions that produce selective exposure. According to the proposed paradigm, degree of preference for supportive information increases with the magnitude of uncertainty. Thus, attempts should be made to identify the adaptive requirements producing highly certain criterion states, and to measure the original state of confidence regarding current orientations and behaviors.

The search for individual difference correlates of partisan selectivity has been largely unsuccessful, although dogmatism remains a possible contributor to biased reception patterns.

Beyond Selective Exposure

The selective exposure issue has distracted research attention from a systematic examination of other instrumental and consummatory factors that produce general information seeking. It must be kept in mind that the need for reinforcement information is only one of many motivations for message selection. Indeed, it is probably of minor significance in most situations. Even when mass media messages are highly partisan, support seeking may not be the most important factor determining exposure. For instance, the partial correlation between candidate preference and attention to advertisements in the Political

Advertising study was only + .15, leaving a vast proportion of the variance unexplained.

A number of other determinants must also be considered. First, information seeking can be traced to needs for surveillance, guidance, and performance information. The role of these factors in combination with needs for reinforcement information requires further investigation.

Second, the contribution of message costs and receiver resources has also been suggested. Anticipated expenditures for obtaining and decoding a message have an important impact on many exposure decisions. These factors should be explored both in isolation and in conjunction with the various components of message reward value.

Third, the important contribution of topical interest to information seeking has been demonstrated in many of the studies presented in this paper. Perhaps intrinsic interest in the subject matter is the primary determinant of exposure to most types of mass messages. If this is the case, researchers should direct more attention to the process of interest formation. One line of research might examine how recurrent instrumental needs affect the development of intrinsic uncertainty about certain topic areas to such an extent that information is sought independently of specific extrinsic adaptive requirements.

Fourth, the entertainment value of a message cannot be ignored in a discussion of information seeking. An individual may expose himself to mass media content partially because it provides pleasurable sensation. This attribute of a message may supplement the informational reward value to produce exposure that might not otherwise occur. Researchers such as Mendelsohn (1972) have begun examining the role of entertainment attributes in stimulating increased information seeking.

Finally, rewards expected from the input of message content can be distinguished from "process" rewards associated with the act of obtaining and decoding a message. For instance, an individual may derive consummatory gratifications from the process of viewing television or reading a magazine. Even if the content itself is not rewarding, it may be satisfying to relax and escape from worries, avoid loneliness, or combat boredom.

Such behavior may also serve instrumental purposes when the individual tries to maintain his social status by using certain types of media messages and excluding others due to normative expectations of peers of authority figures, or when the act of attending certain messages serves to bolster his self-image as a user of some types of messages and an abstainer from others. Thus, an all-American male may watch football games to enact his social role and a factory worker may avoid reading The New York Times for fear of embarrassment, or a person who thinks of himself as a connoisseur of high culture may buy Atlantic magazine and shun James Bond movies.

Thus, the analysis of message exposure patterns cannot ignore these process factors. Although some research has dealt with this type of determinant (Stephenson, 1967), it is not clear how much of the variance in information seeking can be attributed to non-content attributes of a message. Subsequent research should seek to identify those process needs of the individual and qualities of the message that provide major contributions to information seeking.

A Proposed Model

The conceptualization and data described in this paper represent an initial attempt to understand the instrumental determinants of mass-media information seeking. However, any comprehensive model of the message selection process must include the various other factors in addition to instrumental utilities. This final section presents a preliminary outline of the basic elements affecting the exposure act.

An individual will select a mass media message when his estimate of its reward value exceeds his expectation of expenditures involved in seeking or avoiding it. Message reward value interrelates the individual's needs for informational and entertaining stimuli with the message's content and process attributes.

There is a positive reward value when exposure benefits exceed liabilities. Benefits are derived when the individual's needs are satisfied by the process of exposure and the input of message content. Both instrumental utilities and consummatory gratifications combine to produce the overall benefit factor.

Liabilities may occur occasionally when message exposure increases extrinsic uncertainty or creates aversive emotional arousal. For instance, a newspaper editorial may challenge the individual's prior attitude, or a war film may be sickening to the viewer. Process liabilities are particularly salient when social norms proscribe the open usage of certain forms of mass media output.

There are three basic components of the individual's mass communication needs. The need for information is a function of (a) extrinsic uncertainty produced by a perceived discrepancy between his current level of certainty and a criterion state determined by the importance of environmental objects to his adaptive requirements, and (b) intrinsic uncertainty generated by a perceived discrepancy between his present condition and a goal state of knowledge determined by his degree of personal interest in an object.

The need for entertainment is a function of (c) intrinsic desire for pleasurable emotional arousal created by a perceived discrepancy between his current condition and a criterion level of enjoyment.

Messages that reduce intrinsic uncertainty or increase enjoyment provide immediate consummatory gratifications during exposure. These two classes of satisfaction probably account for a vast proportion of variance in information seeking and entertainment seeking. The main concern here has been with messages that reduce extrinsic uncertainty. These have instrumental utilities for the receiver, serving as a useful aid in solving practical problems.

A given message may simultaneously provide multiple satisfactions. Thus, the message may be sought as an input in decision-making, because it describes an interesting topic, and because it is presented in an entertaining style.

Such benefits must be weighted against expenditures as well as liabilities. As discussed earlier, the expenditure concept relates the individual's resources to the message's cost attributes. It varies positively with expenses of obtaining and decoding the message, and negatively with avoidance expenses.

Turning to the modes of information transaction, there are several classes of message exposure or non-exposure, depending largely on the type of relationship between reward value and expenditures. Although overall reward value involves both informational and entertainment elements, the relative importance of each factor can be used to classify the message-handling activity. Information transaction is defined as message selection where the informational component contributes to more benefits than the entertainment component.

The act of message selection may be due to information seeking or occasional information yielding. *Information seeking* subsumes two modes of exposure, where the reward value of the message outweighs the positive expenditures of obtaining and processing it. *Information search* refers to seeking behavior that is purposefully initiated in response to an explicit question about a topic; the individual actively approaches a particular mass medium source with the overt intention of becoming exposed to either the general content or a specific message. *Information receptivity* describes an openness to question formulation resulting from encounters with topic-related cues during routine scanning of messages; selection occurs if the message-induced question arouses cognitive uncertainty.

Information yielding occurs when the individual is exposed because avoidance expenses exceed the seeking expenses. In this mode, the reward value of the message is typically zero or negative, as with redundant television commercials or discrepant front-page news stories.

Non-selection of messages usually results from simple information-ignoring, along with infrequent cases of information avoidance. In the *information ignoring* mode, the positive expenditures are greater than the value of the message to the individual; although the information may be slightly rewarding, it is not worth expending the resources necessary to obtain the message and process the content.

Information avoidance is non-selection due to a motivated effort to escape contacting a message with an overall negative valuation. The individual expects that the message will have liabilities in that it may increase extrinsic uncertainty. In order to qualify as avoidance, the individual must be aware of the message and the seeking expenditures should be fairly low.

Therefore, the individual will respond to various states of uncertainty by seeking out some messages, avoiding others, and ignoring the vast majority. Occasionally, the prominence of a message will lead to yielding when benefits are not present. The distinctions drawn among these types of information transactions offer one scheme for a more precise usage of message exposure terms.

CONCLUSION

The detailed conceptualization of instrumental utilities and the brief presentation of other relevant factors provide a framework for assessing the various determinants of mass media exposure patterns. The basic model represents one approach that can be used to organize and synthesize the assortment of previously unintegrated findings from hundreds of mass communication and social psychological investigations. It demonstrates the extremely complex nature of the message selection act, and outlines some of the variables that should be given prime consideration.

It should be pointed out that this conceptual framework is not limited to information seeking from the conventional mass media. Uncertainty and enjoyment discrepancies may generate seeking from interpersonal and institutional sources. The basic elements in the model can be extended to cover general scanning of the total message environment for the most appropriate source. The model can also be applied to new mass communication technologies as they can develop in future.

REFERENCES

ATKIN, C. K. (1970) Re-assessing Two Alternative Explanations of De Facto Selective Exposure. Paper presented at annual conference of American Association for Public Opinion Research, Lake George, N.Y.

――― (1971) "How imbalanced campaign coverage affects audience exposure patterns." Journalism Quarterly 48: 235-244.

――― (1972) "Anticipated communication and mass media information seeking." Public Opinion Quarterly 35: 188-189.

ATKIN, C. K., L. BOWEN, O. NAYMAN, and K. SHEINKOPF (1973) "Quantity vs. quality in televised political advertising: Patterns of reception and response in two gubernatorial campaigns." Public Opinion Quarterly 37 (in press).

ATKIN, C. K., W. CROUCH, and V. C. TROLDAHL (1973) The Role of the Campus Newspaper in the New Youth Vote. Paper presented at annual conference of International Communication Association, Montreal, Canada.

ATKIN, C. K., J. GALLOWAY, and O. NAYMAN (1973) Mass Communication and Political Socialization Among College Student Voters. Paper presented at annual conference of American Association for Public Opinion Research, Asheville, N.C.

BAUER, R. (1960) "Consumer behavior as risk taking," pp. 389-398 in Dynamic Marketing For a Changing World. Chicago: American Marketing Association.

BERELSON, B., P. LAZARSFELD and W. McPHEE (1948) Voting. Chicago: University of Chicago Press.

BERELSON, B. and G. STEINER (1964) Human Behavior. New York: Harcourt, Brace, World.

BLUME, N., and S. LYONS (1968) "The monopoly newspaper in a local election: The Toledo Blade." Journalism Quarterly 45: 286-292.

BLUMLER, J., and D. McQUAIL (1969) Television in Politics. Chicago: University of Chicago Press.

BUSS, L. J. (1967) "Motivational variables and information seeking in the mass media." Journalism Quarterly 44: 130-133.

BUTLER, D., and D. STOKES (1969) Political Change in Britain. New York: St. Martin's Press.

CAMPBELL, A., G. GURIN, and W. MILLER (1954) The Voter Decides. Evanston: Row, Peterson.

CLARKE, P., and J. JAMES (1967) "The effects of situation, attitude intensity and personality on information seeking." Sociometry 30: 235-245.

COX, D. (1967) Risk Taking and Information Handling in Consumer Behavior. Boston: Harvard Business School.

DAVISON, W. W. (1959) "Political significance of recognition via mass media―An illustration from the Berlin Blockade." Public Opinion Quarterly 22: 327-332.

DERVIN, B., and B. GREENBERG (1972) "The communication environment of the urban poor," pp. 195-233 in F. G. Kline and P. J. Tichenor (eds.) Current Perspectives in Mass Communication Research. Beverly Hills: Sage Publications.

DIAB, L. (1965) "Selectivity in mass communication media as a function of attitude-medium discrepancy." Journal of Social Psychology 67: 297-302.

FESTINGER, L. (1957) A Theory of Cognitive Dissonance. Evanston: Row, Peterson.

――― (1964) Conflict, Decision and Dissonance. Stanford: Stanford University Press.

FREEDMAN, J., and D. SEARS (1963) "Voters' perferences among types of information." American Psychologist 14: 375.

――― (1965) "Selective Exposure," pp. 57-97 in L. Berkowitz (ed.) Advances in Experimental Social Psychology. New York: Academic Press.

GLASER, W. (1965) "Television and voting turnout." Public Opinion Quarterly 29: 71-86.

GRUPP, F. (1969) "Magazine reading habits of political activists." Public Opinion Quarterly 33: 103-106.

HERZOG, H. (1944) "What do we really know about day-time serial listeners?" pp. 2-23 in P. Lazarsfeld and F. Stanton (eds.) Radio Research 1942-43. New York: Duell, Sloan, Pearce.

Journalism Educator (1972) "Cosmopolitan will receive ASJSA publishing citation." Volume 27 (July): 5.

KATZ, E. (1968) "On reopening the question of selectivity in exposure to mass communications," pp. 788-796 in R. Abelson et al. (eds.) Theories of Cognitive Consistency. Chicago: Rand McNally.

KATZ, E., and J. FELDMAN (1962) "The debates in light of research: a survey of surveys," pp. 173-223 in S. Kraus (ed.) The Great Debates. Bloomington: Indiana University Press.

KAY, H. (1954) "Toward an understanding of news-reading behavior." Journalism Quarterly 31: 15-32.

LANZETTA, J., and J. DRISCOLL (1968) "Effects of uncertainty and importance on information search in decision making." Journal of Personality and Social Psychology 10: 479-486.

LAZARSFELD, P., B. BERELSON, and H. GAUDET (1948) The People's Choice. New York: Columbia University Press.

LOWIN, A. (1967) "Approach and avoidance: Alternative modes of selective exposure to information." Journal of Personality and Social Psychology 6: 1-9.

MASLOW, A. (1963) "The need to know and the fear of knowing." Journal of General Psychology 68: 111-125.

McGINNIES, E., and L. ROSENBAUM (1965) "A test of the selective exposure hypothesis in persuasion." Journal of Psychology 61: 237-240.

McGUIRE, W. (1968) "Selective exposure: A summing up," pp. 797-800 in R. Abelson et al. (eds.) Theories of Cognitive Consistency. Chicago: Rand McNally.

McLEOD, J., C. ATKIN, and S. CHAFFEE (1972) "Adolescents, parents, and television use," pp. 173-313 in G. Comstock and E. Rubinstein (eds.) Television and Adolescent Aggressiveness. Washington: Government Printing Office.

McLEOD, J., D. WACKMAN, W. HURT, and H. PAYNE (1965) Political Conflict and Communication Behavior in the 1964 Political Campaign. Paper presented at annual conference of Association for Education in Journalism, Syracuse, N.Y.

McLEOD, J., S. WARD, and K. TANCILL (1965-66) "Alienation and the uses of the mass media." Public Opinion Quarterly 29: 583-594.

MENDELSOHN, H. (1972) Some Reasons Why Information Campaigns Can Succeed. Paper presented at annual conference of American Association for Public Opinion Research, Atlantic City, N.J.

MILLS, J. (1968) "Interest in supporting and discrepant information," pp. 771-776 in R. Abelson et al. (eds.) Theories of Cognitive Consistency. Chicago: Rand McNally.

NAYMAN, O., C. ATKIN, and W. GILLETTE (1973) "The four-day workweek and mass media use: A glimpse of the future." Journal of Broadcasting 17 (in press).

RARICK, G. (1970) "Political persuasion: The newspaper and the sexes." Journalism Quarterly 47: 360-364.

RILEY, M., and J. RILEY (1951) "A sociological approach to communications research." Public Opinion Quarterly 15: 445-460.

ROGERS, E., and C. ATKIN (1972) Patterns of Information Seeking about Abortion. Proposal submitted to National Institute of Child Health and Human Development.

ROKEACH, M. (1960) The Open and Closed Mind. New York: Basic Books.

ROSEN, E. (1964) "Factor analysis of the need for cognition." Psychological Reports 15: 619-625.

SAMUELSON, M., R. CARTER, and L. RUGGELS (1963) "Education, available time, and use of mass media." Journalism Quarterly 40: 491-496.

SCHRAMM, W., and R. CARTER (1959) "Effectiveness of a political telethon." Public Opinion Quarterly 23: 121-126.

SEARS, D. (1968) "The paradox of de facto selective exposure without preferences for supportive information," pp. 777-787 in R. Abelson, et al. (eds.) Theories of Cognitive Consistency. Chicago: Rand McNally.

SEARS, D., and R. ABELES (1969) "Attitudes and opinions," pp. 253-289 in Annual Review of Psychology. Palo Alto: Annual Reviews, Inc.

SEARS, D., and J. FREEDMAN (1967) "Selective exposure to information: A critical review." Public Opinion Quarterly 31: 194-213.

SHANNON, C., and W. WEAVER (1949) Mathematical Theory of Communication. Urbana: University of Illinois Press.

SHEINKOPF, K., C. ATKIN, and L. BOWEN (1972) "The functions of political advertising for campaign organizations." Journal of Marketing Research 9: 401-405.

——— (1973) "How campaign activists use political advertising." Journalism Quarterly 50 (in press).

STAR, S., and H. HUGHES (1950) "Report of an educational campaign: The Cincinnati plan for the United Nations." American Journal of Sociology 55: 385-400.

STEMPEL, G. (1961) "Selectivity in readership of political news." Public Opinion Quarterly 25: 400-404.

STEPHENSON, W. (1967) The Play Theory of Mass Communication. Chicago: University of Chicago Press.

TRENEMAN, J., and D. McQUAIL (1961) Television and the Political Image. London: Methuen.

VINYARD, D., and R. SIGEL (1971) "Newspapers and urban voters." Journalism Quarterly 48: 486-493.

WOLF, K., and M. FISKE (1949) "Why they read comics," pp. 3-50 in P. Lazarsfeld and F. Stanton (eds.) Communications Research 1948-49. New York: Harper.

Chapter 8

A CONCEPTUAL MODEL OF INFORMATION SEEKING, AVOIDING, AND PROCESSING

Lewis Donohew and Leonard Tipton

WITHIN THEIR SYSTEMS, individuals have stored a lifetime of experiences, some of them positively rewarded, some negatively rewarded, and some unrewarded. The sum total of these experiences has led to the formulation of goals, beliefs, knowledges, self-images, and alternative plans for coping with the environment (Miller et al., 1960). This cluster of cognitive elements comprises what we might call an individual's "image" of reality (Boulding, 1956a, b). On the basis of this image, man interprets his environment and chooses strategies for coping with it.

A fundamental part of this strategy-selection process involves communication activities—seeking, avoiding, and processing of information.[1] In some instances it involves initiative on the part of the participant and in others merely "holding still" to permit stimuli to come to him.

In his ordinary waking state, man is witness to a wide variety of stimuli or stimulus clusters. There usually are more stimuli coming at him than he can attend to all at once, and his system has to make decisions about them. Decisions include: which stimuli are important and which unimportant; which are supportive of the bundle of beliefs, goals, etc., and which are discrepant with it; which of the discrepancies are highly threatening to his image and which are only mildly threatening to it.

On the basis of his system's interpretation of the stimuli, he may feel it necessary to become an active seeker of the stimuli or of others related to them

AUTHOR'S NOTE: The process model proposed in the last section of this chapter was developed as part of a project on information behaviors supported by a grant from the University of Kentucky Research Foundation. The authors wish to acknowledge the help of Paul Wagner, research assistant on the project.

(such as seeking reinforcement); he may decide to actively avoid the stimuli; he may choose to "hold still" and take them in; or his system may tune them out without his being conscious that it has done so. The latter may occur through turning his thoughts away from a speaker with a monotonous delivery even though he has wanted to "listen" (Palmgreen, 1971), or because the interpretation his system makes of the stimuli seems so threatening it forces him into something like a miniature state of shock.

CONSISTENCY VS. VARIETY

This brings us to a point of theoretical controversy—whether man tends to be a seeker of *consistency* among his beliefs and actions (e.g., dissonance theory), or whether he tends to be a seeker of *variety*.

The consistency perspective, which has guided much of the research on information seeking, avoiding, and processing, holds that an individual seeks to maintain a steady state by resisting information that conflicts with his current image of reality and seeking information which supports it (Feldman, 1966; Abelson et al., 1968). Underlying the main approaches to these theories (e.g., by Heider, 1946; Newcomb, 1953; Osgood and Tannenbaum, 1955; Festinger, 1957; Abelson and Rosenberg, 1958) is the notion that thoughts, beliefs, attitudes, and behavior tend to organize themselves in meaningful and sensible ways.

In its more sophisticated form, inconsistency among cognitions is seen as the antecedent condition or cue aspect in the motivational framework which gives rise to an arousal or motivational state such as dissonance. This state is thus seen as an intervening variable between the antecedent condition of inconsistency and any consequent behavior. As such, its presence is necessary to the assumption of an active drive state directed at reducing it (which is accomplished by reducing the inconsistency).

Investigators have discovered, however, that consistency studies often produce inconsistent results (Clarke, 1965). Gergen (1968), among others, has argued that the body of evidence simply does not support the idea that consistency is the normal state of affairs. In an effort to increase the predictive power of consistency theories, mediating circumstances have been introduced. Festinger (1964), for example, has considered importance and curiosity as independent variables.

Two of the primary proponents of the alternative position (Fiske and Maddi, 1961) contend that man does not live by consistency alone. They hold that he attempts to preserve a steady state free of stress, but they predict that he does this by sometimes seeking *variety* (see also Maddi, 1968). The basic tenet in their activation level theory is that man attempts to maintain a level of activation to which he is accustomed. Variety is sought when the level of activation is below that desired.

Singer (1966) is primarily concerned with the implications of motivation. He hypothesizes that inconsistency is not absolutely motivating, but that it has an optimal level which is homeostatically regulated—a slight alteration of the usual consistency formulation. He says that inconsistency motivation should be treated as a type of drive, and the drive reduction would be motivating. Inconsistency might then be sought for the reward achieved upon its reduction.

Duffy (1962) finds support for her hypothesis that if other factors are constant, integration of behavior, i.e., consistent goal direction, seems less likely to be maintained when the degree of activation or arousal is either very low or very high. Situations having a high degree of significance will, if other factors are constant, produce a high degree of activation, while situations having a low degree of significance will, if other factors are constant, produce a low degree of activation. Significant situations will produce a strain toward consistency while insignificant situations will result in less of a tendency for consistent behavior.[2]

High activation or arousal can lead to oscillation, where behavior is not controlled. Low activation can lead to behavior that seems to have no direction, and quick changes in direction would be expected.[3]

Thus, it appears to us that although man appears to need a predictable environment (as consistency theorists would hold), he also seems to let a certain amount of uncertainty into his cognitive system. A popular view is that he does this in order to develop skills for coping with change and unfamiliar environments.

We hold with the view that the individual operates between boundaries of variety and consistency (or even redundancy), on the one hand tuning out information if it becomes monotonous in favor of something new, and on the other tuning it out if it reaches a certain threat level.

There is some support for this view from physiological psychology, in which the reticular formation seems to play exactly this gatekeeper function in the attention process—at times letting in new kinds of inputs in the presence of monotony, and at other times keeping them out to protect the individual from too much stimulation (Bakan, 1966).[4] There is strong opposing evidence on the latter point, however (Milner, 1970).

What we are suggesting is a kind of system analogy, postulating that an individual has a preferred "processing state" when he is engaging in information seeking behavior. When his "processing state" goes beyond preferred limits of variety (i.e., he is too aroused), he will tend to reduce his input of variety and seek consistent or even redundant information. When he exceeds preferred levels on the consistency end of this continuum (i.e., his arousal level is very low), he will seek content that is more novel for him. We are assuming the individual must continue his information seeking, rather than correcting internally (e.g., daydreaming) or entering a new situation entirely.

We are unable to specify what might be the components that determine preferred states (if they do indeed exist). We feel it is probably some interface between situation and cognitive style. We feel that the "distance" between preferred levels of variety and consistency varies greatly across individuals, and probably is related to such cognitive personality styles as open- or closed-mindedness and self-esteem, which will be discussed later in this chapter.

We also suggest that on some kinds of information or topics there is a short operating range between the poles, most probably toward one end or another. That is, the individual seeks almost all novel content or almost all redundant content. In other situations with different priorities and different constraints upon him, the range will be much larger. The individual will continue inputting either novel or monotonous information much longer before turning away from it to "correct" his state.

Beyond this we expect that, given a hierarchy of beliefs and goals—the total image of reality—individuals may sometimes appear to defend consistency and sometimes to behave in apparently inconsistent ways because of underlying (and unrecognized) more important cognitions which play an overriding role.

We hold primarily with the consistency position,[5] but contend that, because of the narrow approach of most experiments, support for this position has been mixed, that multi-dimensional and potentially overriding cognitions have not been taken into account (Donohew and Palmgreen, 1971a).[6] We believe that the individual is willing to tolerate inconsistency, and may even seek it at lower levels of his image structure if such behaviors help to maintain consistency at higher levels, i.e., if they help him defend more highly rated basic beliefs or are consistent with more fundamental goals. An example of this might be an individual who watches the television speech of a candidate he opposes because he places great value on his "open-mindedness."

Changes in the basic image tend to take place slowly. Alterations in the cognitions appear to come usually after opposing cognitions have overcome a tendency of the system to avoid or reject them (such as through selective exposure, perception, comprehension, or retention—or the seeking or reinforcement). However, there are cases of apparently rapid conversion (such as a sudden religious or political conversion) in which the belief structure is suddenly altered. In such cases, Boulding (1956a) has suggested, something strikes the nucleus of the belief structure. The old structure is broken down and a radically different structure is organized to achieve a new statis.

It should be noted that these sudden reorganizations are special cases apparently involving different processes and are not common in the day-to-day seeking, avoiding, and processing of information by human beings. This paper will be devoted to what man appears to do most of the time.

The 'Image'

For the purposes of this paper, an individual's "image of reality" is divided into three parts. First are the goals, beliefs, and knowledges which an individual has compiled as a result of his lifetime of experiences. These cognitive "objects" are defined as any concepts, issues, material objects, or ideas which exist psychologically for a person.

Each object can be subdivided into its various "attributes." Attributes are the characteristics, traits, or qualities applied to describe objects as the person perceives them (see Bruner et al., 1956; Brown, 1958; Carter, 1965; Zajonc, 1960, 1969).

In storing information, there is physiological support for the idea that the individual orders or "maps" his image through some hierarchical arrangement of attributes (Guyton, 1962). These attributes have dimensions: prominence, which is the rank of a given attribute along a continuum from those which most nearly characterize an object to those which least characterize it; and valence, which refers to the evaluative ratings of the object on a particular attribute, from most favorable to least favorable (Zajonc, 1969; Donohew and Palmgreen, 1971b).

Thus, one might perceive an object as possessing a certain attribute, consider that attribute to be highly important with respect to the object (high in prominence), and consider that on this attribute the object is "good" or "bad," thus assigning it a valence rating.

The second part of an individual's image of reality is the concept of self. This includes an evaluation of his ability to cope with various situations. A self-esteem measure would tap this dimension, although it would not contain self-evaluations of competency in *specific* situations which probably are considered in the process we are describing.

The third part of the image of reality is an information-handling "set" developed out of past experiences. This "set" probably controls the selection of information used by the individual to cope with the environment. Here, we are talking about an individual's information-seeking and processing "styles," developed according to which style has been successful. Thus, given the basic hierarchy of beliefs, goals, etc., and the variety of situations in which a person might find himself, he permits more or less inconsistent information into his system—either through holding still for it (receiving) or through active avoiding or seeking—according to his previous experiences with processing information.

We think one index of this is dogmatism (Rokeach, 1960; Miller and Rokeach, 1968), or open-to-closed mindedness. For our purposes, we are interested not so much in dogmatism as a personality style but as a predictor of information-behavior style. It refers to the information strategies that a person has learned to use as a general rule.

In his experience with using various information strategies, he may have been rewarded for exposing himself to other points of view, for example, and tend to employ more and broader seeking strategies. Or he might make less use of another device for avoiding stress—discounting the source. These strategies are among several described by Rokeach as characteristics of open- or closed-minded persons. However, we believe they should serve well in an information perspective also (Donohew, Parker, and McDermott, 1972; Donohew and Palmgreen, 1971b).

Chaffee and McLeod (1971) distinguish a similar construct, although in situational terms only. Rejecting the use of the term "image," they describe a "frame of reference." This is a person's mental set that precedes subsequent information-processing behaviors (in time) and that also organizes or shapes the processing approaches a person will use. Frame of reference is a general cognitive style that they separate from "definition of situation."

In terms of our concern with information seeking, frame of reference corresponds to our "image" component. We see definition of situation as being composed of such things as immediate goals, priorities, and availability of information in the immediate situation. While specific situational components may influence processing styles more directly than the broader image, the image should influence and organize the definition of the situation.

BACKGROUND

We have been separately engaged in a number of studies of information seeking, avoiding, and processing (Donohew, 1966; Chaffee et al., 1969; Tipton, 1970; Donohew, Parker, and McDermott, 1972; Donohew and Palmgreen, 1971b). Out of these studies and a review of existing theories in this area, a conceptual model based on the assumptions briefly sketched above has been developed. Before describing the model, we will review some of this work and the evolution in our thinking.

In part, it grew out of our reservations about one of the most popular theories underlying information seeking experiments—cognitive dissonance—and its ambiguous prediction record.[7] These reservations were expressed in an earlier paper (Donohew and Palmgreen, 1971a). We are concerned that a strict interpretation of dissonance—or consistency theories generally—often does not seem to apply when the situation involves some element likely to evoke curiosity or where utility of information is a major consideration.

Furthermore, the expectation of consistently consistent behavior does not seem to square with what other disciplines, such as physiological psychology, seem to tell us about the way the human system works. A variety-seeking point of view, which is not so much a departure from consistency as it appears on the surface, can account for seeking of the apparently discrepant information which has created dissonance among dissonance researchers. It permits us to acknowledge that people do get bored, or curious, or seek information that is *useful* to them even though it may disagree with—or at least does not support—their current beliefs or conception of reality.

In a critical review of dissonance, Donohew and Palmgreen (1971a) also suggested that personality variables, particularly dogmatism and self-esteem, be incorporated into studies carried out under a consistency paradigm (see Clarke and James, 1967).

Underlying Processes

The interpretation of dogmatism as an indicator of information-processing style, described in the introductory section, emerged from a study which sought to incorporate some of the suggestions from our critique of dissonance into an experimental design (1971b). The study examined fundamental processes underlying selective exposure to information. The experiment involved exposing subjects to discrepant and supportive information and measuring the amount of stress produced under varying prominence x valence x personality (dogmatism) conditions in a 2x2x2 repeated-measures factorial design (Winer, 1962).

One of the findings from this study was that discrepant information *did* produce greater psychological stress than supportive information, but with the qualification that this occurred only among low-dogmatic persons. The results provided some empirical support for an hypothesized "open-minded cognition" model of dogmatism. We felt that it might well be that low-dogmatic persons possess such a cognition which motivates them to evaluate fairly *all* types of information, both discrepant and supportive, and that this attempt to "grant the good points" of opposing arguments—possibly requiring a restructuring of cognitions—is highly stressful.

Nonetheless, low dogmatics may be motivated to *expose* themselves to stress-inducing discrepant information because failure to expose themselves to such material would run counter to their open-minded self-concept and perhaps produce even greater stress.

On the other hand, the high dogmatic, when actually confronted with discrepant materials, seems to experience less stress than the low dogmatic. The high dogmatic might therefore manifest less tendency to avoid discrepant information. Yet, lacking an open-minded cognition, he should also possess no motivation to expose himself to discrepant material and should thus manifest relatively less exposure to such material than the low dogmatic. (See Figure 1.)

We had similar findings in two pilot studies (Donohew, Parker, and McDermott, 1972), in which an eye camera was used to record actual selection of discrepant, supportive, and balanced information. Stress was measured with galvanic skin response (GSR) equipment. In both studies, dogmatism was negatively correlated with arousal during exposure to discrepant information. (See Table 1.)

Despite this, open-minded subjects exposed themselves more to discrepant material and closed-minded subjects more to supportive material in one of the studies. Correlations were not significant in the other study.

We see this as supporting our view that in the presence of competing multiple cognitions persons tend to remain consistent with those cognitions that are most highly valued. In this instance, there are two avenues open to the subjects. For those who do not have an "overriding" open-minded cognition (those higher on dogmatism), once they perceive material to be discrepant they may turn away (which they tended to do here). Those who possess the open-minded cognition (those lower on dogmatism), however, are caught in a dilemma. They must endure stress from the discrepant information and the prospect of having to reorder their cognitions or they must endure perhaps even greater stress if they turn away from discrepancy and violate their own "open-mindedness" rule. The option those lower on dogmatism tended to take was to endure the discrepancy.

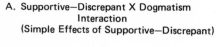

A. Supportive–Discrepant X Dogmatism
   Interaction
   (Simple Effects of Supportive–Discrepant)

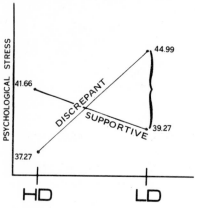

C. Dogmatism X Attribute Prominence
   Interaction
   (Simple Effects of Dogmatism)

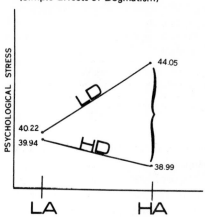

B. Supportive–Discrepant X Dogmatism
   Interaction
   (Simple Effects of Dogmatism)

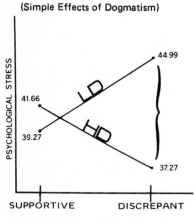

D. Dogmatism X Attribute Prominence
   Interaction
   (Simple Effects of Attribute Prominence)

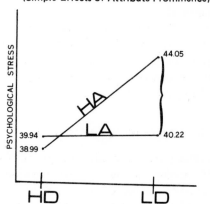

Source: Donohew and Palmgreen (1971b)

Figure 1: INTERACTIONS IN PSYCHOLOGICAL STRESS STUDY

TABLE 1
CORRELATIONS OF PERSONALITY AND AROUSAL
GSR

	Discrepant	*Supportive*	*Balanced*
Dogmatism			
Study 1	−.78	a	a
Study 2	−.73	.72	a

SOURCE: Donohew, Parker, and McDermott, 1972.
a. Correlations not significant at .05 level.
Study 1: p < .05 if r > .45.
Study 2: p < .05 if r > .42.

We think this was because for them open-mindedness was a more highly valued belief.

Unfortunately, we cannot offer proof of the validity of this explanation. We did not ask subjects if they perceived themselves as open-minded. Thus, at this point, our evidence for avoidance by turning away is based on the one small study above; for avoidance by "discounting"—which we think illustrates the same rule of staying with the higher-valued cognition—it comes from two studies: the Donohew and Palmgreen experiment cited here using psychological measures, and a previously unreported study (Donohew and Baseheart, forthcoming) of the same subjects using a physiological measure (galvanic skin response).

All this refers to what persons do when *confronted* with discrepant information. What they do in situations in which they have the option of *seeking* information to help them cope with various situations is another question. Here we are concerned with identifying various information strategies utilized by individuals.

Information Seeking Strategies

There are many different questions that must be asked in connection with information seeking strategies. The most basic, probably, is: what is information? For our immediate purposes, we are defining the concept as any message (probably verbal) that a person expends any effort to attend to (including holding still for it). Such situations generally involve using that information to make some decision or to perform some task.

Much information seeking research is intertwined with decision making. Dissonance theorists operate from the premise that pre-decisional information seeking is unselective (Festinger, 1964) in the sense that the individual has no content preferences, other than that the content be relevant to the decision. This probably is not meant to be taken too literally. Any act of information seeking involves some selection. A study by Chaffee and Tipton (Chaffee et al., 1969) indicates that even in pre-decision states, there is a preference for messages containing attributes that can be used to discriminate choices.

Another consideration is the order in which information is sought. There is some evidence that a preferred order is first a neutral (i.e., not obviously biased) orientation toward a topic, followed by information that presents a favorable view of a position, followed by content that attacks a position or view (Tipton, 1970).

Still another strategy consideration that we have studied involves the point at which the individual exerts closure—that is, the point at which he decides to quit seeking information. The Chaffee-Tipton study seemed to indicate that subjects felt it was a good idea to delay closure as long as possible. Experimental studies have tended to indicate that subjects generally seek more information than is necessary (Edwards, 1962).[8]

We are assuming that in a great many information-seeking situations closure is not as much a function of sufficiency of information as it is a function of factors such as running out of time to seek information. In these cases the strategy an individual adopts becomes of crucial importance, because he may be forced to close before he would really like to. Thus he is forced to go with only that information he collects at that point. Some strategies should be better than others for maximizing the probability that the individual has "good" information at that point to go with.

Our thinking has led us at this stage to consider two strategies individuals might use. We call one *broad-focus* and the other *narrow-focus*. In our view a broad-focus strategy is one that initially involves identifying potential sources of information and inputting them on a relatively non-selective basis—i.e., mapping a number of possible sources. Then the broad-focuser would review his information, select the "best," and organize his other information around it—given his image, pressures for closure, availability of sources, etc.

A narrow-focus strategy, on the other hand, is one in which the individual at first focuses on one source of information and adds sources and ideas as he comes across them.

To give an example, assume two students doing a term paper on dissonance theory. A student using a broad-focus strategy might look under "dissonance" in the card catalogue, make extensive use of such title sources as Psychological Abstracts, if available, and compile a long list of titles. Not until then would he begin to look at specific content.

A student using a narrow-focus strategy might begin with one key article (or book), check the footnotes and titles of other articles, etc., and build his sources from the center outward until he decides he has enough, or is forced to close because of deadlines.

For a more homely example, a gardner faced with the problem of bugs on his roses might begin by a trip to the library to locate some books on the topic, if he were a broad-focuser. The narrow-focuser might try one source to get some advice and continue his information search only if the information were not available on the first try.

In other words, a broad-focuser approaches his topic gingerly; a narrow-focuser jumps right in.

While the examples present these strategies as dichotomies, we recognize that they more realistically should be viewed as "poles" of a continuum. But we assume that these two kinds of strategies generally describe approaches people actually use. One of our concerns is with identifying variables that lead an individual to adopt one or the other. We would expect the image may have much to say about it, especially such personality characteristics as tapped by dogmatism or self-esteem.

We also recognize that situational components would seem to be more useful in predicting strategies. Availability of information and time pressure are bound to be important. Work by Stamm (Chaffee et al., 1969) identified a curiously consistent finding about the effects of time pressure and available information. In a variety of situations, Stamm presented subjects with a puzzle they had to work and with choices between three sets of messages—Set A, Set B, and Set A and B. In all situations, Set A and B was the "best" choice. Stamm also manipulated time pressure. He consistently found that his subjects chose the Set A *or* Set B when presented with the choice under maximum time and minimum time to study the information and decide on a game plan. Those in the middle-time pressure conditions tended to choose the Set A *and* B message.

Stamm's protocol is important. He first presented subjects with the game they were to play. Then he varied the time element by the stratagem of pretending to be called away before actually allowing the subjects to choose information. In the minimum time pressure, he was not called away. For other conditions, he would allow time lapses of 2 to 11 minutes in one experiment and 45 to 90 seconds in another.

It may be that there is a "need to move" (or perhaps a sense of panic as an extreme case) that arises in most individuals when first presented with a decision or task assignment. Stamm's minimum-time pressure subjects were presented with the alternatives and the opportunity to act immediately. The subjects in the middle conditions were given a chance to wait out an initial "panic" reaction.

Although the fit is not good, we see Stamm's A-or-B choice as somewhat akin to narrow-focusing in our scheme, A-and-B to broad-focusing. Time pressure should require a narrow-focus strategy. If there is no perceived time pressure, an individual could use a broader approach (perhaps a safer strategy, but certainly more time-consuming). One might expect, then, narrow-focusing from people under time pressure and from people confronted with a choice and the opportunity to seek information immediately. Otherwise one might expect a broad-focus approach.

A PRELIMINARY STUDY

Before laying out a plan for further research, we felt we had reached a point where we needed to try out some indicators of an individual's image of reality, his assessment of a situation, and his information-seeking styles, and to look at the relationships among these variables. At this stage, before defining more controlled experimental situations, we wanted to insure that we were, as Carter and Ruggels (1968) put it, "avoiding the tendency to look for the 'lost coin' under a convenient light rather than in the place where it was dropped."

For our study we used an upperclass course in communication theory, taught by one of the authors, where students would be seeking information for a term paper. Although we had some informal expectations about what should go with what, we hedged on specific hypotheses. The data collection involved measures of personality and self-reports on goals and strategies. In the study we used measures of the following:

Image. (1) Personality—self-esteem (Rosenberg, 1965); dogmatism (Troldahl and Powell, 1965), and variety-seeking (Zuckerman et al., 1964). (2) Goals—grade aim, intent to go to graduate school, and interest in communication theory. (3) Knowledge—prior knowledge of the topic.

Situation. Time pressures and availability of information.

Information seeking. Number of topics considered, number of literature sources cited, number of interpersonal sources consulted, variety-seeking behavior, information search style (broad-focus versus narrow-focus), and time of closure.

Measure of success. Final grade.

This gave us an opportunity to gather data from people in a realistic and relatively uncontrolled information-seeking situation in which we had some notion of the time order of behaviors and could gain an overview of the sequence of events.

The students were told about the term paper assignment early in the semester and soon afterward filled out the personality measures. Later, after they had done some initial work on the assignment, they filled out a brief questionnaire on goals (grade aim, intent to go to graduate school, and an intellectual goal—interest in communication theory), other demands on their time, and availability of information.

The students were also required to keep a diary of their work on the term paper, including why they chose items, their notes from the items, records of conversations, and notes on reactions or thoughts during their work. All of the students were called in at least once for a consultation with the authros or a research assistant a few weeks after the project began for a review of the diaries and a briefing on their record-keeping. Although we had intended the diaries to be a major data source, we were reluctant to give the students more than a broad, general idea of the kinds of entries we wanted because of the danger of forcing them to follow our expectations and hunches.

We were able to get complete data (personality measures, questionnaires, diaries, and finished term papers) from eighteen students.

Four of us coded the diary entries, using the following criteria:

Availability. We looked for statements that the student was having problems getting access to books or articles. If no such statements appeared, we assumed there was no trouble. We used three judgmental categories—high (N=3), middle (N=7), and low (N=8).

Prior knowledge. The students generally would indicate why they were interested in a particular topic. Those who noted they had been exposed to the topics in other classes were coded as having high prior knowledge (N=9). Middle (N=6) and low (N=3) were also coded.

Variety-seeking behavior. This variable was based on students' statements expressing preference for fresh and novel material or an interest in exploring new fields. These coded as high (N=6), middle (N=5), and low (N=7).

Broad-focus/narrow-focus. Students who went first to card catalogues (or equivalents) to begin building sources were coded as broad-focusers (N=6). Those who first went to one or two key sources (even though they may have found them through the card catalogue) and built outward were coded as narrow-focusers (N=7). Students who could not be clearly identified as being one kind of strategist or the other were coded as mixed (N=5).

Closure. Early closure (N=9) was coded for those students who took notes on only one topic and stuck with it through the semester, even though they may have reported they were considering other topics. Middle closure (N=5) was coded for those students who considered up to four topics, and wrote on the second or third considered. Late closure (N=4) involved more than four topics.[9]

We also used the diaries for other information-seeking measures. For number of topics considered, number of literature sources consulted, and number of interpersonal sources consulted, we simply counted from the notes in the diary.

Results

The data analysis reported below involves zero-order correlations. For a sample of 18, correlations of at least .39 are required for a two-tailed probability of .10, and .46 for a probability of .05.

Ideally, our research design would involve a more powerful procedure which would help us establish causal relationships. This is not possible here because of the limited sample size. However, for clarity we have arranged the major variables in a time order which resembles a path analysis scheme, with our image variables first, then those we associate with priority arrangement and assessment of situation, then information-seeking measures and strategies, and finally the measure of "success," the student's final grade.

Image

The data indicate that many of the components of the image do not predict directly to information strategies. Instead, they seem to predict to other image components which may follow in point of time—personality to goals, for example—and to other variables which we might call "situational perspectives." These, in turn, predict to information strategies. The personality components, in other words, seem to determine such things as immediate goals, perceived availability of information, time pressure, and prior knowledge, and these to influence the information strategies adopted.

To support this, let us look at the reported correlations. Dogmatism is negatively correlated with grade aim (r=-.44), but not directly related to any other variables.

Variety-seeking is positively related to graduate school aim (r=.43), but not to any other variables outside the personality cluster.

Self-esteem is the one personality variable which *does* reach outside the cluster. It is related not only to the kind of grade aspirations persons have in the course (r=.42) and to graduate school aim (r=.45), but also to an information-seeking behavior—use of printed sources (r=-.63).

This negative relationship is somewhat puzzling unless one explains it with a rule of thumb offered by MacLean. He and one of the authors (Donohew) were presenting papers at an international meeting. MacLean (whose paper listed no outside sources) told Donohew (who had offered many) that the number of sources cited was an index (inversely related) of self-esteem. He was jesting (we think) but he may be right.

Other image components are more fruitful in indicating information strategies. Our measure of immediate goals (grade aim), for instance, correlates negatively with variety-seeking behavior (r=-.68) and with narrow-focus strategy (r=-.51). It would appear that students aiming for a higher grade tend not to attach much importance to searching out novel material but rather tend to stay with more conventional (possibly less risky) subject matter. In terms of our system analogy presented earlier, they seem to have a narrow "range" between variety and consistency, located toward the consistency end of the continuum. They also tend to use the strategy of building a large list of potentially useful titles before beginning to seek information that will develop their topic.

Another goals measure, aspiration to go to graduate school, revealed some curious results. It was negatively correlated with the number of printed sources consulted (r=-.52). As something of a validation, the measure was also correlated negatively with the number of sources listed in the term-paper bibliography (r=-.38). On the other hand, this goals measure was related to the grade the student received (r= .54).

Prior knowledge of the topic for the term paper was related with going to the heart of the matter as an information search strategy, i.e., narrow-focusing (r=.59). On the other hand, it served to increase problems with finding specific sources, i.e., the higher the prior knowledge, the lower the availability index (r=-.54). Those who had higher prior knowledge perhaps knew more specifically what sources they wanted. They reported more difficulties in finding these specific sources, whereas those with less knowledge seemed more willing to go with whatever they found available on the shelves.

Situation

We had two variables loosely tied under the heading of assessing the immediate situation: time pressure and availability of information.

The time pressure measure was an index of several questions asking about other demands upon the student's time. The higher this index, the more the student had problems finding information available (r=.49). Time pressure as a situational constraint did little by itself in predicting to information-seeking variables. We had anticipated that this index would correlate with both closure and narrow-focusing as a strategy. It correlated positively with (late) closure (r=.42) but not with narrow-focus.

Information-Seeking Strategies

We have already noted the variables in our study that preceded (in time order) our strategy measures and that were correlated with them. Some of the interrelationships among search strategies, variety seeking and closure are also worth noting.

The broader the focusing strategy used, the later the students closed their information search (r=-.52). Narrow search is positively correlated with variety-seeking behavior (r=.43). There was no significant relationship between closure and variety. The broad-focusers then, seem to be those students with high grade aim and lots of time to spend on assignments (maybe because they start earlier on their information seeking). They consider several topics (r=-.56 between narrow-focusing and number of topics considered) and close relatively late. The broad-focuser in this instance also has the better success (r=-.42 between narrow-focus and final grade).

Remarks on the Study

In the introduction to this preliminary study, we indicated that it was not our intent to test specific hypotheses, as is done in many studies of information seeking which use it as a convenient situation to test an established psychological theory. Rather, we were concerned here with information seeking per se, maintaining that research should proceed from a perspective that attempts a broader coverage of the information process. It seemed to us that the researcher ought to try to visualize the larger perspective by attempting to treat factors that *precede* and those that *follow* specific information situations. We sought to do this by following a situation from stimulus presentation (here, assignment of a term project) through the information search that followed it.

All of this is leading toward presentation of a model of information seeking, avoiding, and processing. We have already introduced the principal components in a broad, general way. Now we have tried out some measures. The correlations observed here form a "common sense" pattern of regularities that is generally consistent with our expectations. However, our results indicate that many of the core components of our tentative model described in the introduction— personality measures, for instance—do not predict directly to information strategies. Instead, they seem to predict to what we might call "situational perspectives," which in turn predict to strategies. This is not a result of our ordering variables according to time. It was the way correlations occurred in a zero-order matrix of all variables. The core components, in other words, seem to determine such things as immediate goals, perceived availability of information, time pressure, and prior knowledge, and these, in turn, to influence the information strategies adopted.

The present study made no real attempt to tackle the consistency formulation that we spent so much time on in the introduction to this paper and in previous studies even though it appears to be an important factor in information seeking. We were more concerned with checking out our view of strategies and whether or not they seem to be viable descriptions of the ways subjects actually behaved. Variety seeking as it was measured here seems to be something different from what occurs at the presumed consistency checkpoint in the human system. In the latter, the first thing the brain does when it gets an input is to compare that input to what is stored in the system. Instead, variety-seeking behavior in this study is an information search strategy.

We will offer a consistency checkpoint in our model, but to test it we will need some more comprehensive way of assessing the preferred "processing state" of a person between poles of consistency and variety, as discussed near the beginning of this paper. We will also need to determine where he is in relation to that state at the time he makes decisions in various situations. The Sensation Seeking Scale (Zuckerman et al., 1964) employed in this study was not as helpful here as we had expected. If the formulation to be proposed is to advance, much more work also needs to be done in developing adequate "cognitive mapping" procedures to cover basic components of the image of reality, such as is being done by Kline and Davis (1971), or was done in a more situation-related way by Edelstein and Hollander (1969). The procedure proposed by Donohew and Palmgreen (1971a) may be too laborious for effective use in a comprehensive study.

Our attempts to account for the correlation patterns point to adding the factor of "risk-taking" as another image/situation component. The term-paper situation is presumed to have a high degree of significance for all subjects and thus should result in less risk-taking. That is, given the importance of doing well in a course, subjects should generally tend to inhibit their variety seeking and to choose safer routes. We had not, however, included any specific consideration of safe versus risky strategies in our operations. We might argue that variety seeking is a riskier strategy than concentrating upon the familiar area. In this case, variety seeking tended to be shown by those subjects who had lower goals. We might also expect the more open-minded persons to choose riskier strategies than those who are closed-minded, although the relationships we found among dogmatism, prior knowledge of topic, and variety seeking did not support this .expectation.

Another distinction that should be made in other studies is the difference between information seeking in what we call a "decision phase" and that in a "task phase." We had originally considered a "topic selection" phase and a "topic development" phase, but did not anticipate the real importance of such a distinction. In terms of utility, for instance, Atkin (1970, and this volume, Chapter 7) carefully separates decision utility from communicatory utility, and it seems clear that this is what we are faced with here. Topic selection is decisional; topic development concerns what information the student will look for to use in his own paper. Atkin limits the term communicatory utility to situations where a person intends to use information in interpersonal discussion only. We prefer a broader definition. Information has communicatory utility if the person wants to include it in any kind of output—conversation, speech-making, writing a report or whatever. The decision phase appears to be more theoretically interesting, and most of the variables we discuss in our introduction are more relevant to this first phase. Future studies should build in a distinction between information seeking to decide what action to take and information seeking to find ways to implement that decision.

Another aspect of information strategies which now appears worth investigating is the question of printed versus interpersonal sources. We had not expected the marked differences we found between the two in this kind of situation. The interpersonal sources appear to be the more complex of the two. People go to printed sources only to *seek* information. But Clarke (1973) noted three reasons people might go to (and are qualified to report on) interpersonal sources: to seek information about a topic, to give information about a topic, and to seek information about the other person. The diaries suggested a fourth: to find out something about "self." (Am I on the right track; is what I'm doing consistent with my goals, etc.?) Jones (1967) advanced the proposition that people tend to go to expert (impersonal) sources when they have already reached closure about "moving" from one psychological state to another. When they are undecided but leaning toward not moving or not changing, they consult a "co-oriented peer." Some of the diaries suggested that the students would consult with the professor when they were about ready to switch to a new topic, and would announce the decision (in their diaries) after that session. If they were continuing along previous lines, their interpersonal sources tended to be friends. Since we have no real assessment of what these conversations were like (compared to the notes we asked them to take on their readings) we have no real inputs for this as a research question.

Our process model will be deliberately aimed at being broad enough to encompass a variety of information-seeking situations. Obviously, not all components or points in the model are needed to describe behaviors in all situations. Our next efforts should be directed at developing protocols that will allow us to "compress" the process—i.e., an information-seeking situation extending over a matter of hours instead of a matter of months as in this study. Also needed are protocols that allow more control over such things as availability of information, content, and time pressure and permit development of clearer criteria for decision points in the model. These seem to us to be necessary steps before proceeding to more focused experimental procedures.

A PROCESS MODEL

The model proposed here will demonstrate how the three parts of the image of reality described earlier—(1) goals, beliefs, knowledges; (2) evaluation of self; and (3) information-handling "set"—are used by the individual in acting upon a cluster of stimuli which define a situation in the environment.

In some instances, man might be called upon to react to collections of stimuli which he believes affect fundamental parts of the image. Most of the time, however, he probably is facing routine challenges to his system's efforts to maintain a steady course. For example, he may be assigned a report to write, be told that he's not caring for his teeth properly, have to decide how to vote on an issue, or have to choose between job offers.

Even the latter two of these messages might be called routine in that they probably do not affect fundamental components of the image, as might happen if a person were challenged to give up his studies for the ministry on the grounds that conventional religion is "harmful to mankind."

The homely examples we have offered here involve situations in which a person is largely triggered into a seeking or processing mode. However, holding still to receive, or taking action to avoid, are also behaviors that need to be included in a general model of seeking, avoiding, and processing of information.

A situation of this kind might be the appearance on the television screen of a political candidate who has previously said things the viewer found upsetting. The receiver can hold still here, or actively avoid by turning off the TV set or leaving the room. This model is an attempt to demonstrate how the individual arrives at various responses.

A Flow Chart of the Model

Our interpretation of the process involved here is presented in flow chart form in Figure 2. The chart is tentative and is presented for heuristic purposes only. It contains elements we have abstracted from theory and a review of studies (including our own), but the actual *order* of the steps is somewhat arbitrary.

We will begin with a cluster of stimuli being brought into close enough proximity to the person's sensory apparatus that they are capable of arresting his attention. For our purposes, we might classify these clusters into two types: those requiring further information seeking, and those that do not.

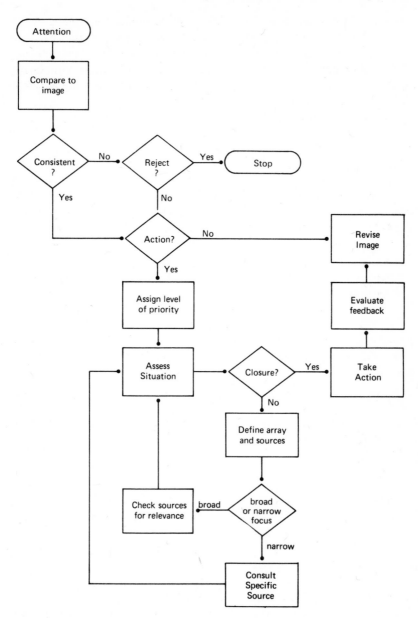

Figure 2: A FLOW MODEL OF INFORMATION SEEKING, AVOIDING, AND PROCESSING

From a physiological perspective, the first test they must pass is an *attention* check. The stimulus characteristics must possess a minimal level of color, intensity, movement, or other attention-arresting properties to pass an attention check conducted by his system. What is "minimal" for passing this test probably depends on the individual's state of arousal at a given moment (Berlyne, 1960, 1968; Fowler, 1965).

A second preliminary attention test has to do with the cognitive (content) characteristics of the stimuli. The stimuli in most instances must at the very least be recognized. It is at this point that most studies of communication behavior begin.

Following the attention check, the stimulus cluster is compared to the individual's set of beliefs, goals, and knowledges, and the individual makes a decision about the possible relevance or non-relevance of the stimuli to his *image of reality*. Somewhere about here he also is likely to determine the amount of *consistency* which exists between the "old" image of reality and this new stimulus cluster. If the new information is so inconsistent that it seems to be threatening to the individual or if the new material is so consistent that it is monotonous the person may tune it out.

The individual's next step is decisional: "Does this cluster require some *action* of me?" If, as in the case of the term paper, the answer is yes, he must begin the process of choosing the appropriate response. If action is not required, the information may become a part of the *image*.

Before deciding what action to take, several factors come into consideration: The individual's assessment of the situation (including his own state of boredom or stimulation), prior experience (including beliefs, goals, and knowledges), his concept of self (whether or not he is capable of employing a particular strategy, or coping with the situation by himself), and his information processing "style" (e.g., seeking or avoiding).

Based on these considerations, the individual makes a decision: "Am I ready to take action on the cluster of stimuli?" In other words, the individual determines if he is ready to exert closure. If the answer is yes, the person may take what he deems to be the appropriate action. However, the individual may feel that he requires further information before taking action.

On the basis of the prominence and valence ratings stored in his image—i.e., how important he feels the topic to be, how strongly he feels for or against it—and his assessment of the urgency of the need for action, the new stimulus cluster also is assigned a *level of priority* relative to other clusters. In the example of the term-paper assignment, the student might assign this a very high priority ranking if he perceives it to be an important determinant of his grade in the course, and if grades are important to him.[10]

The preceding study has suggested that some judgment probably is made about what kind of risks the person is willing to take. If the topic is quite important to him, he probably will choose a conservative information-search strategy, i.e., one which has high probability of processing the desired information. If it is not, he may gamble on getting the "right" information without using the dragnet technique of the broad-focusers.

Given a decision to seek further information, he enters what Berlyne calls an "extrinsic" information-seeking mode: He has at least a general idea of what his informational needs are, and he formulates a strategy for gathering sufficient data to exert closure. In the case of everyday situations such as checking a weather forecast to decide what clothes to wear, this may be a simple strategy which he has frequently employed and found rewarding—in the sense that the action decision was found to be "appropriate." Less common (more uncertain, in Berlyne's terms) situations, such as a term-paper assignment, may require the design of a more complex strategy.

We may also chart this procedure. First, the individual must *define his information needs,* at least in the sense of specifying objects or attributes he needs information about. It should be noted that here we are talking about what has been called *information preference* (Chaffee et al., 1969; Tipton, 1970), i.e., a definition of specific content desired. This construct appears to be more a function of acquired cognitive structure than *information search,* the behavioral act itself.

He must also define potential sources that may supply information. Both of these things must be done before the individual can start to seek information. At least one object or attribute and one source must be identified.

If there are multiple (two or more) sources, the strategy becomes more complex. At the very least, the individual must decide whether to approach sources broadly—to check all (or some part) of them to determine those specific ones that are potentially able to provide the information—or whether to approach them narrowly, such as focusing on one source. In either case he *consults a specific source* and makes a decision on closure: Do I need still more information, or do I now take action? If he needs still more information, he re-enters at the define array and sources point.

The term-paper example would work like this: The topic is balance models. The initial array definition included dissonance, congruity, and coorientation. The source definition included teachers, books, other students, encyclopedias, journals, *Handbook of Social Psychology,* etc.

He may focus broadly—looking over the table of contents or index of all the books he initially identified. Or he may focus narrowly—pick one that looks most promising and go directly to it. If that one pass contains all he thinks he needs, he closes. If not, he redefines his sources (note that this "point" probably includes some priority ordering of sources) and makes another pass.

Any of these source consultations may cause him to redefine his array (by introducing new objects he had not previously recognized, or considered part of his problem or situation), or add sources—additional books, authors, etc.

Following *closure,* the *action* itself is taken. But the model does not end here.

After taking action the individual may *monitor feedback* to his action. He is interested in evaluating the effectiveness of his action in fulfilling the demands of the situation.

Finally, based on this evaluation of the action, the individual may consider *revision of his image* in at least three ways. First, he may alter the content and the prominence and valence of his knowledges, beliefs, or goals, or some combination of them. Second, he may incorporate the new coping strategy into his set of strategies or reinforce an old strategy. Third, based on the degree of success he has just had, he may alter his self-concept. The consideration of these relatively long-term revisions of the image comprises the final step.

NOTES

1. The intended meanings of "seeking" and "avoiding" are similar to those commonly used in the literature. "Processing" here refers to evaluation of inputs against those previously stored in the system and the eventual integration or rejection of these inputs into the image of reality. In our model, it is something that takes place *after* a decision is made to seek no further information and after a plan for coping with a situation has been carried out.

2. Pepitone (1966) has noted that it is "intuitively obvious" that predictions as to whether or not the individual will act and to how he will act depend upon the degree of significance the inconsistency has for him personally. Zimbardo (1960) and Brehm and Cohen (1962) report results of dissonance theory research that indicate that importance of the situation is a determinant of inconsistency reduction behavior. Donohew (1966) and Donohew and Palmgreen (1971b) report supporting results indicating prominence, defined as importance, to be a major consideration in consistency research.

3. The authors wish to acknowledge the work of Lee Becker, a former graduate student of the University of Kentucky, in reviewing much of this literature. Persons interested in some methodological objections to this line of theorizing should consult Looft (1971) and Looft and Baranowski (1971).

4. The reticular formation is a type of nerve tissue in the subcortical region of the brain. It has been suggested as a mediator of two elements in the attention process—arousal and stimulus selection. We have noted earlier that this bears a remarkable resemblance to the homeostatic function described or inferred in cognitive consistency theories. Vernon (1966) suggests that this tissue appears to have the power to inhibit neuronal transmission of some stimuli (generally unpleasant to the receiver) to the higher brain centers while facilitating the transmission of (generally pleasant) others.

5. Underlying consistency assumptions is the extension of physiological homeostasis into a psychological realm. This would hold that the individual seeks to restore order among cognitions once something inconsistent has intruded to upset that order, to a "steady state." The kind of homeostasis we refer to assumes that the "steady state" incorporates the effects of experience, thus representing a new equilibrium point on successive occasions, which has been described as "dynamic homeostasis."

6. One example of an underlying but overriding cognition would be a person's perception of himself as being "open-minded" (Rokeach, 1960). Such a person might be willing to hold still and endure the pain of exposing himself to communications which threaten to upset his belief structure or even to seek discrepant information on an important topic if he also places great importance on the view of himself as an "open-minded" person. Thus, an "open-minded" cognition might be the overriding one in this instance. We have found some experimental support for this view.

7. We follow the view that *avoidance* is something other than the failure to *seek*. As noted in the second paragraph of this paper, we think the process includes active seeking, holding still to receive, and active avoiding. There is another apparent option which is harder to measure, but which is roughly equivalent to holding still and avoiding. This is the "discounting" option we talked about in the preceding discussion of dogmatism. Use of this option seems to be more characteristic of persons on the "closed-minded" end of the continuum.

8. Thus, closure may be defined as the point at which not only the information seeking stops but also the individual feels he has sufficient information to proceed to action. We distinguish two kinds of sufficiency: "formal" as defined by some external observer (maybe one who controls the situation), and "psychological" as defined by the seeker. It seems to be generally true that requirements for psychological sufficiency exceed those of formal sufficiency (Edwards, 1962).

9. One student's diary indicated some of the difficulties we had in coding. This student vacillated for long periods of time, picking one topic, rejecting it, picking and rejecting another. She intuitively seemed to be late closure, but the operational definition did not fit in her case. We eventually resorted to a procedure here that we applied in a few other instances where we were having difficulty—performing what we called "negotiated reliability" between coders: all of us would read it and thrash out what it seemed to be in terms of our tentative conceptualization.

10. Assignment of ratings and priorities bears some similarity to what Barker (1966) calls "regrouping" in his model of intrapersonal communication.

REFERENCES

ABELSON, R. P., ARONSON, W. P. McGUIRE, T. NEWCOMB, M. J. ROSENBERG, and P. H. TANNENBAUM [eds.] (1968) Theories of Cognitive Consistency: A Sourcebook. Chicago: Rand McNally.

ABELSON, R. P. and M. J. ROSENBERG (1958) "Symbolic psychologic: A model of attitudinal cognition." Behavioral Science 3: 1-13.

ATKIN, C. K. (1970) "Communicatory utility and news information seeking." Presented to Association for Education in Journalism convention. Washington, D.C.

BAKAN, P. [ed.] (1966) Attention. Princeton: Van Nostrand.

BARKER, L. L. and G. WISEMAN (1966) "A model of intrapersonal communication." Journal of Communication 16: 172-179.

BERLYNE, D. E. (1960) Conflict, Arousal and Curiosity. New York: McGraw Hill.

——— (1968) "The motivational significance of collative variables and conflict," in Abelson et al. [eds.] (1968).

BOULDING, K. (1956a) The Image. Ann Arbor: University of Michigan Press.

——— (1956b) "General systems theory—the skeleton of science." Management Science 2: 197-208.

BREHM, J. W. and A. A. COHEN (1962) Explorations in Cognitive Dissonance. New York: John Wiley.

BRUNER, J. S., J. J. GOODNOW, and G. A. AUSTIN (1956) A Study of Thinking. New York: John Wiley.

BROWN, R. (1958) Words and Things. Glencoe: Free Press.

CARTER, R. F. (1965) "Communication and affective relations." Journalism Quarterly 42: 203-212.

CARTER, R. F. and W. LEE RUGGELS (1968) Prototypic Projective Protocols. Seattle: University of Washington (mimeo).

CHAFFEE, S. H. and J. McLEOD (1971) "The construction of social reality," in J. Todeschi (ed.) The Social Influence Processes. Chicago: Aldine.

CHAFFEE, S. H., K. R. STAMM, J. L. GUERRERO, and L. TIPTON (1969) "Experiments on cognitive discrepancies and communication." Journalism Monographs 14.

CLARKE, P. (1965) Some Correlates of Selectivity in Information Seeking. Presented to Association for Education in Journalism convention, Syracuse, N.Y.

——— (1973) "Teenagers' co-orientation and information-seeking about pop music." American Behavioral Scientist 16: 551-566.

CLARKE, P. and J. JAMES (1967) "The effects of situation, attitude intensity and personality on information seeking." Sociometry 30: 235-245.

DONOHEW, L. (1966) "Decoder behavior on incongruent political material: A pilot study." Journal of Communication 16: 133-142.

DONOHEW, L. and J. BASEHEART (forthcoming) "Information Selection and Galvanic Skin Response." Journalism Quarterly.

DONOHEW, L. and P. PALMGREEN (1971a) "A reappraisal of dissonance and the selective exposure hypothesis." Journalism Quarterly 48: 412-420.

––– (1971b) "An investigation of 'mechanisms' of information selection." Journalism Quarterly 48: 627-639, 666.

DONOHEW, L., J. M. PARKER, and V. McDERMOTT (1972) "Psychophysiological measurement of information selection: Two studies." Journal of Communication 22: 54-63.

DUFFY, E. (1962) Activation and Behavior. New York: John Wiley.

EDELSTEIN, A. S. and NEIL HOLLANDER (1969) Perception of Social Conflict, Education, and Communication with Respect to Vietnam. Presented to Association for Education in Journalism convention, Berkeley, Calif.

EDWARDS, W. (1962) "Dynamic decision theory and probabilistic information processing." Human Factors 2: 59-73.

FELDMAN, S. [ed.] (1966) Cognitive Consistency. New York: Academic Press.

FESTINGER, L. (1957) A Theory of Cognitive Dissonance. Evanston, Ill.: Row, Peterson.

––– (1964) Conflict, Decision, and Dissonance. Stanford: Stanford University Press.

FISKE, D. W. and S. R. MADDI (1961) Functions of Varied Experience. Homewood, Ill.: Dorsey.

FOWLER, H. (1965) Curiosity and Exploratory Behavior. New York: Macmillan.

GERGEN, K. (1968) "Personal consistency and the presentation of self," in C. Gordon and K. J. Gergen, eds. The Self in Social Interaction. New York: John Wiley.

GUYTON, A. C. (1962) Textbook of Medical Physiology. Philadelphia: W. B. Saunders.

HEIDER, F. (1946) "Attitudes and cognitive organization." Journal of Psychology 21: 107-112.

JONES, E. E. (1967) Untitled study in E. E. Jones and H. R. Gerard, Foundations of Social Psychology. New York: John Wiley.

KLINE, F. G. and D. K. DAVIS (1971) "A Formal Model of Cognitive Structure." Preliminary draft, University of Michigan.

LOOFT, W. R. (1971) "The unimodel preference-for-complexity function: artifact?" The Journal of General Psychology 85: 239-243.

LOOFT, W. R. and M. D. BARANOWSKI (1971) "An analysis of five measures of sensation seeking and preference for complexity." Journal of General Psychology 85: 307-313.

MADDI, S. R. (1968) "The pursuit of consistency and variety," pp. 267-274 in Abelson et al. [eds.] (1968).

MILLER, G. A., E. GALANTER and K. H. PRIBRAM (1960) Plans and the Structure of Behavior. New York: Holt, Rinehart, Winston.

MILLER, G. R. and M. ROKEACH (1968) "Individual differences and tolerance for inconsistency," in Abelson et al. [eds.] (1968).

MILNER, P. M. (1970) Physiological Psychology. New York: Holt, Rinehart, Winston.

NEWCOMB, T. M. (1953) "An approach to the study of communicative acts." Psychological Review 60: 393-404.

OSGOOD, C. and P. H. TANNENBAUM (1955) "The principle of congruity in the prediction of attitude change." Psychological Review 62: 42-55.

PALMGREEN, P. (1971) "A daydream model of communication." Journalism Monographs 20: 1-32.

PEPITONE, A. (1966) "Some conceptual and empirical problems of consistency models," in Feldman [ed.] (1966).

ROKEACH, M. (1960) The Open and Closed Mind. New York: Basic Books.

ROSENBERG, M. (1965) Society and the Adolescent Self-Image. Princeton: Princeton University Press.

SINGER, J. E. (1966) "Motivation for consistency," in Feldman [ed.] (1966).

TIPTON, L. P. (1970) "Effects of writing tasks on utility of information and order of seeking." Journalism Quarterly 47: 309-317.

TROLDAHL, V. and F. POWELL (1965) "A short-form dogmatism scale for use in field studies." Social Forces 44: 211-215.

VERNON, M. D. (1966) "Perception, attention, and consciousness," pp. 37-57 in P. Bakan [ed.] (1966). Also pp. 137-151 in K. K. Sereno and C. D. Mortensen [eds.] (1970) Foundations of Communication Theory. New York: Harper, Row.

WINER, B. (1962) Statistical Principles in Experimental Design. New York: McGraw-Hill.

ZAJONC, R. B. (1960) "The process of cognitive tuning in communication." Journal of Abnormal and Social Psychology 61: 159-167.

––– (1969) "Cognitive theories in social psychology," in G. Lindzey and E. Aronson (eds.) Handbook of Social Psychology. Volume 1. Reading, Mass.: Addison-Wesley.

ZIMBARDO, P. G. (1960) "Involvement and communication discrepancy as determinants of opinion change." Journal of Abnormal and Social Psychology 60: 86-94.

ZUCKERMAN, M., E. A. KOLIN, L. PRICE, and I. ZOOB (1964) "Development of a sensation-seeking scale." Journal of Consulting Psychology 28: 477-482.

Chapter 9

INFORMATION PROCESSING AND PERSUASION:
COUNTERARGUING BEHAVIOR

Donald F. Roberts and Nathan Maccoby

MOST PEOPLE have experienced situations in which someone has attempted to change their opinion about some event, object, or issue. Moreover, at least on some occasions people who have been the target of a persuasive message have argued back, either overtly or covertly, attempting to refute the persuasive appeal.

Indeed, instances of such counterarguing behavior are common, even when there is no possibility of affecting the source of the persuasive message. All of us have probably seen someone, if not ourselves, argue with a televised speech, a newspaper editorial, or a radio commercial, in spite of the obvious fact that "refutations" of the message were unlikely to pass beyond the walls of one's own home. And those of us willing to introspect a bit further can probably recall instances when we have counterargued brilliantly, totally shattering (in the eyes of any reasonable man) the persuasive import of the message directed at us, only later to find ourselves adopting the position we had so ruthlessly annihilated for the very reasons we had so cleverly debunked. In short, regardless of whether our comments are overt or covert, regardless of whether the persuader is present or absent, regardless of whether or not our counterarguments facilitate resistance to the appeal, it seems clear that one characteristic way of dealing with a persuasive message is to argue with it.

Although attitude researchers have long noted that counterarguing is a common response to persuasive appeals, the counterarguing process as such received surprisingly little attention until recent years. Even though some of the

AUTHOR'S NOTE: The work reported here was conducted under a contract from the Office of Naval Research, No. N00014-67-A-0112-0032, entitled "Some Basic Processes in Persuasion."

early work on persuasion—for example, the primacy versus recency studies of Lund (1925; also see Rosnow, 1966) and the work on one-sided versus two-sided messages (e.g., Hovland et al., 1949; Lumsdaine and Janis, 1953)—assumed, either implicitly or explicitly, that counterarguing influenced message acceptance, primary concern was with optimal message strategies for achieving attitude change rather than with counterarguing itself. For the most part, counterarguing behavior was assigned the role of intervening variable, usually appealed to in post-hoc discussions of the relationship between a variety of manipulated independent variables (presumed to mediate learning) and attitude change.

Even in the early sixties, when the growth of interest in resistance to persuasion began to focus attention on counterarguing per se, conclusions about the role of counterargumentation were based more on inferences than on measurements. Studies were designed in which factors presumed to facilitate or inhibit counterarguing were manipulated, but the mediating role of counterarguing was inferred on the basis of attitude change data (e.g., McGuire, 1964; Festinger and Maccoby, 1964).

Recently, however, counterargument production has acquired the status of a dependent variable in its own right. Several investigators have explored various procedures for making manifest the counterarguments that receivers are presumed to generate when exposed to a persuasive message (e.g., Cook, 1969; Osterhouse and Brock, 1970; Maccoby and Roberts, 1971). One result of this relatively new direction in persuasion research has been to enable more direct examination of the presumed relationship between counterarguing and opinion change and between counterarguing and factors thought to influence counterargument production. Another important dividend of this attempt to elicit counterarguments in measurable form has been the opportunity to move a step closer to some of the cognitive strategies which may occur as an individual processes persuasive information.

The following pages present a brief review of research on counterarguing behavior, report some of our own work on the problem of monitoring counterarguments as they occur, and speculate on a possible model which attempts to integrate our own findings with those of earlier studies.

RESEARCH ON COUNTERARGUING AND RESISTANCE TO PERSUASION

For the most part, studies concerned with counterarguing behavior focus on resistance to persuasion. They can generally be classified under one of three headings. Studies of inoculation against persuasion (McGuire, 1964) and of the distraction hypothesis (e.g., Festinger and Maccoby, 1964) have attempted to manipulate counterarguing as an independent and/or intervening variable while maintaining attitude change as the primary, if not sole, dependent variable. The third set of studies can be viewed as something of a convergence of the two preceding approaches. They have manipulated many of the same independent variables presumed to influence counterarguing behavior, but have also employed counterargument production as a primary dependent variable. That is, conclusions about the counterarguing process are based on measurements of counterargument production.

Inoculation Studies

William McGuire's (1964) work on inducing resistance to persuasion provides a large body of data relevant to counterarguing behavior. His inoculation theory stems from a medical analogy that likens a viral attack on an organism's biological system to a persuasive attack on a person's belief system. In the biological case resistance to a massive viral attack may be stimulated either by pre-exposure to a weakened dose of the virus (inoculation) or by augmenting health via adequate rest, vitamin supplements, and so forth (supportive therapy). Similarly, resistance to a persuasive attack on the belief system may be stimulated either by inoculation—prior exposure to a mild version of the attack to stimulate defenses against a later, massive attack; or by supportive therapy—augmenting of the initially held opinion to bolster that opinion in the hope that the stronger it is the more impervious to attack it will be.

McGuire notes that organisms raised in "germ-free environments" appear vigorously healthy but are highly vulnerable to massive doses of disease virus. Analogously, beliefs developed in "germ-free environments" can appear healthy but may succumb to attack if it occurs. He terms such beliefs "cultural truisms," describing them as "beliefs that are so widely shared within the person's social milieu that he would not have heard them attacked, and indeed, would doubt that an attack were possible" (McGuire, 1964: 201).[1] Since in the case of both the biological system and the belief system a supportive treatment is similar to maintaining an aseptic environment, inoculation therapy should be more effective than supportive therapy for inducing resistance to attack.

Two fundamental assumptions underlie inoculation theory: (1) that resistance to attack on a belief is a function of practice at defending that belief (i.e., counterarguing against attack); (2) that practice at defending is a function of motivation to engage in practice. Supportive therapy, which consists simply of bolstering or augmenting an existing belief prior to attack, fails to meet these assumptions. While such a treatment may provide some material useful for defending against subsequent attack, it neither creates awareness of impending threat to the belief nor does it specifically provide counters which could be used in event of attack. In other words, supportive therapy fails to motivate practice at defending and to provide counters to be practiced.

An inoculation treatment, on the other hand, meets the two assumptions. It consists of exposing a person to a mild attack on his belief and, in the same message, presenting counterarguments against the attacking points. Exposure to attacking arguments creates threat, which motivates one to practice defending; presenting counters against the threatening arguments serves to insure that the inoculation dosage is not so strong as to be fatal, and simultaneously augments the defensive armory by supplying defensive materials to be practiced.[2]

Thus, given that cultural truisms are highly vulnerable for the very reason that they have never been threatened, the relative efficacy of the two pre-attack treatments derives from their differential ability to fulfill the conditions of the basic assumptions. That is, people have never been motivated to practice defending a cultural truism, hence lack defenses with which to counter an attack. A pre-attack supportive treatment should simply maintain this condition. An inoculation treatment, however, should both motivate practice and supply the defensive armory.

A series of experiments, more fully described elsewhere (McGuire, 1964), tested both the efficacy of inoculation treatments for inducing resistance to persuasion and the validity of the assumptions underlying the inoculation model. McGuire and Papageorgis (1961) showed that although supportive therapy engendered more strengthening of a belief prior to attack, only the inoculation treatment produced significant resistance to persuasion subsequent to an attack. Papageorgis and McGuire (1961) found increased resistance to persuasion regardless of whether arguments refuted in the inoculation session were the same as (refutational-same) or different from (refutational-different) those encountered in the later attack session. In other words, not only was inoculation superior to supportive therapy, but it effectively induced resistance to persuasion even when the opposition's specific arguments were not anticipated.

Both the superiority of inoculation over the supportive threatment and the "paper tiger" effect found for supportive therapy buttress the assumption that motivation (via threat) is an important precursor to resistance. Moreover, other studies increased threat via forewarning (McGuire and Papageorgis, 1962), decreased threat via prior reassurance (Anderson, cited in McGuire, 1964), and manipulated both threat and reassurance by varying the number of arguments mentioned and refuted during the inoculation session (McGuire, 1964). In each case, increment or decrement in threat, hence motivation, mediated increment or decrement in resistance.

Results also point to the importance of practice. Assuming that the threat produced by the refutational treatment remains constant, results showing that subjects who read a paragraph refuting inoculation arguments (passive treatment) were slightly more resistant than those who wrote a paragraph refuting those arguments (active treatment) (McGuire and Papageorgis, 1961), and the slight, immediate superiority of the refutational-same over the refutational-different treatment (Papageorgis and McGuire, 1961) indicates that practice at defending increases resistance. That is, the difference between these treatments seems to lie in the number of immediately relevant counters made available, hence practiceable. The passive and the refutational-same treatments appear to provide more such materials.

Other studies indicate that as the number of arguments refuted during the inoculation session increases, so too does resistance (McGuire, 1964); that combining supportive and inoculation treatments induces greater resistance than either treatment alone (McGuire, 1961b); that a passive treatment is superior using refutational-same arguments, while the reverse is true using refutational-different arguments, and that combining passive and active participation during the defense session enhances a refutational-same treatment more than it does a refutational-different treatment (McGuire, 1961a). In each case, the superior treatment was the one in which subjects can be assumed to have encountered and/or generated more, immediately relevant materials with which to counter an attack.

Tannenbaum and his associates (Tannenbaum, 1967) provide further information about the nature of the defense process.[3] For example, Macaulay (1965) found that when, during the defense session, the ostensible source of an impending attack on a belief *denied* making an attack *and* took an explicit position supporting the pre-attack belief, resistance was increased. Similarly, Tannenbaum (1967) reports that pre-attack derogation of the source of an impending attack led to increased resistance.

In the Macaulay case, it can be argued that the denial served as a warning motivating defensive preparation, while statement of a pro-belief position provided at least some material which could be used defensively. The source-derogation treatment employed by Tannenbaum can also be viewed as containing both a motivational component and useful defense materials with which to counter the attack. Given that it is difficult, if not impossible, to separate the source of a message from the message itself—that linking a source to a statement influences both the attitudinal acceptability (Lorge, 1936) and the meaning (Asch, 1948) of that statement—pre-attack source derogation should provide threat enough to motivate practice defending against that source and materials with which to conduct that defense, regardless of the issue on which the source takes a position. Indeed, under some conditions it may be easier to counter a persuasive appeal by defending against its source than against its arguments.

A number of studies, then, indicate that treatments designed to motivate people to prepare to defend their beliefs *and* to provide defense materials (or conditions amenable to acquisition of defense materials) with which to conduct a defense increase resistance to persuasion. It demands no great leap of logic to infer that subjects use the acquired counters to defend against attack. The fly in the ointment, of course, is the word "infer." There are no direct measures of counterarguing behavior.

Moreover, the mechanisms McGuire assumes to underlie induced resistance need further clarification. For example, the threat inherent in the inoculation procedure may motivate some *direct* disposition to resist, rather than or in addition to a disposition to practice defenses. Though the two processes are difficult to separate, there is a difference.

Distraction Studies

Festinger and Maccoby (1964) assumed that to the extent an individual comprehends the argument of a persuasive message, and to the extent that he is relatively involved with or concerned with the issue dealt with by the message, to that extent yielding to or resisting a persuasive appeal is a function of the supportive and/or counter responses (overt or covert) he generates as he processes the message. They reasoned that if these assumptions are true, then distracting a receiver from arguing against a counterattitudinal appeal should lower his resistance to that appeal.[4]

Their seminal distraction study (Festinger and Maccoby, 1964) tested this hypothesis by exposing fraternity men and independents to a film the sound track of which advocated abolition of college fraternities. For half the subjects in each group, the film visuals illustrated and reinforced points in the message (non-distracted group); remaining subjects (distracted group) saw a totally unrelated, humorous, silent film selected to create just enough distraction to interfere with counterarguing by fraternity men and pro-arguing (agreeing) by independents, but not enough distraction to interfere with any group's learning of the message.

At schools where the fraternity issue was salient, interfering with concurrent countering or agreeing responses respectively decreased resistance to or acceptance of the message.[5] Distracted fraternity men were less resistant and less likely to derogate the speaker than were non-distracted fraternity men, who were not at all affected by the message. Conversely, although the difference did not reach statistical significance, results for non-fraternity men were in the opposite direction, distracted independents agreeing less with the message than did non-distracted independents.

Subsequent distraction studies, using different issues and distraction procedures, produced varied results. Freedman and Sears (1965) and Dorris (1967) found distracted subjects to be marginally more susceptible to persuasion than were non-distracted subjects. Rosenblatt (1966) and Kiesler and Mathog (1968) demonstrated increased yielding under distracting conditions, although results of the latter study occurred only with a highly credible source. Rule and Rehill (1970) found an interaction between distraction and self-esteem, distraction increasing yielding among high self-esteem subjects but having no effect among low self-esteem subjects. Osterhouse and Brock (1970) showed that distraction reduces resistance to persuasion—results which are greatly strengthened in that they measured counterargument production and also showed less counterarguing among distracted subjects.

On the other hand, Breitrose (1965) and Gardner (1966) report no difference in opinion change between distracted and non-distracted subjects. And directly counter to the distraction hypothesis, Haaland and Venkatesan (1968) and Vohs and Garrett (1968) found that non-distracted subjects manifested *more* attitude change than did distracted subjects.

Several explanations have been offered for this rather mixed bag of results (Osterhouse and Brock, 1970). The most convincing deal with the degree to which various studies meet the assumptions underlying the distraction hypothesis.

McGuire (1966) noted that a learning theory approach to persuasion would predict non-distracted subjects to be more susceptible to persuasion since they should be better able to learn the substance of the persuasive message. Although this position somewhat misses the point of the distraction hypothesis, it does serve to explain some of the studies which failed to find greater susceptibility among distracted subjects. That is, Festinger and Maccoby (1964) conceived of the distraction manipulation as a procedure for interfering with subjects' cognitive responses to a persuasive message, *but not with reception of that message.* Indeed, if distraction is too strong or the message does not contain enough redundancy to guarantee learning of the message, then consequent persuasion gain due to interfering with counterarguing could be more than offset by message reception loss.

In this context, it is notable that studies which failed to support the hypothesis *and* which included a learning measure (Breitrose, 1965; Gardner, 1966; Haaland and Venkatesan, 1968) found distracted subjects less able than non-distracted subjects to reproduce message content.[6] On the other hand, studies supporting the hypothesis found no differences in subjects' ability to reproduce message content. Thus, to the extent that message reception (i.e., learning) is not hindered, the distraction hypothesis tends to be supported. Indeed, Zimbardo's (Zimbardo et al., 1970) finding that distracted subjects who attended primarily to the persuasive message were less resistant than distracted subjects who attended primarily to the distraction task also fits nicely with the reception loss explanation. Focusing attention on the distraction task could well have interfered with message reception, hence with learning, hence with attitude change.

Osterhouse and Brock (1970) also point out that unless the issue addressed by the persuasive message is involving enough to motivate counterarguing under normal circumstances (issues which may also be expected to elicit increased attention), then the mediating role of counterarguing cannot be expected to operate. Hence distraction cannot create interference. Of the studies failing to support the distraction hypothesis, both Breitrose (1965) and Gardner (1966) used issues which were highly unlikely to motivate counterarguing, and some question can also be raised about the motivating impact of the Vohs and Garrett (1968) issue.[7]

Another hypothesis offered to explain Festinger and Maccoby's results holds that yielding by distracted subjects may have derived from a positive affective response due to the use of a humorous film as the distractor McGuire, 1966; Vohs and Garrett, 1968; Kiesler and Mathog, 1968). This, however, ignores the lack of yielding among distracted non-fraternity men in the original study.

Moreover, subsequent studies have used a wide enough variety of distractors to discount this possibility.[8]

Finally, it has been suggested that expending effort to attend to a counter-attitudinal message creates dissonance which can be reduced by realigning one's attitudes to concur with the message. For example, Zimbardo (1965) had subjects read a counterattitudinal message under varying degrees of delayed auditory feedback (i.e., effort) and found that the greater the delay the greater the attitude change. However, such an explanation overlooks Festinger and Maccoby's results with distracted non-fraternity men. In addition, Kiesler and Mathog (1968) directly compared an effort justification with a distraction explanation, finding strong support for the distraction hypothesis and no evidence for an effort justification interpretation. Indeed, one could attribute Zimbardo's (1965) results to distraction, arguing that delayed auditory feedback created distraction which made counterarguing difficult.

It appears, then, that when the assumptions underlying the distraction hypothesis are considered—when the persuasive message addresses an issue which can be expected to elicit covert or overt supportive or counter responses under normal conditions, and when message reception, hence comprehension, is unimpaired—then interfering with such counter (supportive) comments increases (decreases) yielding. From this we can infer that concurrent counterarguing or agreeing by receivers mediates either resistance or acceptance.

As with the inoculation studies, however, most distraction evidence concerning the counterarguing process is inferential. Only two distraction studies attempted to get more directly at counterarguing: one failed to find a relationship between resistance and self-reports of counterarguing (Zimbardo et al., 1970), and the other found a strong relationship between resistance and a direct measure of counterarguing (Osterhouse and Brock, 1970).

Counterarguing Studies

The studies gathered in this section all obtained some direct measure of counterarguing against a persuasive message.[9] Generally such studies manipulate various independent variables that are hypothesized to mediate different amounts and/or kinds of counterarguments. Then, in addition to collecting opinion scores, the researcher intervenes at some point in the experimental procedure and asks subjects to make overt their cognitions (counters, thoughts, comments, etc.) about the message. From these, counterarguing scores are computed. Conclusions are based on between-condition comparisons of counterarguing scores per se and/or on correlations between counterarguing scores and opinion scores.

For example, Greenwald (1968) reports some of the more straightforward evidence that receivers' cognitive responses mediate opinion change. His model regards persuasive situations as complex stimuli that evoke cognitive reactions (e.g., agreeing comments, counterarguments) among receivers which range along a positive-negative dimension. By virtue of their rehearsal in the persuasion situation, such responses are assumed to become conditioned to the opinion topic, leading to a shift in attitude toward that topic in the direction represented by the new response content. Thus agreeing responses should mediate acquiescence and disagreeing responses should mediate resistance.[10]

Greenwald (1968) asked receivers to "collect their thoughts" about a persuasive message immediately following message reception but prior to completing opinion scales. Listed thoughts were judged to agree or disagree with the message, assigned weights indicating intensity of agreement or disagreement (from which a directional content index was computed), [11] and classed as either externally originated (e.g., derived directly from points in the message), recipient modified (e.g., modifications such as illustrations, qualifications, or reactions to points in the message), or recipient generated (e.g., ideas dealing with the issue but not traceable to specific points in the message).

Across several experiments subjects who generated more agreeing remarks favored the advocated position; subjects who resisted gave more disagreeing remarks. The largest proportion of listed thoughts fell into the recipient generated category, and only those comments correlated significantly with post-test opinion scores. In other words, the important "cognitive responses" were those generated by the subjects themselves as opposed to reactions elicited in direct response to points in the message.

Clearly, the results of this and other counterarguing studies depend on how the counterarguing measure is operationalized, and a wide variety of procedures have been employed. For example, in addition to the three categories defined and the scoring procedure used by Greenwald (1968; Greenwald and Mayer, n.d.), counterarguing measures have included: (1) a simple count of comments in any way disagreeing with specific persuasive points (Cook, 1969); (2) classification of "counter" comments as directed at either the source or the content of a message and a count of the number of words in each comment (Baron and Miller, 1969); (3) a count of the number of comments that could be identified as declarative statements against the persuasive appeal *and* which mentioned a specific undesirable consequence of the advocated position *and* which were not paraphrases of the appeal's conclusion (Brock, 1967; Osterhouse and Brock, 1970); (4) a count of the number of paragraphs in which at least one spontaneous comment fell into one of six different characteristic categories (Janis and Terwilliger, 1962).[12]

The nature of counterarguing scores is also a function of when subjects' responses are obtained and how much time they had to generate comments. Counters have been elicited prior to message reception (anticipatory counters) (Brock, 1967; Baron and Miller, 1969); during message reception (Janis and Terwilliger, 1962; Cook, 1969), and after message reception (Greenwald, 1968; Miller and Baron, 1968; Osterhouse and Brock, 1970). Time available for subjects to comment has ranged from one minute (Baron and Miller, 1969) to ten minutes (Brock, 1967) to apparently as much time as subjects desired (e.g., Greenwald, 1968). And finally, while most studies obtain subjects' comments in writing, Janis and Terwilliger (1962) tape-recorded verbalized comments.

Given the diversity of measurement procedures, not to mention the many independent variables manipulated in various studies, there is remarkable consistency in results. Almost all experiments have found an inverse relationship between counterarguing and yielding under some conditions, and no study has found a positive relationship.

For example, in several studies counterargument production was a function of source credibility. Greenwald and Mayer (n.d.) report that a low credibility source elicited more counter comments while a high credibility source led to more agreeing comments. Cook (1969) noted reduced counterarguing (and increased yielding) in response to a high credibility source but no effect on counterarguing or yielding when the source had little credibility. And two studies (Miller and Baron, 1968; Baron and Miller, 1969) found that credibility interacts with whether the receiver is oriented toward the source or the content of the message. When oriented toward the source, low source credibility leads to increased counterargument production. In general, then, there is good evidence that source credibility and counterargument production are inversely related. Whether this effect is due to reduction in counterarguing with a highly credible source (Cook, 1969), an increase with a low credibility source, or both, appears to depend on several factors, among which are receiver orientation and how counters are defined and scored.[13]

Various manipulations of threat have also been shown to affect counterarguing behavior. Janis and Terwilliger (1962), using a standard fear-arousal paradigm and the issue of smoking and cancer, found that high fear led to increased counterarguing and decreased yielding.[14] Brock (1967) manipulated threat via forewarning of intent to persuade and found threatened subjects produced marginally more counters. Osterhouse and Brock (1970) varied threat by leading students to believe that a tuition increase advocated by the message was either likely or unlikely to occur. Their results indicated that high threat led to more counterarguing only when subjects perceived that their responses might influence the likelihood of the tuition increase.

Osterhouse and Brock also produced convincing support for the distraction hypothesis. Varying several levels of distraction, they found not only that distraction reduced counterargument production and increased yielding, but also that the trend across levels for counterarguing scores and opinion scores was significantly linear.

Additional studies have also found that a two-sided message produced less counterarguing (and more yielding) than a one-sided message (Greenwald, 1968), indicating that undercutting of existing counters reduced the effectiveness of a receiver's defenses; that counterargument production can be increased by a priming manipulation (providing subjects with an example of a counterargument), but that this increase does not mediate increased resistance (Brock, 1967); and that as the plausibility of the persuasive arguments decreases, counterargument production increases (Greenwald and Mayer, n.d.). Greenwald (1968) also found a strong effect on both counterarguing scores and yielding due to discrepancy between the receivers' position on an issue and the position advocated by the message. As discrepancy increased, so too did counterarguing and resistance.

To summarize briefly, the counterarguing studies noted above have added significantly to the list of variables which mediate counterarguing. These include source credibility, controvertedness of issue, plausibility of persuasive arguments, threat, fear-arousal, perceived influence, message structure, and communication-recipient discrepancy. In other words, many of the same variables which have frequently been shown to mediate persuasion are, when approached from a different perspective, also mediators of counter-argumentation.

Finally, it should be noted that, taken together, studies which have measured counterargument production provide substantial evidence that counterarguing often functions as a *causal* intervening variable. This conclusion is based on the numerous negative correlations reported between counterarguing scores and message acceptance, the general tendency for independent variables which produced significant F ratios for opinion scores to also produce significant F's for counterarguing scores, and the wide variety of procedures employed to obtain these results. And most convincing, both Cook (1969) and Osterhouse and Brock (1970) report analyses of covariance wherein the effect of counterarguing scores was removed from opinion score variance, with the result that between-group F values for opinion scores were significantly reduced. That is, with the counterarguing effect removed, there were no between-group differences in yielding—a clear indication that a causal role is attributable to counterarguing.

Thus, studies which have measured counterarguing have provided direct support for many of the inferences drawn in inoculation and distraction studies.

Some Unanswered Questions

Research conducted thus far, however, has raised more questions than it has provided answers.

We might ask, for example, if counterarguments produced after message reception (e.g., Greenwald, 1968; Miller and Baron, 1968; Osterhouse and Brock, 1970) are adequate indicators of counterarguing as it occurs during message reception. At least under some conditions they may well be rationalizations of post-message positions, resistance mediating counterargumentation rather than the reverse. While Osterhouse and Brock (1970) cogently argue against this possibility, there have been no comparisons between counters produced during reception and counters produced after.

Similarly, the "anticipatory" counters collected by Brock (1967) and Baron and Miller (1969) pose severe problems of interpretation. Although receivers' pre-message comments can be defined as arguments for or against a particular issue, it is difficult to conceive of them as counterarguments in the strict sense of the term. They are not responses to points or issues raised by a message; they do not "counter" anything other than some anticipated position on an issue. Pre-message comments may provide an indication of a receiver's defensive armory, or even of his pre-message position on an issue. However, if we are willing to assume that aspects of the total persuasive stimulus can and do influence both how a receiver processes persuasive information and his final opinion position, then counters generated before an attack are not isomorphic with those used during an attack. That is, they do not speak directly to the question of if, when, and how available counterarguments are employed *during* the processing of a persuasive message.

Given the different definitions of counterarguments employed across the various studies reviewed above, there are also questions to be raised about the nature of the counterarguing process itself. For example, does the content or focus of a counterargument make a difference? Baron and Miller's (1969) comparison of source counters and content counters and Greenwald's (1968) distinction between "recipient generated," "recipient modified," and "externally originated" counters indicate a need for more attention to the substance of the counters themselves, not to mention to the various conditions under which the focus of counterarguments might vary. We can also ask what constitutes a counter. Need it be the strictly limited declarative statement required by Brock (1967), or can it simply be any comment indicating disagreement with the message? And what is the best measure of counterargument production? Is it the number of counterarguments, however defined, produced? Or the intensity of counterarguments? Or the ratio of counterarguments to agreeing responses? Or the number of words contained in all counterarguments? Or some combination of these?

And clearly, further specification of the relationship between counterarguing and resistance and between various independent variables and counterargument production is needed. At least one study reported by Tannenbaum (1967) found that a supportive treatment increased resistance to persuasion. Hence, while there was no direct measure of counterarguing, his results imply that counterargumentation may not be a necessary condition for resistance. Similarly, the interactions found by several investigators (e.g., Keisler and Mathog, 1968; Rule and Rehill, 1970; Baron and Miller, 1969), and Brock's (1967) demonstration that a priming manipulation increases counterarguing but not resistance, all point to the conclusion that there are conditions under which counterargumentation is not sufficient to mediate resistance.

FURTHER EXPLORATIONS IN COUNTERARGUING

The Research Questions

Our own research on counterargumentation has been aimed at some of the questions raised in the preceding pages. A primary interest has been in the nature of counterarguing as it occurs *during* message reception—in whether counter-arguments produced during reception resemble those produced after reception, and whether they relate to resistance in the same way. This demanded development of a procedure for obtaining receiver responses during communication exposure.

In addition, we were interested in exploring further whether qualitative differences among counters (e.g., whether they are directed at a specific point in the message, or at the source, or whatever), in locating differential resistance, and in examining the relationship between countering responses and agreeing responses. Finally, we wanted to experiment with several techniques for scoring counterarguments.

We have also been interested in further specification of some of the conditions assumed to mediate counterarguing behavior and resistance to persuasion. In the most general terms, these are the same factors that underlie most human behavior. Counterargumentation is at least a function of *availability* of defensive materials (as demonstrated by inoculation research), of *opportunity* to use these materials (as shown by distraction studies), and of *motivation* to use these materials (as indicated by studies in all three of the research traditions reviewed earlier). There remain, however, questions about the operation of these conditions which have not been investigated.

For example, although limiting opportunity to counterargue has been at the heart of all tests of the distraction hypothesis, the effect of an *increase* in receivers' opportunity to generate counterarguments has not been ascertained. Hence, while there is evidence that inhibition of counterarguing reduces resistance to persuasion, we have no idea whether facilitation of counterarguing increases resistance. We can also ask whether increasing receivers' opportunity to counterargue affects the nature of their responses in terms of the kinds of defensive materials they bring to bear.

We were also interested in addressing several questions about the motivation variable. Frequently, prior research has confounded manipulations of motivation with other variables, particularly counterargument availability, making it difficult to draw precise inferences about the role of motivation in the counter-arguing/resistance process. For example, most studies of counterargumentation have employed relatively controversial issues in order to insure that counterarguing occurs. Osterhouse and Brock (1970) argue that a necessary condition for the distraction effect is the use of a "controverted" issue—one advocating "action having negative consequences for the recipient" or contradicting "a strongly held opinion in an area having important implications for the individual." Both the description and the rationale hold for counterarguing studies as well as distraction studies. The rationale is that such issues are likely to incur counterarguing on the part of receivers, and that some counterargumentation is necessary if the researcher is to make comparisons between various levels of independent variables. Hence, participants in most counterarguing studies can be assumed to have been at least moderately motivated to counterargue by virtue of the nature of the persuasive message alone.[15]

The prevalence of such controverted issues in counterarguing research has several implications. First, most experimental manipulations of motivation to counterargue have proceeded from a baseline which is probably well above zero (or even low) motivation. Second, because controverted issues are not only motivating but also those about which recipients are likely to have an ample supply of defensive materials, we cannot be certain about the independent roles of counterargument availability versus motivation. As the supply of counterarguments increases, so too might the likelihood of using them, independent of any motivation to resist a persuasive appeal.[16] And finally, the use of controverted issues makes it difficult to determine whether there is any need for a distinction between motivation to counterargue and motivation to resist.

Both distraction studies and counterarguing studies assume that resistance is a function of counterargumentation. They conceive of manipulations as affecting motivation to engage in counterarguing. A possibility which has not been investigated, however, is that motivation to resist may be independent of motivation to counterargue. Conceivably a person could be motivated to yield to or resist a persuasive appeal, regardless of whether or not he is motivated to counterargue. Conversely, he could be motivated to counterargue but not to resist. Or manipulations of motivation could affect both behaviors (if, indeed, they can be separated). These possibilities recall our earlier questions about whether counterarguing is either necessary or sufficient for resistance.

What seemed called for, then, was the use of a counterattitudinal appeal which was not, in and of itself, highly motivating with regard to counterarguing and/or resistance. The use of an issue on which people are willing to take either a positive or negative stand, but about which they do not feel deeply, should enable manipulation of motivation to defend or to resist that is relatively independent of any motivation inherent in the issue per se. Moreover, to the extent that the issue is not esoteric, receivers can be expected to have a moderate number of counterarguments available should they choose to defend against attack, but not so many that the sheer number of available counters could account for any experimental effect.

Given these questions, we needed to design a study which manipulated an increase in subjects' opportunity to engage in counterarguing and an increase in motivation to counter and/or resist which was independent of that inherent in the persuasive issue. We also needed to collect subjects' comments, agreeing or countering remarks, both during and after message reception.

Experimental Procedures

Overview

We employed a 2 x 2 x 2 factorial design varying commitment to a position on an issue (our operationalization of motivation), temporal opportunity to counterargue, and two modes of "storage" (memory versus written) of whatever comments subjects produced. The purpose of the latter manipulation was to obtain counterarguments produced during and after reception.

The experimental session was represented as a study of what people think about when listening to newscasts, and included a pre-message questionnaire, presentation of the persuasive message, and a post-message questionnaire. Depending on experimental treatments, written comments about the message were obtained either during and after, or only after, reception. Opinion scores were obtained either before and after, or only after, message reception.

These procedures enabled analysis of both opinion post scores and change scores, and comparisons of counters obtained during and after reception, both within and across subjects.

Introductory Procedure

Subjects were 163 male and female junior college students randomly assigned to experimental conditions. They met with experimenters in groups of from 5 to 12 persons. They were told that the study was designed to find out what people think about when listening to news broadcasts, that they would hear a recording of a "news commentary," and that following the recording they would be asked questions about the "broadcast," but that they would not be tested on what they learned.

Our interest in counterarguing was not mentioned, nor was there any indication beyond the use of the word "commentary" that the message would attempt to persuade.

The tape-recorded message was introduced as having been produced by graduate students at an Eastern school of communication. Pilot studies showed this source to have moderate credibility, a desirable condition in order to avoid source influences on counterargument production (Cook, 1969). The message lasted eight and a half minutes and advocated abolition of all "editorial" and "persuasive" content from the news media. Pilot testing showed that most people disagreed with the position advocated but were not strongly involved in the issue. It also appeared to be an issue about which people were capable of producing a reasonable number of counterarguments when asked.

Pre-message Questionnaire and Commitment Manipulation

Following introductory instructions, subjects completed a short questionnaire containing various demographic questions and six opinion statements. The opinion items dealt with various aspects of print and broadcast journalism in the

United States. Subjects were asked to indicate amount of agreement with each statement on fifteen-point scales ranging from "strongly agree" to "strongly disagree."

Commitment was manipulated by presenting half the subjects with the same opinion statement that served as the post-message opinion measure for all subjects—a statement summarizing the conclusion of the persuasive message. We assumed that having subjects commit themselves to a position on the issue immediately prior to the message by means of a questionnaire which they knew would be available to the researchers, would serve to motivate them to defend their position more than if they had not taken a pre-message position. The key item, the first of the six opinion statements, read:

> Persuasive attempts, such as editorials, columns, and news commentary, are dangerous and misleading and should be abolished from our press system.

Non-committed subjects responded to an item dealing with journalistic coverage of state and local politics. The remaining five statements were identical for all subjects and served as control items.

Opportunity and Storage Manipulations

Opportunity to counterargue was manipulated by varying time available to subjects to generate and rehearse comments as they listened to the message. What we have termed "storage condition" was varied by means of a note-taking versus no-note-taking manipulation.

Subjects were told that our interest was in what people think about while listening to news broadcasts, and that they should pay close attention to their own thoughts about the message because they would be asked about these reactions. Half the subjects from each commitment group were further told that the recording would be stopped for a few seconds at various points in the broadcast in order to give them time to "collect their thoughts." This group (Stop group) heard the recording with a twenty-second pause after each major point in the message, for a total of eleven pauses. Remaining subjects heard the message under normal conditions, the tape running continuously from beginning to end (Continuous group). This procedure constituted our manipulation of normal versus high opportunity to counterargue.

Finally, half the subjects in each of the preceding groups were provided with blank scratch paper under the guise that since they were going to be asked questions about their reactions to the broadcast they might want to make notes on their thoughts *as they listened* (Write group). Remaining subjects were instructed to make "mental notes" on their reactions, retaining as many thoughts as possible (Think group).

This manipulation was introduced not because of an interest in the effect of "storage" or rehearsal possibilities implied by the write versus think conditions, but because it provided a means for obtaining comments *during* reception from half the subjects, as well as an independent set of responses obtained after reception. This allowed comparisons between the two.

Message Presentation and Data Collection

Following instructions, the tape recording was played either with or without pauses and with or without note-taking. Since commitment was manipulated by means of individually read questionnaires, pre-tested and non-pre-tested subjects could be combined during reception phases of the experiment.

At the conclusion of the tape recording, Write subjects were asked to place their "notes" under their chairs and to refrain from referring to them. Subjects then completed the post-message questionnaire.

The questionnaire included the six opinion statements and associated fifteen-point scales of agreement/disagreement which appeared on the pre-message questionnaire, with the exception that all subjects received the statement advocating abolition of persuasive materials from the media—the opinion dependent variable. Following the opinion items, subjects were asked to list whatever thoughts they had about the message:

> Please spend the next few minutes listing all thoughts you have about the message you have just heard. These thoughts may consist of statements either favorable or unfavorable to either side of the issue, of your own personal values on the issue, of the information presented in the message, of your thoughts about that information, or any other thoughts you have, even though they may seem unrelated to the issue.

Results

Coding Procedures

Three judgments about each comment were made: (1) *directionality*—classification of the comment as supportive of, counter to, or irrelevant to the advocated position; (2) *intensity*—strength of the comment regardless of directionality (i.e., strongly, moderately, or slightly counter or supportive); (3) *category*—qualitative classification of focus of the comment (e.g., aimed at source, a specific point, etc.).

Category definitions were derived from the preceding literature review and from analyses of both pilot test data and fifty randomly selected experimental protocols. Six content categories were defined on the basis of both face validity and the appearance of comments exemplifying each in the preliminary sample of protocols.

Comments were classed as being aimed at (a) the *conclusion* of the message, (b) the *source* of the message or the style of the *communication*, (c) a specific *point* in the message, (d) the general *issue* of the message, or (e) as being *subject-generated*—agreement or disagreement with the subject of the message but related to content not specifically in the message. The sixth category included comments *irrelevant* to the message. Comments were also assigned weights ranging from -3 (strongly counter) to +3 (strongly supportive). Scores for each individual category and for a "Total" category were then computed in five different ways: counts of the number of counter and of supportive comments, the number of supportive minus the number of counter comments (directional index), the algebraic sum of intensity weights (intensity scores), and the intensity score divided by the number of comments (weighted intensity).[17]

Intercoder Reliability [18]

Three coders independently coded all subjects' comments. Pearson correlation coefficients for all possible pairings of scores assigned by each coder for scores in the Total category ranged from .86 to .90 (p < .001 with N=163).

Calculation of the Kendall Coefficient of Concordance, *W*, for each content category produced coefficients ranging from .45 to .94, all significant by chi square (p < .001).[19] Coefficients less than .80 were obtained only for the conclusion, issue, and irrelevant categories, none of which played a significant role in the following analyses.[20]

Reliability of coding procedures was judged acceptable and final counterarguing scores were based on the mean of the scores assigned to each subject by each of the three coders.

Total Comments Generated

The mean number of comments produced by all subjects, without regard to experimental conditions, was computed for both notes produced during reception (during-comments) and thoughts listed after reception (after-comments). Table 1 summarizes means and appropriate category proportions for the two sets of comments. Since the various content categories do not represent similar levels of generality, statistical comparisons among categories of comments produced either during or after reception were inappropriate. Due to large variances, within content categories tests of the proportion of during-comments versus the proportion of after-comments did not reach statistical significance. However, the patterns revealed in Table 1 are instructive.

First, the larger proportion of comments produced after reception countered the position advocated (56 percent to 44 percent) while comments produced during reception favored the advocated position (63 percent to 37 percent). Second, the Point and Subject-Generated categories accounted for over 80 percent of all comments, both during and after, while the Conclusion and Issue categories, between them, never accounted for more than 4 percent of total comments (further analyses of these last two categories will not be reported). Third, Point comments tended to be supportive while Subject Generated and Source/Communication comments tended to be counter.

TABLE 1

A. MEAN NUMBER AND PROPORTION OF TOTAL COMMENTS PRODUCED BY ALL SUBJECTS (N=163) AFTER MESSAGE RECEPTION

Content category	Number total comments	Proportion total comments	Number supportive comments	Proportion total comments	Proportion supportive comments	Number counter comments	Proportion total comments	Proportion counter comments
Total	6.86	1.00	3.00	.44	1.00	3.86	.56	1.00
Conclusion	.15	.02	.04	.01	.01	.11	.02	.03
Point	2.32	.34	1.71	.25	.57	.61	.09	.16
Source/communication	1.10	.16	.27	.04	.09	.83	.12	.21
Subject generated	3.23	.47	.96	.14	.32	2.27	.33	.59
Issue	.05	.01	.02	.00	.01	.03	.00	.01

B. MEAN NUMBER AND PROPORTION OF TOTAL COMMENTS PRODUCED BY ALL SUBJECTS (N=79) DURING MESSAGE RECEPTION

Content category	Number total comments	Proportion total comments	Number supportive comments	Proportion total comments	Proportion supportive comments	Number counter comments	Proportion total comments	Proportion counter comments
Total	7.68	1.00	4.81	.63	1.00	2.87	.37	1.00
Conclusion	.28	.04	.16	.02	.03	.12	.01	.04
Point	4.76	.62	3.98	.52	.83	.78	.10	.27
Source/communication	.82	.11	.27	.04	.06	.55	.07	.19
Subject generated	1.81	.23	.38	.05	.08	1.43	.19	.50
Issue	.02	.00	.02	.00	.00	.00	.00	.00

Turning to the effect of experimental manipulations on overall production of comments, the mean numbers of all comments (supportive + counter) produced by subjects in each of the experimental groups are summarized in Table 2. (This table also includes the number of subjects participating in each experimental group.) As indicated by the overall means, the various experimental manipulations did not mediate differences in the total number of after-comments.

TABLE 2

MEAN NUMBER COMMENTS PRODUCED AFTER
AND DURING MESSAGE RECEPTION AND NUMBER OF
SUBJECTS PER EXPERIMENTAL CONDITION

Experimental condition *Comments*	*Pre-Post*				*Post Only*			
	Continuous		*Stop*		*Continuous*		*Stop*	
	Think	*Write*	*Think*	*Write*	*Think*	*Write*	*Think*	*Write*
Overall number of comments produced after reception	7.11	6.93	6.75	6.00	6.82	6.43	7.86	6.85
Overall number of comments produced during reception		6.70		9.39		4.57		10.17
Number of subjects	22	20	19	19	22	20	21	20

For comments produced *during* reception, however, there was a clear effect for opportunity, with subjects in the Stop conditions producing many more comments ($F=26.55$; $df=1,75$; $p<.001$), and an interaction which approached significance ($p<.10$). This was due to pre-tested subjects producing more comments than post-tested subjects in the Continuous condition but not in the Stop condition.

These differences attest to the success of the opportunity manipulation and, to some extent, of the commitment manipulation. Moreover, given that manipulations of independent variables mediated differences in total production of during-comments but not after-comments, the results support our earlier contention that post-message measurements of counterargumentation may not characterize counterarguing during reception.

Counterarguing Effects

Because an initial interest was to compare a number of possible measures of counterargument production, the five different "counterarguing scores" mentioned earlier were computed for comments in the Point, the Source/Communication, the Subject Generated, and the Total categories. [21] This procedure gave five scores for each content category. Since the various scores were highly correlated within categories and produced similar results when submitted to analysis of variance, we will simplify discussion by presenting only directional index scores and mean number of counter comments and supportive comments produced. Neither of the intensity measures produced results significantly at variance with those reported here, and neither was a more powerful measure than those based on straightforward counts of the number of various comments produced.

As the means in Table 3 indicate, with after-comments, there was a consistent main effect on counterarguing due to the opportunity manipulation. That is, subjects in the Stop conditions produced more counter (and/or fewer supportive) comments than did their counterparts in the Continuous conditions. This result obtained regardless of the particular measure of content category examined. Indeed, of the 20 analyses of variance conducted, [22] the expected effect for opportunity was statistically significant 9 times (p < .05 or beyond), approached significance 5 times (p < .10), and was in the predicted direction the remaining 6 times.

TABLE 3

SELECTED MEAN COUNTERARGUING SCORES BY
EXPERIMENTAL CONDITIONS FOR COMMENTS PRODUCED
AFTER MESSAGE RECEPTION

Counter-arguing score	*Pre-post*				*Post only*			
Experimental condition	*Continuous*		*Stop*		*Continuous*		*Stop*	
	Think	*Write*	*Think*	*Write*	*Think*	*Write*	*Think*	*Write*
Total								
Directional index	.23	.67	−3.00	−.42	−1.51	.30	−1.98	−1.18
N supportive	3.67	3.80	1.88	2.79	2.65	3.37	2.94	2.83
N counter	3.44	3.13	4.88	3.21	4.17	3.07	4.92	4.02
Point								
Directional index	1.08	1.55	.16	1.60	1.03	1.87	.57	1.00
N supportive	1.79	2.00	1.37	1.84	1.48	2.10	1.44	1.70
N counter	.71	.45	1.21	.25	.45	.23	.87	.70
Source/communication								
Directional index	−.05	−.25	−.58	−.72	−1.11	−.50	−.92	−.33
N supportive	.53	.35	.09	.25	.29	.25	.32	.08
N counter	.58	.60	.67	.96	1.39	.75	1.24	.42
Subject generated								
Directional index	−.83	−.67	−2.49	−1.35	−1.23	−.92	−1.57	−1.60
N supportive	1.23	1.35	.40	.60	.88	1.02	1.08	1.02
N counter	2.06	2.02	2.89	1.95	2.11	1.93	2.65	2.62

After-comments also revealed a main effect for storage condition within the Total and the Point categories. Subjects in the Think conditions gave more counter comments than did subjects in the Write conditions, the difference reaching statistical significance on four measures in each category.

This effect was probably due to an experimental artifact. Think subjects, who produced the less positive scores, were listing comments for the first time, while Write subjects were performing the task a second time. The fact that Write subjects were asked to enumerate their thoughts a second time probably attenuated responding, perhaps because they tired of the task, or perhaps because they summarized several earlier responses into a few later responses. This explanation is borne out by the slightly lower overall mean number of after-comments produced by Write subjects (see Table 2).

There were also several isolated interactions which are probably trivial in that neither the statistical effect nor the pattern of means was repeated across measures or content categories.

The experimental means summarized in Table 3 also support the overall patterns revealed in Table 1-A. With two minor exceptions, Point scores tended to be supportive. That is, although high opportunity subjects gave fewer supportive Point comments than did low opportunity subjects, the overall thrust of their Point comments tended to be supportive. Conversely, the balance of comments in the Source/Communication and Subject Generated categories tended to be counter, with high opportunity subjects more counter than low opportunity subjects.

Finally, the means for number of supportive and number of counter comments produced under the various experimental conditions, and analyses of variance performed on these scores, indicate that increasing opportunity to comment had the effect of both increasing the number of counter comments and, to a lesser extent, decreasing the number of supportive comments across all categories of after-comments.

A somewhat different pattern emerged among comments produced *during* reception (see Table 4). First, mean counterarguing scores in the Total category were all positive (supportive) as opposed to the generally negative scores for after-comments. Second, although high opportunity subjects generally produced more counter comments than did low opportunity subjects, they also produced more supportive comments. Indeed, in the Total and Point categories, Stop subjects gave many more supportive than counter comments.

And finally, the only striking differential effect on counterarguing of increasing opportunity was limited to Subject Generated comments. This was the only category in which measures other than simple counts of supportive and counter comments revealed significant differences, and the only category in which those scores were both negative and large. That is, while subjects in the Stop conditions gave significantly larger numbers of counter and supportive comments in the Total and Point categories, the main effect for opportunity within the Subject Generated category was significant ($p < .05$ or beyond) not only for number of supportive and number of counter comments, but also for the directional index and for the intensity measure.

Recall of our earlier points—that during reception high opportunity subjects produced significantly more comments overall (see Table 2), that the majority of all during-comments were Point comments (62 percent), and that most of these

TABLE 4
SELECTED MEAN COUNTERARGUING SCORES BY
EXPERIMENTAL CONDITIONS FOR COMMENTS
PRODUCED DURING MESSAGE RECEPTION

Counter-arguing score / *Experimental condition*	Pre-post		Post only	
	Continuous	*Stop*	*Continuous*	*Stop*
Total				
Directional index	2.83	2.12	1.53	1.30
N supportive	4.77	5.75	3.05	5.73
N counter	1.93	3.63	1.52	4.43
Point				
Directional index	3.22	4.09	2.17	3.38
N supportive	3.83	4.58	2.67	4.87
N counter	.62	.49	.50	1.48
Source/communication				
Directional index	−.07	−.39	−.20	−.45
N supportive	.42	.61	.07	.02
N counter	.48	1.00	.27	.47
Subject generated				
Directional index	−.47	−1.67	−.50	−1.60
N supportive	.28	.40	.15	.68
N counter	.75	2.07	.65	2.28

NOTE: Contains only subjects serving in Write conditions (N=79).

were supportive (83 percent)—helps to explain these results. Clearly the preponderance of Point comments accounts for the positive scores found in the Total category.

And it is worth noting that while Total scores for high opportunity groups are supportive, they are less supportive than for low opportunity groups. That is, while increased opportunity mediated an increase in supportive comments, it mediated an even greater increase in counter comments.

The significant increase in counters occurred in the Subject Generated category (although the means were also in the predicted direction for Source/Communication comments). To a large extent the less supportive total scores for high opportunity groups can be attributed to the significantly more counter Subject Generated scores for the high opportunity groups. Indeed, if we were to compute a directional index score omitting only Subject Generated comments, scores for the high opportunity conditions would be more supportive than scores for low opportunity conditions.

Analyses of during-comments also revealed two effects for commitment, one approaching and one reaching statistical significance. Committed subjects gave marginally ($p < .10$) more counter comments in the Point category than did non-committed subjects, an effect due solely to high opportunity, non-committed subjects producing more counters than subjects in any other group (interaction p <.05). Given the minimal number of counter comments in the Point category and the relatively consistent effect for opportunity on number of comments across all content categories, we are inclined to attribute this effect more to increased opportunity than lack of commitment.

The main effect due to committed subjects producing more supportive Source/Communication comments is more difficult to explain. It is probably a chance effect, particularly since the Source/Communication category accounted for only 11 percent of all during-comments, making the reliability of such scores suspect.

Opinion Effects

Experimental effects on subjects' opinions were assessed via three separate analyses. The first was based on the post-message opinion measure and included all 163 subjects in all experimental conditions.

The second was based on change scores, hence included only those 80 "committed" subjects who responded to the pre-message opinion item.

The third was based on post-message opinion scores, but included only the 79 subjects who participated in the "note-taking" conditions. This last analysis was necessary for comparisons to be reported in the following section. Table 5 presents mean opinion scores for experimental conditions.

Analysis of variance for post scores including all eight experimental conditions revealed a single significant effect due to an interaction between commitment and opportunity (F=5.87; df=1,155; p <.05). As revealed by the means in the first row of Table 5, subjects who were committed *and* given increased opportunity to produce counterarguments resisted more (produced lower opinion scores) than did subjects in any other condition.

A similar result obtained when change scores produced by Pre-post subjects were submitted to analysis of variance. This analysis, of course, included only two factors, hence the significant effect was a main effect for opportunity, subjects in the Stop condition manifesting considerably less change than their Continuous condition counterparts (F=11.61; df=1,76; p<.01). No other F ratio exceeded a value of 1.

TABLE 5

MEAN OPINION SCORES BY EXPERIMENTAL CONDITIONS

Opinion Score	*Experimental condition*	Pre-post				Post only			
		Continuous		Stop		Continuous		Stop	
		Think	Write	Think	Write	Think	Write	Think	Writ:
Post score		6.82	7.20	4.42	4.32	6.55	6.35	7.05	6.80
Change score		2.82	2.80	.95	.05	—	—	—	—

NOTE: Higher scores indicate greater acceptance of the position advocated.

Finally, the two-factor analysis of variance on post scores including only subjects who participated in the Write conditions continued the same pattern, although the obtained interaction between commitment and opportunity fell just short of statistical significance (F=3.46; df=1,75; p<.10). Again, subjects who responded to the pre-test and who were given increased opportunity to comment manifested more resistance.

Counterarguing and Resistance

As Table 6 indicates, bivariate correlations between after-comments and opinion scores and between during-comments and opinion scores revealed significant relationships between counterarguing behavior and resistance to persuasion. That is, opinion scores varied with counterarguing scores. The inverse relationship between counterarguing and persuasion is most clearly seen, of course, in the negative correlations obtained using number of negative comments.[23]

As noted earlier, however, relationships between measures of counterarguing and resistance do not mean that the former cause the latter. Since after-comments were elicited following subjects' responses to the opinion measure, the relationships in Part A of Table 6 may derive from subjects' attempts to justify or rationalize their opinion position rather than the reverse.

TABLE 6

Content category	N positive comments	N negative comments	Directional index	Intensity score	Weighted intensity
A. CORRELATIONS BETWEEN OPINION POST SCORES AND AFTER-COMMENTS (COUNTERARGUING MEASURE)					
Total	.37[c]	−.22[b]	.37[c]	.41[c]	.43[c]
Point	.29[c]	−.28[c]	.36[c]	.40[c]	.42[c]
Source/communication	.12	.08	−.03	.01	.09
Subject generated	.28[c]	−.23[b]	.36[c]	.38[c]	.38[c]

NOTE: Includes all 163 subjects.

Content category	N positive comments	N negative comments	Directional index	Intensity score	Weighted intensity
B. CORRELATIONS BETWEEN OPINION POST SCORES AND DURING-COMMENTS (COUNTERARGUING MEASURE)					
Total	.15	−.34[b]	.30[b]	.37[c]	.38[c]
Point	.10	−.21	.16	.25[b]	.31[b]
Source/communication	−.03	−.05	.03	.03	.07
Subject generated	.26[a]	−.33[b]	.40[c]	.40[c]	.39[c]

NOTE: Includes 79 subjects who participated in Write conditions.

a. Z>1.96; p<.05.
b. Z>2.58; p<.01.
c. Z>3.09; p<.001.

During-comments, on the other hand, since they preceded subjects' taking of an opinion position, are more easily viewed as possible mediators of the position taken. Still, even with during-comments there is the possibility that the relationship is not causal. Increased opportunity may independently mediate an increase in counterarguing and a decrease in persuasion—the former not influencing the latter at all.

That counterarguing behavior need not necessarily mediate resistance to persuasion is shown by comparison of the patterns of means obtained for counterarguing scores and for opinion scores (Tables 3, 4, and 5). Counterarguing score means typically reveal that increased opportunity to comment engendered more counter comments (or fewer supportive comments); however, opinion score means reveal that increased opportunity engendered lower opinion scores *only* when pre-message commitment accompanied increased opportunity. In other words, comparisons of these means indicate that increased counterarguing need not lead to increased resistance.

On the basis of these means, we hypothesized that counterarguing *mediated* resistance when subjects were previously committed to a position. Support for this hypothesis required at least two steps: (1) a statistical demonstration of a dependent relationship between counterarguing scores and opinion scores, and (2) a logical argument to establish that counterarguing mediated resistance rather than the reverse.

Analysis of covariance provided the means to accomplish the first step, and the results of the covariance analysis in the context of our experimental design offered the means to attempt the second.

First, consider the demonstration of a dependent relationship between counterarguing scores and opinion scores. Our hypothesis holds that counterarguing mediated opinion scores, hence that the effect on opinion scores of the opportunity manipulation was due to the effect of that manipulation on counterarguing behavior. It follows that if we remove the influence of counterarguing scores from opinion scores via covariance analysis, then the effect of the opportunity manipulation on opinion scores should be attenuated. Such attenuation would enable us to at least infer a dependent relationship between the two variables. Since the hypothesis is relevant only to committed subjects, we report analyses using only those who participated in the Pre-post condition.

Table 7 presents F ratios for the effect of the opportunity manipulation on opinion scores before and after covariance analyses. [24] The obtained F ratios demonstrated that removing variance accounted for by counterarguing scores attenuated the effect of opportunity on opinion scores.

Looking first at analyses using after comments as covariates, we discover that some decrement in F value was obtained for each of the various measures in each of the content categories. The largest decrement occurred using measures in the Total category, and none of the analyses totally removed the effect for opportunity. Indeed, in no case was the F ratio reduced to less than statistical significance ($p < .05$).

TABLE 7

F VALUES FOR THE EFFECT OF OPPORTUNITY MANIPULATION
ON OPINION SCORES FOR PRE-TESTED SUBJECTS
BEFORE AND AFTER COVARIANCE ANALYSES

	Comments produced	
Covariate/dependent variable	*After reception*	*During reception*
None	9.14^c	5.56^b
Total		
Directional index	5.89^b	5.33^b
N supportive	6.27^b	5.31^b
N counter	7.66^c	4.18^b
Intensity	5.55^b	5.14^b
Weighted intensity	5.60^b	5.17^b
Point		
Directional index	8.01^c	5.21^b
N supportive	8.46^c	5.16^b
N counter	8.10^c	6.23^b
Intensity	7.44^c	5.40^b
Weighted intensity	7.56^c	5.29^b
Subject generated		
Directional index	6.41^b	3.18^a
N supportive	7.75^c	6.37^b
N counter	8.22^c	3.09^a
Intensity	6.22^b	3.29^a
Weighted intensity	7.27^c	5.20^b

NOTE: Contains only Ss in committed conditions. Intensity measures are included in this table to give the reader a better sense of the pattern of the data.

a. $p < .10$.
b. $p < .05$.
c. $p < .01$.

Turning to during-comments, a different pattern emerged in that, with the exception of the number-of-counters measure, changes in F ratio due to covariance in the Total and Point categories were trivial. Only in the Subject Generated category was there any meaningful attenuation of the pre-covariance F ratio.

As with after-comments, removing the effect of differential counterarguing during reception attenuated, but did not completely remove, the effect of the opportunity manipulation. While F values after covariance were reduced to less than the .05 level of significance, it must be kept in mind that the F value before covariance was $p < .05$ (where, for the larger N included in analyses of after-comments, the pre-covariance F ratio was $p < .01$).

Although there is no direct statistical procedure to test differences between F values, computations of the Omega squared statistic (Hays, 1963: 325) indicated that in both sets of analyses the opportunity manipulation accounted for approximately 10 percent of the variance in opinion scores before covariance and for about 5 percent of the variance after covariance (when counterarguing measures which most reduced F values were used as covariates).[25]

In other words, approximately half the effect of the opportunity manipulation appears to be attributable to a dependent relationship between counterarguing scores and opinion scores.

We must still ask whether subjects' counterarguing behavior mediated opinion scores or whether their post-message opinions mediated counterarguing scores. Our argument rests on two considerations: (1) the temporal ordering of counterarguing scores and opinion scores, and (2) the patterns of counter comments across content categories obtained with after-comments as opposed to during-comments.

Since subjects responded to the opinion measure before listing comments, after-comments could be either indicators of the kind of responses that occurred during reception, or they could be justifications of the position taken after reception. Thus, some questions about the causal role of counterarguing can be raised for after-comments.

Such is not the case for during-comments. Not only were during-comments obtained before subjects gave their opinions, but they were obtained before subjects even knew they would be asked for post-message opinions. Hence, for during-comments there is no question of the temporal ordering necessary to infer causality.

Turning to the second part of our argument, it also seems that if counters are produced in order to justify an opinion already adopted, then these counters should be distributed across all content categories and be most manifest in the Total category. Certainly there is no reason to expect that a post-hoc attempt to justify a position would lead to counters within only one category. Such a distribution of counters across all content categories is precisely the pattern obtained with after-comments.

On the other hand, there is admittedly no reason to assume that comments which truly mediate an opinion would not be distributed across all content categories. However, when *effective* counters *do* cluster within a single category, it seems reasonable to impute a causal role to them (and to question scores distributed across all categories). And this is precisely the pattern of results obtained with during-comments.

Taken together, then, the results of the covariance analyses, the fact that during-comments fulfill the necessary temporal conditions to infer causality, and the fact that one specific category of during-comments accounted for almost all of the obtained relationship between counters and opinions—all point to the conclusion that counterarguing engendered by the opportunity manipulation and measured during reception mediated some of the obtained resistance to persuasion.

DISCUSSION

Results show a clear difference in the nature of counterarguments produced during and after message reception. For example, while a slight majority of after-comments countered the message, a large majority of during-comments supported it. While a plurality of after-comments fell into the Subject Generated category, the large majority of during-comments fell into the Point category.

These data are probably best explained in terms of the time available to subjects to comment. During reception, subjects must simultaneously produce comments and process incoming information. Thus, it is probably easier to simply respond to a point in the message—accounting for the large number of during-comments in the Point category, and the fact that they were mainly supportive.

Conversely, after reception, when subjects had time to think, they appear to have integrated more of their own belief system into their responses, resulting in an increase in the number of Subject Generated comments. This interpretation receives support from the increase in Subject Generated comments found during reception when opportunity (time) was increased.

Finally, it appears that during-comments mediated resistance to persuasion, while after-comments may have been rationalizations of the opinion position adopted. In short, there is good reason to question whether comments listed after message reception—a procedure followed in many of the studies reviewed earlier—are accurate indicators of counterarguing which may have taken place during reception.

It is also clear that increased opportunity mediated an increase in overall production of comments, and that there was a tendency for these comments to be counter to the message. Although the overall increase in counters is clearest in analyses of after-comments, it is probably more important to examine the results for during-comments. During reception, subjects given opportunity to list their thoughts (Stop group) manifested increases in the number of both supportive and counter comments. Most supportive comments, however, fell into the Point category, the only one to produce a positive directional index. Increased opportunity produced more counter comments within the Source/Communication and Subject Generated categories.

Indeed, the Subject Generated category was the only classification which produced a significant difference on the directional index—a difference indicating that more time led to more counterarguing.

It is also interesting to note that this was the only category of during-comments clearly related to opinion scores. As mentioned above, it appears that when subjects had time to process persuasive information, an effective way of operating was to interpret and evaluate the message in terms of their own belief system, rather than simply responding to external stimuli per se. Thus, the most "functional" comments appear to have been Subject Generated. These results dovetail nicely with those of Greenwald (1968). They are also congruent with results of role-playing studies (Janis, 1968) which have shown that subjects who generate their own counterattitudinal arguments are more influenced than subjects who simply present arguments produced by someone else.

Finally, our most intriguing results have to do with the relationship between counterarguing and resistance to persuasion. These results are especially revealing in the context of the opportunity main effect obtained for counterarguing scores and the opportunity-by-commitment interaction obtained for opinion scores. Given earlier persuasion research, it is somewhat surprising that neither opportunity nor commitment produced a main effect on opinion scores. That is, the results of various distraction studies—McGuire's (1964) report that resistance increased with the number of attack arguments refuted, and the generally inverse correlations between counterarguing and yielding reported in counterarguing studies—all lead one to expect a linear relationship between counterarguing and resistance.

Similarly, there is at least tentative evidence to suggest that resistance might be a function of commitment to a position (McGuire, 1969: 261-262),[26] although there is also evidence to suggest that a pre-test does not always successfully commit subjects (e.g., Lana, 1959). Our results suggest, however, that the expected relationship between counterarguing and resistance obtains only when some degree of commitment has occurred (or that a relationship between commitment and resistance may depend on subjects' counterargument production).

Our data reveal that neither counterarguing nor commitment, at least when the latter is operationalized in the form of a pre-test, is sufficient to insure resistance.

The critical question, then, becomes what is there in the nature of having responded to a pre-test *and* being provided an opportunity to counterargue that engenders resistance to persuasive attack? There appear to be several possibilities.

First, to the extent that the critical effect of the opportunity manipulation was the counterarguing it engendered, it may be that the pre-test acted as a catalyst or triggering mechanism for the resistance-inducing components of the counterarguments. That is, given time, most of us could probably generate arguments on either side of a relatively unfamiliar issue, but production of such pro and con comments may be little more than an intellectual exercise unless we have some structure or reference point to which these counters can be linked (Roberts, 1971). It may be that taking a position on the pre-test provided such a reference point, acting to make the arguments "meaningful" vis-a-vis resistance.

Second, the process could be reversed. Rather than the pre-test "activating" the counterarguments, the production of counters might make meaningful or salient the commitment inherent in responding to a pre-test. McGuire (1969) argues that a person's initial belief should become more resistant to the extent that he internally thinks about that belief. Thus, it may be that producing counters—particularly Subject Generated counters—recalled to the receiver the fact that he had taken a pre-message position.

Third, both of the above may be correct. The interaction may be dynamic, the pre-test catalyzing meaning in counters and counters making the pre-test more salient.

And fourth, the opportunity manipulation may have engendered more than counterarguing, high opportunity subjects having time not only to generate counters but also time to think back about their pre-test position independent of counterarguing.

Implicit here is something of an additive model wherein Stop subjects used part of the time to think about their initial belief and part of the time to weaken the persuasive attack by countering at least some of its arguments, but did both of these things independently.

Although available data do not provide a complete test of the preceding possibilities, they do provide tentative evidence that whatever is engendered by combining a pre-test and opportunity to comment operates to affect both commitment and the impact of counterarguments. Even though the opportunity manipulation located significant differences in counterargument production but not in resistance to persuasion, bivariate correlations that ignored commitment revealed a positive relationship between counterarguing and resistance. Such relationships provide some support for the contention that counterarguing at least mildly weakens the force of a persuasive attack, regardless of commitment.

More to the point, however, analyses of covariance revealed that counter-arguments accounted for some, but not all, of the variance in opinion scores located by the commitment manipulation. Given the resistance engendered by combining pre-test and opportunity, counterargument production mediated some resistance. But commitment, or some other unexplicated variable inherent in increased opportunity or in responding to a pre-test, accounted for another part of the obtained resistance. [27] At the least, it appears that both counter-arguing and responding to a pre-test simultaneously added to and gained from each other.

TOWARD A COUNTERARGUING MODEL

In light of the studies reviewed earlier and the results of our own research, we can begin to formulate a possible model of counterarguing behavior and resistance to persuasion.

In 1964 Maccoby speculated about a neo-Guthrian approach to persuasion. Briefly, his formulation posited that reception of a persuasive message, understanding it, and being persuaded by it all take place immediately and simultaneously—that the immediate intake of a persuasive message might lead to immediate persuasion.

Following a modified contiguity learning theory, however, he argued that such persuasion can be easily supplanted by subsequent counter-persuasion—including self-generated counter-persuasion. For example, if one receives a message counter to what one holds near and dear, the contention is that understanding of the message and, for the nonce, persuasion by that message, occur simultaneously. However, almost immediately afterwards, one can say to oneself, "This is hogwash because . . ." and think up or rehearse counter-arguments of various sorts. Hence, the initial immediate persuasion is nullified by an even more recent message—one that is self-generated.

This is not to say that only the most recent stimulus (e.g., single most recent counter) will determine the response. Persuasive propositions, like any others, may be built up and supported by a number of related propositions. Thus, Maccoby contended that the configuration of all comments that a receiver generates and/or rehearses during reception exerts strong influence on the final response.

Greenwald's (1968) cognitive response formulation of attitude change posits a very similar model. Greenwald contends that receivers' cognitive responses rehearsed during reception can be classified in terms of their directionality (supportive of or counter to the persuasive appeal). Such responses become incorporated into the cognitive attitude structure leading to a shift in the central tendency of that structure.

Thus, an overt attitude or opinion response represents the direction in which the attitude structure has been "conditioned" by the total configuration of cognitive responses made during reception. And of course, Greenwald's research indicates that internally generated responses are of primary importance.

The following assumption is implicit in both these formulations, as well as in inoculation and distraction research: To the extent that configuration of a receiver's cognitive responses made during reception can be characterized as countering a persuasive appeal, he should resist that appeal. While this assumption seems fundamentally sound, our research implies that there needs to be at least some minor modification or elaboration of the general model it leads to. Our results indicate that counterarguing need not always mediate resistance, and that some kinds of counters may be more important than others.

Both the present study and Greenwald's (1968) work indicate that Subject Generated comments play a mediational role. Moreover, in the present study counters were primarily effective when preceded by a mild commitment manipulation. Given these results, it seems to us that what must be considered in analyzing approaches to the resistance mediating effect of counterarguing is the concept of "meaning" as it occurs during information processing.

Just as the meaning of any overt communication depends on the receiver's existing cognitive structure—of his "image" of the situation he is in (Roberts, 1971)—receivers also interpret internally generated responses relative to their cognitive state when that response is made. Indeed, their image of a situation at any given moment probably mediates the nature of whatever internal responses or cognitions they generate. In other words, depending on how a receiver perceives a total communication situation, what appears on some objective level to be a counterarguing response may not be, on a subjective level, a counter-argument at all.

For example, a debater, who is required to argue both sides of an issue, is perfectly capable of producing arguments directly opposite to what he believes. While to an observer his comments may appear to be counters, to the debater they may be little more than conventional responses demanded by the situation. He may be arguing vigorously, but covertly, for the opposite point of view.

Similarly, a reasonable case can be made that, at least in this culture, we are trained to generate counterarguments simply because we are socialized to value critical examination of objects, events, or issues. In these instances, our counters are not so much indicators or mediators of resistance as they are responses to other aspects of the situation (e.g., it's time to play the devil's advocate; I must be a critical, thoughtful person; etc.).

What all this means is that counterarguments, at least as we usually conceive of them, may not be counterarguments at all unless we have reason to resist an appeal and "decide," so to speak, that we should fight back. Once we have made such a "decision," then the substance of a given counter probably "means" something different than it might have had we not made such a decision.

This returns us to our earlier point about the possible need for a distinction between motivation to resist and motivation to counterargue. The model we are proposing posits that if a receiver truly deals with a message,[28] both motiva-tions, but particularly motivation to resist, must be present for resistance to occur.

On the one hand we might generate counterarguments all day, but as long as the overt attitude response required of us is perceived to be of little importance, resistance need not follow. Our counters have done little or nothing to attenuate the strength of the persuasive appeal—they do not "mean" resistance. This case is exemplified by non-pretested, high opportunity subjects in the study just reported.

On the other hand, we might have reason to resist a persuasive attack, but to the extent that we truly deal with the message and are unable to counter its arguments, we will probably yield. This case would describe that rare instance when a persuasive source totally overwhelms opposition arguments, and to some extent probably explains the "defusing" effect of two-sided messages and of McGuire's (1964) inoculation treatment.

To summarize, then, our proposed model holds that, at least in this culture, when people truly attempt to process persuasive information (perhaps any information), they will probably produce "counterarguments" of some kind. The "meaning" of such counters, however, will vary with a receiver's motivation to resist.

Motivation to resist may derive from many sources: The nature of the issues dealt with (the more important, the more resistance), perceptions of source (disagreement with an incompetent or untrustworthy source regardless of issue), a need to maintain or appear to maintain consistency (defending a position taken on a pre-test, as in the present study), or many other conditions that have been demonstrated to mediate more or less opinion change.

Given motivation to resist a persuasive appeal, receivers will interpret their own counterarguments—give them meaning—in terms of how well they refute points in the attacking message. Resistance per se, then, will be a function of how successfully the receiver perceives himself to have refuted the attack.

Finally, we contend that the most "successful" counters will be internally generated (Subject Generated comments). By their very nature they are more congruent or meaningful to the receiver's existing belief system.

This model is not too different from those proposed by Maccoby (1964) and Greenwald (1968). It holds that resistance will depend on the configuration of supportive and counter responses generated by a receiver during reception of a persuasive message. It simply elaborates on prior models in its separation of counterargument production and motivation to resist, arguing that the meaning, hence the effectiveness, of the former depends on the nature of the latter.

This new model has the advantage of accounting for instances when apparent counterarguing does not lead to resistance. Perhaps more important, it points to the value of considering persuasion in the context of information processing, particularly as it relates to meaning.

NOTES

1. A set of health propositions (e.g., "It's a good idea to brush your teeth after every meal if at all possible.") were found to conform to this conceptualization of truism in that upwards of 75 percent of all respondants checked the most extreme agreement point on a 15-point scale of agreement with the propositions. Such propositions provide the issues used in most inoculation studies. Regretably, no one has reported experiments on the relative efficacy of the two resistance-inducing treatments using controverted issues.

2. It is worth noting how neatly some of the results of research on one-sided versus two-sided messages mesh with the assumptions underlying inoculation theory. For example, consider Hovland, Lumsdaine, and Sheffield's (1949) finding that both men with more education and men initially in strong disagreement with a message arguing that the war with Japan would continue for some time after Germany's surrender were more affected by a two-sided message. To the extent one is willing to assume that more educated men are better prepared to counterargue with a persuasive message, and that men initially opposed to an advocated position are more motivated to defend against a persuasive attack, the results can be interpreted to imply that among these men the two-sided message may have undercut the basis for resistance for much the same reasons that inoculation is presumed to stimulate the basis for resistance (also see Hass and Linder, 1972).

3. The investigations reported by Tannenbaum (1967) approach induction of resistance to persuasion from the perspective of congruity theory (Osgood and Tannenbaum, 1955). While these, and a number of experiments left uncited, support predictions derived from congruity theory, this is not the place to examine that approach to persuasion. Suffice it to say that a number of the findings, albeit not all of them, fit nicely into the counterarguing model underlying inoculation theory.

4. Similarly, distracting a receiver from generating agreeing comments about a pro-attitudinal appeal should result in less acceptance of the appeal. Both results assume the issue dealt with by the persuasive message is involving enough to the receiver to motivate agreeing or disagreeing under normal conditions.

5. Not surprisingly, at schools where the existance of fraternities was not an issue, thus where counter comments were less likely to occur, the distraction effect was not obtained.

6. Although Vohs and Garrett (1968) did not measure learning, earlier work by Vohs (1964), using a similar distraction technique, showed that distraction led to less learning.

7. Gardner (1966) used a marketing communication and Breitrose (1966) a message about the political situation in New Zealand, neither of which can be considered very involving. The motivating impact of the Vohs and Garrett (1968) issue is somewhat more equivocal in that they used a pro-Ku Klux Klan message. However, although most people hold anti-Klan opinions, it can be argued that the Klan is something of a dead issue, therefore would not be likely to engender much counterarguing.

8. In addition to the irrelevant film used by Festinger and Maccoby (1964), other studies which have supported the distraction hypothesis have used such distractors as viewing of irrelevant slides (Rosenblatt, 1966), orienting receivers to attend to the speaker's personality (Freedman and Sears, 1965), proofreading while reading the persuasive communication (Dorris, 1967), copying a list of digits (Keisler and Mathog, 1968), and attending to a panel of flashing lights (Osterhouse and Brock, 1970).

9. It should be noted, however, that in several of the experiments counterarguing behavior was not the central or sole concern of the study (e.g., Janis and Terwilliger, 1962; Greenwald, 1968), and in several others counterarguments were produced in *anticipation* of a persuasive message (Brock, 1967; Baron and Miller, 1969).

10. Greenwald and Mayer (n.d.: 2) write: "Positive reactions would correspond to acceptance of the communicated opinions or arguments and might consist of overt or covert agreement with the communication, thinking of or voicing arguments supporting those stated in the communication, deciding to take action suggested in the communication,

reviewing the positive qualifications of the communicator, etc. Negative reactions would amount to rejection of the communication and might consist of overt or covert disagreement with or denial of the communicated opinions and arguments, counterarguing, deciding to take action opposed to that suggested, derogating the communicator, etc. By virtue of their rehearsal in the persuasion situation, such cognitive responses are assumed to become *incorporated* into cognitive attitude structure—in other words, conditioned to the attitude object or opinion topic specified in the communication. This process constitutes a cognitive attitude change—i.e., a shift in the affective central tendency of the cognitive repertory conditioned to the attitude object—in the direction (positive or negative) represented by the new response content."

11. A "directional content index" was computed by subtracting weights for opposing thoughts from weights (ranging from one to three in each instance) for supporting thoughts and dividing by the sum of weights for all thoughts. To the extent that index scores were negative, subjects' comments can be conceived as countering the message.

12. Janis and Terwilliger classed comments as either affective or evaluative reactions. The former included (a) expressions of worry, affective disturbance, emotional tension, or (b) references to unpleasant aspects of cancer. The latter included (a) major criticisms such as rejection statements about specific arguments, (b) minor criticisms such as unfavorable comments about style or objectivity, (c) major favorable comments, (d) minor favorable comments, and (e) paraphrases of arguments in the message.

13. Baron and Miller (1969) found that when low source credibility was anticipated, personality orientation led to more counterarguing when both source and content counters were combined in the scoring procedure. However, when only content counters were scored, there was a marginally significant crossover interaction such that source oriented subjects produced more counters when expecting a low credibility source and content oriented subjects produced more when expecting a high credibility source.

14. More precisely, increased fear led to more "rejection statements," a category very similar to many definitions of counterargument.

15. The exceptions, of course, are the cultural truisms employed in inoculation studies (McGuire, 1964; Tannenbaum, 1967) and by Cook (1969). By definition a cultural truism is not a controverted issue.

16. It should be noted that although inoculation studies start with issues about which recipients have few available defensive materials, the inoculation procedure simultaneously manipulates motivation (via threat) and counterargument availability (via refutation of threat), rendering independent comparisons of the two variables impossible.

17. Detailed definitions, coding instructions, and scoring procedures may be obtained from the authors. It should be noted that the *Source* and the *Communication* categories were collapsed when so few comments obtained in the final experiment were classed into either one alone. Our subject-generated category was based on Greenwald's "recipient generated" category.

18. Determination of intercoder reliability focused on subjects rather than comments. Our concern was not with whether any single comment was similarly coded by all coders, but with whether scores summarizing all comments produced by any single subject were similar across coders.

19. If we assume that the score assigned by each coder to each subject represents that subject's rank among all subjects scored by that coder, then W, which measures the relationship among more than two sets of rankings, provides an estimate of whether the three coders scored subjects' comments similarly.

20. Each of these categories accounted for very few comments, creating many tied ranks with score = 0, thus attenuating W.

21. The Total category summarized not only scores in the Point, Source/Communication, and Subject Generated categories, but also included those few comments classed as belonging to the Issue and Conclusion categories.

22. An analysis of variance on scores obtained on each of the five measures for each of the four categories was computed. Detailed summaries of mean scores and analyses of variance may be obtained from the authors.

23. Within condition correlations revealed the same pattern of results, although obtained coefficients were not statistically reliable due to the small N within each experimental group.

24. In the interest of brevity, measures in the Source/Communication category, which lacked reliability and which failed to correlate with opinion scores, are omitted. These scores are, of course, included in the Total category.

25. Omega squared (W^2) provides an estimate of the amount of variance in a dependent variable accounted for by differential treatments on an independent variable. Hence the difference between W^2 values computed before and after covariance should provide at least a rough estimate of the variance due to a manipulation attributable to the variable used as covariate. In the present case, for analyses using after-comments, $W^2 = .096$ before covariance and $W^2 = .055$ after covariance (using the intensity measure in the Total category as covariate–the measure most reducing the F value). For analyses using during-comments, $W^2 = .104$ before covariance and $W^2 = .058$ after covariance (using the directional index in the Subject Generated category as covariate).

26. McGuire (1969) also points out that stability of commitment is a function of how public such commitment is.

27. It should be kept in mind that the failure of covariance analyses to remove all of the variance in opinion scores due to the opportunity manipulation may simply derive from error inherent in our measurement procedure.

28. Of course, a receiver could decide to resist and simply ignore the persuasive message.

REFERENCES

ASCH, S. (1948) "The doctrine of suggestion, prestige, and imitation in social psychology." Psychological Review 55: 250-276.

BARON, R. S. and N. MILLER (1969) Credibility, Distraction, and Counterargument in a Forewarning Situation. Paper presented at the 77th Annual Convention of the American Psychological Association, Washington, D.C. (September).

BREITROSE, H. S. (1965) The Effect of Distraction in Attenuating Counterarguments. Ph.D. dissertation. Stanford: Stanford University.

BROCK, T. C. (1967) "Communicator discrepancy and intent to persuade as determinants of counterargument production." Journal of Experimental Social Psychology 3: 296-309.

COOK, T. D. (1969) "Competence, counterarguing, and attitude change." Journal of Personality 37: 342-358.

DORRIS, J. W. (1967) "Persuasion as a function of distraction and counterarguing." Los Angeles: University of California, Psychology Department (mimeo).

FESTINGER, L. and N. MACCOBY (1964) "On resistance to persuasive communication." Journal of Abnormal and Social Psychology 68: 359-367.

FREEDMAN, J. L. and D. O. SEARS (1965) "Warning, distraction, and resistance to influence." Journal of Personality and Social Psychology 1: 262-265.

GARDNER, D. M. (1966) "The effect of divided attention on attitude change induced by a marketing communication," pp. 532-540 in R. M. Haus (ed.) Science, Technology, and Marketing. Chicago: American Marketing Association.

GREENWALD, A. G. (1968) "Cognitive learning, cognitive response to persuasion, and attitude change," pp. 147-170 in A. G. Greenwald, T. C. Brock, and T. M. Ostrom (eds.) Psychological Foundations of Attitudes. New York: Academic Press.

GREENWALD, A. G. and L. S. MAYER (n.d.) "Cognitive responses to persuasion as a function of source credibility: A study of the acceptance process in persuasive communication." Athens, Ohio: Ohio State University, Department of Psychology (mimeo).

HAALAND, G. A. and M. VENKATESAN (1968) "Resistance to persuasive communications: Thedistraction hypothesis." Journal of Personality and Social Psychology 9: 167-170.

HASS, R. G. and D. E. LINDER (1972) "Counterargument availability and the effects of message structure on persuasion." Journal of Personality and Social Psychology 23, 2: 219-233.

HAYS, W. L. (1963) Statistics for Psychologists. New York: Holt, Rinehart, Winston.

HOVLAND, C. I., A. A. LUMSDAINE, F. D. SHEFFIELD (1949) Experiments on Mass Communication. Princeton: Princeton University Press.

JANIS, I. L. (1968) "Attitude change via role playing," pp. 810-818 in R. P. Abelson, E. Aronson, W. J. McGuire, T. M. Newcomb, M. J. Rosenberg, and P. H. Tannenbaum (eds.) Theories of Cognitive Consistency: A Sourcebook. Chicago: Rand McNally.

JANIS, I. L. and R. TERWILLIGER (1962) "An experimental study of psychological resistance to fear-arousing communication." Journal of Abnormal and Social Psychology 65: 403-410.

KIESLER, S. B. and R. R. MATHOG (1968) "Distraction hypothes inattitude change: Effects of effectiveness." Psychological Reports, 23: 1123-1133.

LANA, R. E. (1959) "Pretest-treatment interaction effects in attitudinal studies." Psychological Bulletin 56: 293-300.

LORGE, I. (1936) "Prestige, suggestion and attitude." Journal of Social Psychology 7: 386-402.

LUMSDAINE A. A. and I. L. JANIS (1953) "Resistance to 'counter-propaganda' produced by one-sided and two-sided 'propaganda' presentations." Public Opinion Quarterly 17: 311-318.

LUND, F. (1925) "The psyology obelief: IV, The law of primacy in persuasion." Journal of Abnormal and Social Psychology 20: 183-191.

MACAULAY, J. R. (1965) A Study of Independent and Additive Modes of Producing Resistance to Persuasion Derived from Congruity and Inoculation Models." Ph.D. dissertation. Madison: University of Wisconsin.

MACCOBY, N. (1965) "Arguments, counterarguments and distraction," pp. 33-42 in D. E. Payne (ed.), The Obstinate Audience. Foundation for Research on Human Behavior Report. Ann Arbor: Braun, Brumfield.

MACCOBY, N. and D. F. ROBERTS (1971) Cognitive Processes in Persuasion. Paper presented at the American Marketing Association Attitude Research Conference, St. Thomas, Virgin Islands, November.

McGUIRE, W. J. (1961a) "Resistance to persuasion confirmed by active and passive prior refutation of the same and alternative counterarguments." Journal of Abnormal and Social Psychology 63: 326-332.

——— (1961b) "The effectiveness of supportive and refutational defenses in immunizing and restoring beliefs against persuasion." Sociometry 24: 184-197.

——— (1964) "Inducing resistance to persuasion: Some contemporary approaches," pp. 191-229 in L. Berkowitz (ed.) Advances in Experimental Social Psychology, Volume 1. New York: Academic Press.

——— (1966) "Attitudes and opinions." Annual Review of Psychology 17: 475-514.

——— (1969) "The nature of attitudes and attitude change," pp. 136-314 in G. Lindzey and E. Aronson (eds.) The Handbook of Social Psychology, Volume 3, The Individual in a Social Context. Reading, Mass.: Addison-Wesley.

McGUIRE, W. J. and D. PAPAGEORGIS (1961) "The relative efficacy of various types of prior belief-defense in producing immunity against persuasion." Journal of Abnormal and Social Psychology 62: 327-337.

——— (1962) "Effectiveness of forewarning in developing resistance to persuasion." Public Opinion Quarterly 26: 24-34.

MILLER, N. and R. S. BARON (1968) "Distraction, communicator credibility and attitude change." Minneapolis: University of Minnesota, Department of Psychology (mimeo).

OSGOOD, C. E. and P. H. TANNENBAUM (1955) "The principle of congruity in the prediction of attitude change." Psychological Review 62: 42-55.

OSTERHOUSE, R. A. and T. C. BROCK (1970) "Distraction increases yielding to propaganda by inhibiting counterarguing." Journal of Personality and Social Psychology 15, 4: 344-358.

PAPAGEORGIS, D. and W. J. McGUIRE (1961) "The generality of immunity to persuasion produced by pre-exposure to weakened counterarguments." Journal of Abnormal and Social Psychology 62: 475-481.

ROBERTS, D. F. (1971) "The nature of communication effects," pp. 349-387 in W. Schramm and D. F. Roberts (eds.) The Process and Effects of Mass Communication. Rev. ed. Urbana: University of Illinois Press.

ROSENBLATT, P. C. (1966) "Persuasion as a function of varying amounts of distraction." Psychonomic Science 5: 85-86.

ROSNOW, R. L. (1966) "Conditioning the direction of opinion change in persuasive communication." Journal of Social Psychology 69: 291-303.

RULE, B. G. and D. REHILL (1970) "Distraction and self-esteem effects on attitude change." Journal of Personality and Social Psychology 15, 4: 359-365.

TANNENBAUM, P. H. (1967) "The congruity principle revisited: Studies in the reduction, induction, and generalization of persuasion," pp. 271-320 in L. Berkowitz (ed.) Advances in Experimental Social Psychology, Volume 3. New York: Academic Press.

VOHS, J. L. (1964) "An empirical approach to the concept of attention." Speech Monographs 31: 355-360.

VOHS, J. L. and R. L. GARRETT (1968) "Resistance to persuasion: An integrative framework." Public Opinion Quarterly 32: 445-452.

ZIMBARDO, P. (1965) "The effect of effort and improvisation on self persuasion produced by role playing." Journal of Experimental Social Psychology 1: 103-120.

ZIMBARDO, P., M. SNYDER, J. THOMAS, A. GOLD and S. GURWITZ (1970) "Modifying the impact of persuasive communications with external distraction." Journal of Personality and Social Psychology 16, 4: 669-680.